Implementing Person-Centered Planning
Voices of Experience

John O'Brien & Connie Lyle O'Brien
Editors

Volume II
INCLUSION PRESS
Toronto

National Library of Canada Cataloguing in Publication

Implementing person-centered planning:
voices of experience

John O'Brien & Connie Lyle O'Brien, editors

Includes bibliographical references and index.
ISBN 1-895418-50-X

1.Handicapped-Services for. I. O'Brien, John, 1946-
II. O'Brien, Connie Lyle

HV1568.I46 2002   362.4   C2002-904990-3

Preparation of this publication, and of Chapters 3, 6, 11, 20, and 21 was partially supported through a subcontract to Responsive Systems Associates from the Center on Human Policy, Syracuse University for the Research and Training Center on Community Living. The Research and Training Center on Community Living is supported through a cooperative agreement (number H133B980047) between the National Institute on Disability & Rehabilitation Research (NIDRR) and the University of Minnesota Institute on Community Integration. Members of the Center are encouraged to express their opinions; these do not necessarily represent the official position of NIDRR.

Inclusion Press
24 Thome Crescent
Toronto, Ontario M6H 2S5 Canada
www.inclusion.com

Cover design: Catherine Hollands
Cover photo: Preah Kahn, Angkor Wat, Siem Reap,Cambodia
©1998 Jack Pearpoint

Contents

Previously Published in
A Little Book About Person-Centered Planning

The Power in Vulnerability

Judith Snow places person-centered planning in the context of interdependence and community.

> *When I am in relationship with other individuals and if these others are networked with each other and especially if these others are different from each other, the possibility exists for all of us to have a rich life, drawing on each other's gifts. Differences in each other's physical and cognitive functioning, our interests, history and experience, our possibilities, our possessions and resources only add to the mix of possibilities that increase our total capacity.*

Learning to Listen

John O'Brien and Connie Lyle O'Brien reflect on listening, the foundation skill for person-centered planning.

> *People come to life when they make contact with someone who works actively and faithfully to understand what they want to say. When people communicate in unusual ways, or when they have been rendered invisible by an environment that discounts the worth of their communication, the effects of listening can be profoundly energizing.*

Person-Centered Planning Has Arrived… or Has it?

Connie Lyle O'Brien, John O'Brien, and Beth Mount identify issues that arise as service systems mandate person-centered planning.

> *We believe that implementations of person-centered planning will be disappointing if people rigorously apply a procedure without sufficient regard for the context of relationships and agreements necessary for it to thrive.*

Think Before You Plan

Michael Smull defines issues for facilitators to consider before agreeing to plan.

> *Be sure to think before you plan. Thinking about a few issues before you get started can help you achieve a better outcome, prevent problems, avoid unnecessary struggle, and save you from public embarrassment. {Plans are} ordinary, day to day efforts to*

*understand how someone wants to live and what we are going
to do about it. The overriding principle is that a plan is not an
outcome, the life that the person wants is the outcome. The only
acceptable reason to plan is to help someone move toward the life
they desire.*

The Politics of Person-Centered Planning

John O'Brien and Connie Lyle O'Brien situate person-centered planning in
terms of enduring conflicts that arise at the intersection of individual and
family life, community, and human service policy and practice.

*Person-centered planning belongs to the politics of community
and disability. It is not a way to avoid conflict; it is one way to
seek real and enduring conflicts in collaboration with people with
disabilities who want to consider a change in their lives.*

Revisiting Choice

Michael Smull identifies common abuses and misunderstandings of
"choice" in the lives of people with disabilities and provides guidance on
dealing with situations when it seems impossible to honor a person's choice,
finding balance between choice and safety, creating the kind of opportunities that increase capacity to honor people's preferences about how they
want to live, and increasing people's control over their lives.

*What opportunities we provide, hold back, encourage
people to find or protect people from depends as much on
our values as they do on the preferences and capacities of
the people we support. We need to listen to ourselves when
we say that someone is not ready or that they should be able
to do something simply because it is their choice. Our values influence and often control what we support. We need
to talk about what our values are so that we understand
the basis on which we are making decisions. We need to
remember that the opportunities that are made available
depend on the values of those with control.*

Positive Ritual and Quality of Life

Michael Smull raises consciousness about the routines and rituals that structure our days and embody our relationships.

*As we look at supporting people in their communities we
need to remember that much of the richness of community
comes from the relationships that we have and the ritu-*

als that celebrate and build those relationships... In our rapidly changing, mobile, and fragmented society, positive rituals deserve attention for all of us regardless of the presence of disability. For people who need substantial support to get through life, developing positive rituals should be a priority.

More Than a Meeting

Beth Mount identifies the benefits and limitations of person-centered planning, identifies ten conditions associated with positive changes in people's lives and outlines the framework for person-centered development projects.

People interested in the future of person-centered planning must look past the lure of the quick fix toward the long journey of learning to do things differently on personal, community, and organizational levels. The resources of the system can be used to support safe havens where people can learn the art of person-centered development. The continuing challenge is to create environments which nurture the concern, commitment, and caring that engenders true relationships.

The Quest for Community Membership

John O'Brien and Connie Lyle O'Brien use the image of a quest to explore the relationship between person-centered planning and community building.

How can person-centered planning contribute to building communities competent to include people with developmental disabilities as contributing members? Failure to actively and thoughtfully engage this tough question unnecessarily limits the effectiveness of the growing variety of approaches to person-centered planning.

After the Plan

Michael Smull outlines a learning process for closing the gap between how people want to live and how their services are supporting them to live.

Whenever people are empowered a dynamic situation is created. The process of listening and then acting on what has been heard is an ongoing cycle. What people want today will be different from what they want tomorrow. The process is lifelong and interactive. The only thing worse than never listening is only listening once.

Participation Through Support Circles

Judith Snow moves outside the confines of a disability focus to describe the steps to circle building.

> *Circles empower circle members because they are unpredictable. Energized by multiple, complex relationships they often become magnets of synergy, taking advantage of lucky accidents —opportunities that cannot be predicted or bureaucratically managed into existence. This living essence of circles drives out the deadening spirit of disability thinking.*

A Circle Check-Up

John O'Brien and Jeff Strully offer a list of questions that support circle members can use to assess their contribution to supporting people.

> *Circle members hold responsibility for developing a deep, accurate and clear account of the person's interests, preferences and dreams and assuring that this understanding guides the day-to-day behavior of the people who provide assistance.*

The Ethics of MAPS and PATH

Jack Pearpoint and Marsha Forest define dangers and safeguards in the use of person-centered planning and provide a checklist for good facilitation.

> *Good facilitators hold questions with people, then wait, and listen to the silence. The tension in this silence creates a safe space for people to fill with their deep yearnings and simple unspoken needs, the real stuff of life. As facilitators we open an inviting space for the focus person and insure that their ideas and wishes are heard. Then the hard work begins.*

Telling New Stories

John O'Brien and Beth Mount differentiate person-centered planning from planning that serves systems by contrasting two different sorts of stories about people's lives and the role of service providers with them.

> *Burton Blatt said, "Some stories enhance life; others degrade it. So we must be careful about the stories we tell, about the ways that we define ourselves and other people."*

Finding a Way Toward Everyday Lives: The Contribution of Person-Centered Planning.

John O'Brien and Herb Lovett identify what different approaches to person-centered planning have in common, discuss the ways person-centered planning influences change, consider its limitations, and define some of the controversies among practitioners.

> Person-centered planning can invite, align, and direct shared
> efforts to create positive community roles for people with dis-
> abilities. It allows people to exercise their practical wisdom to
> work for more inclusive, more just communities... The future of
> person-centered planning depends on the willingness and ability
> of its practitioners to improve through critical reflection on the
> effects of their work in the lives of people with disabilities and
> their families.

A Guide to Personal Futures Planning

John O'Brien considers the role planning plays in improving the lives of people with substantial disabilities, defines five essential accomplishments of human services as a perspective on service quality, and outlines a very early version of the procedure for personal futures planning.

> None of us creates our lives alone. We each create better quality
> life experiences with the other people who form our social net-
> work. And usually we are resources to each other without much
> formal planning. Like all of us, people with severe disabilities
> develop in relationship. But because they rely on other people's co-
> operation to an unusual extent, and because human services often
> play a larger than ordinary role in their lives, people with severe
> disabilities count on other's planning and organizing skills.

Authors

Betty Boomer is the Associate Executive Director for the Waterloo and Wellington-Dufferin Branches of the Canadian Mental Health Association. With a background in psychiatric nursing, Betty has worked for many years in clinical and community mental health settings and does training for the Collective for Community Action on a variety of topics related to mental health. E-mail: boomerb@cmhawrb.on.ca.

MaryJo Alimena Caruso is from Pittsburgh, PA, where she lives with her husband and three children, Griffin, Mackenzie and Connor. Her role as a facilitator of person-centered plans began in 1990 and since then she has added on the hats of trainer, mentor and writer. She enjoys the opportunity to help others think about how values influence our work and ways to apply person-centered thinking and tools to a variety of situations.

Patricia Fratangelo is Executive Director of Onondaga Community Living, where she has worked since 1990. She has worked in the field of developmental disabilities for 22 years, beginning as a direct care worker. She remains a close friend with several people with disabilities that she previously worked for, vacationing and spending holidays with them. She lives in Trumansburg, NY, with her husband, John King. Onondaga Community Living. 518 James Street, Suite 110 Syracuse, New York 13203 E-mail: patfrat@aol.com.

Rob Greig is National Director of Implementation for Valuing People –the English national strategy for learning disability. Previously he was Director of Organisational Development at the Institute of Applied Health and Social Policy at King's College London. Earlier experience included managing learning disability services in both the health and social care field. E-mail: Rob.D.Greig@doh.gsi.gov.uk.

Steve Holburn I am a Research Scientist at the New York State Institute for Basic Research. I spent much of my career trying to help people with intellectual disabilities and serious behavior problems, but my impact was often blunted if the person lived a poor lifestyle in a bad environment. I was struck by person-centered planning because it sought to change such conditions and bring about better lifestyles. It offered a sensible starting point. However, I have been equally struck by how difficult it is to *do* person-centered planning and how few attempts have been made to empirically demonstrate its effectiveness. Many professionals are eager to dismiss person-centered planning as a fad or a panacea. For these reasons, I and my colleagues have been trying to find ways to (a) assess and implement person-centered planning faithfully, and (b) measure its effects over the long term. While some may see a contradiction in applying "science" to a "counter-science" approach such as person-centered planning, I believe the blending will contribute to the survival and evolution of this approach. E-mail: holbursc@infi.net.

John Jones is the Chief Executive Officer of the Waterloo Regional Branch and the Wellington-Dufferin Branch of the Canadian Mental Health Association. John has over twenty-five years of experience as a funder, administrator, and consultant with boards, staff, people supported, and volunteers of human service organizations. E-mail: jonesj@cmhawrb.on.ca.

Susannah Joyce is the Director of Realizations Training & Resources. She works internationally with people who have disabilities, families, and service organizations on person-centered planning, circles and friendships, positive approaches to challenging behavior, leadership, and systems change. Visit her website at www.realizationstraining.com. E-mail: susannahjoyce@sprint.ca.

Jo Krippenstapel offers consultation and training focused on enhancing quality lives for individuals, more responsive organizations, and richer community life. She provides support to individuals with disabilities, families, and staff to create teams of people who learn and take action together. Jo lives in Cincinnati, OH. She can be reached by E-mail: Jokripp@cs.com.

Sandy Landis lives and works in rural Perry County, OH, where she is involved in projects designed to increase community capacity and improve the quality of day to day experience for local citizens.

Kathy Lee is a native of Meadville, PA, where she lives with her roommate Connie and their 2 dogs and 3 cats. She has been actively involved in thinking, planning, teaching and writing about person-centered planning and circles of support since 1991. Kathy travels about occasionally and talks to others about the importance of community for everyone.

Debra McLean. I am a practitioner of employment and person-centered planning processes since 1988. I have lived and worked in Oregon since 1979. I have provided consultation and training to families, individuals and agencies on those topics, both locally and nationally. I owe a huge debt to those families and individuals who allowed me to learn from them how to successfully enter the world of work. I work at Oregon Technical Assistance Corporation. E-mail: dmclean@otac.org.

Karen Green McGowan is a clinical nurse consultant with 38 years of experience in developmental disabilities. She specializes in teaching clinicians and service providers to work with those persons perceived as medically fragile and difficult to serve because of major movement disorders and other health obstacles. She has been appointed to several court oversight panels, and currently monitors services to persons in Massachusetts nursing homes who are also identified as having developmental disabilities. She has developed a number of publications on health issues for persons with disabilities, including an electronic instrument to identify health risk. For more information, see her website at www.mcgowanconsultants.com.

Beth Mount. For the past 25 years I have been searching for new ways to discover, affirm, and describe the beauty and strength in the lives of people with disabilities, their families, and the people who support them. During the past twelve years, I have been involved with person-centered planning and community building in New York City. Living in New York City has given me the opportunity to deepen my understanding of the universal themes in the spirituality and artwork of world cultures. As another way to help tell people's stories, I work on my fabric art while my son does his homework. Visit www.capacityworks.com.

Connie Lyle O'Brien and **John O'Brien** work together to learn about building more just and inclusive communities from people with disabilities, their families, and their allies. They use what they learn to advise people with disabilities and their families, advocacy groups, service providers, and governments and to spread the news among people interested in change by writing and through workshops. They work in partnership with a group of friends from 12 countries. They are affiliated with the Center on Human Policy at Syracuse University and the Marsha Forest Center for Inclusion, Family, and Community. Connie's E-mail: connielyleobrien@mac.com John's E-mail: rsa315@cs.com.

Anne O'Bryan has twenty years of experience in developing, managing, and improving services for individuals with learning difficulties in the United States and Europe. She is currently providing support and technical assistance to individuals, their families, employers and support services. Anne lives near Bath in England and can be reached by E-mail: anneobryan@compuserve.com.

Jack Pealer. Some of his friends once called Jack an "Ohiopatriot". He has spent the last 32 years in Ohio trying to help people with disabilities find or make "home" for themselves. E-mail: jackjr158@earthlink.net.

David Pitonyak can be reached at Imagine, 3694 Mt. Tabor Road, Blacksburg, VA 24060 For additional information, log onto David's web site: www.dimagine.com.

Pete Ritchie works for Scottish Human Services Trust (SHS). SHS is a non-government organization working with others to build more inclusive communities and more responsive services. SHS offers encouragement, training and consultancy to people and organizations who are learning about person-centered planning. You can contact SHS at www.shstrust.org.uk or at 1a Washington Court, Edinburgh, EH11 2HA and reach Pete directly at pritchie@shstrust.org.uk.

Mary Romer. To paraphrase the lyrics from John Lennon's song, "Imagine," some say Mary is a dreamer and she is glad she is not the only one. She is exceedingly grateful to have grown up in a family that promoted her ability to dream, both for herself and for people labeled with a disability. For the past 29 years, she has worked along with people with disabilities, their families, and people who provide services striving to give life to the dreams people hold. E-mail:mromer@seanet.com.

Fredda Rosen and her colleagues at Job Path in New York City support people with developmental disabilities in their efforts to make choices about their lives. Job Path, which was established in 1978, strives to be a reflective organization where staff carefully listens to people and thoughtfully considers the implications of their work.

Martin Routledge is the Valuing Support Team Regional Advisor for the North West of England. Martin's work over the past few years has been in service management and development. Prior to joining the VPST he was co-ordinator of the North West Training and Development Team, which is funded to work with self advocates, families and service agencies in the region to promote the full inclusion of people with learning disabilities. Martin can be contacted at Martin.Routledge@doh.gsi.gov.uk.

Helen Sanderson works part-time for the North West Training and Development Team. She has a Masters in Quality Assurance in Health and Social Care, and has recently completed her Ph.D. in person-centred planning with people with profound learning disabilities. Helen is the primary author of the book *People, Plans and Possibilities* and has written extensively on person centred planning. Helen is an essential lifestyle planning mentor trainer, and much of her work is around the practice and development of person centred planning processes and systems. Helen lives in Manchester with her partner Andy, and three daughters, Ellie, Laura and Kate. E-mail: helen.sanderson@nwtdt.com.

Sally Sehmsdorf lives in Seattle with her husband Art Gomez and her children Johann and Kayta. She works for the Center for Community Support, a project of TASH, under Mary Romer's leadership. For the past seven years, she has had the privilege of sharing life and dreams with many people with disabilities and their families. E-mail: salliese@attbi.com.

Mayer Shevin has worked at various times as a professor of special education, a psychologist at a large state institution, and a teacher in the areas of positive approaches to behavior change, advocacy, and communication development. He directed the "Home-made Futures Project," developing person-centered planning resources in North Dakota. He is an associate of the Facilitated Communication Institute at Syracuse University, where he edits their newsletter, the Facilitated Communication Digest. In his private practice as a trainer and consultant he supports individuals seeking to progress toward their personal goals despite challenging behaviors and communication impairments, their families, and the agencies that support these individuals.

Michael Smull plays a key role in developing and disseminating Essential Lifestyle Planning. To contact him and read much more of his work visit www.allenshea.com/friends.html.

Jeff Strully I am the Executive Director of Jay Nolan Community Services. I have held this position for the past ten years. I have been involved with people with developmental disabilities for over 32 years in a variety of capacities and environments. My wife and I are the parents of three adults with developmental disabilities. Visit the JNCS website at www.jaynolan.org.

Marsha Threlkeld has been creating plans and working on behalf of people with disabilities for 17 years. She is also a choreographer and has performed with individuals with disabilities at The Kennedy Center. Marsha gets bored, looks for new ways to entertain herself, and likes to be recognized and appreciated for work well done. She assumes everyone else does too. Marsha works at Washington Initiative for Supported Employment in Seattle. Visit the Initiative's web site at www.theinitiative.ws.

David and Faye Wetherow share their lives with an adopted daughter who has complex mobility and communication challenges. They have long been involved in innovative service development, teaching, facilitating and community-building. You can reach their website at www.communityworks.info.

Voices of Experience

John O'Brien and Connie Lyle O'Brien

Four years ago, when we assembled *A Little Book About Person-Centered Planning* (1998) by collecting frequently copied papers from the early developers of person-centered planning, we predicted that there would soon be material enough for a bigger book incorporating the voices of more practitioners. In fact we underestimated. Four good sized books appeared in 2002.

The first book, *One Candle Power,* edited by Cathy Ludlum, collects stories and learning about person-centered work from the point of view of people with disabilities and their families and friends; these accounts are especially valuable because they cover years of living –from the excitement of expressing a dream through the difficulties and disappointments and rewards and new problems that go with living a full life. Cathy's collection makes an essential contribution, not only because of the wisdom of the people who tell its stories, but because the perspective of people with disabilities and families has been underrepresented in written accounts of person-centered planning (for an important exception see Snow, 1998).

The second book, *Person-Centered Planning: Research, Practice, and Future Direction*, edited by Steve Holburn and Peter Vietze, collects research and commentary on two important questions: "Does person-centered planning really work?" and "How can we best adopt person-centered planning to maximize its effectiveness?"

The third, this book, collects the reflections of people who facilitate person-centered planning and people who work to increase the availability of good quality person-centered planning in order to build more just and inclusive communities. We want this volume to continue and extend the discussion begun in *A Little Book About Person Centered Planning.*

The fourth book, *Planning with People: Towards Person-Centred Approaches* issued by the Department of Health as policy guidance for publicly funded services in England, marks a turning point in the development of person-centered planning. It positions person-centered planning as one key tool for achieving a deep shift in a nation's culture and practice of services and defines a long term organizational change strategy to create a context in which person-centered planning can make sense. How successful this bold effort will be remains to be seen, but it is the best effort that we know to think through the strategic implications of implementing person-centered planning. You can read about it in Chapter 28 of this book.

Many book reviewers approve of uniformity of voice and style in an edited book. Such uniformity isn't here. The authors we asked to contribute to this book have consistent commitments but diverse voices. We invited people whose work we know and admire and asked them to write about something that they want other people interested in doing person-centered planning to know. Some people had already written something we wanted to include, but eighteen chapters were written specifically for this book. We encouraged people to write in whatever style matched their message. So you can read, among other things, a family memoir, text from official government guidance, a polemic in favor of ordinary life experiences based on 37 years of professional engagement in the lives of people with profound disabilities, a yarn about a long and instructive relationship, and a fictional short story and a formal academic paper both by the same author. You can also read about developments in the UK: four chapters come from England and Scotland. We have standardized spelling throughout the book, but not usage. When you read about "people with learning disabilities" you are reading about "people with developmental disabilities", and vice-versa. When you see an unfamiliar word order –"disabled people" or "people with disabilities"– you are seeing the author's respect for the clear preferences of the people they work with. And "person-centred" in the book title above isn't a mis-spelling.

We have kept within the boundaries we set for *A Little Book About Person Centered Planning*. While some chapters describe the ways an initiative has developed or enumerate the steps of a change process, we have not tried to replace the growing number of manuals, videos, and trainings that teach people how to do person-centered planning.[*] We continue to present the perspective of practitioners reflecting on what they have learned from their work.

Within these boundaries, there are at least two serious omissions that we know about.

---

[*]For a comprehensive and well-annotated list of resources on how to do person-centered planning, see Sanderson, Kilbane, & Gitsham, 2002.

- People with developmental disabilities themselves have begun to facilitate person-centered plans outside the boundaries of formal service organizations –usually in the context of a self-advocacy group and often in partnership with other facilitators. Family members have begun to do the same –often through networks formed through participation in leadership development programs like Partners in Policy Making (see www.nwtdt.com/pinp/default.htm). The people we invited to tell us about these important developments were too busy with their own work to write about it here. Soon, we hope, they will write about what they have done and what they have learned.
- Lots of person-centered planning happens with children and their families and in schools. Apart from reflections on projects assisting young people to move from school to adult life, reports on this vital work are missing from this book, an omission we want to remedy in a later volume.

Different voices, common commitments

All of the authors share a commitment to inclusion. They each believe –for different reasons that matter deeply to each of them– that love and justice demand sustained effort to open up ordinary public facilities, schools, associations, workplaces, and housing so that people with disabilities can fully participate in valued roles. All of the authors share a commitment to freedom. They each believe –for different reasons that matter deeply to each of them– that love and justice demand a sustained struggle to respect and support each person's autonomy in living up to the responsibilities in their relationships and their duties as citizens.

These commitments are not exceptional. Many people believe that people with disabilities should live, learn, work and play in community. Many people believe that the services that people with disabilities require should promote choice and self-determination. What we admire about the people we invited to contribute to this book is their attitude toward their commitments. They are among those agents of deep change who can acknowledge the gaps between espoused beliefs and beliefs in practice. They can see and name these gaps in their own lives and work. They don't just point their finger at a society that still invests heavily in the segregation and restriction of people with disabilities, and in service organizations that talk community and choice but practice congregation and control. They also know from personal experience that what is possible for people with disabilities can be transformed by those willing to build trusting relationships and learn how to try another way.

The reason to have commitments is so that we can acknowledge gaps between our values and our actions and take responsibility for learning from these gaps. Person-centered planning offers one important way to guide this learning so that it engages people's freedom and creativity. Often the victories are frustratingly small, hard won, and fragile despite best efforts, but the people who wrote this book find enough to sustain their hope in walking with others to build ways to belong to more inclusive communities.

Common commitments leave plenty of room for differences. The authors of the chapters that follow this one have different roles, work in different settings, prefer different ways of going about person-centered planning, and feel called to work with people with different impairments. As you will see by reading their chapters, they could find plenty to differ over on such important questions as the way person-centered planning figures in strategies to change service systems, the worthwhileness of person-centered planning in service settings that are not committed to deep change in their ways of assisting people, the balance of benefits and threats in measuring the ways person-centered planning is done and the outcomes associated with it, the desirability of formally adopting a particular method of person-centered planning, and whether person-centered planning is better understood as a clinical intervention or as a sort of art.

Two levels of implementation

The purpose of person-centered planning is to inform action that makes life better for people with disabilities and the people who know and love them. Thinking about this purpose suggests two implementation questions:

- What does it take for people to gain access to an effective way to plan?
- What does it take to move plans into action that makes a positive difference in people's lives?

As understandable as the appetite for simple, easy-to-do answers to these questions may be, this book can't satisfy that hunger.

We have seen situations where person-centered plans came together with minimal effort and were translated into action with little fuss or bother. But this only happens when the gap between a person's vision of a desirable future and their current reality is easily bridged by a known and immediately available solution.

There is a hard way and an easy way to narrow the gap between current capacity and vision enough to make implementing person-centered planning simple. The hard way involves increasing capacity so that a system finds it easier to offer personalized supports and a community is more familiar with people with disabilities as active participants. The easy way shrinks vision to match current capacity by keeping people's expectations within whatever a system can do without changing much. People get stuck within the box made by whatever a system finds easiest to do. Person-centered planning activities can serve either people who choose the easy way or people who choose the harder way.

The voices of experience assembled here don't spend many words on person-centered planning along the easy route except to worry about its bad effects. They write about building and sustaining trusting relationships through the long struggle for life circumstances that allow people's gifts to shine through. They write about the challenges of active imagination and creative action. They write about the assumptions they have taken pains to uproot in their own work about what is possible for people with disabilities, what is possible for our communities, and what effectiveness means in the world of services. They write about the importance of facilitators seeking not just technical skills but personal support to keep growing in their own capacity to contribute to meaningful change.

Those who learn from this book will shape the future of person centered-planning, and, far more important, they will play their part in building up a more inclusive community wherever they live and work . Our opportunities for constructive action will be shaped by two sorts of forces, a changing environment that demands person-centered planning on a large scale, and a set of practices that emerge from nearly 25 years of work with person-centered planning.

A changing environment means rising demand

Four rising trends shape the environment for person-centered planning and create new contexts for its continuing development by demanding more person-centered planning for more people.

First, more service systems want person-centered planning done on a large scale. Typically, this demand is associated with a larger system-reform. For example, in Michigan person-centered planning is part of a state-scale initiative to change the way services are funded and delivered. In England it is a key element in an overall change in national policy designed to increase choice and inclusion (See Chapter 28). This greatly increases the demand for people to facilitate person-centered planning (Chapter 13 and 14 describe long-term efforts to prepare and support facilitators). As person-centered planning grows more visible by being required, reasonable people ask for evidence of its effectiveness (see Chapter 7 for a sense of how far there is to go to provide good answers to this reasonable question).

Second, many people have worked hard over the last 25 years to develop technologies, deliver services aligned with the values of inclusion and choice, design policies that allow people control of individual funding, and discover ways to mobilize community members and associations. This work revolutionizes what can be for people with developmental disabilities. The extent of implementation of each of these forms of organized support varies greatly, and the number of places competent in more than one or two of them is currently very small indeed. Nevertheless, it is now possible to see person-centered planning in the context of a set of initiatives that significantly increases people's chances for a good life in community (Chapter 8 connects person-centered planning with efforts to offer positive behavior support and self-determination. Chapters 22 and 23 explore person-centered planning in relationship to supported employment. Chapter 27 describes the transformational changes necessary for an agency to offer personalized supports). Most accounts of good practice in family support, inclusive education, supported employment, and supported living call for person-centered planning to guide the work of personalizing assistance.

Third, there is a growing interest in re-shaping service systems to provide people with developmental disabilities with effective control of the public money available to pay for the services they use (Bradley, et al. 2001; Dowson, 2002). Most people involved in this important reform think that increasing disabled people's control of services requires a major shift in the way services are planned and coordinated (see Chapters 4 and 28). While some understandably criticize the temptation of resistant service systems to substitute talk about person-centered planning for real change in power over public money (Nerney, 2001), most advocates of self-determination see a place for person-centered planning (or something very like it) in their vision of a reformed system (Cumming, 2002).

Fourth, interest in person-centered planning begins to grow outside the fields of special education and services to people with developmental disabilities. (Chapter 18 outlines the way users of mental health services have collaborated in modifying person-centered planning procedures to suit their own preferences and Chapter 2 was written to introduce people in the mental health field to person-centered planning.)

Evolution from within

Biologist Humberto Maturana makes a key point about the relationship between conservation and change. Biological evolution and human history, he thinks, are a process of transformation based on what is being preserved. "What we choose to conserve determines what is free to change," he says (Maturana & Bunnell, 1999, p. 82).

The voices of experience gathered here have a lot to say about what is worth conserving as growing demand creates new contexts and attracts the creative energies of many new practitioners. Some of these messages take the form of reflections on history: personal history (Chapters 8, 9 and 17), organizational history (Chapters 24 and 27), and the history of person-centered planning (Chapter 3). These are not just reminiscences but stories of change that say what it is important to hold onto when confronted with the possibilities (and seductions) of a new environment. We think it would be a mistake to imagine that the conditions prevalent when person-centered planning began are described here as reminiscences: despite much talk about self-determination tens of thousands of people with disabilities have no alternative but to exist in the captivity of congregate services.

Some of these messages are appeals to hold onto person-centered planning as the practice of a creative art. A different kind of listening and a different kind of action proceeds from people who are finding ways to create together than follows from the time-metered completion of a state defined person-centered planning procedure (Chapters 10, 11, 12, 13 and 19).

Some of these messages arise from the writers' engagement with such difficult issues as…

- Balancing what people want for themselves with concerns about safety and health (Chapter 15).
- Supporting participation by people with severe communication impairments (Chapter 16).
- Responding well to people with profound movement disorders and other obstacles to good health (Chapter 17).
- Inviting older parents and their children to plan with heightened expectations (Chapter 19).
- Encouraging young adults and their families who are on the track for segregated lives to reach for community opportunities (Chapters 20 and 21).
- Building commitment to action outside current understandings of disability and community (Chapter 5).
- Incorporating the requirements of a well made plan into daily service routines by creating effective staff teams (Chapter 26).
- Finding hope to continue when things get difficult (Chapters 8, 9, and 13).

There is no way for us to tell how person-centered planning will change in response to these environmental demands to scale-up the capacity for person-centered planning. Those who call for much more person-centered planning might make the sustained investments necessary to supply capable and committed facilitators and the even bigger and much scarier investments necessary to transform systems that segregate and control people. In that case, person-centered planning will be one contributing factor in a major social change. Or, those who require much more person-centered planning can choose the easy route and invest only enough to discover personal visions that generate no real tension with their current practice. In that case, person-centered planning will continue to make a positive difference to those people who are willing to work at the system's edges, with whatever resources they can scrounge.

References

Bradley, V., et al. (2001). *The Robert Wood Johnson Foundation Self-determination Initiative: Final impact assessment report.* Cambridge, MA: Human Services Research Institute. (Download from www.hsri.org.)

Cumming, E. (2002). *Personal agents and independent brokers.* Center on Self-determination. (Download from www.self-determination.com)

Dowson, S. (2002). *Not just about the money: Reshaping social care for self-determination.* Bury St Edmonds: Community Living (Download from www.emprise-international.com/njam.htm)

Holburn, S. & Vietze, P. (Eds.) (2002). *Person-centered planning: Research, practice, and future directions.* Baltimore: Paul Brookes Publishing.

Ludlum, C., (Ed.) (2002). *One candle power: Seven principles that enhance the lives of people with disabilities and their communities.* Toronto: Inclusion Press.

Maturana, H. and Bunnell, P. (1999). The biology of business: Transformation through conservation. *Reflections: The Society for Organizational Learning Journal, 1* (1), 82-86.

Nerney, T. (2001). *Filthy lucre: Creating better value in long term supports.* Center on Self-determination. (Download from www.self-determination.com.

O'Brien, J. & Lyle O'Brien, C. (Eds.) (1998). *A little book about person centered planning.* Toronto. Inclusion Press.

Sanderson, H., Kilbane, J. & Gitsham, N. (2002). Person-centred planning: A resource guide. In Department of Health, *Planning with people: Towards person-centred approaches.* London: DoH. Pp. 83-121. (Download from www.doh.gov.uk/learningdisabilities)

Snow, J. (1998). *What's really worth doing and how to do it: A book for people who love someone labeled disabled (Possibly yourself).* Toronto: Inclusion Press.

2

A Turn for the Better

Pete Ritchie

What is person-centered planning?

Person-centered planning is a way of organizing around one person to define and create a better future. This way of working has evolved over the last twenty years, mainly in North America and the UK.

Thousands of people and families have used person-centered planning to help them make decisions and changes in their lives.

Typically in person-centered planning the person invites people who know and like them to come to a meeting. One or two facilitators guide and record the discussions and decisions. After the meeting, people do what's been agreed.

This hardly sounds revolutionary. But the frame which is put around the meeting, the questions the meeting asks and the way the meeting is organized often mean that new possibilities emerge, new understandings develop, new alliances are formed and people's lives take a definite turn for the better.

In this chapter, I describe the defining features of person-centered planning; give an everyday example of person-centered planning in action; and suggest better and worse ways of using the power of person-centered planning to help people with mental health problems be included in their community and their society.

The defining features of person-centered planning

Person-centered planning is a philosophy and an approach, not just a set of tools and techniques. However, the family of tools which are used in person-centered planning provide a practical demonstration of philosophy in action.

Person-centered planning has evolved as a philosophy, a method and a craft over the last twenty years. Key figures in this evolution include Marsha Forest, Susan Burke-Harrison, Herb Lovett, Connie Lyle O'Brien, Beth Mount, John O'Brien, Jack Pearpoint, Michael

A version of this chapter was previously published in P. Bates, Ed. (2002) *Making social inclusion a reality for people with severe mental health problems.* London: Sainsbury Centre for Mental Health and is printed here with permission of the publishers.

Smull, Judith Snow and Jack Yates. David Sibbet's work on group graphics (Sibbet, 1977) was also an important influence.

For an account of the evolution of person-centered planning, see O'Brien and O'Brien (2000). For an overview of person-centered planning, 'its limitations, conditions for success, and contribution to organizational renewal', see O'Brien and O'Brien (1998). Sanderson et al. (1997) provide a full account of how the different tools have been applied in a UK context.

Person-centered planning tools share an underlying four part structure, which is diagrammed on the facing page. They also share common features. Person-centered planning also relies on a distinctive style of facilitation, and uses a number of distinctive questions and frames to explore and understand people's situation.

Steeped in values

Person-centered planning grew out of a commitment to inclusion as a social goal and was consciously designed as an inclusive process. There is a fundamental coherence between goal – what person-centered planning is helping people to achieve –and process– how person-centered planning works.

For example: we think that there are people out there who are willing to help in new ways if we ask them properly –so person-centered planning invites contribution from the people present at the meeting.

We think that many disabled people experience a lack of control in their lives and feel they are managed by the service system rather than managing their services. So person-centered planning gives people as much control and direction as possible –over who comes to the meeting, when and where it is and how long it lasts.

We think that many disabled people live in enforced absence from communities –so person-centered planning always makes sure they are present.

We think that many people labelled disabled have gifts and capacities that go unnoticed and unused in our communities –so person-centered planning draws attention to people's gifts and capacities and takes these as the starting-point.

We think that what happens to people labelled disabled is powerfully shaped by mental models: the person's sense of her own identity, and how she and the people around her see each other and understand the part they play in each other's lives. So person-centered

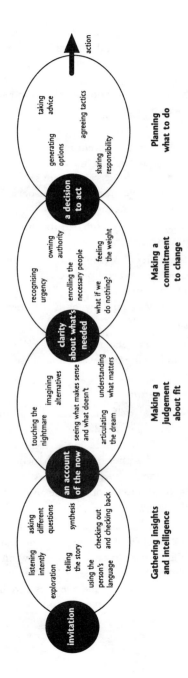

The Underlying Structure of Person-Centered Planning Tools

planning asks 'who is this person' and offers a space for the person to assert a new identity and for others both to affirm this identity and confirm their investment in it. Person-centered planning invites people to enlarge their understanding of the person and to see them through different lenses. As they do this, they also reconsider their own place in the person's world.

Accountability to the person

Person-centered planning is an event in the person's life, not a procedure of the service system. As much as possible, it takes place in the person's world, with the service system seen as part of the environment. So for example 'here' means the person's house, 'there' means the hospital or the day centre.

The facilitator is accountable to the person who is the focus of the plan. Jo's meeting is Jo's meeting.

The tools and techniques of person-centered planning can be used to manipulate the person into compliance with the service system or with powerful others. However, this is not person-centered planning, any more than sawing up firewood is carpentry.

A commitment to action

While an assessment can stand alone as a description of the person and her situation, a planning process without a commitment to action is unfinished.

Focus on the whole person

Traditional assessment starts from a 'categoric' perspective. The frame around the assessment is 'what do people who have this diagnosis typically need?' The discussion is steeped in assumptions about 'people like Jo' – that they belong with 'people like them', that other people will find them a burden, that they don't know their own mind. In this sort of discussion, people are not seeing Jo at all, just her diagnosis.

In a more individualized approach to assessment, people do focus down on Jo and try to set aside the 'group' frame. However, they focus on Jo's disability –what Jo can't do, what's wrong with Jo and what would make Jo better. This makes sense, because disability is what the different professionals and agencies have in common. Being an expert in disability qualifies someone to participate in the assessment.

Person-centered planning, though, is about Jo and not about Jo's disability. Jo's disability is acknowledged and respected as one of her identities —but the focus of the plan is on Jo's aspirations —what Jo longs to do; on her preferences — what Jo loves to do; on her relationships —who Jo needs to see; and on her contribution —what Jo, the unique, fascinating, multi-sided Jo, can offer the world.

The planning focuses on how Jo can use her gifts to connect with others, not on how Jo can be fixed. The planning starts from the assumption that Jo is OK, that she is just fine as she is. This doesn't mean she doesn't need help —in fact she might die in 12 hours without help —or that it wouldn't be helpful for her to learn some new things if she wants to change things in her life. But Jo is already a whole person, not a part person.

Unique events

Although all person-centered planning shares a common architecture, every planning event is different. All four elements of the planning process are interactive exchanges, and the planning is what happens during and after these exchanges. What happens depends on who is there at the time, and what happens will be different next time.

Each meeting is consciously planned —where should it be, who is being invited by whom, how will we use the space, what sequence of questions might work— and is under continuous review —are we getting stuck, are we staying focused on what matters to the person, are the right people being heard, what is not being said.

By contrast, 'care planning' meetings often follow a standard format and have a similar feel even when significant people are absent or when one person from an agency has substituted for another.

The graphic record is the planning's footprint —the evidence that planning passed this way. The real plan is not in the paper but in what people do next. Person-centered planning is an event, not a document.

By contrast, an assessment is given objective status as a document and can be discussed and passed on independently of the person or of anyone involved in producing it.

Facilitation

Person-centered planning relies on facilitation to move the energy in a situation to a more productive state.

There can be many reasons why the energy in and around the person is not being well-used. For example, the person herself may not be allowed to shape her own future or even to know what is being planned. Sometimes, families and friends are not involved at all, or are told only what someone else thinks they should hear, or their views and their contributions are discounted even before they are heard. Sometimes, the professionals around the person are working in parallel or at cross purposes, and sometimes this continues even when people know it is happening. Sometimes, people's perception of who the person is constricts their imagination about what might be possible, and often people start from the service solution end 'have we got a place for Jo?' and are stuck because there are no slots to slot Jo into.

But most of all, the energy is poorly used because people are not thinking about Jo.

Facilitation is a skilful process of realigning the energy around Jo and Jo's aspirations —eliciting, confirming, relating, summarizing, re-presenting, questioning, inviting, reflecting, focusing, pushing, encouraging, interpreting, checking out..

It is difficult to facilitate a plan when you have a close interest in what happens afterwards or when you are a big part of how things got to be the way they are —because your own hopes and fears for the future or your own defensiveness about the past are noisy and stop you hearing other voices.

Some people might imagine that if someone facilitates her own plan she has more choice, control and status, but the reverse is true. Having a facilitator to help you plan is like having someone cut your hair —they can see all the way round.

Gerry Smale and colleagues describe three models of assessment: the questioning model, the procedural model and the exchange model (Smale, 1993). In the questioning model, the professional's role is to apply her professional expertise to the situation to determine the correct diagnosis and asks questions from that perspective. In the procedural model, the professional is also very much in control of the process, but her starting-point is her administrative authority to allocate resources.

In the exchange model it is assumed that all people are expert in their own problems and that there is no reason to assume that the worker will or should ever know more about people and their problems than they do themselves, and certainly not before they do" (Smale, 1993.) The professional's authority derives from her skill in facilitating and negotiating exchange between the people involved in the situation.

Person-centered planning is firmly within the exchange model.

Exchange is a source of energy and insight. When people with different perspectives and different requirements engage in dialogue, new understandings can emerge and new solutions can be generated to problems. Equally, if only half the stakeholders are present, consensus may be more easily achieved but the hard work of engaging with difference has only been postponed. As far as possible, person-centered planning puts 'the whole system in the room' and works with the difference.

Facilitators use marginality – being on the boundary – to assist people to exchange. They dance on the edge between the person and the people close to her. They dance on the edge between the 'ordinary' world of the person and her family and the 'special' world of services and professionals. They belong in neither world. If they lean too far towards persuasion or coercion they lose their authority.

However, facilitators are not neutral. They believe that abuse and neglect are wrong, that people's civil and human rights should be upheld, that people should flourish and not just exist. They are biased towards inclusion.

Use of graphics

Person-centered planning typically uses graphic facilitation. In very small meetings, the back of an envelope will do, but when there are more than two or three people a large sheet of wallpaper works better. A graphic has a distinctive power which has nothing to do with people's ability to read.

The graphic creates a focus of attention for the whole group –people watch the paper, not each other.

The graphic confirms that people have been heard. People who are used to not being heard soon see that their words become real when they go on the paper. If people think the facilitator missed or misunderstood what they said, they can point this out and see it being corrected then and there.

A good graphic conveys emotion and vibrancy through color and shape and size and helps to keep depth and richness in the room. It stores energy and makes it available throughout the meeting.

The graphic shows the relationship between one issue and another. A traditional written report has only one dimension – words go before or after other words. A graphic has two dimensions so it is easier to see patterns.

The graphic helps the facilitators to recap from time to time, pointing to what people have said.

The graphic is unique – and is handed to the person at the end as the only shared version of events.

Because the graphic uses shape and color and position and icons as well as text, when people go back and look at the graphic, it is much easier to remember the meeting and who said what than when people go through a written minute.

Asking different questions, using different language

Person-centered planning asks different questions, because it is interested in getting to a different place. Each question has a rationale, and the phrasing of each question is considered carefully, for example:

What's the story?

This simple question is deeply layered. 'The story' is what people choose to tell, there and then on the day. 'The story' is also the dominant account of who the person is - an account which the person may or may not accept and which may or may not be deeply damaging. 'The story' is both more than and less than 'Jo's story'. There is no space here to discuss the idea of 'story' fully.

What's the dream?

Allowing and helping people to dream unlocks the present. Most people do not know what their dream is until they tell it to others. Having your dream heard and respected generates a feeling of safety, often for the first time. The dream is a source of energy, and contains the seeds for what to do next.

What's the nightmare?

For many people, running away from the nightmare is a more powerful force than working towards the dream. So naming the nightmare and bringing it out into the shared daylight can be hugely liberating.

What brings out the best in Jo?

This beautiful question gets people to think carefully and positively about Jo in relation to others; about Jo as a person who is different in different environments; about how to work with what works for Jo. And while Jo knows some of the answers already, she doesn't know them all, and the conversation helps everyone get a clearer understanding.

Person-centered planning in practice: John's experience

John is a man in his 40s who lives near Edinburgh. He currently lives on his own with support from Connect Housing Association. His parents live a few miles away and they have just gone on holiday together to Cyprus. John is a part-time college student and is learning to use computers. Most evenings he visits a couple of close friends who live locally and they often play pool. John is currently looking for work either as a cook or a gardener.

For many years John lived in a privately managed small hostel for people with mental health problems. He had to fit in with the other six people. Bed was at 9.30, lights out at 10.00. He went to a mental health day centre during the week. At the weekend he only got out for half an hour. The social worker used to come to see him and ask how he was getting on. John would say "I'm not coping" and she would say "you'll just have to grin and bear it".

John was referred to Connect Housing when the manager of the private hostel retired. He moved into a shared house managed by the housing association and around the same time he got a new social worker. John was invited to use person-centered planning to think about his future and how he wanted to lead his life.

John's person-centered plan

Before the meeting John chose a few people who knew him well and, with one of the facilitators for the plan, went to ask them some questions – questions like 'what do you admire about John?' and 'what makes a good day for John?'

John invited various people to come to the first meeting – his parents, his social worker, someone from the day centre, someone from the housing association and a couple of friends. They met in the housing association office and used a large sheet of 'wallpaper' to record the discussion and the decisions. As John says:

*It was a bit strange. People were saying good things about
me. I managed to get through it all. Dad came out with a
lot of good things.*

*It was a blank sheet before we put pen and paper to it.
What came out of it? A lot! My past is my past —let's look
forward. My future holds a lot this year.*

Since then, John has moved to his own house; stopped going to
the day centre; taken a college course; established some close friendships with people living locally; taught a friend to play pool (he's
too good now, he always wins) learned to manage everyday tasks
like cooking stir fries and doing the ironing; and worked out some
coping strategies for the ups and downs ("I've been going in even if
I feel miserable –I never skip art.")

The group has kept meeting every few months to help John take
stock and plan ahead:

*I look forward to these meeting... when they're finished I'm
glad to get home. We've had about four meetings, everything's come out positive. Every time it came round I got
more confidence about dealing with the bad things.*

What's different about person-centered planning?

- Different people come – John's friends and family are equal con-
tributors in the meetings, alongside professionals. As John says
*This was the first time they've felt involved. Before then it
was just decisions made.*

- People come by invitation – it's up to John to say who he wants
at the meeting, nobody has an automatic right to be there. John
in turn has been invited to help a friend of his to plan.

- There's a different style – the facilitators keep the meeting focused on helping John work out what he wants to do and how he
wants to go about it. The meetings are positive and lively, and the
graphic recording helps to track and summarize the discussion.

- Everyone is involved in follow-up work after the meeting –John's
task last time was to sort out getting a computer and setting it up.

- The meeting asks different questions. John's negative reputation
preceded him to the housing association. It would have been easy
to focus on John's problems and on how to 'fix' John or where to
'place' him. Person-centered planning focused instead on John's
gifts and capacities and on where he wanted to go with his life.

- There is a very practical respect for John's preferences. John said he wanted to live on his own.

    My parents weren't quite sure. Now my Dad comes on a Sunday, helps with the grasscutting. He's taught me to play golf.

    John said he wanted his own garden, and this is now an important part of John's life. John did a person specification for his support worker and then used this as the basis for interviewing and choosing Linda.

    I wanted someone nice, kind, my age who was good at pool (but now I've found someone else to play with) who isn't bossy and is good at listening.

- Person-centered planning is not about doing things to John or for John – but nor is it about saying "here you go, John, you're on your own now, you can do everything yourself". It's about people who know and like John doing things with John, and recognizing that John –like all of us– needs other people's support to be his own person.

    Living on my own is perfect.. I can do what I want, come home when I feel like it… it's my weekend,

Better and worse ways of using person-centered planning

Like every innovation, person-centered planning has its champions and its critics, people who want to sell it and people who want to buy it. It will deliver more than its detractors wish and less than its enthusiasts claim.

A thoughtful person –wherever they stand in the mental health world– will go back a stage before deciding how best to use this approach, and will ask: *What is the problem person-centered planning is designed to solve?*

Person-centered planning is designed to overcome inertia –the tendency for things to continue in a straight line. For many disabled people, the status quo is isolation, invisibility, and dependence. Their identity is defined by others, they live to other people's clocks, their life is restricted by the absence of their own power or by the misuse of other people's power.

Many people are detained, often kindly, in serviceland –both in the old serviceland, physically behind the wall, and in the new serviceland, physically in and among the real world but subtly separate, out of phase, never quite connecting to ordinary life.

Practitioners of a method of service evaluation called PASS (Wolfensberger and Glenn, 1975) ask the question "What are the likely consequences for this person if current practice does not change?" For many people the answer is "more of the same" —left to itself, the current situation will not generate change. Person-centered planning focuses energy around the person so they can choose a different path. It intentionally bends social space-time.

Sometimes inertia is too strong and the best planning in the world is unable to deflect the forces constraining the person's life. Sometimes there is plenty of room to work and only a light touch is needed to chart a new direction.

If this is the purpose for which person-centered planning is designed, a thoughtful person would quickly see the dangers of seeking to assimilate person-centered planning in the service system. Even their best friends would admit that service systems are experts in inertia —at keeping on keeping on.

Danger one: the belief that services are what people need most

The aspirational nature of person-centered planning takes it outside the context of service planning; much of what people need and want is not available within the mental health service system. Person-centered planning does not demand that the service system provides these things; rather it acknowledges the limitations of the service system and invites people to engage with the person in working for what they want outside the system.

Danger two: having no locus to act when change is called for

People can learn to use the tools and apply the techniques of person-centered planning within a context where all people are going to be allowed to have is what they have already got; and service workers who have promoted person-centered planning in good faith find that they cannot honour their commitments. Unless the system is willing to disinvest and reinvest, at least at the margins, then person-centered planning from within the service system will lead to cynicism.

Danger three: cut-down versions

The leading practitioners in person-centered planning have been learning for over twenty years. It is entirely possible to take their work, strip out the philosophy, ignore the underlying theory, dull the edge of their questions, forgo their commitment to uniqueness, confuse their purpose and discount their dilemmas.

It is easy to make a thin, shiny thing and call it person-centered planning and produce computer templates for people's plans. This proceduralisation starkly relocates person-centered planning within the administrative nexus: we can generate your plan from our template. These attenuated versions of person-centered planning may cause a slight rash for a few days but will certainly inoculate the system against the real thing.

Danger four: expecting person-centered planning to do the system's work

It doesn't need person-centered planning to see that services are letting people down. Making services more responsive and relevant; freeing up money so that people get direct control over the services they use; having professionals on tap not on top; confronting poor quality – none of these depend on person-centered planning. There is a danger of systems postponing reform until they have finished doing their person-centered plans.

Danger five: covering up some or all of dangers 1-4

The real danger is when people refuse to look at what is really happening.

So, what's a better way of using person-centered planning?

First, recognize that the system needs its systems, and that person-centered planning should remain marginal to these. Aim for person-centered thinking to infect rather than inoculate the system, but don't try to build in or mandate person-centered planning as a specific process.

Second, invest in developing a community of practice over time. Invest in initial learning, do a few plans well. Recruit people with natural talent as facilitators from different backgrounds and give them time to become skilled and discerning. Encourage people engaged in person-centered planning to meet, reflect and write.

Third, get system managers to listen to people who have had plans and to facilitators who have been planning with people. See what the patterns are and think about how the system could flex a little.

24

References

Lyle O'Brien C. and O'Brien J. (2000) *The origins of person-centered planning: a community of practice perspective* Syracuse, NY: The Center on Human Policy. (Also in this book.)

O'Brien J. and Lyle O'Brien C. (Eds.) (1998) *A little book about person-centered planning.* Toronto: Inclusion Press.

Sanderson H. , Kennedy J. Ritchie P. and Goodwin G. (1997) *People, plans and possibilities: exploring person-centered planning.* Edinburgh: Scottish Human Services Trust.

Sibbet, D. (1977) *"I see what you mean!" An introduction to group graphics.* San Francisco: The Grove Consultants.

Smale, G. and Tuson, G. (1993). *Empowerment, Assessment, Care Management and the Skilled Worker.* London: HMSO.

Wolfensberger W. and Glenn L. (1975) *Program Analysis of Service Systems (3rd edition).* Downsview, ON: National Institute on Mental Retardation.

3

The Origins of Person-Centered Planning
A Community of Practice Perspective

Connie Lyle O'Brien and John O'Brien

Like other efforts for social change, person-centered planning has been used and misused, complicated and simplified, lengthened and shortened, trivialized, legalized and lionized. As an aid to those who use person-centered planning to improve life conditions for people with disabilities, this chapter offers one account of how the family of approaches to person-centered planning developed. We describe the context shared by the first four methods to emerge (Personal Futures Planning, Individual Design Sessions, Getting to Know You, and Twenty-four Hour Planning) and indicate some of their formative influences.

This is recent history as viewed by insiders. We understand person-centered planning as a systematic way to generate an actionable understanding of a person with a developmental disability as a contributing community member, and we can identify twelve distinct and mostly related approaches that developed during what we think of as its formative period: 1979 to 1992. To prepare we interviewed some of the originators of each approach and collected and read training materials, reports, manuals and accounts of person-centered planning published before 1992.*

Because we are remembering our own thoughts and activities as well as interviewing friends and reading familiar documents, we can make no claim to distance, much less any approximation of

---

Thanks to the people who participated in interviews or reviewed this paper: Brian Abery, Marcie Brost, Emilee Curtis, Marsha Forest, Charles Galloway, Susan Burke Harrison, Teri Johnson, Susannah Joyce, Jo Krippenstaple, Sandra Landis, Marijo McBride, Karen Green McGowan, Beth Mount, Jack Pealer, Cindi Pitonyak, David Pitonyak, Michael Smull, Steve Taylor, Alan Tyne, Ann Turnbull, John VanDenBerg, Terri Vandercook, John Winnenberg, Wolf Wolfensberger, and Jack Yates.

* References identify published versions of materials that usually circulated for some time before finding their way into print, so dates in the bibliography are not a reliable guide to when things were first written and used. Most materials passed from copy-machine to copy-machine and can be hard to locate. We have tried to partially remedy this in O'Brien & Lyle O'Brien (1998).

objectivity. Our engagement may have amplified some influences at the expense of others or blinded us to distinct approaches to person-centered planning that developed outside our own network. Such omissions arise from ignorance (or maybe from defining what could be considered a distinct approach as a variation of one of those we identify), not from any claim to act as the arbiter of what is or is not person-centered planning. These omissions are more likely in the time between 1985 and 1992 as the ideas and tools of person-centered planning were more and more widely disseminated.

Communities of practice

It is reasonable to look at person-centered planning as a collection of techniques each of which has particular defining features and a distinct history associated with particular leaders. However, we have chosen another way to organize this discussion. We want to explore the emergence of person-centered planning from the point of view of communities of practice, a way of understanding how knowledge and skill are created and shared that puts learning in the context of social engagement (Wenger, 1998). *Communities of practice are groups of people informally bound together by shared expertise and a passion for a joint enterprise.* (Wenger and Snyder, 2000, p. 139). People select themselves into communities of practice because of personal interest in building and exchanging knowledge with others who share their commitment to an issue or a task. Communities of practice develop knowledge and invent necessary skills by allowing people to build up and act in terms of a shared context: a set of common meanings and stories that allow them to understand a social world that matters to them and take effective action to change it.

We have an agenda to promote by adopting this point of view. We notice that agencies that want to benefit from person-centered planning often act as if person-centered planning were a sort of tool box of techniques which staff could be trained to use in workshops by studying protocols, hearing about ideas, and perhaps trying out a technique or even two for homework. Such context-free training no doubt teaches something, but we think it deprives learners of the kinds of social supports for inventive action that were available to the people who developed the first approaches to person-centered planning. This seems to us like a prescription for a system fix destined to fail in its purpose of promoting better lives by disclosing people's capacities and gifts.

The community of practice that shaped all of the earliest approaches to person-centered planning functioned between 1973 and about 1986 among people from across North America who shared a passion for understanding and teaching how the principle of normalization might be applied to improve the quality of services to people with developmental disabilities. As the work spread to Britain in 1979, this community of practice became transatlantic, generating cross-national exchanges that extended available perspectives and skills and offered a ready channel for sharing and refining approaches. (For a very helpful account of person-centered planning in Britain, see Sanderson, Kennedy, and Ritchie, 1997). This community of practice provided the originators of person-centered planning with a laboratory for closely observing how services affect people's lives, a forum for discussing the difficult questions that arise in the work of providing services and formulating ideas grounded in their experience, a workshop for inventing new ways to explore the experience of people with developmental disabilities, and a medium for communicating new ideas and techniques.

In describing the community of practice from which these first approaches emerged we are not yearning for the good old days. We do think it wise for those who want proficient person-centered planning to invest in the kind of long-term, regular, face-to-face sharing of activities, stories, and questions that will build communities of practice able to create knowledge and skills relevant to today's opportunities and challenges. We also hope that describing some of the beliefs and assumptions that shaped the emergence of person-centered planning will help those who were not then involved to make sense of what has developed.

A family of approaches

In 1979, Karen Green-McGowan and Mary Kovaks began a series of workshops on 24-hour planning for people with severe disabilities sponsored by the Canadian National Institute on Mental Retardation. By 1980, Beth Mount was training her Georgia colleagues in Personal Futures Planning, Jack Yates was leading people in Southeastern Massachusetts in Program Design Sessions for people moving out of Dever State School, and Marcie Brost, Terri Johnson and their co-workers were planning with people from three county service boards as a way to define the capacities Wisconsin's system would need to develop in order to deliver individualized services. As we will see, these distinct efforts grew from common roots in a network of normalization teachers and their originators. It is the genesis of these four initial efforts that will primarily concern us here.

By about 1988, person-centered planning had grown well beyond the immediate reach of the people who developed the first dozen approaches. More and more people were moving the techniques they learned in workshops or by reading into new settings for new purposes. A few regional and state administrators were considering the question of how to make person-centered planning routinely available on a large scale. Over the four following years, interest continued to grow. In June 1992, the Pennsylvania Office of Mental Retardation sponsored a conference that gathered people involved in various approaches to person-centered planning to inform the implementation of the state's strategic plan (O'Brien and Lovett, 1992). We have chosen this event, with its debate about the costs and safeguards for mandating person-centered planning as a matter of state policy, to mark the close of its formative period.

This family tree identifies twelve early approaches to person centered planning that developed between 1979–1992 and suggests generational influences among them. (Brief references to approaches other than the first four will be found in the last section.)

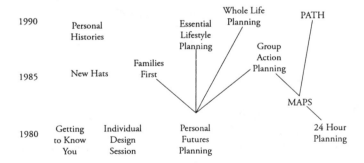

Since 1992, many more variations have developed as a growing number of practitioners and agencies have adapted these approaches to new circumstances and developed their own methods. Today, some approaches, like Essential Lifestyle Planning, are widely practiced and continuing to spread; others, like Individual Design Sessions, continue to develop in the niche where they were born; still others, like Getting to Know You, have nearly dropped from use.

The heading *person-centered planning* became common by 1985. It expresses the family resemblance among these different methods and suggests that they share common genes. This heritage was said to embody four themes (Mount, 1992):

- Seeing people first rather than relating to diagnostic labels
- Using ordinary language and images rather than professional jargon
- Actively searching for a person's gifts and capacities in the context of community life
- Strengthening the voice of the person and those who know the person best in accounting for their history, evaluating their present conditions in terms of valued experiences, and defining desirable changes in their lives

Person-centered planning did not emerge full blown. Scores of people worked out its methods in their common attempt to support people with disabilities to compose their lives. People did not begin to purposely apply these approaches to individual planning until about 1979, but the four at the base of the family tree have common roots in the community of practice that promoted the adoption of the principle of normalization between 1973–1986.[*]

Understanding the origins of person-centered planning requires both a broad sense of trends shaping disability services and a more particular sense of the evolution of understanding and practice among the people interested in teaching and applying the principle of normalization in the development of community services.

New perspectives and possibilities

After taking a course in recent American history, one of our nephews observed, "A lot of the '60s happened in the '70s." For social change minded people with disabilities and their allies the 1970s

---

[*]The first intensive, practicum-based training in the application of the principle of normalization through PASS (Program Analysis of Service Systems) (Wolfensberger and Glenn, 1972, 1975) was held in 1973. By 1986, the network of people working to promote the principle of normalization had divided on questions of the proper role of human services in society and in people's lives, the significance of innovations like supported employment and supported living for the future role of congregate services, the aims and methods of teaching, and Wolfensberger's re-conceptualization of the principle of normalization as social role valorization. After 1986, an international group of teachers affiliated with Wolfensberger continue to provide intensive training in social role valorization, but most of those involved with person-centered planning have moved into other ways of learning and teaching for social change.

crackled with hopeful activism. Many drew strength and strategies from the struggle for civil rights, the struggle for women's rights, and the struggle against the Viet Nam War. In this brief review of a decade, we focus on events and ideas which engaged and influenced many members of the community of practice that created the first approaches to person-centered planning.

In *The Origin and Nature of Our Institutional Models*, Wolf Wolfensberger (1969) used an intellectual history of mental retardation services to vividly sketch the powerful and mutually reinforcing connection between how society sees people with disabilities, the shape of the services professionals consequently offer, and the impact of these services on the lives of people who rely on services. He illuminated the practical differences it makes to understand people with disabilities as citizens and developing persons rather than as sub-human, as menaces, as objects of ridicule, as sick, as burdens of charity, as eternal children, or as holy innocents. This perspective offers a powerful tool for deconstructing common service practices and points a way to improve life conditions by emphasizing personhood, citizenship, and developmental potential. This analysis appeared alongside the first written expression of the principle of normalization (Nirje, 1969) in a volume commissioned by the recently formed President's Committee on Mental Retardation to explore changing patterns in services. This influential volume was followed by the publication of Wolfensberger's more theoretically rigorous definition of the principle of normalization (1972), a definition operationalized in Program Analysis of Service Systems (PASS) (Wolfensberger and Glenn, 1972 and 1975).

The growth of community service systems sufficiently powerful to support all people, regardless of the severity of disability – in Nebraska's regional system, in Macomb-Oakland Regional Center in Michigan, and in Eleanor Roosevelt Developmental Services in New York's Capital District– laid a practical foundation for action on the increasingly incisive criticism of institutionalization emerging from Syracuse University's Center on Human Policy (e.g. Blatt, 1973; Bogdan, Taylor, deGrandpre, and Haynes, 1974, Biklen, 1977).

The National Institute on Mental Retardation (NIMR), sponsored by the Canadian Association for the Mentally Retarded (CAMR), built a national initiative around these US regional service achievements, aiming to demonstrate regional comprehensive community services systems that would make institutions unnecessary. This initiative, called COMSERVE, gave Wolf Wolfensberger a base to refine, teach, and publish his ideas about planning and implementing comprehensive services, evaluating service quality, renewing voluntary organizations, and creating citizen advocacy programs. COMSERV also supported the first series of training and consultation events that drew together a community of practice around normalization teaching. When Wolfensberger founded his Training Institute at Syracuse University, these efforts began to include and influence more people in the US.

Legal work aimed at social change for people with mental retardation excluded from school or trapped in institutions developed rapidly (Kindred, Cohen, Penrod, & Shafer, 1976). Exposé and landmark legal cases further discredited institutionalization, reinforced an understanding of people with disabilities as a disadvantaged and segregated minority, and fueled the move to develop comprehensive services in local communities. The fact that many professionals continued to defend institutions and advocate for congregate services and segregated special education opened deep questions about the legitimacy of the professional perspective. Much service activity seemed to fall under the shadow of handicapism (Biklen and Bogdan, 1976). As Burton Blatt (1981) pointed out, it is possible for well meaning professionals to destroy lives by telling stories that demean people's capacities for development and community membership.

Physically disabled activists incorporated the Berkeley Center for Independent Living in 1972, organized to override the veto of the 1973 Rehabilitation Act with its application of civil rights language in section 504 to forbid discrimination on the basis of disability, and committed civil disobedience to force the Secretary of Health, Education, and Welfare to sign implementing regulations. Near the end of the decade, this spirit touched survivors of mental retardation institutions, who organized to proclaim that they are People First, to attack the process of labeling that justifies their exclusion from the opportunities of everyday life, and to make their voices heard in the governance of services.

Powerful ideas about the practical contrasts between typical and valuing ways of understanding disabilities grew out of the lived experience of disabled activists. These ideas crystallized in a number of versions of these two paradigms. (From normalization teaching materials developed in 1979 based on DeJong (1979).)

	Rehabilitation View	Independent Living View
Terms for defining the problem	Impairment/ skill deficiency	Dependence on professionals, relatives and others who take over control of your life.
Where is the problem located?	In the person	In the environment & the way services do their work
What's the solution?	Professional intervention	Removal of barriers, advocacy, consumer control, & self-advocacy
Who is the person?	Patient/client	Person/citizen
Who's in charge?	Professional	Citizen
What defines results?	Maximum possible individual functioning as judged by professionals	Living independently (being in control of your life regardless of how much assistance you need to do so)

Political action and litigation by parent advocacy groups resulted in growing state investments in community services as well as in state and then federal legislation establishing a right to education for children of school age. Legislative requirements of individual planning as a foundation for special education, rehabilitation, community services, and institutional services provided opportunities to discover both the power of the multidisciplinary professional voice and the service system's very limited capacity to differentiate and respond to individuals that was covered up by the welter of activities surrounding the writing of "I (fill in the blank with the appropriate letter) P's" (Weatherly, 1979).

The work of researcher-practitioners like Marc Gold (1972), Lou Brown (1976), and Tom Bellamy (1979) and their colleagues and students clearly demonstrated that people with severe disabilities were habitually, reflexively, and profoundly underestimated by almost all of the professionals who assessed their capacity to learn and to work. As the American Association for the Education of the Severely and Profoundly Handicapped (AAESPH, later TASH), formed in 1974, set up conferences and a journal to broadcast their findings, more and more people built on them. The contrast grew between people's potential with good assistance and the lives that too many people were forced to live by professionals who would rather attribute incompetence to people with disabilities than face what they themselves did not know how to do.

The engagement of sociologists who brought qualitative methodology and a phenomenological perspective to understanding the daily lives and social possibilities of people with developmental disabilities had a powerful effect on the development of person-centered planning (Bogdan and Taylor, 1975; Taylor and Bogdan, 1977). Framing developmental disability as a social construct opened new space for seeking to understand the experience of labeled people from their own perspective.

Developments in the normalization teaching community of practice

From 1973 to around 1986, the normalization teaching community of practice provided the people who originated the first approaches to person centered planning with a laboratory, a forum, a workshop, and a medium for communication. Each of these functions played a direct role in shaping the early years of person-centered planning.

This community of practice grew up among people who found PASS a powerful way to understand the relationship between disability, service policy and practice, and community life. Though designed primarily as an instrument for quantitative program evaluation across all of the human services (and still presented in that way by Wolfensberger and his associates, see Flynn, 1999) and secondarily as a way to teach the normalization principle, many teachers found most benefit in PASS as a way of learning about the relationship between people with disabilities and service programs from the perspective of normalization.

PASS workshops were intensive, taking five demanding days and typically involving between 60 and 70 participants who worked as a large group to learn the conceptual foundation and in teams of 10-12 to practice the process of looking at services from the perspective of the principle of normalization. Team practice, guided by an experienced team leader and usually an assistant team leader, included at least one practicum visit to assess a service program. Practica included observation and extensive discussion of program quality from the perspective of the 34 dimensions of the normalization principle defined by PASS and 16 dimensions of program quality relating to administrative effectiveness.

For many reasons, PASS did not catch on widely as an official evaluation tool, and, except in a few regions, PASS training was not particularly well or systematically funded (see Thomas, 1999). A workshop required a number of teachers, typically 10 to 14. By the late 70's there were as many as 40 workshops a year in North America and Britain and some workshop sponsors made a practice of inviting some teachers from other places to join in building up their local cadre of teachers. The hard work of offering training on a controversial way to understand services built many strong relationships.

Only a very few people tried to make a living doing normalization training, so most teachers had other work, usually in the human service professions or in human service administration. A number of parents of people with developmental disabilities and a few people with disabilities participated in the workshops but only a few who were not also employed in the field became teachers. Most workshops were substantially subsidized by teachers' regular employers allowing them released time and more than a few teachers used their own vacation time to contribute to the work.

In addition to basic workshops there were occasional advanced workshops and a number of consultation assessments which invited experienced PASS practitioners to assist a program, typically a program led by another member of the network.

A laboratory

The various activities created by members of the normalization teaching community of practice provided a laboratory for the close observation of how service programs functioned. While practitioners of either qualitative or quantitative research could find much to criticize in the process, PASS encouraged looking carefully at a program from the point of view of the people the program serves. Observation, and the following evaluative discussion, focused on a set of questions and criteria derived from the principle of normalization, and the practice of seeking consensus among team members on conclusions about each dimension of service quality stimulated extensive discussion of the sort that often surfaced different understandings, values, and mindsets among team members. Feelings often ran high in these discussions as participants struggled to digest the implications of what they had observed. Writing reports on consultation assessments demanded deeper thinking and offered a vehicle for disseminating ideas.

Members of the community of practice had repeated chances to look at the same world that they functioned in everyday, but from the position of outsiders charged to identify and think about what the people served experienced through the program. A discipline of accounting for what teams observed rather than explaining why service programs were constrained from doing better built awareness of the potential damage human services can unknowingly inflict. Many participants changed their own practice based on what they learned by assessing another program.

Through the lenses provided by PASS, the originators of person-centered planning learned difficult lessons. They learned that opportunities for improvement which are evident to people with disabilities and those who care about them as people are very often obscured, ignored, or dismissed by powerful people in their lives as "impossible" or "unrealistic" based solely on the untested assumptions of the powerful person. They learned how difficult it is to consistently and intensively provide people assistance that is truly relevant to their development. Even those individual plans that specified relevant assistance typically did not predict what people did day-to-day with the staff available to them. They learned that people's social worlds were typically very constricted, even when they were served in ordinary looking buildings on ordinary local streets. They learned that alternatives to controlling and disciplining people with disabilities in groups of stigmatized people were rare and themselves raised significant dilemmas. They learned to expect a disconnection between a program's stated aims and its daily activities and they found that only a rare few service organizations had any way at all to discuss and work toward closing this gap. They learned that meeting ordinary needs for the security of a comfortable home, and people to love and care for, and good work to do is typically beyond the reach of a human service that is not consciously and systematically committed to developing its own organizational capacity.

There was good news as well as hard lessons. Many network members avidly collected examples of good practice. Stories and data about people with disabilities pioneering employment, supported living, and membership in community networks and associations traveled quickly and widely to an audience sensitized to appreciate their importance.

A few projects were funded to apply what community of practice members had learned in new contexts. Two, which were widely discussed among the network, focused on linking individual plans to individualized budgets. One project assessed the capacity of three Wisconsin county service boards based on plans and individual budgets developed with 92 people and their families. This study pursued a two part question:

> *What specific goods, services, and other supports does each individual need to be a respected, participating member of his/her community?*
>
> *What needs to happen for these services and other supports to be made available by the right people in the right place at the right time?* (Brost & Hallgren-Ferris, 1981 p. 1).

The second project focused on a single individual, responding to a judge's order to develop effective community supports for an institutionalized young woman (Galloway, 1981). In it's framing of Sharron T's move from the institution as a "passage to community participation", this detailed plan made imaginative use of the PASS teaching notion of designing services based on "culturally valued analogues". This means asking,

> *What does this service compare to in the world of valued citizens and what would it take to offer the same variety of opportunities to people who rely on services?*

As the graphic below indicates, pursuing this question and viewing the work as assisting someone to journey safely from surviving in the culture of an institution to moving competently in the unfamil-

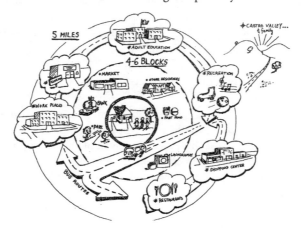

iar culture of community defined a far different setting for Sharron and her two "Teaching Companions" than the specialized group home design anticipated by the service system.

The people who gave shape to the first approaches to person-centered planning knew from their time in this laboratory that mission statements, and regulations, and inspections, and policies, and individual plans on paper are useless unless people act on a commitment to each other. They knew the hellish difficulty of overcoming isolation from community life and escaping reproduction of the web of control that surrounds most people with developmental disabilities. They knew that with disciplined effort and careful listening it is possible to learn a little bit about a person's perspective on their life and what they think would improve it. They knew from experience that attending closely and openly and thoughtfully to a person with a disability –even for a little while– could draw one into caring about how that person's life goes on.

A forum

Every careful look at a service program raised more and deeper questions about the relationship between disability, organized services, and community. Looking closely and thinking carefully about brief snapshots of people's experience troubled the understanding of each term.

For example, the struggle to realize the value of social integration, understood as the active opportunity to grow in a variety of good relationships with others, including people without disabilities, made the shared understanding of community deeply problematic. Members of the community of practice knew that such relationships were possible. Indeed, all of the originators of the various approaches to person-centered planning had (and have) such relationships themselves. But services very seldom do well in facilitating such relationships outside their own boundaries.

In the forum created by ongoing teaching, members explored both the meaning of social integration and some of the means to build good relationships. This made news from citizen advocacy initiatives (local organizations that match and support people in a variety of one-to-one relationships) and the growing number of circles of support relevant, especially in the development of Personal Futures Planning (Mount, 1984; Mount, Beeman, and Ducharme, 1988).

The continuing forum for refining and developing new ways to understand and explain the relationship between disability, community, and organized services led some to explore alternative ways of framing the search for service quality. The most elaborated such understanding found expression at about the same time that the first approaches to person-centered planning emerged. Interest in the work of Thomas Gilbert (1978) led Charles Galloway and John O'Brien to re-think service effectiveness in terms of accomplishments (Galloway, 1978, O'Brien, Poole, and Galloway, 1981). The idea of accomplishments provided part of the conceptual structure for Getting to Know You, Personal Futures Planning, and 24-Hour Planning, though the number and labels for the accomplishments bounced around for a time before settling at five dimensions of experience in which service practice can make a significant difference to the lives of people with disabilities: community presence, choice, respect, competence, and community participation (O'Brien, 1987).

A workshop

Members of the network of normalization teachers regularly faced groups of people with different outlooks, different values, and different styles of learning. Normalization teaching provided a workshop for inventing and testing new ways to facilitate learning about the effects of services on the quality of people's daily experience and their connections to community life. Three innovations in the process of normalization teaching were of particular importance in the development of person-centered planning.

As experience grew, it became clear that PASS teams benefited from spending time in thoughtful discussion of the overall situation of the people who rely on the service whose quality the team is assessing before jumping in to a discussion of service particulars. Two simple questions guided these discussions, which often moved the group to surface and work through significant differences among themselves. These questions are, *Who are the people served?* and *What are their most important human needs?* These discussions proved most fruitful when people used ordinary language to describe people's needs and the consequences of their impairments rather than taking refuge in professional jargon.

By adding only one question to these two, *What would have to happen to meet these needs?*, Jack Yates developed a format for engaging staff in reviewing their own program, which he called Program

Design Sessions. When Bertha Young, the director of a community service agency and an active member of the normalization teaching community of practice, asked Jack Yates, *Why not work through these questions around one person instead of a group of people?*, the format for Individual Service Design emerged. Exactly because these questions are so simple, facilitating a discussion that moves below superficial comments and clichéd understanding requires great mastery on the part of the group leader. Repeated practice in teaching PASS helped a number of community of practice members develop such mastery, though such experience was not the only source of the necessary skill, as Herb Lovett's long and creative use of Individual Service Design demonstrated.

Over time, the power in striving to look at a service program from the point of view of the people who rely on the program led a number of teachers to shift the service assessment's perspective. Teachers learned simple, effective ways to pair team members with particular people a program served in order to encourage them to view the program from that person's place within it. For example, team members might look very closely at what happens for a person who needs assistance eating during a meal or during a time scheduled for training. As team members considered their observations, they asked *What are the likely consequences for the people we met if current practice does not change?* (Note that the focus is on noticing what happens; team members are not asked to pretend to understand the other person's inner experience.)* This provided the originators of person-centered planning with a good deal of practice in facilitating groups' thinking from a person's point of view. Twenty-four-hour planning makes explicit use of this kind of predictive question, asking, *What is this person at greatest risk for, if we do not change his or her life?* (Green-McGowan and Kovaks, 1984).

Graphic facilitation (Sibbet, 1977) introduced a way of guiding discussion and information gathering by combining words and simple graphics. It also stimulated the creation of graphic templates and tasks to structure the collection and display of information. Photocopies of a growing number of these templates and tasks passed

---

*Though he had practiced a comprehensive approach to individual planning for many years, Wolfensberger (1983) strongly disagreed with this move in the context of program evaluation. He believes that looking at a program from the point of view of a few of its participants rather than considering the program as a whole compromises PASS (or its younger cousin PASSING) as objective instruments for service evaluation.

from hand to hand for several years until they were collected in a handbook (O'Brien, 1981). Some level of graphic facilitation found application in 24-hour planning and Individual Service Design and it became a hallmark of Personal Futures Planning.

A medium of communication

Year on year the community of practice grew, engaging most of the originators of person-centered planning with one another and with a growing number of people who shared the demanding and exciting experience of teaching people about normalization through PASS. As person-centered planning took shape, some of the members of this growing network would become early adopters of an approach, others would collaborate in developing the approach, others would sponsor projects that refined and extended the reach of the approach, still others would become its critics.

People in the community of practice spoke a common language and could count on each other to have some skill in facilitating and usefully recording discussions about the tough questions and interesting possibilities at the intersection of people's lives and the daily reality of services. When Jack Yates (1980) wrote about his preferred format for a meeting's "wallpaper", he knew that his readers would be thinking about writing with water-based markers on big sheets of paper taped to the wall and when he referred to "age-appropriateness" he could be confident that most of his readers would grasp the nuances of the issue and not misunderstand it superficially as a crusade to tear beloved stuffed animals from the arms of adults with developmental disabilities.

This common language and skill set made it reasonably easy for people across the community of practice to try out different person-centered planning approaches and to provide originators with fast feedback on results and news about variations they invented to deal with particular problems arising in practice.

A common agenda

The first approaches to person-centered planning shared a common agenda which reflected their originator's involvement in the normalization teaching community of practice. The themes of increasing choice, avoiding de-personalizing labels and difference-making procedures, honoring the voices of the person and those who know the person best, building relationships, individualizing supports based on high expectations for the person's development, and demanding that agencies adopt new forms of service and organization to provide newly conceived supports express an agenda that each approach to person-centered planning followed in its own distinct way. A typical way to communicate what person-centered planning was all about was to draw a strong contrast between usual practice and belief and person-centered practices and beliefs, as illustrated by the two tables below, quoted from documents widely circulated in early training.

Perhaps the most powerful idea underlying person-centered planning is that the way a person who needs services is seen and understood by those who deliver that service generates a powerful internal consistency in the ways the person is served. Trying to make changes in procedures or settings offers far less leverage for changing services than shifting the understanding of a person. This table (Mount, 1984) expresses a contrast that deconstructs the logic of the activity center that currently serves George and outlines a common sense response to him as a person which is masked by the internal consistency of George's current program.

The person-centered planning process makes three important moves. One, it re-frames differences in performance that justify diagnostic labels in terms of differences in life experience. George acts age-inappropriately, in part, because those close to him treat him as

Congregate Service Perspective		Connections Perspective	
Who is George?	What does he need?	Who is George?	What does he need?
A person with a mental age of 4 years 3 months	A program for children	A 40 year old man who has missed most typical experiences and has never had a real job	A lot of experiences
A person with IQ >30	To be protected from the world		A real job
A person who is severely mentally retarded	To learn very simple tasks	A person with no income who is poor	An income
A person who has "an indication of organicity, including difficulty with angles, closure, retrogression, over-simplification and an inability to improve poorly executed drawings."	To learn these skills separately from non-disabled people because he is so different from them	A person who has been isolated all his life	To be included and present in the community
		A person who has no contacts or connections to the wider community	Relationships to other people, connections to community
	Highly specialized staff who can address issues of retrogression, closure, etc.	A person who has little control over the direction of his life	Friends
			Vision for the future and support in getting there
	An environment where his temper can be controlled	A person who has more difficulty learning new skills than most people	Someone who can speak out on his behalf
A person with acute temper flare-ups directed at staff			A lot of support for learning
	To be repaired and sent back to the real world when he is better controlled	A person who is treated as a child by his mother	More people who see and treat him as an adult
		A delightful man who makes a difference in the lives of those who care about him	People who can enjoy him

a child. He needs more people in his life who see and treat him as an adult and facilitate his participation in the adult world of work and community. Two, it directs attention outside the orbit of service programs. George is poor and has missed many typical experiences. He needs a real job of the sort only available in the real world and not at his group's table in the activity center. Three, it brings George's capacities to the foreground. George is a delightful man to those who know him. He needs more people to enjoy him. Those who think inside the logic of congregate services will experience dissonance if they make these three moves. This dissonance can motivate change but, paradoxically, it can also stimulate a re-commitment to the familiar logic of congregation. To support their retreat, people re-cast person-centered planning in terms that make it consistent with service-as-usual. Managing this paradox in ways that preserve person centered planning's leverage for system change continues to trouble its originators (Lyle O'Brien, O'Brien, and Mount, 1997).

Typical individual planning happens inside the logic of the sponsoring service program. The way individual planning is done reflects and reinforces the assumptions underlying the program. Person-centered planning confronts these assumptions explicitly and seeks to build its practice on a different logic. This table, taken from the manual for *Getting to Know You* (Brost and Johnson, 1982, pp. 6-7), expresses a criticism of usual individual planning approaches in terms familiar to members of the normalization training community of practice.

Our Assumptions	Perspectives on Traditional Approaches
1. All people, with and without disabilities, share the same basic needs. As human beings, all of us are concerned about having experiences throughout our lives that provide us with: a) autonomy and independence, b) individuality, c) love and acceptance through presence and participation within a family and community, d) stability and continuity, e) continuous growth and learning, f) community status, g) security with respect to personal finances as well as	1. "Even though you say you value me as a person, my experiences tell me that you are unable to distinguish me from my disability. Your assumption seems to be that people with disabilities are more different than like you who are non-disabled. Your society operates as if my disability and the problems it presents are the most important, and perhaps the only thing worth mentioning about me. From here it is a short step to you seeing me as "a problem."

protection of our legal and human rights. People who have disabilities do not have qualitatively different kinds of needs.

---

2. Description of disability is relevant only to the extent that the disabling condition complicates the fulfillment of the above-mentioned needs. What people who are disabled do not have in common with non-disabled people is the independent ability and means to create conditions, situations, and experiences in their lives to meet some or all of their basic human needs.

2. "Once I, as a person with a disability, am seen as 'a problem', it becomes increasingly difficult for you to view me as a real human being. The question of 'What do I as a person need?' becomes 'How do you deal with me, this problem?' Too often, your thinking begins to follow this logic:

- "This person is disabled!"

- "His/her disability is a problem!"

- "This problem needs to be fixed!"

- "Special people are needed to fix it!"

- "It can only be fixed in special places!"

- " It needs to go to one of those special places to be fixed!"

- "It can only come back, or come out, when "it" is fixed!"

This scenario is one of the most real and most overwhelming barriers that stand between me and the rest of the world.

---

3. Because disabilities complicate people's lives in ways that ultimately make it more difficult for them to meet their own needs independently, some form of help is required. "Help" can be provided in a variety of ways, in many places, by many people. The form of help and the ways in which it is designed and arranged determine whether or not people get their basic human needs met. It is com-

3. "Your line of thinking prevents you from asking the right questions about me and other people with disabilities and our needs. The questions that you ask focus on what is wrong with me and are designed to determine my levels of functioning and the degrees of severity of my disability. The results are usually a short perfunctory list of my 'strengths' well as lists of services that need to be purchased

mon to hear phrases such as "Joe Smith needs speech therapy." A more accurate wording would be: "Joe Smith, like all of us, needs to be able to communicate effectively in order to express his needs and preferences and to socialize. His disability interferes with communication ability in several specific ways. Speech therapy is one form of organized paid-for assistance that might help him meet his communication needs."

in order to 'fix' me."

"When I as a person with a disability become a disability and then become the problem, my needs are only seen as services. When my needs become defined as service types, professionals, and places (e.g., 'he needs physical therapy, a behavior management expert, a group home'), it is easy to lose sight of my more basic human needs that your services were meant to address in the first place

---

4. The goal of the human services system should be to join forces with natural unpaid support networks (families, friends, neighbors, co-workers, citizen advocates, etc.) to create conditions and support for people with disabilities to live within their local communities. Services should be designed and delivered to enhance each person's capacity for growth and to convey the conviction that each person can participate in some valued role in the community. This goal is valid regardless of a) the type of disability or problems presented, b) the extent to which the disability complicates service provision, c) current lack of services required by the person, d) scores achieved on tests or scales, e) past involvement with the service system. If we view people with disabilities as individuals first and the difficulties they encounter as a result of disability as secondary issues, our vision of their needs will focus on ordinary human needs and the multitude of forms of assistance possible to help meet those needs.

4. "Too often your services are designed and arranged in ways that ignore my current and potential natural, unpaid supports and in ways that restrict my growth, maintain my dependency, and deny me opportunities for community presence and participation"

"Assessment becomes a way to rationalize excluding me on the basis of type or extent of my disability, test scores, past experiences, or lack of appropriate services."

"If you view me and other people with disabilities as disabled first, then your vision of our needs will focus on fixing or alleviating our problems through paid services, and you will overlook opportunities to involve our families, friends, neighbors and co-workers."

Distinctive methods

Because people can belong to and be influenced by more than one community of practice at a time, and because over time people can move from one community of practice to another, the idea can help explain how approaches with common roots and common agendas differentiated from each other. Differences grew because practitioners engaged distinct issues and settings, drew on different theories and tools to shape their processes, and formed new communities of practice around each approach.

Different issues

As the diagram below suggests, person-centered planning developed in the context of an overlapping set of communities of practice that grew up around some of the issues that shaped the field of service to people with developmental disabilities from 1975 to 1985. These were concerned with directly improving life for people with developmental disabilities in school, in the transition to adult life, in employment, in the move from institution to community, especially when difficult behavior or severe disability threatened to leave people no alternative to institutionalization.

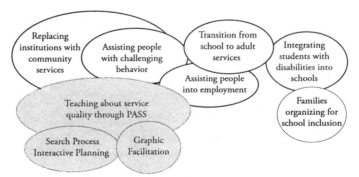

Twenty-four-hour planning grew from a concern for people whose chances for effective community services were significantly reduced by the complexity of their disabilities. Drawing on their own successful work in creating effective services for people with profound, multiple disabilities, Karen Green and Mary Kovaks developed training and consultation that focused service development on careful individual plans that specified the exact settings and supports a person would need in order to engage in functional and meaningful activity. Here is an example from a plan developed with a 20 year old man identified as "the most medically fragile" person in a 1,200 person institution at the request of his family. Given the perception of Jerry as embodying a devastating disability and the resulting institutional service arrangements that the system assumed were essential to his survival, a plan that called for Jerry to live in his own place with non-disabled peers and make choices among community activities profoundly challenged the imagination and skill of those responsible for Jerry's services (Green-McGowan and Kovaks, 1984, p. 9-10). In their formulation, these goals presume that the institution cannot offer Jerry what he needs to grow and develop. As might be imagined, this made the plan the locus of controversy between advocates for institutional improvement and advocates for institution closure; a controversy in which Jerry's advocates prevailed.

---

1. **Jerry's goal for community presence**

   From: living in a ward with 60 persons labeled "medically fragile" in an institution of 1200; being worked with by nurses and aides who bathe, feed, dress, change and give medication; getting one hour of "music therapy" a week, staying in bed when he had seizures

   To: living in a home with at least one non-handicapped age peer and no others with handicaps; being worked with by his peer on experiencing five other environments per week (i.e., leisure time, basic necessity, watching/helping with real work); being allowed individualized recovery time after seizures.

2. **Jerry's goal for rights and personal interests**

   From: crying, grabbing, grunting, eye pointing and withdrawing; having no consequences for decisions

   To: head signals for yes or no; eye or finger pointing to eight to ten symbols representing persons, objects, places; making two to five choices for breakfast, lunch and dinner; choosing daily apparel.

This style of planning blended a deep understanding of how to assist people with significant disabilities in very practical and detailed ways with the task of forming an appreciation of the unique identity of each person. It gave people who knew and loved a person with profound disabilities a privileged voice in formulating their sense of the person's individuality and worth as a community member and in defining what mattered in a person's life. It gave people with specialist knowledge and skills the chance to define how these things that mattered could be supported and to specify the exact conditions of service under which professionals could most effectively practice. Accordingly, 24-hour plans were more technically specific and detailed across people's days, evenings and weekends, and nights than the other three approaches and they appealed especially to people with specialist training. They became one instrument in gathering a community of practice of nurses and occupational, physical, and speech therapists committed to creating powerful supports for community living for people with very complex bodily needs.

Getting to know you was designed as a way to define the capacities a service system requires in order to provide individualized supports. It enlisted people with disabilities and their families as collaborators in system evaluation and service development rather than as the consumers of a planning process and available services. Plans are precise about the assistance that people need, but far less detailed about how support must be delivered than those constructed in 24-hour planning. Many of the 92 people and families who chose to test their county service system by clearly specifying their individual needs and the costs of meeting them reported some benefit for themselves in making the plans, but what they created also influenced the evolution of their county and state's developmental disabilities services system.

Individual Service Design guided service workers to a deeper understanding of a person's experience and thus to increased empathy and personal identification with the person they assist. It gathered people to reflect on a person's identity by carefully reviewing personal history, thoughtfully drawing out connections between the individual's experience and the processes of social devaluation that shaped institutional living and comparing and contrasting life experiences between the focus person and other members of the group. By imaginatively pursuing a search for socially valued analogues –defined by asking *How does this ordinarily happen for valued citizens?*– the group constructed a test for its own practice. For example, if the focus person lived in a group home the question "What is 'home' like for the rest of us here?" would be followed by the question "In what ways is our group home like and different from what the rest of us consider 'home'?" and "What changes would offer this person more of the benefits of home?"

Personal Futures Planning intersected several communities of practice as Beth Mount's work took her from helping people move into employment from a work activity center in a rural South Georgia county, to assisting people to move from institutions into community living settings in Northeast Georgia, to doctoral research with young African-American adults and their families who were completing special education in places that had very limited service funding, to work with people identified as having the most severe behavioral problems in Connecticut's institutions. At each step, new issues and problems tested, refined, and extended the approach as new colleagues brought new skills and knowledge. Beth's involvement with Citizen Advocacy, a program that makes and supports one-to-one relationships between people with disabilities and other citizens, and with Circles of Support, a way of organizing a person's allies around shared concerns, focused Personal Futures Planning on organizing and extending a person's social supports (Mount, 1988).

Two approaches with distinct roots

Two streams of person-centered planning developed apart from the community of practice concerned about normalization teaching. **New Hats** grew from Emilee Curtis' recognition that many of the dreams and potentials of the people with developmental disabilities she worked with in an activity center were easily overlooked. Indeed, she concluded that service workers too often tried to extinguish people's dreams. Encouraging people to communicate their dreams has led her to develop a variety of powerful aids to thinking, deciding, and communicating. Links to other approaches with person-centered planning emerged later as she made connections to their practitioners and incorporated some of their ideas into her unique formats.

MAPS developed when concern for including children in a residence for children with profound disabilities in a neighborhood school led Marsha Forest to learn about 24-hour planning. A growing community of practice driven by the desire of Ontario parents to open neighborhood schools and their classrooms to students with disabilities re-shaped the 24-hour planning format. The questions of how a school might welcome and support a student with disabilities whose needs for adaptation challenged typical classroom practice and how a student whose place in school was threatened might get the support to belong and to learn provided the context for MAPS development (O'Brien and Forest, 1989). Two Ontario Separate (Roman Catholic) School Boards, in Hamilton-Wentworth and Kitchener-Waterloo, committed themselves to full inclusion and their schools became sites for visits by educators and family members from around the world. Visitors went away having learned about what it takes for all children to be welcomed as active learners, including the usefulness of MAPS. Efforts to promote inclusion in schools across Canada convened a ten year series of summer institutes at NIMR and McGill University that gathered parents, people with disabilities, teachers, and administrators and, among many other things, taught them how to use MAPS as a foundation for inclusion (Forest & Lusthaus, 1989). Collaboration with Judith Snow, who lives with the support of a circle and has a deep and powerful interest in assisting people to guide their lives by listening to their dreams (Snow, 1992), extended the MAPS process and built strong bridges between MAPS, the creation of circles of support, and Personal Futures Planning.

Different theories and tools

Different interests in planning theories and tools among their originators also differentiated approaches from each other. Individual Service Design stayed very close to its roots in PASS training. Getting to know you blended the normalization teaching perspective on gathering information and understanding people's needs with an approach to human service needs assessment and case management that constructed General Service Plans specifying services that would respond holistically to an individual's needs.

Balancing participation in order to assure that professional voices did not drown out the contributions of those who knew and loved a person deeply concerned the originators of 24-hour Planning. They adopted nominal group process techniques (Delbecq, Van de Ven, and Gustafson, 1975) as a way to assure equality of involvement and a balance of influence on the group's results.

Personal Futures Planning incorporated the most extensive exploration of ideas about planning of any early approach to person-centered planning. Some of these ideas came from Beth Mount's doctoral study in public administration, which brought her into contact with research on people-centered development efforts in Asia (Korten, 1981) and with the processes of life/work planning created to assist former clergy and displaced engineers to discover new career paths (Crystal and Bolles, 1974). Some came from her shared reading and discussion with a sub-group of the normalization training community of practice interested in applying the insights of feminist thinkers in disability practice (for one key example, see French, 1985). Some came from her engagement with a community of practice concerned with service planning that intersected the normalization teaching community of practice.

Incorporating lessons from systems planners

A much smaller community of practice involving people concerned about designing community service systems overlapped the normalization teaching network. Under the leadership of Allan Roeher, The Canadian Association on Mental Retardation's National Institute on Mental Retardation (NIMR) became the hub for this network, which gathered associates from across North America and sent them to work with advocates and bureaucrats across Canada. Based in part on his work at NIMR, Wolf Wolfensberger created and repeatedly presented a six day course on planning community service systems through the Training Institute he founded after his move to Syracuse University in 1973.

Experience led to disappointment with the kind of rational planning that assumed it was possible to systematically implement a fully designed system from the top down. It proved nearly impossible to gather sufficient political power to pull off the complete implementation of a blueprint for comprehensive services. Worse for some members of this network, the approximations of a comprehensive solution that did get implemented –viewed from the perspective of the people and families they served– demonstrated that the prevailing idea of "system" was too mechanistic and inflexible to support people in valued community roles.

This disappointment pushed Alan Roeher and John O'Brien to look for different ways to understand planning and systems, a concern that led them to collaboration with David Morley at York University's Faculty of Environmental Studies. The Faculty was powerfully influenced by its engagement with Eric Trist, a seminal thinker in understanding and designing adaptive social systems. Through this collaboration, the process of the search conference and the social systems theory behind it became available in the normalization teaching network. (For a current overview of this process and theory, see Emery, 1999 and Trist, Emery, and Murray, 1997.) Involvement with other faculty members brought contact with complementary systems theories and planning practice developed by Russell Ackoff and his colleagues (1974) under the heading of interactive planning.

These links provided four key ideas.

- Rapid and connected change means that people and their organizations live in a turbulent environment. In such an environment, it is possible for people to find ways to steer but it is not possible for them to sustain walls strong enough to keep change far enough away to permit successful control from the top. Self-organization leads to success.

- The best way to understand human situations is to look at them whole, in terms of their interactions and purposes, rather than breaking them down into ever smaller pieces and then trying to think up ways to reassemble the pieces.

- There are important benefits to gathering people with diverse and conflicting interests to discuss the trends and forces shaping their shared environment, to assess the consequences of not changing, and to create vivid images that communicate shared possibilities for a desirable future.

- A shared vision of a desirable future provides a far more robust mechanism for coordinating action in a rapidly changing world than any bureaucratic blueprint for command and control.

Once people in the normalization teaching network began to gather people for search conferences around topics like family support and employment opportunities and attendant care, all that was necessary was for someone to notice that the search conference process could be adapted for a group of people who gathered to focus on one person's future. This is the step that Beth Mount and her collaborators made into Personal Futures Planning.

Continuing development

By 1992 four approaches had become at least twelve.

One additional approach, **Personal Histories**, drew directly from the normalization teaching community of practice to encourage those who acted as planning assistants to invest time and imagination in helping people with developmental disabilities to construct and communicate an account of their life story (Landis and Pealer, 1990). Initially incorporated into the work of Residential, Inc, a pioneer supported living agency in New Lexington, Ohio, Personal Histories formed a part of the consultation Sandra Landis and Jack Pealer did with agencies in Ohio until about 1990.

The other approaches built on Personal Futures Planning and MAPS as their originators brought different ideas about planning and services to bear on different situations. John Butterworth (1993) and his colleagues in Connecticut developed **Whole Life Planning**, a way to match planning procedures to the individual preferences of people with developmental disabilities who were seeking employment. Ann and Rud Turnbull created **Group Action Planning**, adopting ideas from Personal Futures Planning and MAPS to empower families to plan, especially families like their own who are concerned to realize great expectations for family members with behavioral challenges (Turnbull and Turnbull, 1996; Turnbull and Turnbull, 1999). Families First, a project of ARC-Ohio, conducted workshops to support parents in building brighter futures for their young and school aged children, linking family controlled individual planning with organizing for the local and state system changes necessary to align education and human services with visions shared among families. (Holden, 1990). PATH supported individuals and groups in charting strategies for achieving valued futures when sustained and coordinated action is required (Pearpoint, O'Brien, and Forest, 1992).

After exploring Personal Futures Planning, Michael Smull and Susan Burke Harrison (1992) responded to the opportunity to specify what community services would provide for people so profoundly isolated and deprived by their years of institutionalization that they could not articulate a dream for themselves and lacked anyone to join a support circle who knew them beyond their reputation for challenging behavior. **Essential Lifestyle Planning** (ELP) aimed to discover and gain service provider agreement to address the simple but important issues for each person which, if ignored, lead to mistrust, unhappiness, and power struggles. A growing community of practice around Essential Lifestyle Planning has generated an array of tools for discovering what matters to people, building a very finely grained understanding of the rituals and routines that allow people to express their uniqueness, reviewing the quality of plans, incorporating the perspective of skilled service providers, dealing with conflicts, supporting necessary organizational changes, and bridging to other person-centered approaches as a person's dreams grow bigger and stronger and a person's relationships with potential allies grow wider and deeper.

Keeping person-centered planning alive

Person-centered planning grew from passionate concern to discover the gifts hidden by disabling assumptions and to create paths to valued participation for people segregated by social devaluation.

Shared passion brought people together in ways that generated communities of practice. These communities of practice developed skills and knowledge that moved their members into alliances with people with developmental disabilities and their families and friends. These alliances put person-centered planners' knowledge to work supporting one person at a time to add their capacities to the task of shaping more just and more inclusive communities. This bold vision melds personal and social change. Discovering and realizing ways for marginalized people to claim opportunities and contribute to community life serves justice in small and significant ways.

Person-centered approaches that lose touch with this almost presumptuous vision of will drown in the swamp of bureaucratic requirements. Practitioners without lifelines to a community of practice that renews and refines their energy by firing imagination and creating knowledge will wither into servants of rules and regulations. The meaning in person-centered planning today lies where it has since its beginnings. Meaning lies in belonging to a community of practice that, over months and years, shares stories, lessons, and support. Meaning lies in serving people as they move from being segregated and being controlled toward community participation and the support to compose lives that matter.

References

Ackoff, R. (1974) *Redesigning the future: A systems approach to societal problems.* New York: John Wiley.

Bellamy, G.T., Horner, R, and Inman, D. (1979) *Vocational habilitation of severely retarded adults: A direct service technology.* Baltimore, MD: University Park Press

Biklen, D. and Bogdan, R, Handicapism: A slide presentation. Syracuse, NY: The Center on Human Policy.

Biklen, D. (1977). The politics of institutions. In B. Blatt, D. Biklen, and R. Bogdan, eds. *An alternative textbook in special education.* Denver: Love Publishing Company. Pp. 29-84.

Blatt, B. (1973). *Souls in extremis: An anthology of victims and victimizers.* Boston: Allyn & Bacon.

Blatt, B. (1981). How to destroy lives by telling stories. *Journal of Psychiatric Treatment and Evaluation, 3,* 183-191.

Bogdan, R, and Taylor, S. (1975). *Introduction to qualitative research methods: A phenomenological approach to the social sciences.* New York: Wiley.

Bogdan, R. and Taylor, S. (1976). The judged, not the judges: An insider's view of mental retardation. *American Psychologist 31(1),* 47-52.

Bogdan, R., Taylor, S., de Grandpre, B., and Haynes, S. (1974). Let them eat programs: Attendant's perspectives and programming on wards in state schools. *Journal of Health and Social Behavior, 15(2),* 141-151.

Brost, M., Hallgren-Ferris, B. (1981). *Getting there: Developing individualized service options.* Madison, WI: Bureau of Developmental Disabilities.

Brost, M. and Johnson, T. (1982). *Getting to know you: One approach to service assessment and planning for individuals with disabilities.* Madison, WI: Wisconsin Coalition for Advocacy.

Brown, L., Nietupsky, K, and Hamre-Nietupski, S. (1976). The criterion of ultimate functioning. In M. Thomas (Ed.) *Hey, don't forget about me! Education's investment in the severely, profoundly, and multiply handicapped.* Reston, VA: CEC.

Butterworth, J. (1993) *Whole Life Planning: A guide for organizers and facilitators.* Cambridge, MA: Institute for Community Integration.

Crystal, J. and Bolles, R. (1974). *Where do I go from here with my life?* Berkeley, CA: Ten Speed Press.

DeJong, G. (1979). Independent living: From social movement to analytic paradigm. *Archives of Physical Medicine and Rehabilitation, 60,* pp. 435-446.

Delbecq, A., Van de Ven, A., and Gustafson, D. (1975). *Group techniques for program planning: A guide to nominal group and Delphi processes.* Glenview, IL: Scott-Foresman.

Emery, M. (1999). *Searching: The theory and practice of making cultural change.* Philadelphia: John Benjamins Publishing.

Flynn, R. (1999). A comprehensive review of research conducted with the program evaluation instruments PASS and PASSING. In R. Flynn and R. Lemay, eds. *A quarter century of normalization and social role valorization: Evolution and impact.* Ottawa: University of Ottawa Press. Pp. 317-349.

Forest, M. & Lusthaus, E. (1989). Promoting educational equality for all students: Circles and MAPS. In S. Stainback, W. Stainback, and M. Forest. *Educating all students in the mainstream of regular education.* Baltimore, Paul Brookes . Pp. 43-57.

French, M. (1985) *Beyond power: Women, men, and morals.* New York: Simon and Schuster.

Galloway, C. (1978). *Conversion to a policy of community presence and participation.* Presentation to The 1978 Regional Institute in Law and Mental Health, USC Schools of Medicine and Public Administration, Los Angeles, CA.

Galloway, C. (1981). *Passage to community participation: A plan for Sharron T. and those who follow.* Sacramento,ca: Author.

Gilbert, T. *Human competence: Engineering worthy performance.* New York: McGraw Hill, 1978.

Gold, M. (1972). Stimulus factors in skill training of retarded adolescents on a complex assembly task: Acquisition, transfer, and retention. *American Journal of Mental Deficiency, 76,* 517-526.

Green-McGowan, K. and Kovaks, M. (1984) Twenty-four hour planning for persons with complex needs. *The Canadian Journal on Mental Retardation, 34,* 1, 3-11.

Holden, L. (1990) *Building brighter futures for our children.* Columbus, OH: ARC-Ohio.

Kindred, M., Cohen, J., Penrod, D., & Shafer, T. (1976). *The mentally retarded citizen and the law.* New York: The Free Press.

Korten, D. (1980). Community organization and rural development: A learning process approach. *Public Administration Review, 41, 6:* 480-510.

Landis, S. and Pealer, J. (1990). *Personal Histories.* Chillicothe, OH: Ohio Safeguards.

Lyle O'Brien, C., O'Brien, J., and Mount, B. (1997). Person-centered planning has arrived... or has it? *Mental Retardation 35,* 480-484.

Mount, B. (1984). *Creating futures together: A workbook for people interested in creating desirable futures for people with handicaps.* Atlanta: Georgia Advocacy Office.

Mount, B. (1988). *What are we learning about circles of support?* Manchester, CT: Communitas.

Mount, B. (1992) *Person-centered planning: A sourcebook of values, ideas, and methods to encourage person-centered development (1992 edition).* New York: Graphic Futures.

Nirje, B. (1969). The normalization principle and its human management implications. In R. Kugel and W. Wolfensberger, eds. *Changing patterns in residential services for the mentally retarded.* Washington, DC: President's Committee on Mental Retardation.

O'Brien, J. (1981). *Normalization training through PASS: Team leader manual (version 1.0).* Decatur, GA: Responsive Systems Associates.

O'Brien, J. (1987). A guide to lifestyle planning. In B. Wilcox and T. Bellamy, eds. *A comprehensive guide to the activities catalog.* Baltimore: Paul Brookes.

O'Brien, J. and Lyle O'Brien, C., eds. (1998). *A little book about Person Centered Planning.* Toronto: Inclusion Press.

O'Brien, J. and Forest, M. (1988). *Action for inclusion.* Toronto: Inclusion Press.

O'Brien, J., Poole, C. and Galloway, C. (1981). *Accomplishments in Residential Services: Improving the Effectiveness of Residential Service Workers in Washington's Developmental Services System.* Decatur, GA: Responsive Systems Associates.

Pearpoint, J., O'Brien, J., and Forest, M. (1992). *PATH.* Toronto: Inclusion Press.

Sanderson, H., Kennedy, J., and Ritchie, P. (1997). *People, plans, and possibilities: Exploring person-centered planning.* Edinburgh: SHS, Ltd.

Sibbet, D. (1977). *"I see what you mean!" A guide to group graphics.* San Francisco: Author.

Smull, M. and Burke Harrison, S. (1992). *Supporting people with severe reputations in the community.* Arlington, VA: NASMRPD.

Snow, J. (1992). *What's really worth doing and how to do it: A book for people who love someone labeled disabled (Possibly yourself).* Toronto: Inclusion Press.

Taylor, S. and Bogdan, R. (1977) A phenomenological approach to mental retardation. *In B. Blatt, D. Biklen, and R. Bogdan, eds. An alternative textbook in special education.* Denver: Love Publishing Company. Pp. 193-203.

Thomas, S. (1999) Historical background and evolution of normalization-related and social role valorization related training. In R. Flynn and R. Lemay, eds. *A quarter century of normaliza-*

tion and social role valorization: Evolution and impact. Ottawa: University of Ottawa Press. Pp. 353-374.

Turnbull, A. P. and Turnbull, H. R. (1996). Group Action Planning as a strategy for providing comprehensive family support. In L. Koegel and G. Dunlap (Eds.), *Positive behavioral support: Including people with difficult behavior in the community.* Baltimore: Paul Brookes. Pp. 99-114.

Turnbull, A. P. and Turnbull, H. R. (1999). Comprehensive lifestyle support for adults with challenging behavior: From rhetoric to reality. *Education and Training in Mental Retardation and Developmental Disabilities 34(4),* 373-394.

Trist, E. Emery, F. and Murray, H., Eds. (1997). *The social engagement of social science: A Tavistock anthology. Volume III: The socio-ecological perspective.* Philadephia, PA: The University of Pennsylvania Press.

Weatherly, R. (1979). *Reforming special education: Policy implementation from state level to street level.* Cambridge, MA: MIT Press.

Wenger, E. (1998). *Communities of practice: Learning, meaning, and identity.* Cambridge, UK: Cambridge University Press.

Wenger, E. and Snyder, W. (January-February 2000). Communities of practice: The organizational frontier. *Harvard Business Review,* 139-145.

Wolfensberger, W. (1969). The origin and nature of our institutional models. In R. Kugel and W. Wolfensberger, eds. *Changing patterns in residential services for the mentally retarded.* Washington, DC: President's Committee on Mental Retardation. Pp. 51-179.

Wolfensberger, W. (1972). *The principle of normalization in human services.* Downsview, ON: National Institute on Mental Retardation.

Wolfensberger, W. and Glenn, L. (1972 and 1975). *Program Analysis of Service Systems (PASS), 2ⁿᵈ and 3ʳᵈ editions.* Downsview, ON: National Institute on Mental Retardation.

Wolfensberger, W. (1983). *Guidelines for evaluators during a PASS, PASSING, or similar assessment of service quality.* Downsview, ON: National Institute on Mental Retardation.

Yates, J. (1980) *Program design sessions: OOP (optional operating procedure).* Author.

4

A Plan Is Not an Outcome

Michael W. Smull

Person-centered planning is our label for learning how people want to live, to learn what is important to them in everyday life and to discover how they might want to live in the future. But, a plan is not an outcome. The only reason to do the planning is to help people move toward the life that they want and person-centered planning is only the first part of the process. Whether anyone can get the life described is also determined by their access to resources and the rules for using those resources.

When you put these two things together, planning for your future and control over resources, you have self-determination. Not too many years ago this was not an issue, most of the groups pursuing self-determination were individual agencies that believed in helping people with disabilities chart their own destinies. They gathered circles of caring people around each person to discover what they might want and used their resources to help people move toward the life that was described. Now some of the public agencies that fund and manage services are mandating person-centered planning. They are requiring that everyone get a person-centered plan. Whether this will result in people moving toward the lives that they want will depend in part on the quality of the planning but also on the control that people will have over the resources.

Those who are the best at both the planning and helping people have control over their resources recognize that it is as much a journey as it is a destination. It is about helping people find and maintain a balance in their lives. It is a journey because what people want changes over time (sometimes quickly and often slowly). Everyone has to try things to see what they like and what they like changes as they grow and mature. It is about helping people find a balance because real life is complicated. Most of us want mutually exclusive things (e.g. to be thin and eat all the fattening food we want). Most of us need to take into consideration the desires and preferences of other important people in our lives. Many of us have more that we want than we can afford. Resources are finite, so we have to decide how to prioritize what we want. Good plans are a snapshot that takes of this into account (implicitly or explicitly) at a moment in time. They reflect the current balance that someone wants and give direction for the future.

Good person-centered planning requires that you be able to learn what is important to each person, separate what is important to the person from what is important to others, and communicate what you have learned in a way that others understand. Implementing plans is also about supporting a journey. In trendy business terms, it reflects using a learning wheel. We begin by listening and trying to understand what we hear. We record what we learn in a plan. As we act on what we have learned, we see how it works. And then begin again by listening and understanding.

Those who fund and regulate need to change the current reality. For most people with disabilities, who receive services, the present reality is a world of programs. Most of the current resources are fully committed to buy capacity, to buy slots. There are people living in group homes and going to segregated day services who have told us that they hate their roommate and are bored during the day. There are high school students attending educational programs they find meaningless because they do not prepare them for the future that they desire for themselves. Where people want change, planning without real action simply creates cynicism for everyone. One of the traps that this creates for planning is that what is available now shapes what is asked for.

In trying to not be limited by what exists we have learned that the kinds of questions that you ask and the order in which you ask them make a difference in the outcome. Ask about what is important before asking where it could happen. Learn what is important in everyday life and then look at all the different ways that it could happen. Look at what is happening in the rest of the world. We now have enough best practice, enough pilots, that what people have in mind is likely to already exist. It may not be next door, it may have been developed on the other side of the US, or in the UK or in Canada, but it is likely to exist. Only after people have explored what is possible should they look at what is available now. Where what someone wants is not offered the next question is how do we develop it here? Knowing that it has been done elsewhere gives people the sense that it can be done and someone to learn from.

Clearly this is easier to do with people who are just coming into the community system, people who are leaving their family homes or are leaving institutions. When we plan with those people who are already receiving services we are facing a number of new challenges. One of these is that people are not used to looking outside of their current ways of doing things. Plans that started with what was wrong with someone were typically part of a professional ritual where good paper counted more than good lives. These plans were written with those who spent the least time with the person having the greatest input. They were read only by those who wrote them (and those who inspect), and were not used in everyday life. This part of professional culture continues and interferes with implementing person-centered plans. To change the culture we have been recommending that those who manage or visit ask some simple questions after the person-centered plans are written. Ask those being supported and those providing the day to day supports: How is the plan working? What have we learned? What have we tried? What else could we try? What else do we need to learn? Ask these questions often and in as many ways as makes sense. Write the answers on the person-centered plans. Where this is done those who provide the support see what they learned incorporated in the plans. They see that what they do and how they do it changes as we all learn. Those who are supported and those who provide the supports feel respected, and part of a partnership. The plan becomes a living document that is changed as our understanding deepens and as the person changes.

If we want to change the system we need to look for incremental change as well as revolutionary change. At any moment, we can create best practice for a few people if we put in enough effort and resources. However, if the many are not to be left behind we need to move our entire system incrementally toward best practice. One way to do this is to think of the changes as happening in phases. Start by looking for every opportunity for best practice and seize each one. Then think about how to start incremental change. For many it begins with simple person-centered plans where we ask what is important to people in everyday life, compare that with how they are living now, and change what can be changed now. Change what can be changed without having to make major changes in structure or practice.

Making the easy changes is a good way to start, but an unacceptable place to stop. If people with disabilities are to get the lives that they want, change has to continue. Planners, managers, and those who support have to look at what people want and compare that with their capacities to deliver what is being asked for. Where there is a deficit in capacity they need to look at what needs to change. Does the deficit in capacity reflect a deficit in skills, knowledge, or competencies? Does the development of new capacity require changes in policy, practice, or structure? Is the deficit a reflection of problems in how we think or in the unwritten rules for how we act, is there a problem with organizational culture? Again, this is most easily seen as a learning wheel where we are looking at what individuals want and using that to change the system.

Those who mandate the planning will need to make changes in funding, practices, and structures if plans are to reflect what people want and be implemented. They need to invest in the new vision of quality. They will need to build structures that are rooted in values of respect, trust, and partnership. They will have to change a provider agency culture that sees the funding that people receive as the agency's money and uses the language of ownership about people with disabilities. And they need to do this with a minimum of wreckage.

Those who get the support need to be able to say that I am moving and I am taking my money with me. However, those who are left behind need to be able to continue to live as they wish. The change literature makes it clear that there is no change without loss but we can make change without wreckage. We need to make sure that those who provide the supports are offered the technical assistance to find the win-win solutions. Most will need help to learn the new skills and make the changes in practice and culture needed to move from a relatively static system of supports to one that has the flexibility needed to support people in their evolving visions of how they want to live.

5

Community-Building &
Commitment-Building
with PATH

David Wetherow and Faye Wetherow

When people first learn about PATH, they tend to think of it as a planning tool –after all, that's part of the title: Planning Alternative Futures with Hope (Pearpoint, O'Brien & Forest, 1995). If they are involved in supporting people with disabilities, they are likely to be interested in the prospect of a colorful, engaging, positively-oriented alternative to traditional individual program planning, education planning, and service planning processes.

PATH is certainly a powerful planning tool, but in addition, and, perhaps even more importantly, it is a very powerful tool for *invitation*, *community-building* and *commitment-building*.

PATH and traditional planning processes

Unlike a service plan, a PATH is not defined by or constrained by the limitations of what the service system is prepared to offer, nor by the prescribed mandate of an agency, school, or service system. The creative conversation at the heart of PATH extends well beyond any agency mandate, and the invitation to participate should extend well beyond the boundaries of the service system.

PATH is not an ISP, IPP, IEP, Health Care Plan or Rehabilitation Plan. When it is thoughtfully undertaken, it offers a broad view of the person's vision for their own life, a vision sometimes developed in collaboration with friends and family members, especially when people have great difficulty communicating. With that broad vision in mind, it becomes possible to derive a service plan that is consistent with the PATH.

The service plan derived from PATH is one of a larger set of understandings and commitments. It is the response of *one* of the parties to the person's future (the agency, the school, the system's representative) to a larger expression of the person's life direction. It gives an agency a way of saying, "We see the overall direction and understand our role in supporting that direction. The ISP that we will develop next week will reflect how we can support Shirley to pursue the elements of her PATH that fall within our mandate."

The school might say, "We understand the broad direction that Jack and his family want to take with his education, and we're clear about our role in supporting that direction. Next month, we will develop an Individual Education Plan to reflect what the school is able to offer Jack to assist him on that PATH."

Sometimes the PATH graphic depicts the intention to create a relevant service plan as one of the many steps that will contribute to the goal, but by now it is clear that the service plan does not define the goal, and it is well understood that the vision is not limited by the mandate of the service system.

Community-building and commitment-building begin with strategic invitation

When we are organizing a personal PATH, one of the general strategies we have in mind is the idea of following the threads of a person's interests, gifts, dreams, and passions in the direction of community connection, companionship and contribution. We know that a great deal of energy is released when it becomes apparent that the personal interests of the pathfinder intersect with the personal interests of community members, caregivers and other allies.

With this strategy in mind, we encourage the pathfinder and his allies to think expansively, creatively and courageously about whom to invite to the PATH session. We mention family members, friends, neighbors, colleagues, people who may have been important to them in the past, and especially members of the larger community. We emphasize people with whom they might share a particular interest or passion, or people with whom they share a strong identity –perhaps people who attend the same church, members of common cultural groups, and so on.

One person's question about how to deal with the bugs in her garden without using pesticides might be welcomed by community members who might be involved in permaculture, organic gardening, or saving the local river estuary. We could pursue the possibility that a brief connection based on that question might evolve into a more extended involvement, companionship and contribution to the cause of a less polluted planet. If someone were interested in music, we would encourage them to invite people who are involved in making music, even if they were relative strangers.

Church and cultural connections can be particularly fruitful, even
if they don't appear to include common interests other than a shared
cultural identity. Remember the old nursery rhyme,

Here is the church,
Here is the steeple,
Open the door,
And see all the people!

When we think about it, each one of 'the people' goes some place
during the day, so a connection that begins with the church has the
potential to reach into hundreds of places in the community. Each
of the members is also connected with other friends, neighbors,
interest groups, community associations, workplaces, and so on, so
a single connection has the potential to reach into hundreds of additional 'places' in the community.

If we limit the PATH invitation to the usual cast of characters
–service managers, immediate family members, caregivers, system
advocates– we may be missing this rich set of potential connections.

***

A few years ago, we visited a facility-based day program that
was searching for a new direction. One of the young women who
attended the program particularly enjoyed the activity of baking
muffins every Wednesday afternoon. Program staff described the
benefits: an enjoyable hour or two; a tasty dessert to share with
friends and family, learning outcomes related to reading and following recipes, development of "functional" cooking skills, and
so on.

Since many of the people in the program expressed the desire
for more companionship and connection in their lives, we began
to explore the idea of *moving from activity to connection*.* When
the staff began thinking about cooking-with-a-focus-on-con-
nection, one of them quipped, "We need to stop cooking and
start looking". Being a good detective became an interesting new
element in their job descriptions.

As our conversation evolved, we helped Sara and her mother
create an invitation list for a personal PATH. Initially, Sara
thought about inviting a couple of program staff, her social
worker and her mother. We asked Sara if she might want to
invite some other people in her community who cared about her.

---

* To read more about this idea go to www.communityworks.info/articles/activity.htm.

She said yes, she would invite the pastor from her church.

On the day scheduled for the PATH, we arrived at the apartment building where Sara and her mother lived, and encountered a rather distinguished-looking English gentleman. We introduced ourselves and learned that he was the pastor that Sara had talked about. "I'm not sure what I'm doing here," he said, "I don't know anything about disability." "That's alright," we said, "We're really glad that you're here. Our guess is that you'll have a lot to offer."

Sara had been in the day program for some time, and program planning normally took the form of asking "what activity should we add to the calendar?" –focusing on personal interests and skill development, but not particularly focusing on connections. But now, because Sara's PATH included the idea of moving from activity to connection, several new opportunities presented themselves. And it turned out that Pastor Martin held the key to almost all of the connections.

As soon as we mentioned the idea of "cooking as connection," Martin came up with the idea of introducing her to the group of women who met every Saturday afternoon at the church to make muffins for the Sunday service. 'Gardening-as-connection' led to Martin's vision (included by Sara on her PATH!) of planting 5,000 daffodils in the garden beds at the foot of the church. "It will be spectacular in the Spring! And we won't just have people digging and weeding alone –we'll make sure that people do this together and have a picnic whenever they get together at the church."

Sara was interested in social dancing, and this activity had always taken the form of a little group of people from the day program being driven to the pub by staff on Thursday evenings. But when Martin learned that Sara loved folk dancing, he came up the idea of starting an English folk dance group in their small community. Martin had a personal interest in this –he missed the folk dancing that was part of his life in England before he came to Canada, and he knew that there was no such group in their town.

Martin absolutely understood what we were working on. He understood that Sara was a catalyst for community-building –that she would make his community stronger. And, he was able to make connections that nobody else could make– because he was a connected person. This gentle man who was so nervous at the outset, ended up making the strongest set of commitments at Sara's PATH –and he kept his promises.

***

We thought about what made this work.

We limited "the ask". When we made the invitation, we only asked for involvement for the duration of the PATH session itself; we didn't ask for a lifetime commitment. In essence, we said, "Martin, we wonder if you could help us by spending a couple of hours thinking with Sara about her life and thinking about how her interests might be encouraged."

Although we didn't ask for a commitment beyond the PATH session, we did hope for it. There was no way of predicting or controlling the outcome, but the outcome would have been certain if Sara hadn't made the invitation. Making the invitation requires courage —but it's worth it.

Each of the elements of PATH offered an opportunity for engagement. Martin became engaged at many distinct points in the overall PATH process. Each of the steps in PATH offers a unique opportunity for engagement:

Hearing the Dream, people often begin to get the feeling that they are on sacred ground —in a tender place— and they respond with considerable empathy. As the deeper parts of the Dream are spoken and heard, people begin to see the other person in themselves; and they see themselves in the other person.

With the pathfinder's permission, we offer all participants the opportunity to add something to the Dream —something that reflects their knowledge of the person, reveals the person's gifts and interests, or is an expression of *their* dream for the person. We always check in with the pathfinder to see if each element corresponds with their own personal vision.

The inquiry about the Goal is framed in a way that allows participants to feel that it is not just desirable, but possible, and they begin to sense what might become their own role in making those possible things happen. In Sara's PATH, the question "What would be happening if we were doing good work in this direction for a couple of years?" allowed Pastor Martin to visualize his own place in the picture, and to see that this role was within his means, because it was balanced by the roles that others played. "I know these women who bake at the church on Saturdays, and I know I can help Sara make that connection."

As the PATH develops, each of the participants begins to envision their particular role in making things happen. In their imaginations, they begin to experience the sense of satisfaction that comes from contributing to a desirable outcome, and begin to relish the part they can play in making this positive future possible.

Creating a snapshot of What's Happening Now may engender recognition of difficulty, but it also contributes to an awareness of resources and opportunities. "Sara spends a lot of time alone" is balanced with "She makes wonderful muffins, and I know one woman in the group who would really appreciate her skill in that area. Mary would be a perfect bridge builder for the Saturday group."

Who Do We Need to Enroll? is a question that often marks a change in the energy level of a PATH. We recognize that we need to enroll ourselves; and we see that if others can be enrolled the effort will be more broadly shared – making our contribution possible. It becomes clear that a continuing strategy of enrollment is one of the things that will eventually bridge the gap between where we are now and where we want to be.

What Do We Need to Do to Get Stronger? Identifying General Strategies, and Identifying Milestones on the way to the goal are all steps that engage the creativity and the problem-solving energy of the participants, create additional opportunities to see oneself in the picture, and increase the sense of shared effort and possibility.

Committing to First Steps is a crucial opportunity for each participant to declare their personal commitment and hear and celebrate the commitments of others.

The final check-in offers an opportunity to recognize and declare a sense of delight, safety and commitment, and to relish hearing that expression on the parts of others.

The PATH process engages participants in problem-solving, and they experience a growing sense of involvement and investment.

***

Joe's vision of owning his own home galvanized the 17 people who had gathered to participate in his PATH. "I bought the house!" Joe said in the 'Goal' section of his PATH. "Great," we said, "How did that happen?" Joe was a bit stumped, but half a dozen of the people who had gathered with him 'remembered' what made it possible to buy the house:

"We used some of the money that Joe's mother had set aside for him to make a down payment."

"I got my friend Charlie, the bank manager, to come to a circle meeting about a month after we did this PATH. He saw Joe's vision, and he also realized that the circle was a source of real strength – it gave Charlie the security he needed to feel comfortable about making the loan."

"We had a big painting party one weekend. All of us showed up with our families. We painted and gardened and picnicked, and had a great time. Mary brought one of her famous apple cobblers!"

Joe's group needed a real estate agent who would operate with integrity – they couldn't afford to make a big mistake in purchasing a house – and one participant in the group remembered that she knew someone who would fit the bill. "My friend Janna is a real estate agent who is very honest. We can share Joe's PATH with her so she understands what we are trying to do, and she can help us find a place that we can afford that won't have any hidden problems. Also, she'll know that seventeen people will be watching – that will keep anybody honest."

The real estate agent showed up later in the PATH as one of the 'People we Need to Enroll', and the person who had the strongest personal connection with her included contacting her as one of her personal First Steps. Other participants celebrated this contribution, and in a very subtle way, are prepared to encourage and support that participant to take that important first step. If the group makes good use of the PATH graphic, they can re-visit the story each time they meet, and hold themselves accountable for their personal and collective commitments.

***

As participants begin to get engaged in active problem-solving, the experience of making these active contributions deepens their sense of commitment and shared purpose.

The inquiry helps pathfinders and their allies become more strategic in their thinking.

***

As a long-time recipient of rehabilitation services, John had adopted a rather closed, binary model of thinking about how he might make progress in his life. Significant gains were either to be achieved alone —through independent effort— or they could not be achieved alone, in which case he needed to go back to the service system for further rehabilitation and training.

Years of immersion in special education and rehabilitation services had never raised the prospect of enlisting his personal support network in helping with his search for meaningful employment, quitting smoking, or moving towards more authenticity in his relationships – all of these had been interpreted as matters of individual skill or will.

The pattern of inquiry and reflection in PATH opened up some new possibilities. John can use the graphic record to remember the strategies he created, to share his vision and plan with his friends, and to reconnect with the energy that was attached to these discoveries.

***

The inquiry encourages the pathfinder to recognize the importance of identifying individuals and groups to enlist, to get very specific about what they plan to ask people to contribute, and to make very specific plans to contact those potential supporters.

Even when potential supporters are absent, pathfinders and allies see that they can use the PATH graphic to effectively share their vision with friends and family members. The prospect of gaining understanding, commitment and practical support from this extended community is exciting and highly motivating.

PATH may help redefine stuck roles, releasing a lot of energy.

***

The staff members who worked in the four-person residence that was Walter's home had become rather bored with their jobs. The Nursing Plan (in a big blue binder full of charts) not only defined the work of the shift, it defined their relationship with Walter, their jobs, and their identities. One staffer said, "We have to check our real lives at the door when we come in to do a shift."

Walter was a man who didn't speak, and he slept most of the time. When we were inquiring about the Dream, it initially began and ended with "Healthy" and "Safe". But when we asked, "When does he wake up?" the staff woke up!

"He loves banjo music. I brought my banjo here one night, and he really seemed to enjoy it."

"He wakes up when he's in fresh air. I had to meet my daughter at the skating rink, so I took Walter with me, and he kind of came alive."

"He loves it when new people are around. I had a couple of friends over for tea one afternoon, and he really liked hearing the sound of people talking together.

As those elements became part of the Dream (connected to a little graphic showing Walter waking up), new elements began to emerge: "Walter surrounded by people who see who he really is", "Part of a larger community." "A gentle, patient teacher and listener."

Then, in the Goal section, the PATH took an interesting twist. Instead of moving in the direction of looking for a music program, a recreation program, and a socialization program, individual staff members began to create little stories about involving Walter in the activities and connections that formed important parts of their own lives. It turned out that one staff member is a very accomplished musician, and that he was connected with dozens of people who make music in the area. He started the ball rolling...

"I can get Walter in when people are jamming ... especially when they're playing Bluegrass music. That'll be a good time for Walter, and it will be a good time for me!"

"I coach competitive skating. If we can free up the van, I can bring Walter to practices. The one time he went, the skaters loved pushing his chair around on the ice."

"For years, I've wanted to be part of the Amnesty International group that meets at the Library. If Walter and I go together, he would be my best reason for finally making that commitment. I wonder if Amnesty works on behalf of people in institutions?"

"Hmm, you know, if we do this with Walter, we can do it with Jane..."

***

The move from caretaker to detective and bridge builder, especially when it involves things that people are personally invested in and passionate about, can be liberating.

We've seen this happen with family members as well.

***

Two sisters said, "Now we know what we can do. Before this, all we could see was Mom beating her head against a brick wall, and we knew we didn't want to do that. But now we see ourselves on Mary's PATH."

***

A father who had long been separated from his family had only spoken a few words during his daughter's PATH. When we reached the last stage (First Steps) he was literally the last person in the room to speak. "This has been great" he said. "We can hold the next PATH meeting at my house." A breakthrough.

***

Community and organizational PATHs

PATH builds community in the context of planning for individuals and families, but it can also directly support a community or a group to develop a clear picture of their direction and commitment. Sometimes, the group has a very specific project they want to work on, but sometimes, they're simply struggling with the question, "What do we want to *be* together *as a community?*"

***

Pastor Martin's small church congregation engaged this question a few months after Sara's PATH. The pattern that emerged surprised and delighted everyone, and opened the door to the church being more purposeful in its commitment to inclusion. One man said, "I want this to be a church where my skepticism is as welcome as my faith," and he received acclamation from all of the other participants. At the end, I said, "If I knew for a certainty that there was a church like this in our community, I'd be there in a second!"

***

Members of a housing cooperative used PATH to regenerate their commitment to be a community. "In the last couple of years we've gotten totally preoccupied with finances and furnaces, and we've lost the sense of why we came together in the first place."

***

Parents, teachers, students and elders created a PATH to re-energize a private school that was based in seven constituent churches. In this PATH, it turned out that the most disaffiliated student was the person who created the biggest breakthrough!

***

In Northern British Columbia, a group of First Nations elders created a community PATH that was initially focused on the question of how to bring back people with disabilities who had moved to urban institutions and nursing homes decades ago. Rather than starting with a vision for a service agency or a hospital board, their vision centered on a 3,000 year-old traditional body of understanding about how individual life, family, clan and community life, life on the land, and connection with the Creator were to be conducted. Then they used this pattern to figure out how they would organize the work of bringing people with disabilities home.

Since then, this community has unrolled their PATH about every six months to work on another question –fisheries, education, economic development, cultural enterprises, and so on. One of the participants said that this PATH was like doing an archeological dig: it is a way for the community to remember together things that they have always known, but now, because the whole pattern can be seen in one place, it is more available for community-building.

***

Walter's PATH includes a tiny graphic depicting "a long, slow, tender journey". PATH-in-practice is a world-wide journey of discovery, connection and contribution. It can be a gift from the disability field to the larger community. People who live with the questions about welcoming people into the heart of community life are discovering many patterns for capacity-finding, community-building, following the threads of gifts and interests, and developing engagement and commitment. Our communities need this.

The picture that is emerging is more like a mosaic than a satellite map. The discoveries about PATH and community-building are being made in the moments, with Walter, and Sara, and Martin. There is no Corps of Engineers or university research facility assembling a giant map. We're more like the early explorers, following tiny trails, canoeing in and out of small bays –the sweet places of community life. If there is ever going to be a 'big map', it will be because the explorers –the people who are reading this book– occasionally take the time to gather together, share their stories, and weave the stories together. We invite you to share your discoveries.

74

Reference

Pearpoint, J., O'Brien, J. & Forest, M. (1995). *PATH (2nd edition)*. Toronto: Inclusion Press.

6

Increasing the Chances for Deep Change
Through Person-Centered Planning

Beth Mount, John O'Brien, & Connie Lyle O'Brien

Some changes come easily: people's requests for something different fall within existing know-how and ability to respond. In these happy circumstances, planning involves getting clear about the request for change, scheduling the necessary steps, tracking progress and troubleshooting. But some changes take people into new territory. These deeper changes call for learning to do new things in new ways, require redirection of existing investments and the discovery of new resources, and often mean saying good-bye to familiar beliefs and habits of practice.

Some communities have established the capacity to assist people with severe disabilities to study in ordinary schools, work at real jobs, and live securely in their own homes. In these places, deeper change has already happened and routine planning and problem solving will usually serve people well. But in many places, available services can't support inclusion without learning to do something very different from their routine offerings. People and families and their allies will have to make the path to a rich, full community life by walking it together.

A change process should be no more complex than the change required. An easy change demands skill in routine planning and problem-solving. Deeper change takes smart, hard work over time. What drives the work is a search for capacity in the person, among family and friends, in communities, and in services. What sustains this work is the desire for a more just and inclusive community and the expectation that publicly funded services should provide personalized assistance. Reflection on the experience of many deeper changes identifies twelve resources that each increase the chances for good outcomes when innovation is necessary. When each resource is strong, it increases the contribution of the others.

Thinking about these resources suggests possibilities for building or maintaining the strength necessary to work for real change. If a resource is missing, don't get discouraged, think about how you might take steps to develop it. If a resource can't be developed, think about how other resources might compensate for the missing one.

Committed, Organized People

A Person with a Strong Desire for Change

The focus person, or someone who cares about the person, wants a change that existing opportunities and supports don't make easy to accomplish. The desire is strong enough to motivate a search for something better and to overcome reluctance to ask others to get involved in the action.

A Support Circle

People who care about change happening for the focus person choose to give their time and resources to working for change. They see themselves as an action oriented group that exists with and for the person, commit themselves to working alongside the focus person and meeting from time to time for as long as it takes to assure that the person has a secure and interesting community life. The more diverse the group's skills and connections the more they can get done. The better they are able to listen and see things from the focus person's point of view, the more the focus person will be strengthened by their support.

At Least One Committed Champion

At least one involved person has a relationship that transcends roles, laws and rules. This person is there with the focus person for the long haul, is very slow to settle for second-best, and wants to do or persuade others to do whatever it takes to keep moving into a positive future.

A Community Builder

A person who is familiar in the local community and brings the community's knowledge and folklore with them either belongs to the support circle or is willing to provide practical help, good leads, introductions, and advice. The community builder knows who needs to talk to whom in order to open doors for the person.

A Skilled Facilitator

A facilitator guides the focus person and the support circle as they create a shared vision, as they figure out the action steps necessary to move toward the focus person's vision, and as they review what they have learned together and deepen their shared understanding of how the focus person can live a rich, full life.

A Productive Process

Defining a vision is only the first step. Real change almost always takes a long time. The focus person and the support circle have ways to keep refining vision and revising action as things develop.

Vision

Positive View of Personal Capacities

Those involved with the focus person find ways to discover and emphasize capabilities and potential for positive action in the focus person, in the community, in the service system, and in themselves.

Personal Vision for A Rich Community Life

The focus person and those involved craft and communicate a lively and interesting vision of the person as an involved, contributing community member. A community vision stimulates creativity and sustains action better than a system-oriented vision that promotes more or better services or seeks compliance with rules or legal requirements.. The circle finds ways to give the vision creative expression through media that have meaning for the person and communicate vividly with others through graphics, sculpture, fabric art, music.

Connections to Resources

Connections to Wider Communities

When members of the support circle are actively involved in community organizations, self-help groups, and interest groups, they can link the focus person to resources and opportunities. Without this connected knowledge, it's possible to get stuck because the support circle is limited to only what the service system can offer. Often these offerings don't match the focus person's interests or preoccupy the focus person and the support circle with fighting scarcity in services.

An Agency Committed to Change

At least one agency involved with the focus person sees a direct connection between change for the focus person and the agency's learning better ways to realize the agency mission.

Influence with People in Authority

Some members of the support circle have direct access to people in positions of authority in the service system. They can negotiate face-to-face for necessary changes to usual system practices and policies.

Flexible Resources to Support Positive Action

There is sufficient time and money for the focus person and support circle members to learn about new possibilities and to try out new ways to do things.

7

The Value of Measuring Person-Centered Planning

Steve Holburn*

Person-centered planning is an alternative to traditional professional methods of program planning and evaluation for people
with disabilities (Mount, 1994; O'Brien & O'Brien, 2002), and it has been
a popular aspiration of traditional service systems in the field of
developmental disabilities for nearly 10 years. Everyone in the field,
including consumers, family members, and employees, seems to
know about the philosophy and objectives of person-centered planning. Person-centered language is so common that it now sounds
platitudinous to say a central theme in person-centered planning
is inclusion. However, what is truly refreshing about the inclusion
position is that the architects of the method seem to have meant it.
For example, it is no secret that some proponents of the approach
believe that conventional congregate/ segregated service approaches
constrain people's lives and much conventional programming wastes
people's time, yet the door is left ajar for traditional methods.

The inclusion premise typically refers to the integration and participation of all people throughout our society, but it also pertains
to an openness to multiple perspectives. A more specific illustration
of this aspect of inclusiveness emerges in a discussion of whether
or not we should subject person-centered planning to conventional
analysis. In lamenting the popularity and widespread misapplica-
tions of person-centered planning, O'Brien, O'Brien, & Mount
(1997) cautioned,

> Now some people want to evaluate the effectiveness of person-
> centered planning by counting its outcomes, sometimes in
> pre-defined categories; for them, people's story's are 'anecdotes.'
> Mindful work involves remembering that people's emerging
> life stories are not anecdotes and that the outside evaluator's
> tally marks are simply one more point of view (p. 483).

---

*This work was supported in part by the New York State Office of Mental Retarda-
tion and Developmental Disabilities. Inquiries may be sent to holbursc@infi.net

The interesting point here is that outcome quantification, a hallmark of traditional analysis, is posited as a threat to the integrity of the process, yet it is not abandoned as a tool for knowledge. It is *included* as "one more point of view." In my involvement in person-centered planning, I have tried to keep that door open.

From my vantage point, person-centered planning is frequently misapplied because it seems to have become a procedural free-for-all resulting in unclear outcomes. I propose a remedy through systematic assessment of the process and outcomes. I believe that facilitators and applied investigators should evaluate the process and outcomes in ways that should increase the effectiveness of person-centered planning. Further, I believe that proper evaluation will contribute to the discovery of procedural variations that will make person-centered planning more do-able within agencies that assist people with disabilities. The obvious starting point is to assess the impact of a "real" person-centered planning endeavor. However, prerequisite to ensuring proper implementation of any process and achieving its purported goals is the capability to know with a reasonable degree of believability whether the process is indeed being implemented and if the goals are being achieved.

To determine if we are truly doing person-centered planning using an observational method, the *process* must first be operationalized (deconstructed into definable and observable components), and then adherence to the partitioned components must be assessed. To reliably demonstrate the degree to which *outcomes* such as community inclusion, relationships, and respect are being accomplished, it is necessary to operationalize them as well before we can measure the degree to which they are occurring. Hypothetically, feedback about the results of the process and outcome measurements will help keep the team on track. However, the challenges in assessing adherence to the process and the extent to which the aspirations are being achieved are significant. Interestingly, there is a potentially important side benefit to assessing the process and outcomes of person-centered planning that may eclipse the importance of person-centered planning itself: If a true empirical analysis of person-centered planning takes place, it means that we have broken new ground in the technology of measurement, suggesting that the principles of science can be applied to issues of greater social relevance.

Will measuring person-centered planning ruin it?

Before discussing the challenges and benefits of measuring person-centered planning, it might be wise to address common concerns and fears about measuring the process and outcomes of person-centered planning. Person-centered planners have good reason to be wary of applying systematic measurement procedures to the process and outcomes of person-centered planning. In evaluating service provision, too often measurement is inaccurate, and worse, it measures the wrong thing. Some of this bad measurement is no doubt due to an incentive system gone wrong. It is all too easy to envision employees in a residential setting busily documenting progress, while the ostensible beneficiaries sit nearby with nothing interesting to do, and with no real plans of going anywhere. Specifically, the voluminous data and other paperwork necessary to convince auditors that there are few or no programmatic, health, or safety deficiencies. This way of measuring of accountability usually forms the basis on which auditors can threaten funding. Unfortunately, this practice of punishing agencies for paperwork failures constitutes a powerful contingency that unintentionally shifts attention away from the person and toward the program auditor. It is no fault of the paper workers; they too are trapped by these unfavorable circumstances. This contingency arrangement, which ironically removes opportunities for assistants to spend time with the person in order to demonstrate that they are engaging the person in activities and providing services that advance quality of life is a continuing problem in much service provision today, and its consequences should serve as a warning to policy and financial planners to loosen the link between funding and record keeping.

With respect to person-centered planning, the problem is obviated by keeping the funding separate from the measured outcomes. This position begs the question, "Then how do we achieve accountability?" However, this chapter does not purport to examine all of the ways that accountability could be achieved in service environments; the point here is that no matter what forms of assessment are used to gage success, when funding is contingent on assessment results, those written results will be biased in the direction of maintaining funding. If blatant fabrication of positive results is too unsettling or conspicuous, one needs simply to resort to the practice of goal recycling, which entails setting goals that are already part of the person's repertoire. Even when challenging goals *are* established, the bias toward positive results as a consequence of the direct link between funding and documentation interferes with the natural feedback system necessary for effective adjustments to strategy. Thus, a prerequisite of establishing reliable and valid measurement is elimination of the penalty for honest reporting of results, whether the results pertain to a toothbrushing goal or learning to make friends in the community.

One reason why funding is not now contingent on accomplishing goals such as friendship, inclusion, and autonomy is the notion that these aspirations cannot be accurately measured. If agency funding *does* become directly connected to the process and outcomes of person-centered planning, the focus will shift to documentation of those goals for auditors, which will probably ruin person-centered planning endeavors. For example, an employee may become adept at *reporting* how the person is participating more in the community and doing more of the things he or she truly enjoys, yet the employee might be unable to spend sufficient time with the person in the community or give a true appraisal of the degree to which the person is doing what he or she wants to do, including going to desired places and being with friends.

Another concern about measurement pertains to the notion that in the act of measuring something, the measurer automatically begins to limit his or her view of other important phenomena, and therefore, the measurer cannot see the whole picture or grasp the totality of the individual or the vision. For example, if a goal of 90 % correct verbalizations during speech therapy outweighs a goal of increased community experiences for an individual, then the measurer will certainly miss the big picture. If multiple aspects of what is important to the individual are measured, the measurer should begin to see larger areas of the picture. A related worry is that measurement might induce a team to teach to the test and neglect other aspects and aspirations. For example, a planning team that has developed goals and methods of assessment might be reluctant to switch gears or add new goals, once the measuring processes have begun. Of course, such concerns relate to the complexity of the measurement and the practical limitations of simultaneous assessment.

A common belief is that it is not possible to validly measure accomplishments such as community participation, respect, happiness, relationships, and autonomy, yet all of these phenomena have been assessed and altered using reliable observational methods, examples of which are described in Holburn (2001 b) and Holburn and Vietze (2000). Another concern is that the measurement procedures might interfere with carrying out the process of person-centered planning, although none of the researchers in the examples referred to above reported that their measurement process interfered with their interventions. In applied research, it goes without saying that the act of assessment is independent of the intervention. If the measurement itself affects the thing that is being measured, the measurement technically becomes part of the intervention, making it impossible to separate the effects of say, person-centered planning, from the evaluator's tally marks. Feedback about the tally marks can help guide the process, but the act of collecting the data should not get in the way. The measurement can be relevant, non-intrusive, and useful to person-centered planners depending on what the team decides to measure and how the measurement is conducted. There is nothing intrinsically counterproductive in assessing processes and outcomes of person-centered planning, although it does have the potential to hinder implementation and thwart the goals if conducted imprudently, and especially if it becomes linked to the operating funds of an agency.

Are we doing person-centered planning faithfully?

Person-centered planning is a complex, long-term process that adjusts its course as it goes along in response to changing circumstances and changing aspirations of the focus person. The fact that the process entails variation in adapting to the person and the circumstances bodes well for discovering new ways of accomplishing goals. However, a drawback to the complexity of the process and its inclusion of various components is increased likelihood of insufficient process integrity. As the process evolves, it requires problem solving, creativity, collaboration, and patience, and many team members, including facilitators, may not have the proper training, support, or time to participate in the process as prescribed. Consequently, improvised planning ventures have emerged, some of which have probably been effective. However, if these modified approaches are not described in detail, we cannot duplicate them, and if they are not carried out as specified, we cannot be sure of what exactly was responsible for their success. On the other hand, even when all the necessary ingredients, skill, and motivation are available to a team, it is possible that the process drifts away from the prescribed principles and procedures unless consistent and accurate feedback is provided on how well team members are conforming to the specified process and achieving their goals.

Person-centered planning is not a chaotic process buffeted by all external influences. Many if not most of its components, principles, and guiding ideas remain stable throughout the planning process. Many of these components can be specified based on the numerous materials available that detail person-centered planning principles, as my colleagues and I have done (see Figure 1). Fortunately, the principles are not conceptually complicated, nor are the procedures difficult to convey. Specifying and assessing such components would seem to be a promising starting point in evaluating the fidelity of a person-centered planning endeavor.

Figure 1 displays an example of a modest measure, the *Assessment of Person-Centered Planning Facilitation Integrity* (Holburn, 2001 a), to assess the facilitation integrity of a person-centered planning project currently under way to assist 10 families headed by parents with intellectual disabilities. To construct the measure, we selected components of facilitation that are important to the integrity of the process and that should not change as the planning process matures. Accordingly, we identified 20 aspects of meeting logistics and meeting facilitation. To assess intervention reliability, an observer who is present during the meeting specifies the presence or absence of each aspect. This assessment focuses only on what occurs during meetings, and therefore does not assess adherence to all aspects of a person-centered planning process.

In the current project, the form is completed by the same person, who is present at the first, second, fifth, and tenth meetings. (There is no cutoff date or final number of meetings, so integrity assessment will likely continue beyond the tenth meeting). Following the meeting in which the evaluation took place, feedback is provided to members of a subgroup of the planning team. The subgroup consists of the facilitator, process evaluator, and project coordinator, who discuss the degree of adherence to each component. This meeting provides an opportunity to suggest alternative ways of adhering to the components of the process. At some meetings, two people complete the form independently, and by comparing ratings, a measure of observer reliability is made possible. So far, inter-rater observer agreement is strong, with the least consensus on question number 9: *The facilitator asked probing, open-ended questions to evoke*

Figure 1: **Assessment of Person-Centered Planning Facilitation Integrity**

Name of focus person _____ Date_____ Meeting number_____

Instructions: Place a Y (yes), N (no), or NA (not appropriate) before each question below

Meeting Logistics

1. ___ Date and time of meeting was convenient for focus person
2. ___ Meeting was held in adequate location with enough space
3. ___ Seating arrangement facilitated discussion
4. ___ Refreshments were available
5. ___ Mapping materials, such as flip charts and markers, were present at the meeting
6. ___ Attempts were made to get relevant people at meeting (e.g., focus person, family members, friends, pertinent employees), including timely notification, and transportation assistance, if feasible

Facilitating the Meeting

7. ___ At the outset of the meeting, the facilitator stated the purpose of the meeting
8. ___ Team progress was reviewed early in the meeting, including status of pending action steps
9. ___ The facilitator asked probing, open-ended questions to evoke detail about the focus person and issues related to the focus person
10. ___ The facilitator kept discussion centered on the interests and desires of the focus person
11. ___ The facilitator was oriented more towards building capacity than correcting deficiencies.
12. ___ Throughout the meeting, the facilitator sought clarification of vague information and cloudy issues
13. ___ If present "system constraints" prevent achievement of the focus person's wish(s), alternative ways of achievement were discussed
14. ___ During problem solving, the facilitator conveyed an optimistic attitude and encouraged creative solutions
15. ___ The facilitator obtained consensus in problem-solving
16. ___ The facilitator gave positive feedback to participants who shared information
17. ___ If mapping was used, it conveyed information in a way that helped team members develop a common understanding of the focus person
18. ___ Strategies and responsibilities for follow up were made clear, and the plan of action was summarized at the end of the meeting
19. ___ All participants gave input during the meeting
20. ___ A record of proceedings of the meeting information was kept throughout the meeting

detail about the focus person and issues related to the focus person. A practical advantage of comparing ratings is that disagreements can be discussed and confusing terms and criteria can be clarified.

To ensure that the evaluator did not interfere with the team process, she was instructed not to interact during meetings. However, the evaluator gradually became interested and involved in all of the meetings, and at this point in the project, she attends each meeting as a contributing member (we have begun person-centered planning with five of the 10 families, and we are on our fifth and sixth meetings at the writing of this chapter). We have discovered that the assessment form can be easily completed after the meeting, which allows the evaluator to continue as a contributing member and also assess the integrity of the facilitation in a way that does not distract or interfere with the process.

A more sophisticated process measure would take into account more aspects of the person-centered planning process. Determining adherence to the aspects depends less on the type of person-centered planning employed than the degree to which its components can be deconstructed into their constituent units for verification. The integrity assessment in Figure 1 is a global measure applicable to many, if not all, forms of person-centered planning. However, if one is interested in assessing adherence to a less global aspect of person-centered planning, say, *developing a personal profile* (Mount, 1992), the steps in this aspect could be identified and evaluated. Most person-centered planning approaches entail a sequence of activities and procedures in a curriculum-like format that are described clearly. These are the bones of the process and they are found in the guidelines, ground rules, mapping methods, problem-solving strategies, checklists and so forth.

However, not all of the ingredients of person-centered planning are easily detected. Some are less objective. For example, the criteria that team members be *committed to change* or *think about the person in a new way* are not as distinct as *all participants gave input during the meeting* (Figure 1, item 19). The former criteria are often considered private information because commitments and thoughts are entities that are held inside; they are not public information to which an evaluator has access, and thus, their constituent parts cannot be observed by an external evaluator, making consensual agreement impossible. Nevertheless, these private events do exist, and they are certainly observable by the person who is experiencing them (Skinner,

1945). Other aspects of person-centered planning are not necessarily internal, yet they still pose a significant measurement challenge. For example, a team might readily agree of the definition of a *personalized vision*, but there can be considerable disagreement on whether the vision is truly personalized. However, irrespective of their degree of privacy or other measurement challenges, aspects that are integral to the process should be assessed. It is possible to deconstruct and verify some of them through observation, but it is also possible to assess their presence through opinion or consensus of opinion, although the latter raises questions about the exact nature of the phenomena under consideration. Nonetheless, it is germane to ask team members, including the focus person, how they feel about the process and to what extent certain components are happening. This approach was used to quantify adherence to six derived elements of person-centered planning for 37 planning teams, about one-half of which were experiencing person-centered planning (Holburn, Jacobson, Vietze, Schwartz, & Sersen, 2000). Team members periodically completed a questionnaire that comprised a *process index* ascertaining the degree of the following: presence of strategic roles, personal relationship with the focus person, desire for change, creation of a personalized vision, commitment to planning and follow-up, and flexible funding/resources. For the *process index*, test-retest reliability was sufficient ($r = .88$), and internal consistency was strong (Cronbach's alpha was .87). The questions can be completed individually and averaged, or the answers may be determined by consensus. Consensus determination is more likely to evoke team discussion about the process and how it can be improved.

Are we honestly reporting person-centered planning outcomes?

The results of person-centered planning endeavors are often presented qualitatively in the form of stories. Many stories of person-centered successes are interesting and compelling. However, just as the process of person-centered planning can drift from its specified procedures, so too can the reports of success. The positive orientation of person-centered planning in focusing on what works is useful in finding solutions to difficult problems, but when its influence affects the perceptions about the impact of the process, it can result in exaggerated claims. In addition, there seems to be a tendency not to report failures of person-centered planning. Today, person-centered philosophy, principles, and language are so pervasive in the mission statements, policies, and even laws that govern practices in the field of disability, that an acknowledgement of a failure in person-centered planning is more like an indictment of the agency than an admission that a given person-centered planning approach simply did not work for a given person under a given set of circumstances. Unfortunately, unreported failures are missed opportunities for learning.

Qualitative accounts of what happened as a result of person-centered planning hang together well and are easier to transmit than a collection of numbers, but a quantitative verification based on observational assessment can complement or form the basis of stories. Many person-centered outcomes can be quantified in terms such as frequency, rate, duration, percentage, and type. Goals such as getting married or finding a job do not fit the quantitative paradigm as singular units, but they can be broken into their component parts, familiarly called task analysis when the deconstruction is done to identify and subsequently teach a sequence of basic behavioral units comprising a complex behavior. However, because of the variation in the ways that people come to marry or land a job, and because of their multifaceted processes, the component parts of each are more like short-term plans or steps along the way. The main challenge in sufficient measurement of person-centered outcomes is the practical problem of evaluating multiple complex outcomes simultaneously.

To exemplify quantification of a difficult-to-assess outcome, let us consider the goal of *respect*, the most indistinct person-centered outcome of O'Brien's (1987) *five essential accomplishments*. According to O'Brien, "Respect is having a valued place among a network of people and valued roles in community life" (p. 179). This description seems to contain quantifiable components. For example, if having a *valued role in community life* means filling the role of a worker and getting a pay check, quantification might be accomplished by developing and assessing functional employment skills (see Bellamy, 1988; Wehman, 1981). The *value* of a particular job for an individual could be assessed through social validity measures (e.g., Wolf, 1978) querying others' opinions about its importance and assessing the consumers desirability of the goal and level of satisfaction with its accomplishment. Having *a valued place among a network of people* might be accessible through a sociometric analysis, such as described by Asher, Singleton, Tinsley, and Hymel (1979), or by conducting a social network analysis as described by Newton, et al. (1994). The

89

later identifies people in the person's social network, the network category (family or friends), and information about the degree and desirability of the social contact.

The measurement of a more distinct goal of person-centered planning, spending time in the community, is displayed in Figure 2, below. This figure shows the number of hours per month in the community over a five-year period during which person-centered planning was taking place on a formal basis for one focus person.

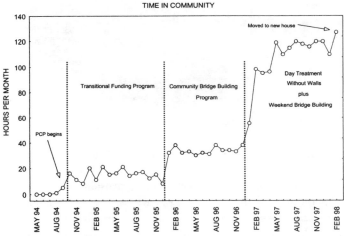

Figure 2: Number of Hours in Community Per Month

From May 1994 to February 1998, there was an increase from zero hours per month to more than 120 hours per month. As Figure 2 shows, the increases are correlated with the three types of interventions designed to increase time spent in the community. Additional information about what is happening can be obtained by cataloging the types and frequencies of activities occurring. For example, focusing in on the third phase of Figure 2, *Community Bridge Building Program*, there was a total of 176 activities, a breakdown of which is displayed in the pie chart in Figure 3, on the following page. Here, one can see the number of activities by category that occurred during this phase. Such breakdowns in each of the four phases permit examination of the relationship between interventions and types of activities. Measuring time in the community and types of community involvement in this way are admittedly gross measures of community inclusion, but they can assist in decision-making during a long-term process, and they are not difficult to do.

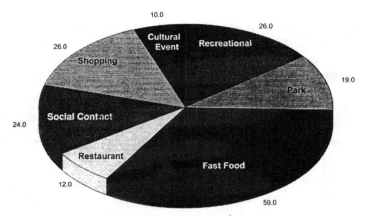

Figure 3: Number of Community Activities by Category
During Bridge Building

Another type of data display is presented in Figure 4. This graph shows the cumulative increase in change scores in five aspects of *Relationships*. *Relationships* is one of nine dimensions of quality of life measured with the *Person-Centered Planning Quality of Life Indicators-Consensus Version* (Holburn & Pfadt, 1995). To complete this assessment, two or more respondents who know the focus person and what is happening in the person's life arrive at a consensus on change in 48 aspects that comprise the nine dimensions of life quality. The change score ranges from -3 (very negative change) to +3 (very positive change). Each aspect is defined by a set of guiding questions. For example, one aspect of the dimension *Relationships* is *Primary Relationships*:

> 19. *Primary relationships. How many people are intimately con- nected to the person and how much time do they spend together? Does the person have a best friend? Any friends without disabili- ties? Any non-paid friends?*

Figure 4 shows that during the approximate 5-year time span, positive changes occurred in some aspects but not in others. *Fam- ily* relationships improved steadily, but *friends* and *social network* improved dramatically upon the third administration. No improve- ments were perceived in opportunities for *intimacy* or involvement in *associations* during the period. Taken altogether, the nine dimensions of quality of life provide useful feedback about the impact of the planning process. Each administration offers a status or profile of met and unmet aspects, and this feedback can assist the team strategically.

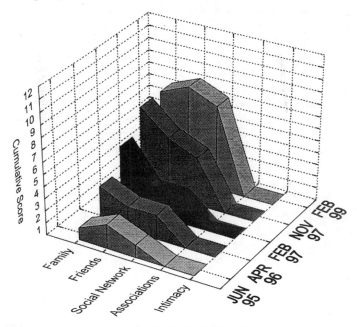

Figure 4: Changes in Relationships

The questionnaire-based approach described above is an attempt to capture information more complex than hours of time in the community or types of activities in the community, but the dimensions of life quality measured by the questionnaire are generally more subjective and harder to reliably quantify. Therefore, it is crucial to question the validity of such data. The more believable the information, the more useful it is in advancing our knowledge about how to best bring about the values of the new paradigm into fruition.

Conclusion

This chapter presents the argument that the field of disabilities has neglected measurement in person-centered planning. In thinking about ways to improve person-centered planning, the word *quanti-*

fication usually does not come to mind. Perhaps the use of numbers to measure how we assist people with disabilities and determine their achievements evokes thoughts of impersonalization, fragmentation, and even manipulation, thoughts that are typically associated with the bureaucratic systems whose negative effects on people's lives gave rise to person-centered planning in the first place. However, the failure to systematically assess the process appears to have resulted in procedural drift that takes the process too far from the intended methods. In some cases, teams have modified the process altogether using whatever ingredients are available. "Accidents" from unintentional drift, as well as intentional compromises of the process, might occasionally result in successful outcomes, but if the altered procedures are not adequately specified or truly implemented as described, others will not be able to take advantage of them. Likewise, if the results of the process are not validly ascertained, why should others repeat what was done?

Some people worry that if we dilute person-centered planning too much it will surely be ineffective, but this assertion is weak if we cannot determine with integrity that the process was employed as stated or that the goals were achieved as claimed. It is true that if we deviate too far from the original process, it will not be person-centered-planning anymore, but this result is not particularly troublesome when we remember that the overall goal is not improving person-centered planning per se -- the goal is better lives for people with disabilities.

Our current measurement technology permits at least rudimentary quantification of most aspects of person-centered planning processes and outcomes, but improvements are needed. It is clear that assessment must be conducted in ways that do not interfere with the process, and the techniques must be relatively easy to carry out. If their complexity constrains the evaluator to measuring too few aspects, the measurement will have limited benefit. If the measurement does not reflect the most important aspects of person-centered planning, it will lack relevance. Examples of measuring basic process and outcome components were offered here not as perfect models, but as illustrations of the many ways one can approach the challenges of assessing the complex aspects of person-centered planning.

To be completely fair, irrespective of whether an account is based on qualitative or quantitative evidence, it must be acknowledged that assessments of human behavior can only be *estimates* of what exactly happens, and they are usually brief samples at that. Rather than pondering the merits of a data-based accounts that yield a high level of certainty of only parts of the picture versus story accounts that yield less certainty but cover the bigger picture, it seems more constructive to merge the two. Resolution of discrepancies can only bring us closer to the truth and ultimately improve person-centered planning.

References

Asher, S. R., Singleton, L. C., Tinsley, B. R., & Hymel S. (1979). A reliable sociometric measure for preschool children. *Developmental Psychology, 15,* 443-444.

Bellamy, T. G. (1988). *Supported employment: A community implementation guide.* Baltimore: Paul Brookes.

Koegel, R., & Koegel. L. (1988). Generalized responsivity and pivotal behaviors. In R. H. Horner, G. Dunlap, & R. L. Koegel (Eds.), *Generalization and maintenance: Life-style changes in applied settings* (pp. 41-66). Baltimore: Paul H. Brookes.

Mount, B. (1994). Benefits and limitations of personal futures planning. In V. J. Bradley, J. W. Ashbaugh, & B. C. Blaney (Eds.), *Creating individual supports for people with developmental disabilities: A mandate for change at many levels* (pp. 97-108). Baltimore: Paul Brookes.

Mount, B. (1992) *Person-Centered planning: Finding directions for change. A sourcebook of values, ideals, and methods to encourage person-centered development.* New York: Graphic Futures Inc.

Newton, J. S., Anderson, S. A., Ard, W. R., Horner, R. H., LeBaron, N. M., Sappington, G., Spoelstra, R. J. (1994). *A residential outcomes system operational manual.* Eugene: University of Oregon, Center on Human Development.

O'Brien, J. (1987a). A guide to life-style planning: Using The Activities Catalogue to integrate services and natural support systems. In G. T. Bellamy & B. Wilcox (Eds.), *A comprehensive guide to the Activities Catalogue: An alternative curriculum for youth and adults with severe disabilities* (pp. 175-189). Baltimore: Paul Brookes. (Another version in *A little book about person-centered planning.*)

O'Brien, J., & Lovett, H. (1992). *Finding a way toward everyday lives: The contribution of person centered planning.* Harrisburg, PA: Pennsylvania Office of Mental Retardation. (Also in *A little book about person-centered planning.*)

O'Brien C. L., & O'Brien, J. (2002) The origins of person-centered planning: A community of practice perspective. In S. Holburn & P Vietze (Eds.), *Person-centered planning: Research, practice, and future directions.* Baltimore: Paul Brookes. (Another version in this book.)

O'Brien, J., O'Brien, C. L., & Mount, B. (1997). Person-centered planning has arrived... or has it? *Mental Retardation, 35,* 480-488. (Also in *A little book about person-centered planning.*)

Holburn, S.(2001a). *Assessment of Person-Centered Planning Facilitation Integrity* New York State Institute for Basic Research in Developmental Disabilities, Staten Island, New York.

Holburn, C. S. (2001b). Compatibility of person-centered planning and applied behavior analysis. *The Behavior Analyst, 34,* 271-281.

Holburn, C. S. & Vietze, P. (2000). Person-centered planning and cultural inertia in applied behavior analysis. *Behavior and Social Issues, 10,* 39-70.

Skinner, B., F. (1945). Operational analysis of psychological terms. Psychological Review, 52, 270-277.

Wehman, P. (1981). *Competitive employment: New horizons for severely disabled individuals.* Baltimore: Paul Brookes.

Wolf, M. M. (1978). Social validity: The case for subjective measurement or how applied behavior analysis is finding its heart. *Journal of Applied Behavior Analysis, 11,* 203-214.

Selected Readings on Measurement
Quantifying Processes and Outcomes of Person-Centered Planning

Steve Holburn

Cummins, R. A. (2002). Proxy responding for subjective well-being: A review. In L. Glidden (Ed.) *International review of research in mental retardation* (pp. 183-207). San Diego: Academic Press.

Conceptual paper that argues for not using subjective proxy measures. Concludes that others' statements about subjective outcomes is inaccurate and unethical.

Felce, D. (1997). Defining and applying the concept of quality of life. *Journal of Intellectual Disability Research, 41*, 126-135.

Conceptual paper on applying and evaluating quality of life that includes discussion of subjective versus objective assessment of QOL.

Hawkins, B. A., Kim, K., & Eklund, S. (1995). Validity and reliability of a five dimensional life satisfaction index. *Mental Retardation, 33*, 295-303.

Example of instrument to assess satisfaction.

Heal, L., & Chadsey-Rusch, J. (1985). Lifestyle satisfaction scale (LSS): Assessing individuals' satisfaction with residence, community setting, and associated services. *Applied Research in Mental Retardation, 6*, 475-490.

A brief and popular instrument to assess satisfaction with life.

Holburn, S.(2001a). *Assessment of Person-Centered Planning Facilitation Integrity* New York State Institute for Basic Research in Developmental Disabilities, Staten Island, New York.

Example of an instrument to quantify adherence to a person-centered planning process.

Holburn, C. S. (2001b). Compatibility of person-centered planning and applied behavior analysis. *The Behavior Analyst, 34*, 271-281.

Conceptual piece that gives examples and references of methods to quantify various outcomes, all of which are common goals of person-centered planning.

Holburn, S., Jacobson, J. W., Vietze, P. M., Schwartz, A. A., & Sersen, E. (2000). Quantifying the process and outcomes of person-centered planning. *American Journal on Mental Retardation, 105*, 402-416.

Describes a measure designed to assess person-centered planning process and outcomes.

Holburn, C. S., & Pfadt A. (1995). *Person Centered Planning Quality of Life Indicators-Consensus Version.* Staten Island, NY: New York State Institute for Basic Research in Developmental Disabilities.

An instrument that assesses of eight dimensions of quality of life typically targeted in Personal Futures Planning.

Holburn, C. S., & Pfadt A. (1995). *Person-Centered Planning Quality of Life Indicators-Consensus Version.* Staten Island, NY: New York State Institute for Basic Research in Developmental Disabilities.

This instrument uses a consensus approach to quantify degree of positive change of 8 dimensions of quality of life associated with Personal Futures Planning

Holburn, S. & Vietze, P. (Eds.) (2002). *Person-centered planning: Research, practice, and future directions*, Baltimore: Paul Brookes.

Many chapters in this book present methods of qualitative and quantitative assessment of person-centered outcomes.

Mount, B., & Holburn, S. C. (1996). *Personal futures planning indicators.* Staten Island, NY: Institute for Basic Research in Developmental Disabilities.

A brief yes/no instrument to assess 11 ingredients associated with successful person-centered planning.

Hughes, C., Hwang, B., Kim, J. H., Eisenman, L. T., & Killian, D. J.. (1995). Quality of life in applied research: A review and analysis of empirical measures. *American Journal on Mental Retardation, 99*, 623-641.

Describes a conceptual model of 15 dimensions of QOL based on an extensive research review.

Jansen, C. G. C., & Vreeke, G. J. (1995). Outcome indicators in the care for people with a mental handicap. *The British Journal of Developmental Disabilities, 41,* 79-90.

A survey of instruments that assess various global outcomes for people with intellectual disabilities.

Kearney, C. A., Durand, V. M., & Mindell, J. A. (1995). Choice assessment in residential settings. *Journal of Developmental and Physical Disabilities, 7,* 203-213.

A summary of instruments to assess choice in residential settings.

Schalock, R. L. (1996). Reconsidering the conceptualization and measurement of quality of life. In R .L. Schalock (Ed.), *Quality of Life: Vol. 1. Conceptualization and measurement* (pp. 123-139). Washington, DC: American Association on Mental Retardation.

Suggestions for various ways to think about and assess quality of life.

Schwartz, A. A., Jacobson, J. W., & Holburn, S. (2000). Defining person centeredness: Results of two consensus methods. *Education and Training in Mental Retardation and Developmental Disabilities, 35,* 235-249.

Describes two methods of defining indicators of person-centered planning.

8

Opening the Door

David Pitonyak

I knocked at the door, but he wouldn't answer. I could see him on the couch, turning under a blanket. It was dark in his living room, shadows everywhere.

"Danny!" I called. "It's me –David."

He pulled the blanket over his shoulders. He wouldn't answer.

Two doors down, an elderly woman was staring at me suspiciously. I smiled at her and she disappeared from her porch like a startled cat. I wondered what she thought of me. I wondered what she thought of Danny.

I knocked again.

Still no answer.

In the darkness, I could see half-empty Styrofoam cups of coffee on the dining room table, television, and floor. They were everywhere. He must have been up all night, I thought. Again.

For months, Danny had been having a difficult time emotionally. He complained that his heart was racing, he couldn't sleep, his head hurt. He was routinely checking himself into the local emergency room for "nerves," but they couldn't find anything wrong and sent him home with short term sedatives and Tylenol.

His entire life had become a chore. Even his shower routine, which he had been comfortable with for years, didn't make sense anymore. He couldn't remember his towel until he had gotten all wet, and by the time he found a towel and dried himself off, he would have

Danny (not his real name) asked me to respect his privacy by changing certain details of his story. I have done so, I think, without altering the basic truth of his story. Danny, you know who you are and I thank you for giving me the opportunity to hold your story and to share it with others. I am thankful to The Edge (not his real nickname) for his support and insight. You, my friend, are making a real difference. I also appreciate the feedback and support I have received from Bruce Anderson, Sherrie Anderson, and Jane Boone. Nothing like good friends to remind you that what you have to offer can be offered more succinctly. Thanks too to John and Connie for waiting patiently as I missed all of my self-imposed deadlines. I am indebted to Cyndi Pitonyak, my wife and best friend. She's the smartest person I know and her feedback is always exactly right, but her love makes all the difference in the world.

forgotten where he left his clothes. At night, he was forgetting how to use the thermostat and was standing by the burners of his electric range for heat. He was getting stuck all day, like someone trying to drive a bicycle through the mud. It made him angry. He knew he could do better.

On top of everything else, Danny's landlord was threatening him with eviction because of regular screaming matches he was having with a neighbor. Danny said the neighbor was playing his music too loudly. The neighbor thought differently. The landlord believed the neighbor.

As if he didn't have enough to worry about, his brother-in-law, Tom, told him that if he "didn't straighten up," he would end up like Andrea Yates, the Texas mother who drowned her children in a bathtub. Danny became so concerned that Tom was right he avoided children for weeks.

Tom routinely says that Danny is "lazy" or "going sick in the head."

I think Danny is lonely.

Loneliness is the only real disability

I believe that most people supported by our human service system are lonely. Profoundly lonely. And much of what we professionals do to help is a colossal waste of resources and time. *Most* (not all) of our rules and regulations, programs and interventions, medicines, buildings, training, coverage –you name it, *most* (not all) of what we do is a physical manifestation of our inability to come to grips with the central reality of people's lives– loneliness.

Look around you. Take the rest of the day to spend time with some people who receive services and supports from your organization or local community provider. My bet is that you will meet lonely people, people who don't have many friends, people who have lost, or are at risk of losing, their connections with family. My bet is that most of the people you meet will be dependent on paid professionals for their day to day support.

My bet is that hardly anyone who receives services will ask you about the Medicaid program or the upcoming audit. No one will be curious about the latest management information software installed on the network. No one will ask you to explain trends in community expenditures or what is happening in the *Journal of Applied Behavior Analysis*. No one.

Someone might grab your hand and refuse to let go. Someone might treat you like a long-lost friend (even though the two of you may have just met). Someone might ask you if you know the whereabouts of a long-lost parent or sibling. Another might ask you to dinner, hoping against hope that you will oblige. No one, I am willing to bet, will ask you for your credentials.

Maybe I'm wrong.

Maybe most of the people you support already have meaningful relationships – enduring and freely chosen connections. If this is true, I am happy for them and you. My point is quite simple, really: I believe that *most* of the people served by our MR/DD system are disconnected from meaningful and enduring relationships. And most of their discontent, most of their suffering, is the result of loneliness, not disability.

On *becoming* a problem

This circumstance –where I am knocking on Danny's door and he is not answering– is not new. We have known each other this way for years. He frequently insists that I wait outside his door, particularly when he is unhappy. I am learning to wait.

I remember one occasion, years ago, when Danny lived in a small apartment adjacent to a group home. His staff were angry at him because he dug up the entire front yard in the middle of the night. He told them that he was digging a flower bed, though in scale it was more like a large garden. I tried to talk with him, but he refused to answer the door. I sat outside in a green plastic chair and tried to figure out what to do.

The manager of the group home, a tall, stately woman, dressed sharply in a dress suit and gold jewelry, arrived in a mini-van. "Jesus, help me Lord" she said, shaking her head as she scanned the front yard. The overnight staff person, looking worried, came out of the front door and raced down the front steps to meet her. "I didn't hear anything, Eiesha. Not a peep! I went to get the morning paper and this is what I found."

Both of them stood for a moment, looking at each other blankly. They were in shock. Slowly, Eiesha turned to me. I could tell from the look on her face that she expected me, as the "behavior consultant," to tell her what to do. I had no idea and shook my head. "I should talk with him." I offered.

"Talk with him?" the overnight person said, pointing to the yard as if I had not noticed that it was missing. "I think we are way past the point of talking. He needs consequences."

Eiesha held him by the arm, "Gerald, calm down. You're not in trouble."

I told Eiesha and Gerald that I thought Danny's intentions were right, that a flower bed would look good in the front yard, but that Danny had gone overboard a bit in scale. "If anything," I told them, "I think he needs gardening advice."

They both looked at me as if I were from the Moon. After what seemed to be an eternity, they both turned on their heels and walked into the house shaking their heads. I knew I had been a bit smug. I tried once more at Danny's door (no answer) and returned to the green plastic chair wondering what *would* be helpful. I couldn't think of much of anything as people slowed down in their cars to view the gone lawn. One guy asked me if a pipe had broken. Another said moles had done the same thing to his front yard years ago. A woman with a baby didn't say anything. She hurried to the other side of the street.

After sitting for a period of time with absolutely no idea of what to do next, Eiesha and Gerald joined me outside. They brought coffee and donuts and I felt a bit easier around them, a bit more willing to admit that I had no idea about what to do, less smug. I tried to be more open about their concerns.

"Danny doesn't listen," said Gerald, his hands shaking as he stirred his coffee. "We told him he could not put in a flower bed and what does he do?" I knew that the question was rhetorical, but I answered anyway, "Dug up the lawn."

"Dug up the lawn" Gerald said, as if he hadn't heard me. "Dug up the lawn!"

Eiesha was concerned about the cost of repairing the lawn. She knew that the Executive Director of her agency would not be pleased and that money for repairs would undoubtedly come from her already thin budget. She told me that finances were tight because Danny required more "supervision" than had been planned. "His needing a one-to-one is not something we expected."

I tried knocking on Danny's door again.

Still no answer.

While the three of us waited outside, Eiesha remembered an old behavior plan that was attached to the files sent by the institution when Danny first moved out. "When I first read that plan, " she said, "I didn't like it. It seemed too harsh. Too controlling. But maybe Gerald is right. Maybe Danny *needs* consequences."

I had seen the plan she was talking about. It *was* horrible. But before I launched into my usual righteous indignation about such things, I thought about how many behavior modification programs I had written over the years that were equally horrible. I asked Gerald to pass me another donut and sat quietly for a moment thinking about the fundamental mistakes I had made during my early years as a "behavior consultant". I was oblivious to my own shortcomings and the fundamentally disrespectful way in which I had been conducting myself. First, I rarely got to know the person I was trying to help (I was too busy being a professional). Second, I rarely involved the person in the development of his or her plan. If it's hard for you to understand why this is a problem, think of one of your behaviors that you need to change. Now imagine that someone you don't know very well has developed a plan to rid you of this unwanted behavior. Without your input or even your consideration. Get the picture? A third reason why so many of my behavior modification programs were unethical is that I often asked other people (staff) who did not know the person very well to implement my plans. When the plans worked, I complimented myself for a job well done. When the plans didn't work, I blamed it on turnover (the average length of stay for residential caregivers, last time I looked, was seven months). Fourth, my interventions sometimes involved punishment, especially in the early years. Imagine someone you don't know very well doing something unpleasant to you every time you exhibit the before-mentioned behavior. No more explanation should be needed. Fifth, my interventions involved positive reinforcement. Now imagine someone you don't know very well trying to be nice to you while completely disregarding your input. And last, but not least, while I promoted these unethical, and yes, nonsensical approaches, the managers of the organizations that hired me were thanking me for my good work. It took me years, and lots of help, to understand that I had *become* a part of the problem.

Something all at once

Trish arrived in a large beat-up Buick, looking a bit beat-up herself. Her face was tired and drawn, her hair was badgered, as if someone had deliberately tried to tangle it into knots, and she was in the sixth month of her second pregnancy. She carried a bag bulging with files and looked as if she might tip over in the street. Her mouth was open as she surveyed the lawn. "What in God's name happened?" she asked.

We told her about Danny's midnight gardening project.

Right then, at that moment, this tired woman, who looked hopeless and beat-up, did something remarkable. Something that all at once gave me hope.

She laughed.

She laughed hard.

She laughed so hard that she dropped her bag , held her hand in the arch of her back, and sucked for air. Tears were rolling down her face. And then, almost as quickly as she had begun laughing, she stopped. She looked at the three of us sadly and with just three words described the essence of Danny's struggle. "He's so lonely."

It's not about coverage

I met a man once who was very much alone in the world. He could have been Danny. They have very similar stories. When he was a young boy, his family sent him to an institution. He had troubling behaviors that would not go away, regardless of the intervention or medications he received. He refused to do things with other people and preferred to isolate himself in his bed room, wrapped tightly in blankets. I believe his troubling behaviors and resistance to relationships were the direct result of the trauma* he endured when he was separated from his family, and from the systematic abuse he suffered at the hands of his "care givers" over a period of years. When I suggested that loneliness and trauma might be at the root of his difficulties, one member of his team said, "He's not lonely. He has one-to-one coverage."

---

*My good friend Al Vecchione, PhD. is a psychologist in Vermont who helps people who have been institutionalized to recover from trauma. He once told me that betrayal is at the root of all trauma. Someone you assumed would keep you safe didn't keep you safe. Someone you thought you could count on was untrustworthy. Whether the promise was explicit or implicit, it got broken. And the remedy for broken promises, Al believes, is predictable, enduring, and freely chosen relationships.

You can, of course, have ten-to-one coverage and be terribly alone. One way I like to explain the difference between coverage and relationships is to ask people to imagine that I have just returned home from a road trip. I pull up in my driveway, and discover that my wife Cyndi is not home. Another woman is standing at the door and I ask, "Where is Cyndi?" She replies, "Cyndi is not home, but don't worry. We have you covered."

People generally laugh at this scenario. It's silly. Preposterous, really. But it is exactly what happens to people who experience our services time and time again. The very fact that people laugh at the joke of another woman "covering" for my wife is indication that they know there is a huge difference between "coverage" and "relationships".* Our field keeps giving people coverage when what they desperately need is to *belong*.

The powerful medicine of belonging

"A sense of belonging," writes Dr. Kenneth Pelletier of the Stanford Center for Research and Disease Prevention, "appears to be a basic human need – as basic as food and shelter. In fact, social support may be one of the critical elements distinguishing those who remain healthy from those who become ill." (1994, pp. 137-138)

Researchers Brent Hafen, Keith Karren, Kathryn Frandsen, and N. Lee Smith (1996) describe the results of a nine-year study of 7,000 people living in Alemada County, California. "The people with many social contacts – a spouse, a close-knit family, a network of friends, church, or other group affiliations – lived longer and had better health. People who were socially isolated had poorer health and died earlier. In fact, those who had few ties with other people died at rates two to five times higher than those with good social ties." (p. 261)

Hafren, Karren, Frandsen, & Smith write that "social support is the degree to which a person's basic social needs are met through interaction with other people. It's the resources –both tangible and intangible– that other people provide. It's a person's perception that he or she can count on other people for help with a problem or for help in a time of crisis." (p. 263)

---

*Epidemiologist Leonard Sagan (1987) writes that it is not the number of people physically present in our lives, but the extent to which we are *satisfied* in our relationships and whether or not we *perceive* ourselves as isolated.

Although the reasons why social support leads to better health are not entirely understood (one theory is that belonging improves immune function), the implications are profound for people who experience our services. It may be that a great deal of what we see as pathology (e.g., poor health, mental health issues, problem behaviors, etc.), is, in fact, the side effect of loneliness.

Sidney Cobb, president of the Society of Psychosomatic Medicine, argues that the data supporting a link between loneliness and illness is overwhelming – that "social support can indeed protect people in crisis from what he calls a 'wide variety' of diseases. Adequate social support, Cobb says, has been proven to protect against conditions from 'low birth weight to death, through tuberculosis to depression, alcoholism, and other psychiatric illness. Furthermore, social support can reduce the amount of medication required, accelerate recovery, and facilitate compliance with prescribed regimens (Pilsuk & Hiller Parks, S., 1986). People who are suffering from a break down in social support are also more prone to cancer, hypertension, and heart disease. (Bai, 1989).

Apparently it's true. You *can* die from a broken heart.

The promises you keep

Trish walked up to Danny's door and knocked.

He answered immediately.

Eiesha, Gerald, and I shook our heads and chuckled. "Danny always opens the door for Trish," Eiesha said. "Always."

I first met Trish at the institution where Danny lived prior to moving to Eiesha's group home. I liked her immediately. She was a no-nonsense kind of person who intuitively seemed to understand that Danny needed a life (as opposed to a program). She did more than make the required number of visits and file reports, she spent time with him, in ordinary, everyday places, doing things he enjoyed. She listened to him over coffee and helped him to find the materials he needed to build a flower bed outside of the administration office. She made sure that anyone who ever came into the building admiring the flowers knew that Danny was responsible. Most importantly, she kept her promises. Whenever they made arrangements to meet, she was there, on time. She told me once that she didn't like to make Danny wait. "Danny has to wait all the time." On occasion, staff would tell Trish that she should not take Danny to lunch because he had "mis-behaved." Trish, who normally kept her cool, would groan at them and pronounce, "I made a promise to Danny and I keep my word."

She groaned at me that way after I suggested that we meet once again with staff at the institution to "iron out" our different approaches. "They don't listen to Danny and they never will" she said. "This is not a place that he, or anyone else, should have to endure." And then, with a tone of voice that simultaneously communicated her appreciation for my efforts to date while warning me that she would throttle me if I suggested any further "negotiations" with the institution staff, she asked, "What are you going to do to help me get him out of here?"

I promised her that I would do anything I could to help. But the central reason why Danny got out of the institution is not because of anything I did. The central reason he got out was that Trish was ferociously committed. She went beyond the requirements of her job. She kept her promises.

In the center of the frame

I still remember that day, years ago, sitting in those green plastic chairs with Eiesha and Gerald, eating donuts and chuckling to ourselves about how quickly Danny opened the door for Trish. The truth, of course, is that it was not so easy. Trish and Danny had known each other for years. Trish had worked hard to earn his trust. They cared about one another.

Years later, when I found myself sitting outside of Danny's apartment on his concrete steps, I couldn't help but wish for Trish. I imagined her pulling up to a parking spot in her big Buick, kids in tow, hair in a knot. She would laugh, undoubtedly, at the sight of me waiting for Danny to open the door.

She would laugh hard.

And Danny would probably let her in.

I stood up from the hard step and looked again through the window. I had become so accustomed to the light of the day I had to wait a few moments for my eyes to adjust. He was still on the couch. He still wouldn't answer.

Sitting back down, I thought about the "gone lawn incident" and all that has transpired since that eventful day. A lot of ground was covered (no pun intended). Trish convinced Danny to sit down with Eiesha and her Executive Director and work out a plan to re-seed

the lawn and build proper flower beds. Trish also took responsibility for organizing a circle of support and the circle met regularly
until she left to care for her newborn baby. When she left, a new
case manager, Caroline, took the lead in helping Danny to schedule
his meetings and develop a personal futures plan with the circle
members.

Danny loved his circle meetings. He liked the fact that he was
in charge of the invitation list. He invited his sister Teresa and
brother-in-law Tom, though they rarely showed up. He invited Trish
and Eiesha and Katherine and Caroline. He invited me. He didn't
invite Gerald, or anyone from the institution, or *anyone* he thought
wouldn't listen. It was *his* meeting. He liked the way people talked
about his gifts and capacities. He hated the old way of doing things,
when people talked about his "problems" and nothing ever got
done. He liked "thinking big" about his dreams, his future. He liked
the little things too – the coffee, the food, the artwork on the big
pieces of paper.

At one particularly memorable meeting, Danny said, "I want my
life back" and everyone in the room sat perfectly still. It probably
only lasted seconds, but imagined that I was watching a movie,
when the camera slowly pulls in for a close up. There he was, in the
center of the frame, looking angry and determined. He was asking
each of us to help him reclaim something that had been taken away
from him – something no less important than his "life."

The stories we hold

I tried knocking on the door again. I didn't even bother to stand
this time. I just knocked on the lower half of his door, pretty sure
that he would ignore me. "Danny. Let's get something to eat. I'm
hungry!"

Still no answer.

The lady down the street, the one who had disappeared from her
porch like a startled cat, was back again. Staring. I waved and she
waved back. I was surprised. I didn't know what to do, so I just
waved again. Thankfully, she missed my second wave when a car
load of people arrived in front of her house and she left her porch
to greet them. Out from the car jumped young children who leaped
into her arms yelling "Grandma!" Their parents, looking exhausted,
hugged her too. The out-of-state tags suggested it had been a long
journey, especially with kids. I watched them hug and laugh and felt

happy for the old woman. She had family who loved her. And by the look of things, her family was growing and changing it's shape. Her child had become a parent. She had become a grandparent. While the mother and father unpacked the car, the children sat with her on the porch and told her stories about the journey. I couldn't hear the details, but I knew they were fighting about who would tell her what. The youngest one, a girl, began screaming, "That's *my* story!"

In my family, we tell stories. Every Christmas, at my brother's house in Vermont, we gather for an evening of food and storytelling. Last year, with the youngest generation at our feet in diapers, we gathered in the den, all of us, and we told stories of the year just passed. We also told stories that we tell year after year. Like the one about my parents taking the five of us into Hubbard Park to cut down a Christmas tree. It was supposed to be a joyful evening, but all five of us were miserable because it was cold and rainy. The older ones wanted to stay home and watch American Bandstand and I felt like I was going to pass out in my tight corduroy snow suit. My father, who was probably hoping for one of those Norman Rockwell moments, was cussing at us all the way up the hill and all the way back. "God damn it, you kids! It's Christmas!"

We love to tell stories.

We hold them for each other.

Who holds your story? My bet is that someone, somewhere, remembers you when you were knee high to a grasshopper. Someone remembers the day you lost your first tooth, or the day you swam to the raft in swimming lessons, your first date, your newborn. Someone probably knows about that hole in your heart or that reason you fear change. I hope someone, somewhere, holds your story.

The problem for many people who experience our services is that no one holds their stories. We know them by their labels or brief social histories (e.g., "mother experienced complications in pregnancy... child was institutionalized at fourteen... home visits became less frequent in 1977..." etc.), but we know nothing, really, about their stories – where they came from, the names of their family members and long-lost friends. We know little of the events that shaped their lives, the achievements and disappointments that gave shape to their sense of self, where they feel connected and where they feel cut off. Thanks to processes such as person-centered planning, we are learning to ask different questions, questions that invite a story to be told. Instead of, "What's wrong with you?" and "How do we fix you?" we're learning to ask "*Who* are you?" and "What do you dream of?" and "How can we help you to move towards a desirable future?"* The rich details that make stories worth telling and retelling are emerging. But for most people served by our system, the preoccupation with deficits and limitations is still pronounced. We not only don't know people's stories. We don't even notice that their stories are missing.†

You could be one of the millions

Danny was institutionalized when he was 23 years old. He had been living with his mother in a broken down apartment. His older siblings, Eddie and Teresa, were long gone. His father, who lived only a few blocks away but whom he never really knew, died in the 1970's. When I asked Danny why he was institutionalized, he told me he had been "flippin' out." I asked him to describe what "flippin' out" means and he said that he "was going after" his Mom and a nephew, Tommy-Boy. He was also threatening to hurt himself.

After Danny was institutionalized, he was subjected to all kinds of abuse, often in the guise of "treatment." Time out, seclusion, cold water showers – *all* were approved by a "human rights" committee. In addition to this sanctioned abuse, he was repeatedly assaulted and raped by a male staff person. He tried to tell people what was happening, but no one believed him. The perpetrator was transferred to another unit – this one serving women only – and the official position was that the "matter had been satisfactorily resolved."

Danny told me that he didn't tell his mother about the abuse for years, but on one visit home during the Christmas holidays, he told her what had happened and it broke her heart. A couple of months later she died of heart failure. To this day, he believes that she would still be alive had he kept the secret to himself.

---

*Thanks to John O'Brien for helping me to think of these questions so succinctly.

†A simple thing to do is to draw a horizontal line on a big piece of paper. On the left hand side of the line, write down the day and year the person was born. On the right hand side of the line, write today's date. Now try to fill in this time line with as many major or significant events you can think of. What do you see? My bet is that there are gaps, spaces of time in which you know very little about the person. My bet is that most of what you know about the person falls in the recent past. A big part of the work, in my view, is to help people to reclaim their lost stories and to make sure those stories are told in a way that is respectful and meaningful.

Danny remembers those early days with his mother as being some of the best and worst days of his life. He remembers fondly the things that his mother would cook for him – spaghetti with meatballs, TV dinners, and mashed potatoes. The two of them watched television together. She told him stories and sometimes he made her laugh. But life could be hard too. There were kids who picked on him when he walked home from school, and sometimes, after enduring their taunts, he would arrive home to find his mother drinking alone or with strange men. He also remembers that Eddie, his brother, struggled with drugs and alcohol. On one occasion, when he was in the hospital for his "behaviors" and his mother was in the same hospital "getting tested for her heart," Eddie broke into their apartment and tore the place apart. "He was looking for money" Danny said. "He ransacked the place." The landlord evicted them, and in what had become an all too familiar pattern, they found themselves looking for a new place to stay. They ended up living with his sister Teresa and her husband Tom, but that didn't work out because Danny's mother didn't get along with Tom. "He was always bossing her around and she didn't like it."

Like nomads, they wandered from one run down apartment to another in a neighborhood in the city's northeast quadrant. Bordering a once prominent port that was host to ships from all over the world, the neighborhood fell onto hard times after the shipping interests moved down river to newer facilities. All kinds of businesses – mom and pop groceries, restaurants, bars, movie theaters – closed. It was like watching dominoes falling as dreams soured and people moved away in droves.

In the 1960's, the neighborhood was literally split in half by a major interstate highway that runs north to south. To get anywhere, you have to follow a maze of narrow streets that snake under the highway. Some of them end abruptly in abandoned lots lined with wire fencing and "No Trespassing" signs. Others lose the light of day as they pass between abandoned warehouses and factories. My favorite is a road that runs directly beneath the interstate for half a mile. You pass by what's left of a neighborhood park and the shell of a burned-out church. Part of the road is cobblestone, a reminder of a time when things were simpler and less hectic. Just before you turn onto Chestnut, the street where Danny lives, there is a massive billboard positioned for southbound travelers on the interstate. It reads, "You could be one of the millions of Americans suffering from generalized anxiety disorder."

Crisis as an opportunity

A lot of things happened after Danny told his circle that he wanted his life back. The wheels of the system finally started rolling his way. With help from Caroline, he hooked up with Ed, who directed the city's self-determination initiative, and in no time at all he got control over his own budget. This meant that he could now make his life what he wanted it to be. He didn't have to take orders from anyone anymore. Staff would now be *his* employees, not the employees of an agency. He was calling the shots.

He found his apartment on Chestnut Street by looking through real estate newspapers with Caroline. It was only blocks from the neighborhood where he grew up and in no time they had it looking like a home. He found a couch, table, chairs, and a bed at a local second hand store, and pots and pans and dishes at the flea market. Someone gave him a VCR to play his movies and he brought his TV and prized stereo –the only thing he owned that was new – from his apartment attached to the group home. In the basement, there was a washer and dryer and out back, in a tiny court yard, there was room enough for his flower beds. At his housewarming party, circle members brought new things –pictures for his walls, a rack to dry his dishes, red and blue towels for the bath. He was on cloud nine.

But less than a year later, life started to unravel –again. He had trouble finding and keeping good staff and the ones he didn't like seemed to stay too long. Managing employees was all new to him. Even though Ed and Caroline were doing their best to help, it was hard to keep track of schedules and hours and the way he wanted things to be. He found himself in that same old "client" role with staff who did little more than watch his television and tell him what to do. He felt depressed and paranoid – he stopped eating, found himself sleeping all day and he began worrying that staff were stealing his money. Tom warned him, "You're going to get kicked out of that self-determination program if you don't straighten up!"

I can only imagine what he was thinking when his entire circle showed up at his house one afternoon. Ed, from the self-determination initiative, took the lead. In a very straightforward and respectful way, he told Danny why we had come. " We're worried about you. And we're afraid that if things keep going the way they have been going, you will get sick from not eating or you'll burn yourself up in a fire by using the stove for heat. You gotta believe us, we care about you. We don't want to intrude, but we also can't ignore the fact that you are doing some dangerous stuff. You said you wanted to be free, but with freedom comes responsibility and we don't think you're living up to your end of the bargain. So, for a time, we want you to give us keys so we can let ourselves in."

I thought Danny was going to be angry and throw us out of his place. But he seemed relieved – *genuinely* relieved. I realized that day that he was not only scaring *us*. He was also scaring *himself*.

Years ago, I heard John O'Brien and Connie Lyle O'Brien talking at a conference about "choice."* As a field, we have finally begun to recognize that people who experience disabilities are entitled to make choices about their own lives. Making choices is an essential part of well-being. Even our "bad" choices can be good for us.† But what do you do when someone you care about is making choices that are destructive or dangerous? Are those choices OK too? That's the question that John and Connie addressed at the conference and that's the question Danny's circle had to consider as his life began to spin out of control. John and Connie encouraged the conference participants to think beyond the "faddishness" of choice in such circumstances and address what matters most –a person's security and well-being. When you care about someone, there is ambiguity at times like these. It might be gray when you want it to be black and white. The person you care about might not want help, might not even consider "the problem" a problem. But if you are in doubt, in my judgment, the responsible thing to do is to talk about it, get advice from people you respect, and do what it takes to assure a reasonable level of safety.‡ People hurting themselves or others in the name of "choice" or "freedom" is nonsense.

---

*September 27, 1993 Conference at Central Virginia Training Center in Lynchburg, VA.

†Some of the most important things I have learned have not been because I have made "right" choices, but because I have made the "wrong" ones. When I think about the totality of what I know (which doesn't take long), at least half of my brain cells are occupied with information I learned because I made mistakes. In short, my brain would have been half full if I had failed to fail.

‡ A good way to figure out how to settle things down is to ask the person what he or she <u>needs</u>. If the person is unable to let you know, because he or she does not have a formal means of communication, or because things are just spinning out of control, it's useful to talk with the people who know him or her best. I like to ask people to imagine that the person is in the next room having a horrible day. Then I tell them I will give them $500 if they go to the person and help him to feel better, and to be safe. People often respond, "Nothing we do works all the time." I tell them, yes, of course, nothing works *all* the time, but imagine I would give you $500 right now if

An equally ludicrous approach to someone in crisis is to respond with unpleasant consequences designed to "teach him/her a lesson" or to become overly-controlling. These reactive strategies are understandable but flawed for several reasons. First, it is unlikely that the person wants to be having a hard time. Most of us would rather be happy rather than miserable. My assumption when I meet people who are in crisis is that they are already feeling badly about their behavior, perhaps embarrassed, and the last thing on earth they need is to be fussed at. Second, the person probably has very little self-confidence because he or she lacks the necessary coping skills to deal with the troubling emotions or difficult situations. Third, the person probably has very little idea about what situations or circumstances lead to a difficult time, and once they confront those feelings they don't know what to do to stay calm (coping skills). Once identified, the person needs to practice those skills during *non*-stressful times. You don't give swimming lessons to someone who is drowning and you don't teach coping skills to a person who is in the middle of a crisis. Fourth, anyone who is repeatedly in crisis has probably learned from experience that things sometimes get out of hand and when they do, something really bad happens (they get hurt, someone else gets hurt, things get broken). A clear set of steps that care givers can take when the person is falling to pieces is critical. When the person regains his or her balance, care givers must be willing to support the person to "get back on track."*

---

you tried something and it worked. What would you do? From here, a list of sensible ideas is usually generated. I then ask people to imagine that I would give them $500 if they made the person feel *worse*. This list comes easily. No one ever says, "nothing we do works all the time." The list of things that people would do to make the person feel worse usually comes easy. It is often a word for word transcription of the current behavior plan. "Settling things down" means that we do more of the things we know work, and less of the things we know that make matters worse.

*A crisis can be an *opportunity* to teach a person the importance of relationships. The Outward Bound program is based on this idea. For example, counselors might take a group of "hardened" kids out into the wilderness. On the bus ride, the kids sit in the back, full of attitude and cool. The adults sit in the front of the bus, discussing logistics and responsibilities. When they arrive in the wilderness, the adults tell the kids that they are going to climb down a 100 foot rock face, and suddenly the kids who seemed full of attitude and cool change their physical proximity to the adults (they get closer). They let everyone know that they are not so confident anymore. In essence, the adults have created a "crisis." The goal of this crisis is to show the kids that the adults can be helpful. They can help them to overcome their fear of heights, help them to master new skills (e.g., using a harness, tying knots, repelling). And one by one, the kids step over the edge of the cliff and make their way safely to the bot-

The importance of *enduring* relationships

I looked at my watch. It was 1:30 PM.

I figured the best thing I could do at this point was to wait for Jennifer who was scheduled to arrive at 2:00. She was Danny's newest staff person, someone who started working for him shortly after the "intervention" with his circle members. Danny likes Jennifer. She helps him with budgeting and grocery shopping. *Together*, they are taking a pottery class at the YMCA. I like Jennifer too. She is real with Danny. She doesn't get all wound up when he is having a bad day, but she doesn't ignore him either. She listens carefully and shows him respect for his fears. She encourages him to take "one day at a time" and can usually help him to find something to smile about.

As I watched the couple down the street pulling the last bags from their car, their kids climbing all over their grandmother, I was reminded of how much I missed my wife Cyndi and sons Joe and Sam just then. I was on another road trip and it seemed like they were a million miles away. Then I thought of Danny and how rarely he sees his family. His mother and father are both gone, and Eddie is nowhere to be found. He visits his sister Teresa and Tom on occasion, but not often. When he does visit, he usually gets an earful of criticism from Tom. Most of the people in Danny's life are like me – *paid* to be with him. Most are good people, mind you, but most don't stay long. If they do, they probably don't come often. I live nearly 500 miles away and have never been a frequent visitor, but I am still one of the most enduring relationships Danny has with a "professional" (we met in 1996). Even Trish, who saved his life when he lived in the institution and who would undoubtedly find a place in his hall of fame, visits infrequently. In Danny's life, people leaving is a constant. People staying is rare.

Jennifer arrived at 2:00 and didn't seem surprised to find me waiting there on the steps. "He had a rough weekend," she said matter-of-factly, knocking on his door. When he didn't answer, she let us both in and a wall of dry, still air hit me as I entered his living room.

---

tom. Not surprisingly, once they unhitch themselves from their harnesses, they cop the same attitude they had at the outset. But something is different now. Through this crisis, the kids have learned that the adults will support them during a crisis and help them to develop mastery over needed skills. Additionally, they now share a *story*.

He was standing in the kitchen in his boxer shorts and a t-shirt, shifting his weight from foot to foot and complaining about Tom. "I went over there for Sunday dinner and he said I had to take a shower or I couldn't eat. Teresa stood and watched me to make sure I did. I must be awful to be told to take a shower or leave."

Jennifer listened carefully and slowly began to pick up the kitchen. She took Styrofoam cups from the table and threw them into the garbage pail. She wiped sugar from his counter. She didn't fuss at him or tell him to clean up *anything*. She was there to help. She was there to help him get back on track. "It must have been awful to be treated that way," she said. "I can understand why you are so upset."

Slowly, Danny began to relax. He apologized for making me wait outside and told me that his stomach had been too upset to eat. Jennifer reminded him that he had an appointment later in the week with a new doctor. "Remember to tell her about your stomach," she said, taking both he and his complaint seriously. Then she asked him if he would help her carry a laundry basket to the basement. He refused. Jennifer simply smiled and carried the basket to the basement by herself. When she returned, she asked him if she could help him to find some clothes to wear. He told her that she could. I heard her say, "I think you are handling things pretty well." I could tell from the look on his face that he was beginning to believe it might be true.

When you begin to believe it might be true

In the months following my wait outside of Danny's door, his life has improved dramatically. He has found a psychiatrist whom he likes very much. More specifically, he likes his psychiatrist's assistant, Dana. "She has red hair and is beautiful" he tells me. "She said I should think of the future rather than dwelling on the past." Dana, I am told, does Danny a world of good whenever they see each other. She takes time with him and doesn't rush things. If she is having a particularly chaotic day at her office, she tells him *why* she is rushed and assures him that she will try her best to spend more time with him on his next visit. Dana keeps her promises and she also expects a lot from Danny. She knows that he doesn't trust medications and is apt to stop taking them, so she asked him to promise her that he would take his an anti-depressant regularly and stop only if the two of them have had a chance to talk. So far, so good.

Another important person in Danny's life these days is Sean. Sean is an independent consultant who works with the city's self-determination initiative. He is a firm believer that Danny can learn the skills necessary to manage his own staff. He helps Danny to convene regular meetings with each of his employees to discuss what's working and not working. These meetings are a structured way for Danny and his employees to "air things out." The regular schedule for the meetings is helping to assure that issues don't get out-of-hand and to assure Danny that he won't have to wait too long to say what he needs to say. Sean is like an orchestra conductor who keeps everyone on the same page. He responds to crises when they arise, but he never assumes that crises are inevitable. He is always working to find a solution to every problem.

Life for Danny has also improved because of "The Edge." That's the nickname I give to Edgerin, Danny's newest employee. An outgoing and friendly man, The Edge is father to three adult children and as many grandchildren. He is a jack of all trades. In the recent past, he was a communications specialist for a telemarketing firm. A few years back he helped adjudicated youth to find instruments so that they could form punk bands. What I like most about him is that he is deeply in love with his wife. When he talks about her, he talks about her with reverence. I tell you this because I think the man knows the importance of getting connected and staying connected. He is one of those guys that seem to connect with people everywhere he goes.

For example, I recently had lunch with Danny, his casemanager Katherine, and The Edge in a part of town that is notorious for its lack of parking. The Edge told me to park on a side street next to an abandoned lot and I was a bit concerned about leaving my car. "Don't worry" he said. "I know those guys." He let out a loud whistle and three men warming their hands over a smoking 50 gallon drum waved. The Edge pointed to my car and one of the three men held up a thumb. "It'll be OK" said The Edge confidently. "You can trust these guys."

The four of us ate at Hooters, a restaurant and bar chain that routinely employs attractive women in tight fitting tops and shorts. It doesn't take a genius to see that Hooters caters to a largely male clientele. (I felt so guilty about being in the place that I thought of calling my wife and explaining to her what I was up to.) When we walked through the front door, we were greeted by a young woman named Sara who recognized Danny and The Edge immediately. "Your favorite table is available, Danny" she said, smiling. "Will it be a Sprite today? I know you're watching your caffeine."

We ordered terrible chicken wings and gallon-sized soft drinks and talked for nearly three hours about what the two of them had been up to. The Edge, who affectionately calls Danny his "CEO," was careful not to talk too much or to do anything that would inhibit Danny from telling *his* story. Whenever Danny forgot a detail (he was frequently distracted by Sara), The Edge would kindly offer him a reminder or ask for his permission to elaborate.

There was a *lot* to tell. In recent weeks, the two of them had built a flower bed in the back yard. Low on cash, they purchased a child's plastic pool, punched holes in the bottom, and filled it with dirt. It wasn't as fancy as a raised bed made of wood, but it would do for now. The two of them were planning a beach vacation together and it was important to save as much money as possible. In the meantime, for fun, they were frequenting a local gardening center looking for new ideas. They had come to know the owner fairly well and Danny was trying to get his courage up to ask for a part-time job. "It's your call" The Edge told Danny during our lunch. "The time will be right when the time is right for you." They talked about the trips they were making to a college radio station after the midnight hour. As long as I have known Danny, he has dreamed of being a DJ. With the Edge's support, he was now routinely visiting the college station at precisely the same hours that he had been fighting with his neighbor over the loud music. Danny told me that the DJ talked with him "on air" the week before our lunch. He asked me if I heard the show.

Katherine, who has known Danny for longer than I, said she hadn't seen him this happy in years. I knew that it was unlikely that his new medication had taken effect so soon, but his good mood was certainly apparent and welcome. I asked him if he knew why things seemed to be looking up. He said he wasn't sure. I asked him if his staff were helping him in ways that made him happy. He said yes. I asked him if he could elaborate and he helped me to construct this list. We call it "The Hooter's List":

They help me to do things I *want to* do.

They help me to do the things I *have to* do and they don't boss me.

They ask me what I want to do each day and let me make decisions.

They know I need time to myself sometimes and leave me alone.

They make funny jokes.

They keep their promises.

After our waitress had removed the last dishes from our table, I asked Danny if there was anything else that should be on the list. He thought about it for a minute and said, "They tell me positive things."

"What do you mean?" I asked.

"They tell me things are going to work out."

"Do you think things are going to work out?"

He looked at me with a pained look. "I don't really know."

I don't really know

My friend Rollin and I have a humorous routine that we perform whenever we see each other. We met 23 years ago when I was a live-in house parent at an Intermediate-Care -Facility in Vermont and he was one of six adolescent boys living there. Over the years, we have become good friends. Whenever we get together, I ask him if he would like me to update his vocational assessment. He laughs and says no. I then ask him if he would rather go get a hamburger. He says, "hamburger, french fries, root beer float." I act all bothered and plead with him for an opportunity to assess his skills and deficits. He belly laughs and tells me that I'm "nervous."

In my judgment, many professionals *are* nervous. We keep trying to fix people who don't need or want to be fixed. We roll out programs and initiatives –new ways of doing things– and keep ourselves so busy we never have to come to grips with the central reason why people are suffering –loneliness.

Danny is beginning to open his door. But I suspect he will close it again if the people he is learning to trust disappear. "To be vulnerable is not necessarily to be in danger" writes Willard Gaylin (1990. p. 136), "to be vulnerable and unloved is the matrix of disaster."

References

Gaylin, W. (1990). *On being and becoming human*. New York: Penguin Books.

Pilisuk, M. and Hillier Parks, S. (1986). *The Healing Web*. Hanover, NH: University Press of New England.

Blai, B. (1989). Health consequences of loneliness: A review of the literature. *JACH* (37)(162).

Hafren, B.Q., Karren, K.J., Frandsen, K.J. & Smith, N.K. (1996). *Mind/body health: The effects of attitudes, emotions, and relationships*. Boston: Allyn and Bacon.

Pelletier, K. (1994). *Sound mind, sound body: A new model for lifelong health* (pp. 137- 138). New York: Simon and Schuster.

Sagan, L. (1987) *The health of nations: True causes of sickness and well being*. New York: Basic Books.

9

Two Is Not Enough

Mary Romer

I recently saw the movie, *about a boy*, based on the book by Nick Hornby (1998). I greatly enjoyed reading this book a couple years back. While it wasn't by any stretch an intellectual read that stirred deep philosophical questions, I found myself alternately laughing out loud and shedding silent tears. The film was a pleasant reminder of why I so enjoyed the novel. Besides its entertainment value I discovered relevance to the ways I think about relationships within my own circle of family and friends. The fictional character Marcus, a 12-year-old boy, well illustrates these views at the end of the story,

> *I can't explain it, but I feel safer than before, because I know more people. I was really scared because I didn't think two was enough, now there aren't two anymore. There are loads. And you're better off that way.*

For many years, I have had the privilege of being invited into the lives of many people with disabilities. Sometimes these invitations have resulted in regular and ongoing connections and sometimes it has meant briefer commitments of time. While honored by these invitations, I am always humbled and nervous about my ability to offer worthwhile help. I find myself wishing that I had retained some of the certainty I had when I was in my twenties. As I recall, I was often filled with the self-assurance of knowing I could change the world. I am, however, grateful for the humility that grows each passing year and leads me to a deeper understanding of the importance of, in Marcus' words, *more people*. It quells my anxiety about attempting to bring meaningful assistance to those asking. And it offers places to begin:

> Are enough people engaged in the person's life?

> Are there people who are imbued with the belief and hope for a brighter, better future for the person?

> If not, how might such people be found or how might that sense of hope be instilled in those committed to walking with a person?

Joanne, a beloved friend of mine, has on many occasions remarked on the gifts that her daughter, Kim, has brought to her life. One gift is finding and forming sustaining relationships with people who she may never have known if not for Kim. I have the good fortune of being one of those people. It is also through Kim's gift of connection, that Leah, her younger sister, came to work with me more than ten years ago. As with most friendships, the mutuality of giving and receiving remains a constant in my relationship with Joanne. Often, when Joanne, Kim and I participate in gatherings and meetings concerned with issues related to the lives of people with disabilities, Joanne remarks on the importance she places on the hope and validation of her dreams for Kim that she believes I bring to our relationship.

Joanne's perception of this gift has led me to contemplate where my own sense of belief and hope for a better world for people with disabilities arises. I am not an exceptionally optimistic person. I often feel a deep sense of despair over the state of our world, the fracturing of relationships and divisions amongst people, and the meanness of spirit that can leak in and permeate our best efforts. Nonetheless, I realize one of my core beliefs is hope for the positive futures of people labeled with disability. Usually I have attributed this to the good company I have kept over the past many years with people with disabilities and their families who have invited me into their lives and allowed me to bear witness as they find their pathways towards more positive futures. Recently, though, I have been thinking about my own experiences within my family.

My Uncle Don died of cancer a year ago. He was 59 years old. A son, a daughter, sisters, brothers and numerous nieces and nephews survive him. His modest estate consisted of a house, a new pick up truck, a college fund for his daughter, and life insurance policies for each of his children. He spent most of his life in upstate New York, not far from the city of Buffalo where he was born. Uncle Don was well known to the older folks around the town where he lived as the guy to call if they needed errands run, things hauled or assistance moving. His reputation was one of honesty, dependability and hard work.

For a brief period in his late twenties, he moved to Los Angeles and found work at the Los Angeles airport loading food unto the planes. I visited Uncle Don with my grandmother once while he was living in Los Angeles. He was a terrific host and was determined that I see as much as possible during the two weeks I stayed with him. A whirlwind tour that encompassed L.A., Bakersfield, San Francisco, San Diego, and Tijuana, Mexico ensued with my sixteen-year-old self doing much of the freeway driving. Driving 80 miles an hour along the California freeways was, according to Uncle Don, as important an experience for me as seeing Disneyland and Knott's Berry farm.

He was happy with his life in Los Angeles but returned to New York because my grandmother asked him. He had always lived with her. While Grandma was fairly protective of him, she was also reliant on him for companionship and help. Upon return from California, Uncle Don was hired at the Fisher Price factory where he worked for over 20 years until the factory closed. He took great pride in the products he was making and loved his job. All of the children in the family were beneficiaries of every Fisher Price toy made during his years of employment there.

In his late thirties, Uncle Don got married. After several years and two children, he was divorced and became the custodial parent for both of his children. He was an enormously proud parent. Like most parents, he was resolute in wanting his children to have opportunities better than his own. In the last year of his life, he was able to see his daughter begin college. By this time he knew he was dying of cancer. Nonetheless, he was unwavering that his daughter follow her dream of moving to New York City and studying theater.

My Uncle Don was an ordinary man who enjoyed life's simple pleasures. He was committed to his children and extended family and gave generously of himself to those who needed his assistance. Family celebrations, parties and events were not to be missed and he could always be counted on to out-stay and out-eat everyone else. Sharing stories, catching up on another's life and eating good food were sources of great enjoyment. Uncle Don was a well loved, contributing member of my family. In return, the extended family was integral in supporting him in any number of ways, including periods of extended care of his children at times needed.

My sister, Katie, is six years younger than me. She has been married for twenty-three years. For the past seven years, she has worked at a restaurant in a nearby town. She has been awarded an Employee of the Year certificate. Katie is such a valued employee that on several occasions the restaurant manager has personally provided transportation to bring her to and from work since she does not drive nor live in an area where public transportation is readily available. Prior to this job, she provided childcare for ten years for the children of her husband's co-worker. She lost this position when the children's mom was laid off from her job.

Katie has a remarkable memory of people, places, dates and events. In family lore, she is the one counted on to remember and acknowledge all of the family birthdays and special occasions. Family members go to her if they want to recount details of past family history. She is warm and friendly, has a great sense of humor and is always willing to pitch in and help.

In addition to a shared reputation of a strong work ethic and good people skills, Katie and Uncle Don were both labeled with a developmental disability as young children. Each spent all of their school years in the special education system. Institutionalization was suggested to my grandparents when Uncle Don was a small child. Fortunately, for Uncle Don and the rest of the family, my grandparents adamantly refused to consider this alternative. This was not suggested to my parents as an alternative for Katie. They were told, instead, that they should bring her home, love her and curb their expectations around her abilities to contribute and participate fully in community life.

Not long ago, I participated in an event with a woman who spoke about painful childhood memories visiting her sister who was institutionalized due to her family's inability to provide her sister with the intensive support she needed. While it is certainly true that our sisters' and families' circumstances and needs vastly differed, her reflections accentuated how each of our experiences shaped our individual perspectives and beliefs in relationship to people with disabilities and their families. It seems that my family unknowingly practiced theories such as normalization, inclusion, and shared space in our everyday lives. A rich web of relationships included extended family, friends, neighbors and members of the broader community. My parents regularly participated in church and civic associations and organizations. In now popular terms, it would be accurate to say that they engaged expansively in activities that gained them *social capital*. (Though, my parents undoubtedly would find this a bizarre term.) It would be further correct to say that they exchanged on the capital they accrued in innumerable ways to address the needs of our family.

Discussions of disability seldom took place within either my immediate or extended family. What I remember was the acceptance of my uncle and sister as valued family members and, though their disabilities were not ignored, the expectation was that they be treated with the same respect as any other family member. It wasn't until I was in my late teens that I realized that my uncle and sister's lives didn't mirror the lives and experiences of a good number of people with disabilities of similar age. During those years and later as I became acquainted with more people with disabilities, I began to pay attention to the subtleties that displayed these differences in life experiences. I was often astounded by the mundane ways that seemed somehow symbolic to me of people's places in their families and their communities. Didn't all children whose families had a religious affiliation attend church and, if Catholic, make their First Communion? Weren't all kids part of the family or neighborhood herd that participated in all the events, activities and festivities associated with family or neighborhood and community life? Wasn't it typical that adolescents from middle-class families got braces to straighten their crooked teeth? The formal service system played a relatively minor role in my family's life. This was not a result of resistance or belief that government or systems were to be avoided. My parents simply found little necessity. My mother, in particular, was quite adept at seeking out and depending on the informal and typical resources available through her relationships and associations. On those occasions where it was essential to interact with more formal systems, such as educational or vocational services, my mother was inclined to call upon people she knew and whose values aligned with those held by our family.

A few years ago, Katie's husband had major surgery that prevented him from driving for several weeks. I flew back to stay with and help them for a couple of weeks. While there, it became apparent that my sister would need a temporary way to get around until my brother-in-law recuperated sufficiently to drive. This necessitated finding proof of Katie's eligibility for the local van service available to senior citizens and people with disabilities. My old high school friend was able to retrieve my sister's school records documenting her eligibility for special education services. I had not, until that time, ever seen any of the diagnostic language used to describe my sister. Seeing this, even after all the years I have spent with people with disabilities gave me pause. It described my sister in ways totally unfamiliar to who she is and how I think about her. What I found most heartrending was the inference arrived at and stated that my mom and dad were irrationally hopeful about their expectations for my sister and her future.

In spite of professional suggestions to the contrary, my parents were tenacious in believing a good life was possible for my sister. I know well that when my sister became a young adult they frequently grew anxious about her leaving their nest. Yet, they were able to balance their trepidation with their belief that my sister had the right to forge a life for herself. As the oldest daughter, my mom began calling me to talk over the various transitions happening in my sister's life. Sometimes, the calls were to update me on the various goings on in the family. At other times it was clear that my mom was seeking validation and encouragement. In particular, I remember the call to tell me my sister wanted to get married... did I think this was a good idea? Should my mom and dad accept this and support it as well? Would I talk with my sister about this decision and make certain she understood the commitment and responsibility? By conferring this role of confidant and encourager on me, my mother inadvertently was my first coach in what has become a large part of the work I do.

While I am writing this chapter, Katie's marriage is in a rocky period. Amidst the uncertainty about the long-term future of this relationship, many new questions are emerging for my sister and our family. How does she envision her life as a single woman? Where does she want to live? Does she have new interests she wants to pursue? What are her capacities? What resources are available for her? What assistance does she need to manage her day-to-day life? Who does she want to provide this assistance and how does she want it arranged? Similar to most marriages, my sister's is built upon reciprocity. Each partner's interests, gifts, capacities and resources guide the give and take of her relationship. And, the reality is that my sister does have daily needs for support and assistance that, at present, are available to her through her husband.

I have suggested that we convene a family conversation with my sister and her husband to build a back-up plan should they decide to end their marriage. Katie thinks it would be helpful for the family to assist in exploring her options. My parent's initial response to this suggestion startled me. According to them, Katie is my parent's responsibility and they will move her to Florida, find her a place to live, a job and assist her in those areas needed. My brother and I, therefore, don't need to worry about her. Our time will come, but not just yet. While I have heard this countless times from the families with whom I spend time, I did not expect to hear it from my mom and dad. It is clear that we have previously only danced around the edges in casual conversations about my sister's future safety net. Perhaps we need to remind one another of the lessons of our earlier life and remember again our capacity as a family to engage in shared action. There are *more than two* who love and care about my sister. Those who love her see her gifts, capabilities and contributions to her family, those around her and the broader community.

Periodically, through the project I manage, I am asked to put together workshops on *working with families*. These requests have come most often from professionals working in organizations offering services to people, though sometimes they are directly from families. In all honesty, such requests bewilder me. I can't quite get my head around what might actually be taught in such a workshop. And, it has somehow struck me as a tad disrespectful to create training around ways to work with families. I am left with the sense that families are perceived as mysterious and, at times, troublesome beings rather than ordinary people who care deeply about their sons and daughters. Is this notion of *working with families* merely a polite phrase for seeking ways to control or quiet people deemed troublesome? That's not to say that I don't understand and have not witnessed what drives such requests. Stories abound and my personal experience attests to the subtle or overt ways in which families can be dishonored, disregarded and disrespected and, of course, the reverse, where families may distrust and disregard the good intentions and good will of those paid to be in service to their sons and daughters. I am not naïve to the fact that the tension that might result can be fairly detrimental to the people with disabilities caught in the cross hairs.

I have come to believe that it has less to do with putting together a good workshop, per se, and more to do with finding ways to value and honor the contributions of each person who cares about and wants to play a part in the life of a person with a disability. This is tricky to do within the confines of a typical training session or workshop. The formality inherent in a sit, listen, and possibly simulate, session constrains the conversations critical to developing the personal relationships needed. Even in workshops designed to elicit deeper conversation, it is typically a capsule in time versus the ongoing, long term commitment required to deepen the communication and trust essential to sustaining relationships. One of the moms with whom I spend considerable time, describes this as needing people in the life of her daughter who will spend the time to know her well enough to "listen to her heartbeat". Person-centered work, as envisioned by originators Beth Mount, Connie Lyle O'Brien and John O'Brien, Marsha Forest, Jack Pearpoint, Judith Snow, Michael Smull and others, coupled with the long term commitment of, at least, a small group of people offers a route to those seeking ways to work together. Person-centered processes approached in the manner described by their creators, open the possibilities and conditions for people to discover each others' humanity ...conceivably finding ways to **work with one another.**

Revisiting the lessons from my own family, the things I learned that have frequently guided me well in my own life and work in relationship to people with disabilities are:

Making a commitment to walk with people over time isn't mysterious or magical.

It is the ordinary, everyday things that count.

One's ability to belong and contribute is not determined by intellectual capacity.

Having "the" answer is often less important than a willingness to keep engaging the questions.

Having a trusted ally who listens and encourages is sometimes all that's needed.

Doing things with people is better than doing them alone.

At its best, our work isn't bound by professional roles.

People care for other people, not their titles or qualifications.

The words of Wendell Berry (1990, p. 9) serve well to remind me of these lessons:

Pursuing originality, the would-be creator works alone. In loneliness one assumes a responsibility for oneself that one cannot fulfill.

References

Berry, W. (1990). *What are people for?* Berkeley, CA.: North Point Press.

Hornby, N. (1998). *About a boy.* New York: Riverhead Books.

10

The Weird Guy

Steve Holburn

Chapter 1

I had to get away to a coffee place or someplace like that to be alone and figure something out, but I was interrupted. He was weird. Nobody said anything about it, but he was weird. He had some kind of light attached to a band around his forehead. It looked like it was a coal miner's light. He seemed well dressed in black but his socks were brightly colored. He ordered a large cup of hot water with an oversized ceramic mug that he had walked in with that read, "17 Jefferson." Then he sat down with his back to everybody, put his big mug down and opened up a very fancy laptop with an unusually big screen. It sprang open to a screensaver of little figures dancing in circles to techno music chirping from the internal speakers. I think this intrusion was annoying to everybody in the room, not just me, because all of the talking stopped. Then the weird guy got up and put a dollar in the CD machine and went into the bathroom, leaving behind a continuous disturbance.

He had transformed a peaceful Sunday morning coffee shop into a wacky scene with computer figures, now dancing to the techno beat booming from the CD, and naturally the CD was out of synch with the chirps and pops that I could hear well because I was right next to the computer wondering what the hell happened. Before the weird guy came in, I was relaxed and beginning to concentrate. I might feel the same if I were an artist, quietly painting a reflection on a still pond and suddenly someone starts throwing rocks in the water and doesn't stop.

The guy was in the bathroom for a long time and by the time he came out the second song was almost over. I was familiar with the tune because it was the same number as the first. He hurried back to the table, took a sip of water and pulled some kind of device from his jacket and plugged it into the back of his computer. He adjusted the light on his head and tapped a few keys and an image came onto the screen that looked like something was moving. It dawned on me that it was not a light but a video camera fixed like a third eyeball on top of his head. It was remotely projecting a scene onto the computer screen of whatever he turned toward. The guy grinned obnoxiously as he turned around toward us all, and he appeared delighted to be bothering us. You could tell that he wanted us to look at the screen of ourselves but we all glared at him and not at the computer screen. We must have looked like angry high school teachers. The grin disappeared. He stopped panning, turned around, and clicked off the camera. The computer screen returned to the dancing figures, as to say "Go to Hell." But that was OK because we had won. There was something unusually satisfying about the moment. It was like a 5-second contest between normal versus weird, and normal won.

Then something else weird happened. A woman rushed in yelling, "My car's on fire! My car's on fire!" This event pretty much guaranteed I wasn't going to be concentrating and resolving any deep problems of my own. The woman was distraught and imploring us to do something about her car. First, a handful of us got up and looked out the window. Sure enough, you could see a car on fire right outside in the street, maybe 50 feet away from the coffee shop. Even the weird guy got up to look, but when he did, he knocked his laptop off the table and it crashed on the floor, instantly turning the screen black. Luckily, the 17 Jefferson mug wobbled to the edge of the table, then settled safely. But weird guy's timing was off. Just after it settled, he clumsily reached for it, causing it too to crash to the floor sending water and ceramic chips flying everywhere. "How fitting," I thought, "Too bad it missed the computer."

We kept looking out the window at the smoking car and then back at the frantic woman, as if to say to her, "What can we do about it"? Someone was calling 911. Certainly others had called too because a crowd was gathering on the street.

The car kept burning and nobody knew what to do or maybe didn't want to do anything, and besides, an old guy was near the car acting like a policeman and yelling to everybody to keep away because the car could explode. The flames were curling around the edges of the hood and smoke was pouring out and the woman was watching and crying. Everyone just watched. Except for the police guy or whoever he was. He was protecting everybody and he stayed at a safe distance but close enough to appear in charge.

This was more than rocks in the pond; this was like an earthquake at the pond, as far as peacefulness went. After a while, the flames started flashing from the bottom of the engine, then pouring back toward the door, and it was clear that the tires would be next, and then the whole car would go up in flames. I wondered how long it would take before the flames were actually inside of the car and burning the interior. It would be a total and spectacular loss. A few of us took turns trying to console the owner of the car. Her crying had reduced to whimpering, as if she too had accepted the inevitable. But to be honest, I wasn't just accepting it −I was stimulated by it. I was feeling a little impatient and hoping that the fire would finish off the car before a rescue truck arrived. I figured the car was already ruined, and it seemed like everybody was safe, so why not see some fireworks? There would be a whole lot more smoke when the tires caught on.

I was too engrossed to notice that the weird guy had left. Out of nowhere, he appeared in front of the window, walking toward the car with a fire extinguisher. I don't know where he got it, but again, his timing was off. It was too late because the fire was now out of control, with black, black smoke rolling at a low angle toward the front of the car then wafting upwards. At first, the weird guy acted like an expert, and I got this image of Clark Kent turning into Superman, but he looked more like a crazy fool, not an expert, and he was ignoring the old man, who we had decided was probably a fireman off duty, and he kept yelling at weird guy to get the Hell away from the car, that it was going to blow.

Weird guy ignored the fireman and approached the car from the front. Smoke and soot were blowing on his suit and into his face and the heat was blowing his hair so that he looked ridiculous. I too wanted him to get away from the car, but despite the danger, it was hard not to laugh, especially with the camera on his head. Then it hit me… the camera! I glanced over at the laptop on the floor. The screen was still black and surrounded with broken mug pieces lying in water. I picked up the computer, hit enter, and there was the car, burning clearly and colorfully. Weird guy was now crawling toward the car like a soldier in combat, still fighting off the smoke and heat. You could tell it was hot because you could see the air rippling around the front of the engine and he was shielding his face with his arm and the heat could have been burning his hair and skin but not enough to stop him. At one point, he got really close but a blast of hot forced him back and now he was just lying prone looking at the car as it burned hotter making for a hopeless scene.

I was looking back and forth between the scene out the window and the close up of it on the computer screen and the whole thing seemed surreal. I felt like I was part of a news camera crew during an emergency, and weird guy now seemed like a mixture of Superman and Geraldo Rivera.

I was the only one who noticed the computer. Most everybody else was fixed on weird guy and wishing he would get away from the car, but all they could do was yell at him with things like "It's only a car!" and "Don't be a hero you idiot!" To our relief, a siren was heard in the distance. But weird guy didn't seem to hear the siren or our yelling, and nobody was dumb enough to try to pull him away because he was too close. Futile as it was, weird guy was now the person in charge, and he was crawling forward again.

The fire was now roaring audibly and the car was approaching the point of total burn that I had hoped for moments earlier, never imagining someone would be doing what this guy was doing. He finally crawled and wriggled close enough to touch the car with the nozzle of fire extinguisher. He pointed it deliberately between the hood and the radiator, as if he had done this a hundred times before, and he pulled the trigger. The flames suddenly disappeared. Instantly gone. That's all it took? One little blast at the right point? But the flames burst back to life, this time from under the car. So he sprayed underneath of the car and the flames were gone again. The crowd was now silent, waiting to see if the fire would pop up again. All you could hear were a few children in the distance who were re-enacting the scene by crawling on the sidewalk and holding sticks and yelling "Get away from there!" and "You're an idiot!" We watched the diminishing smoke as the siren grew louder. Weird guy was strutting around the car, peeking inside, as if to examine his work, but his job was done. Weird guy had put out the fire.

A fire truck rolled up and several firemen jumped down and ran around and doused the smoldering car with a large hose. They were getting ready to smash the windows with an axe so they could flood the interior when another fireman yelled, "No, it's out!"

A van pulled up too. A woman got out and walked over to weird guy, who was standing with the fire extinguisher in his hands and still had the camera on his head. Amazingly it was still projecting onto the computer screen. She said something to him and looked him over. From the screen, I could see her face clearly and I could tell that she knew him because she seemed disgusted with him but also relieved. It was probably his girlfriend or wife. He seemed unconcerned and pointed repeatedly to the coffee shop and I knew what he was referring to. They walked toward me, hand-in-hand, and entered the coffee shop. Before they could say anything I handed him his computer and said, "The computer is OK, and I could see everything on it!"

Weird guy turned his head toward me. He was pointing the camera down at my nose and he gave me that grin again, only this time it didn't seem obnoxious. We both looked at my nose on the screen and this time I smiled back, realizing now that it was really pretty cool to project a remote video camera onto a laptop, not to mention being a hero, but then weird guy did one better than that. He punched in a few keys to show that it had all been recorded. The whole fire scene had been recorded from the top of his head and he was able to play it all back. Now he *really* seemed like Superman mixed with Geraldo. I was feeling like little wimp boy. The problems and solutions I was pondering earlier seemed unimportant compared to what had just happened. You could still hear the children playing on the sidewalk and I began to speculate about how they would reenact my own problem solving. Pitifully, they would sit around a table acting annoyed at anything that disturbed them. Their sticks would be pencils and they would make fun of people who were different from them...

"What happened here?" the woman asked, snapping me out of my little fantasy.

I looked at weird guy and said, "*You* tell her."

"He doesn't talk," she replied. "Can you just fill me in a little?"

Weird guy grinned at me again, as if to say, "Go ahead and tell her how I put out the fire."

"He understands a lot though," she said. "Especially about computer stuff. He got away from us again, and this time he brought his computer and his camera. I work in a group home on 17 Jefferson Street where Tommy lives and we've been looking for him for over an hour." She spotted the jukebox and asked, "Did he play the Jukebox?"

Before I could answer, a burley fireman burst through the door, slapped Tommy on the back, and said "Good Job Tommy! I heard you put out the fire!" (Seems like a lot of people know Tommy, I thought.)

"He helped put out a fire"? She said. "That doesn't surprise me. Tommy's amazing, but he shouldn't be out here alone." She turned to him and said sternly, "Come on, Tommy get your stuff. We gotta go. I gotta write up an incident report and get you something to eat."

As they walked to the van I was feeling small. Almost tricked. How could this guy be a hero? That's not the hero persona that I know. I wasn't feeling small because he had some kind of disability and then did something brave. I felt small because if I was in danger, this strange guy would automatically try to help me, but if the situation was reversed, I doubt I would try to help him. Maybe I would, reluctantly.

As the van was driving by, Tommy waved at me, grinning triumphantly. I gave him a thumbs up. He held his laptop up to the window and pointed to it. The van accelerated and Tommy shifted to the rear window and waved me on, as if to say "come here," but the van kept going. I wondered why he was waving me on. I also wondered what else might be on that computer. Should I pay Tommy a visit? Maybe I could bring him a new mug.

11

Great Questions and The Art of Portraiture

John O'Brien

Among my friend Judith Snow's wise sayings is her definition of a great question. "A great question refuses to be answered, and so it leads us into deeper thinking and deeper connections." Visual play with the word shows that questions contain quests. Great questions move people into the adventure of searching together for something compellingly worthwhile. Such a search can seem too much to manage while juggling the daily requirements of survival or it can threaten too much embarrassment from the risk of seeming a poor imitator of Don Quixote. So, paradoxically, we can easily ignore great questions by refusing time for deeper thinking or withholding energy from deeper relationships. To influence us, great questions need hosts to invite their presence into busy lives and champions to remember their merit in the face of anxiety.

The hosts and champions of great questions need courage, respect, and a discipline. While great questions can be found in any field, what interests me here is the framing of great questions in the lives of people whose capacities easily get lost. Person-centered planning offers a disciplined way to search for great questions in the lives of particular people who choose it, questions that lead to deeper think-ing about a person's identity and contributions and to deeper con-nections to other people who matter for the person's future. Sarah, nine-year old John's mother, has found such a question, and with the question the courage to ask it to a group of family friends:*

> Who will need to know John, and what kind of experience
> will they need to have with each other so that someone
> in our circle will offer John employment when he leaves
> school? What do we need to be doing together over the next
> ten years for this to happen

---

*David & Faye Wetherow (2000). Sarah Jenning's question. *Inclusion News 2000*, p. 3. I am grateful to Dave and Faye for this example and for reminding me of Judith's definition of a great question. To get a copy of *Inclusion News*, visit www.inclusion.com.

This is a great question because it anticipates a co-evolution of resourcefulness over the next decade. John's identity and gifts will develop as those now close to him assist him to know and be known by a wider circle of people. The community John lives in will develop by appreciating his contributions and adapting to make room for him.

Reflection on Sarah's great question suggests a framing question for the person centered planning process. This framing question asks...

> Under what conditions can this person discover and express more of who he or she is as a known and valued contributor to our community?

The answer to this framing question will be another question, a great question like Sarah's if its askers work artfully.

Great questions have their source in an imaginative and respectful understanding of a person's life. The service world that surrounds many people with developmental disabilities seems less comfortable with the image of understanding people as an art than with the image of an objective science of assessment and intervention. Such an image of science appeals, in part, because it promises the sort of steady improvement in the prediction and control of people's behavior that makes service systems more manageable. From this point of view, one gets to know a person in order to discipline need. Talk of art, imagination and great questions can sound like the trumpets of anarchy.[*]

Those experienced in person-centered planning resist arguments for impersonal assessment as the basis of assistance for people with disabilities. A careful confidence grows from living through important changes with people who have hold of a great question about their lives in community. This confidence supports twin judgments on the sort of professionalism that serves managerial command and control in the name of objective science. Such science is dangerous insofar as its predictions trap people in professionally controlled low expectations and segregation. And, such science tells uninteresting stories by abstracting life as particular people experience it into sterile categories and roles. Objective knowledge may suffice for

---

[*]Seymour Sarason trenchantly enumerates the costs psychology incurs from sacrificing art to the pursuit of mechanistic science. See Seymour Sarason (1990) *The challenge of art to psychology*, New Haven, CT: Yale University Press.

those medical treatments that function impersonally (though some physicians would disagree); only art will do for finding and pursuing a great question.

Confidence in the rightness of assisting people to discover and pursue great questions gives practitioners of person centered planning the courage necessary to do their work. It also exposes them to danger. Bad art is at least as common as bad science and the consequences of artistic misunderstanding can be as life-wasting or trivial as the consequences of scientific assessment too often are.

At least three kinds of relationships reduce the risk of poor understanding:

- Maintaining alliance with the people, families, and circles one plans with and making time to reflect on what aids and what hinders their journey
- Joining with other practitioners for mutual support and coaching*
- Linking with complementary disciplines to gain a broader perspective on the work.

Links to complementary disciplines can help by suggesting different metaphors for the work, different practices, and different ethical perspectives. A brief introduction to the work of Sarah Lawrence-Lightfoot talented originator of a complementary discipline follows in the hope that it will persuade practitioners of person-centered planning to meet her by reading three fine books.

The books, in the order I would suggest reading them, are:

- Sara Lawrence-Lightfoot (1999). *Respect: An exploration.* Reading, MA: Perseus Books. Here she applies her approach to the investigation of a virtue that is fundamental to the work of person-centered planning.
- Sara Lawrence-Lightfoot and Jessica Hoffmann Davis (1997). *The art and science of portraiture.* San Francisco: Jossey-Bass. This describes her method in relationship to visual art and to social sciences.
- Sara Lawrence-Lightfoot (1994). *I've known rivers: Lives of loss and liberation.* Reading, MA: Addison-Wesley. Here are wonderful portraits of successful African-Americans told to disclose the kinds of experiences and relationships important for liberation.

---

*For electronic impressions of such a group of practitioners, visit the Circles of Support Mentoring Project at www.toolcity.net/ also see Chapter 14,

In her practice of research as portraiture, Sara Lawrence-Lightfoot, a sociologist at Harvard's Graduate School of Education, offers valuable resources to those who want to host the emergence of great questions in people's lives. She thinks of herself as weaving a tapestry from the elements her subjects share with her and describes her project in words that will resonate and raise helpful questions among practitioners of person-centered planning.

> *Portraitists seek to record and interpret the perspectives and experience of the people they are studying, documenting their voices and their visions –their authority, knowledge and wisdom. The drawing of the portrait is placed in social and cultural context and shaped through dialogue between the portraitist and the subject…* (The art and science of portraiture, p. xv.)

She defines her work as a counterpoint to a social science concerned primarily with defining social problems for an elite audience.

> *Portraiture… seeks to illuminate the complex dimensions of goodness and is designed to capture the attention of a broad and eclectic audience.* (The art and science of portraiture, p. xvi.)

In Sara Lawrence-Lightfoot's hands, the idea of portraiture is fruitful in many ways. Each of her books repays study in new techniques for exploring and presenting people's lives and struggles, in new ideas about the contributions of professionals and researchers, and in civic lessons drawn from people's living wisdom. Here, I will focus on some of the contributions her work makes to my thinking about an important ethical question: **what is the proper relationship between the practitioner of person-centered planning and the people she wants to serve?**

For some practitioners this question has a straightforward answer. They see themselves as reflecting only what people say they want and assisting people to organize available resources to get it. The practitioner meets requirements by performing a two or three step sequence:

- Record the words people say in answer to straightforward questions about their desires and dreams
- Facilitate the writing of an action plan for making it happen; and, sometimes.
- Gather people occasionally to check and revise the action plan.

This answer makes sense as far as it goes. Many people do have clear and achievable ideas about what would significantly improve their lives, ideas that have gone unrealized because they have remained buried under other people's unwillingness to listen to them and act on what they hear. But reflection on Sara Lawrence-Lightfoot's account of the roles she plays with the people who choose to join her in understanding what their lived knowledge and wisdom can contribute to a stronger community shows that this kind of relationship only makes a good beginning. Much more is possible when people consent to share part of their lives with someone who seeks to know them in order to serve both them and their community. As you read the following paragraph, notice the seven roles and associated activities she describes herself as playing in unfolding her subject's lives. Then take a moment to consider the possibilities and dangers each role might hold for the practitioner of person-centered planning. (I have highlighted the roles)..

> As I listen to these extraordinary women and men tell
> their life stories, I play many roles. I am a *mirror* that
> reflects back their pain, their fears, and their victories.
> I am also the **inquirer** who asks the sometimes difficult
> questions, who searches for evidence and patterns. I am the
> **companion** on the journey, bringing my own story to the
> encounter, making possible an interpretive collaboration. I
> am the **audience** who listens, laughs, weeps, and applauds.
> I am **the spider woman** spinning their tales. Occasionally,
> I am a **therapist** who offers catharsis, support, and chal-
> lenge, and who keeps track of emotional mine fields. Most
> absorbing to me is the role of the **human archaeologist**
> who uncovers the layers of mask and inhibition in search
> of a more authentic representation of life experience. (I've
> known rivers, p. 26)

Sara Lawrence-Lightfoot's way of understanding portraiture illu-minates another problem with the notion of the practitioner as sim-ply taking accurate dictation. Portraiture works from the powerful effects of the artist on the portrait, even on a photographic portrait, and does not try to hide behind a screen of objectivity. Such a screen can be made from the fabric of positivistic science and professional-ism; it can also be made from the naïve idea that "I only do what the person tells me." Even mirrors lack objectivity,

> *...through [the arts of] documentation, interpretation,*
> *analysis, and narrative we raise the mirror, hoping —with*
> *accuracy and discipline— to capture the mystery and*
> *artistry that turn image into essence. (The art and science of*
> *portraiture, p. xvii.)*

The possibility of understanding oneself as human archeologist, spider woman, companion, inquirer, and portraitist while doing the work of person-centered planning raises difficult questions about the nature of the agreement between the practitioner and the person she assists. Is the relationship solely to benefit the person, or might it be understood more powerfully as a relationship that exists to benefit both the person and a community that acts unthinkingly against itself by excluding the person and denying the person's contributions? Perhaps person-centered planning could serve the common good by supporting people to represent and deepen their knowledge, wisdom, vision, and authority. And perhaps the subjects of person-centered planning, like Sara Lawrence-Lightfoot's subjects, better disclose their knowledge, wisdom, vision, and authority through engaged conversation with someone they authorize to actively inquire with them and produce a portrait of them. The imbalance of power between the practitioner and the person she assists trouble these questions in ways that raise even more difficulty than they do in the dialogue between Sara Lawrence-Lightfoot and her subjects.

A practitioner of person-centered planning who wanted to add the skills and roles of the portraitist to her repertoire would need to build relationships with people and their families and allies based on commitment to a common project that early trials of those skills and roles could serve. She would also seek connections to others interested in going deeper in their work by trying new ways of engagement and new kinds of representations of people. In this way, study of Sara Lawrence-Lightfoot's work might be the occasion for another great question entering her life.

12

The Art and Soul of Person-Centered Planning

Beth Mount

Tyesast and I look together for photos and objects to tell the story of the things she loves. We made a collage out of the pictures to express her interests. We also made a basket to put in items that represent her interests and hopes for the future. Since Tyesast does not speak, working with images and objects really helps her communicate. She expresses her interests by pointing and clapping her hands. Her accomplishments over the past two years have been wonderful. We just put a beautiful flower in the basket to represent how she has grown from a seed into a flower!

—Louisa Henderson

I am in the process of creating a wimple with Tzvi and his family. In Judaism, a wimple is made from the blanket one was wrapped in as a baby and used during a Bar-Mitzvah ceremony. On it is your life story and things that are most important to you. It is similar to quilting in many ways. After the ceremony, it becomes the covering for the Torah. Tzvi never has had a Bar-Mitzvah, so we will be making this for him in lieu of having the actual ceremony. We chose that as the concept (a theater term used to describe the metaphor for the main idea of the play) for his futures plan because it is the time when we are welcomed in to the community of adult Jews and recognized as an independent person with a life of our own. It is re-birth in many ways. Tzvi was rejected from his own community for an extended period of time, so we thought the symbolism of the event and the wimple was an important way to describe the themes in his life.

— Josh Skolnick

These service workers provide far more than practical assistance. By participating in artistic creation with Tyesast and Tzvi and the others who know and care about them, Louisa and Josh join the body work of helping someone through the day and the mind work of coordinating activities to the soul work of claiming and celebrating each person's human identity and belonging. Their shared creations are beautiful and ordinary. They depend less on formal artistic training than on the pleasure of using everyday crafts in a sacred way to arrange pictures, to collect meaningful objects, to sew a garment rich in symbol.

The simple act of attention to images and objects that tell the story of what Tyesast loves, and their thoughtful collection into a collage and a basket of wonderful things, embodies respect for her interests and helps communicate her identity to people who spend time with her. Resonance with a culturally familiar path of initiation into adult independence as a responsible community member –in which signs of important life events from infancy forward enrobe first the initiated person and then the community's Holy Scripture– gives power and direction to Tzvi's claim on belonging to a community that has not previously known quite how to welcome him as a grown man.

This art grows from and nourishes and transforms relationships. Obvious differences –in status, or ability, or language, or culture, or material wealth or race, or any combination of these– shape relationships among people with disabilities and their families and the people who assist them. How these differences affect the quality of everyone's experience depends, in part, on achieving a living sense of what connects us, differences and all. Part of what connects us is working together toward a jointly meaningful goal. Part of what connects us is our participation in life's ordinary mysteries, the mysteries of life's journey: birth, growth, coming into adulthood, work, relationship, belonging, grief, suffering, and death. Each people, tribe, and family provides resources for encountering these mysteries, and these resources differentiate the ways that we understand and cope with them.

One powerful modern strategy for encountering these mysteries is to reduce them to problems to be solved through the application of expertise. This strategy has many benefits. Among other good things, it makes childbirth safer, instruction more systematic, the pursuit of economic success more rational, and many diseases less threatening. It provides some people with disabilities the means to move about, to learn useful skills, and to communicate. One effect of this strategy is to leave most questions of meaning up to people as private individuals. Access to good health technology means that death comes to many of us later than it otherwise might have, but we must still find a way to face death's uncertainties and those who survive us must still find their way through grief. And, despite the presence of many experts who fill the self-help shelves and the talk shows with advice, relationships remain more wonderful and more maddening than reason can handle.

I am convinced that deep change in the lives of people with substantial disabilities depends on soul work. Soul work does not replace skilled help or good management or political organizing, but it is essential to energizing, directing and sustaining efforts to assure people their place in community life.

A direct support worker who understands her two years of engagement in a person's life as the unfolding of a seed into a beautiful flower has different possibilities for action than a worker who sees her job only in terms of doing the prescribed chores. She can become excited about figuring out how other's can share the beauty and pleasure of Tyesast's interests. She can be alert to the unfolding of new blooms because she knows there has never been a flower quite like Tyesast before. A facilitator who chooses the concept of growth into manhood in community has inspiration to search for the unique combination of opportunities, accommodations, and assistance that will allow Tzvi to enact valued adult roles. The root's of this concept in tradition will carry sustaining energy when others resist or falter in their support of Tzvi's journey into manhood.

I am increasingly interested in how art can serve as a bridge across the differences that segregate people with disabilities and expose them to control by others. Sharing in the creation of artifacts that express what is meaningful honors the ordinary mysteries of human life. Honoring the ordinary mysteries encountered along life's path opens the possibility of mutuality.

Mutuality offers people moments of rest from the strictures of the power-over/under-power positions assigned by staff and client roles. Judith Snow (1998), whose survival depends on the competence and reliability of her personal assistance and whose vocation includes discovering ways to understand people who do not speak, writes of the importance of opening this space in our relationships:

> *Sustained vibrant relationship demands that the person*
> *with a handicap be viewed with a different vision and*
> *listened to with a different ear. Foremost of the alterna-*
> *tive possibilities is to see and hear the person as a welcome*

fellow traveler. We must see our shared life journey as one
of transforming human suffering by creating the supportive
relationships we all need to sustain life and of celebrating
together life's joys, victories and surprises (p. 12.).

Our person-centered planning formats and techniques are meaningless unless they help us open the door to a space of mutuality
where we discover transforming images, and commit to action inspired by deep listening and concern. This is particularly important
for people immersed by prejudice and social devaluation in what
educator Paulo Freire (1994) has exposed as a "culture of silence".
In this state of imposed silence, not only do people lack words and
images for the oppressive states that limit them, but they also lack
awareness of their own sources of life potential, and the conditions
that encourage the emergence of that potential.

The culture of silence is locked in place by a system that offers
necessary assistance in a way that disregards relationships and denies
human mystery in a blind frenzy to reduce people's lives to prob-
lems-to-be-solved under expert tutelage. Such a system encourages
definition of people's lives in terms of their potential to generate
billable hours of service. Such a system reduces person-centered
planning to specification of the terms of clienthood. Such a system
squeezes the life out of people in the name of efficient service.

The role of art and soul is to bring life in. The keys that open the
box of silence that entombs so many people with disabilities are
three: deep listening that leads to discovery of words that name
the structures that enforce silent passivity and images that express
a powerful vision of contribution. These keys can wake-up the
imagination and commitment and voice of small circles of people
and guide their action to shape a community that recognizes and
receives the gifts that they bring.

Sometimes, deeper listening means respectful attention to the
possibilities for social action in what is obvious on the surface.
Douglas's devotion to coffee is apparent in the excitement with
which he talks about it as well as the enthusiasm he brings to finding, preparing, and sharing a cup. As part of the process of gathering
knowledge of Douglas's interests, Nathan Hernandez, a direct support worker, wrote this verse:

I like coffee. Yes I do.
I like coffee. How about you?

I like the taste and I like the smell.
I like the stories that the commercials tell.
When I drink coffee, it just quenches my thirst.
That's why I put coffee always first.
The way sugar and cream just mix together,
Makes me wanna drink coffee forever.
When I don't have sugar or I don't have cream.
That'll be okay cause I'll always have my dream.

Honoring the obvious allowed Douglas and his supporters to generate his own business as a vendor of "Stardust Coffee." The poem invites Douglas's customers into his dream. Along with his coffee cup, it goes everywhere with him.

Sometimes, deeper listening means searching together and collecting clues from which a meaningful image emerges and asks for action. Gathering to share these clues, going out to look for more possibilities, returning to share again builds a rhythm of interest that calls for a powerful image. Color coding bits of information –green for what seems to bring life and meaning to this person and red for what seems to frustrate or block– reveals patterns that point toward well-springs of possibility. Inviting and recording graphic images honors visions and dreams.

The essential capacity in person-centered planning is the ability to listen for, invite, and express images of personal identity and possibility that will energize, guide, and sustain action that transforms the relationship between people with disabilities and their community. This capacity grows with practice. Having assembled photos and objects that are signs of Tyesast's passions, Louisa has opened a way to listen more deeply. Having conceived Tzvi's garment, Josh has opened a way to invite new energies. Having written the verse about the place of coffee in Douglas's life, Nathan has opened a way to keep the dream in view.

This essential capacity also grows with exposure to images and ideas that express the human potentials for transformation. The rest of this chapter comprises a small gallery of images and ideas. See color versions of these images on this book's web page (inclusion.com).

References

Freire, P. (1994). *Pedagogy of hope*. New York: Continuum.

Snow, J. (1998). The power of vulnerability. In *A little book about person-centered planning*. Toronto: Inclusion Press.

The spiral, an ancient symbol of the soul's journey, reminds us that working together for change means sharing a universal journey. We enter that place of wandering, exploration, discovery, and struggle that nurtures the life force in us all. The spiral indicates the path we walk together toward the justice for which our soul's yearn.

Meaning is important for the health, well-being and wholeness of individuals and communities. The presence of symbols in a community, as well as the living out of a belief in these symbols, is a measurement of the health and energies present in the community. Indeed, to live without symbols is to experience existence far short of our unlimited capacity as human beings. Thus every rebirth of the life and purpose of a people is accompanied by the revitalization of that people's symbols.

— The Sacred Tree: Reflections on Native American Spirituality

Through person-centered planning we work together to reclaim
the inherent potential of each person and establish their belonging and connection to community life. When we honor the soul
work in person-centered planning we open the eyes of the heart.
This allows us to feelingly see the yearnings, dreams, possibilities,
and capacities in people. When we share the images that we see
with the eyes of the heart, our voices change. We are no longer
talking heads but whole people giving voice to ourselves.

Let us look at our children and families in our community, not as blurred objects in the
landscape, or by their possible usefulness to us; but to see them with imagination, with
the "eyes of the heart" with faith in their possibilities... It is a great loss when we look
at people from a financial or business point of view and neglect the life side.

—Mamie Hillman

It is important to give form and color to what we see when we look with the eye of the heart. These shields, created by young adults moving from school into adult life, are emblazoned with icons that they have selected to communicate the visions they have come to as they have explored their unique interest and gifts and the opportunities for contribution their neighborhoods and their city offers. Each shield carries visible signs of the young person's identity and serves as a way to stay awake to the possibilities they have discovered and as a guide for telling their story.

The hand print is a sign of the power that arises within us when we act on the urge to make our unique mark on the world by making contributions that reflect our gifts to the world. Hand prints have been found on rocks, icaves, and walls around the world. They transmit the spiritual power of people who made their mark on the world through all of humanity's generations.

Each person bears a uniqueness that asks to be lived and that is already present before it can be lived. You and I and every single person is born with a defining image. We each embody our own idea, and this image does not tolerate too much straying. The heart has it's reasons. This means that each child is a gifted child, filled with data of all sorts, gifts peculiar to that child which show themselves in peculiar ways.

—James Hillman

The Build a New World Quilt grew from the stories of five young people and their families whose bold efforts to seek their dreams have inspired and encouraged others to overcome segregation and seek their rightful place as contributing citizens of New York City.

For as long as we've been around as humans, as wandering bands of nomads or cave dwellers, we have sat together and shared experiences. We've painted images on rock walls, recounted dreams and vision, told stories of the day, and generally felt comforted to be in the world together. When the world became fearsome, we came together. When the world called us to explore its edges, we journeyed together. Whatever we did, we did it together.

—Margaret Wheatley

Enactment, engagement, creation, rehearsal —each of these ways of doing exercise our imagination when they are fed by a desire to realize what we have seen with the eye of the heart. This spirit bird, an icon from Mexico, reminds us to open ourselves to inspiration.

Of course, not all stories are successful. How can we discern whether one telling of events is any a better or more worthy than another? A story must be judged according to whether it makes sense. And "making sense" must here be understood in its most direct meaning: to make sense is to enliven the senses. A story that makes sense is one that stirs the senses from their slumber, one that opens the eyes and the ears to their real surroundings, turning the tongue to the actual tastes in the air and sending chills of recognition along the surface of the skin. To make sense is to release the body from the constraints imposed by outworn ways of speaking, and hence to renew and rejuvenate one's felt awareness of the world. It is to make the senses wake up to where they are.

—David Abram

13

The Rhode Island Facilitators Forum
Reflections on Recent Experiences in Building the Numbers and Capacities of Facilitators

Jo Krippenstapel

> How can we expand the number of people who are competent in facilitating conversations that support better lives for individuals, more competent organizations, and richer community life?

> What will it take for these facilitators to reflect and learn together, over time, in a way that nurtures a community of learning about the art and practice of facilitation?

These were questions that Rhode Islanders asked in response to finding themselves in an all too familiar situation. In spite of investment over the years in person-centered planning, families and agency staff expressed the desire to have more people to turn to in confidence to facilitate planning conversations.

This chapter tells the story of Rhode Island's journey from few facilitators to the formation of a network –The Facilitators Forum– that supports a diverse group of facilitators to grow in the art and practice of facilitation.

This article is written from the perspective of someone who is both an "insider" and an "outsider/consultant". I lived in the *Biggest Little State in the Union* from 1982-1991. During that time I became actively engaged, along with many others, in understanding the service accomplishments, normalization and social role valorization, and approaches to person-centered planning. During that decade of the 1980's there were many informal leaders (parents and mid-level agency staff) who became committed to planning with individuals and organizations based on these shared values.

Central for many of us during this time was the creation of a local network of the informal leaders. This informal network –called the Service Quality Network– came together monthly over a period of many years to share stories, celebrate successes, and plan and deliver training that served to deepen our collective understanding around these principles and values. As convener of this Network, I was able to witness the many ways in which participants became a community of learners who turned to one another to find ways to enhance the quality of individual and organizational life.

Over time, these informal leaders of the 1980's moved into formal positions of agency leadership, and I moved on to live elsewhere. As a result, many people with the capacity and desire to facilitate individual and agency planning sessions no longer had the time or opportunities to do so. Although I was often invited back to Rhode Island to facilitate planning conversations around complex situations, the network of those available to lead planning conversations diminished over time. The need to expand the number of local, competent facilitators became clear.

We knew from experience that simply training more people to become facilitators was unsatisfactory as a stand-alone response. More training usually led to short term increases in activity and interest in facilitation, but many who experienced the training as meaningful did not feel competent or ready to facilitate. And even in those situations where additional training led to an increase in the number of facilitators within an agency (at least for a while) it usually did not expand the opportunities for people to think together across agencies. Clearly a richer response to this challenge was in order.

As we faced the challenges posed in the questions that open this chapter, we found ourselves returning to our experiences with the Service Quality Network and recalling the beliefs that had served us well in the past:

- We have tremendous capacity and we must find ways to bring it forward.
- We learn and grow over time and in community with others who share common hopes and concerns.
- We must turn to one another. We must create a community of facilitators that turns to one another across typical agency boundaries.
- Competence in facilitation requires naming and nurturing our shared values. We must become clear about who we are and what we believe in, as well as what we do. Gathering with trusted others is a powerful way to expand our understanding of who we are and what we believe in.

These convictions led Rhode Islanders to respond with the creation of the Facilitators Forum.* Over the past three years, a group of about thirty facilitators has been gathering on a regular basis. This network – a community of learners - supports one another in growing in the art and practice of facilitation.

My contribution to this unfolding story, as an insider/outside consultant, has been in the facilitation of the initial two-day retreat that launched this Forum and in leading many of the almost bimonthly sessions that have followed. I worked with a core group of local leaders –most with roots in the Service Quality Network– who shared the many responsibilities of arranging the logistics and hosting the sessions, inviting people to attend, and spreading the word of the significance of this effort. The sharing of this story will reveal some of the insights and learning that are emerging from this experience.

The invitation: Talking the walk and other lessons

Reflection on three years of investment in the Facilitators Forum offers some clarity of hindsight about the importance of the invitation to join the Forum. Since few people thought of themselves as facilitators, it was important to tell the story of "who should come" in ways that expanded the possibilities. Creating thoughtful and powerful invitations became central to early success.

From the beginning, two types of invitations have been issued. Written invitations are created for each event. These are often colorful and intriguing, clearly suggesting "this is different".

In addition, those organizing the Forum often make powerful, personal invitations to potential members. These happen through phone calls, e-mails, and personal conversations. The gist of these informal, personal invitations is "This is for YOU. This is connected to the work you do, or want to do. This could help you, and you could contribute as well."

---

*Those who nourished these ideas into the creation of the Facilitators Forum include Lynda Kahn and Maya Colantuano (Rhode Island Division of Developmental Disabilities), Mary Madden (Ocean State Association of Residential Resources) and Doreen McConaghy (Parents for Alternate Living). Others who have joined in the informal leadership of this effort and contributed significantly to the development of this article include Sandy Deryck, Alissa Forleo, Ken Renaud, Diane Westerman, and Theresa Couture. Many others, in countless ways, contribute to sustaining the vibrancy of the Facilitators Forum.

These are some of the emerging lessons about the elements of powerful and successful invitations:

- **Keeping the threshold low.** All that is required for entry and acceptance into the group is interest and curiosity. Welcoming and exploring interest and curiosity become the way into deeper understanding of capacity and contribution. This has contributed to regular participation by a wide range of people, including professional and support staff from service provider and advocacy organizations, State Division staff, parents of people with disabilities, and people receiving services.

- **Clearing the way.** The original conveners of the Facilitators Forum included a small group of leaders from three agencies: The Rhode Island Division of Developmental Disabilities, Parents for Alternate Living (an advocacy organization of families and self advocates), and OSARR (Ocean State Association of Residential Resources). In addition to holding leadership positions in these agencies, the conveners are in close contact with those who provide and receive service. From the start, these conveners have used their contacts to clear the way for people to attend. They are able to use their daily work to notice those who might benefit from and contribute to the Forum. They use their influence with agency leaders to say, "I was just in a meeting with one of your home managers. She was helpful in moving the conversation in a constructive direction. I think she would contribute to and benefit from our Facilitators Forum. Do you think that would be a good investment of her time? Good. I'll tell her we talked."

- **Talking the walk.** The cliche advice to "walk the talk" is sometimes used to express the notion that people simply need to act on what they say they believe. Those organizing the Forum found this admonishment severely lacking (Senge, 2001). In contrast, as the organizers issue personal invitations to the Facilitators Forum they stand this familiar cliche on its head. They ask potential Forum members:

  Where have you been walking?

  Where does your daily journey (as a staff, parent, or person experiencing life with a disability) take you?

  What have you been talking about as you walk through your day?

As people describe their daily journeys and conversations, we have opportunities to listen for ways to connect their every day work and lives to the content of the Facilitators Forum.

- **"Quality conversations"**. Attracting only those who saw themselves as "facilitators" would have meant a certain death for the Facilitators Forum. It would have ignored the many staff, advocates, family members, and people receiving services who encourage positive change through the conversations they have each day. The initial success of the Forum was due, in part, to finding ways to highlight and honor the many ways that participants are in conversation about the future of a person, an organization, or community. Discovering and practicing more meaningful ways to be in conversation expands both the number of individuals attracted to the Forum and the helpfulness of the Forum in people's everyday lives. The reflections of one participant capture this:

  It's more manageable for me if I think of this work as helping to lead more constructive conversations. It feels more accessible, more natural. I think these skills we learn are very important. However, if I concentrate on those too much, I feel too mechanical. Remembering that it's a conversation helps bring this into balance.

- **Bridging and building on other events:** Some people are attracted to the Facilitators Forum because of their experiences with other training and learning opportunities. At the close of a local three- day course on PATH and Creative Facilitation, for example, participants heard this invitation: "If this course was helpful to you, please join a group of people who meet regularly to learn together about facilitation and quality conversations. If you are afraid to take the next step with PATH, you are especially welcome!"

  For others, participation in the Facilitators Forum has been the springboard for involvement in training opportunities that they might not have otherwise experienced. Because of connections made through the Forum, several people participated in the Design for Change Course offered by John O'Brien and Jack Pearpoint. These members have since taken leadership roles in sharing their insights and learning with the other members of the Forum.

Creating a learning community during the Forum gatherings

In its short, three- year life, the Facilitators Forum has become a source of inspiration, learning, and renewal. Participants often use the word "connection" to describe a critical aspect of the experience. This connection exists during the gatherings, and sustains itself between gatherings.

Given the opportunity to reflect on this sense of connection, participants often point to two seemingly irreconcilable aspects of the time spent at gatherings. One aspect is that of the "safe place":

> It's a "safe harbor". I can say what I really think, and say what I don't know.

> I can just show up as myself. I feel accepted for who I am.

> I feel encouragement to become better. As time goes by, I notice I'm bringing more of myself into the room.

> The same spark is inside everybody.

Many participants describe the "safe place" that exists concurrently with the experience of "being stretched out of my comfort zone". The stretching sometimes comes when participants try out a new skill. Sometimes participants feel stretched to think about things in a new way.

> I was scared and nervous, but I felt safe. I didn't feel alone. I was with fellow journeyers. Others in the room are like threads of a parachute for me. I won't just fall. The Facilitators Forum is a place of sanctuary.

After only three years, most participants are reluctant to draw too many firm conclusions about how this can be both a safe place and one that stretches and makes one nervous. At least one participant makes the connection this way:

> Perhaps it is **through** the experiences of stepping out of our comfort zone that we have **moved** to discover together this place of deep comfort and trust.

Sustaining a learning community through collaborative action

Participants today use Forum gatherings to describe an invitation or opportunity to facilitate, seek co-facilitators, ask the group for ideas, and report (most often in hilarious detail) the stories of recent facilitation experiences.

Members call on one another across typical program and agency boundaries. Those whose job or life roles had not previously included facilitation, now engage in facilitating planning conversations. A few of the many stories of collaboration and community building include:

- A woman who receives services attended a PATH and Creative Facilitation Course. She was invited to join the next gathering of the Facilitators Forum. She did so, and used the occasion to recruit facilitators and team members to engage with her in a planning process that focused on making some key changes in her life. She moved to a new home that better suits her interests and desires for greater independence.
- Forum members from one agency invited members from another agency to plan and facilitate the agency annual planning event.
- A Forum member recruited help from others to plan and facilitate a planning day for a statewide advocacy organization.
- A Forum member invited other members to meet with her to think together about a young woman whose supporters "feel stuck". They helped script conversations and planning sessions that are helping staff better understand why the person is acting as she does.

Emphasis today is on the action and collaboration that happens *between sessions*. The sessions are the "pauses between the notes" —a time for finding connections, new ideas, and new skills that contribute to richer action.

There are many factors contributing to sustaining this community. When long-standing Forum members are asked, "What has helped this group become a community that learns together and turns to one another for support and assistance?" they often recount the story of the Sweaty Palms Pledge.

Collaboration and The Sweaty Palms Oath

After the Forum had established a faithful group of "regulars", they created a PATH plan for the Facilitators Forum. Members first engaged actively and creatively in describing the "North Star" that gives meaning to their work. When the group then considered what might be "Positive and Possible" to accomplish together over the next year, one member offered:

> *This is how it goes for me. The phone rings and someone
> says, "We have this challenge, or this mess, or this opportu-
> nity, and we want you to help facilitate a planning conver-
> sation." My palms immediately start to sweat. I consider
> what lies I can tell to get out of the invitation.*
>
> *I think that in order to be a member of this group each
> person ought to take an oath. We could call it "The Sweaty
> Palms Pledge". You swear that you will ask for help when
> your palms are sweating. And if you get a call from a
> fellow member asking for help ("Help, my palms are sweat-
> ing!") you have to say "yes". You have to find a way to help.*

The Sweaty Palms Oath has become a shorthand way to convey a
request for help, or an invitation for collaboration. It brings into the
conversation both the acknowledgement of fear and inadequacy, and
the promise to ask for and offer help. Each promise fulfilled builds a
stronger community of facilitators. In on-going efforts to make this
Oath come alive, members have since created Sweaty Palms plays,
poems, and posters.

Attending to what we do

The Facilitators Forum does not attempt to duplicate training offered on approaches to person-centered planning and change. Some
members are attracted to the Facilitators Forum because of their
involvement in PATH and Creative Facilitation Training, Design for
Change, Personal Futures Planning, or Essential Lifestyle Planning.*
Others have first established a connection with the Facilitators Forum, and allowed this to become a springboard to an opportunity to
learn more about approaches to person-centered planning.

The Forum focuses, rather, on skills and approaches that are helpful in a variety of planning conversations – and in general conversation as well. The group attends to skills and approaches that support
more general " sensemaking" (Weick, 2001). Facilitators can support
sensemaking, and help groups "make sense" together, when they
have useful skills to invite reflection around...

- **Identity** –Who is this person/ organization?

---

*Many of those involved in the launching and support of the Facilitators Forum
have enjoyed years of training, support, and friendship with the authors of these
approaches. We acknowledge that much of what we try to understand and share
through this Forum is built upon this foundation.

- **Events** –What is going on here? What meaning do we make of this?
- **Possibilities for meaningful action** –What do we imagine as possible?

These conversations build meaning and provide direction for action.

Participants have opportunities to experiment with new skills during regular Forum Gatherings. One of the skills that participants have practiced includes identifying and exploring "themes". Illustrating the manner in which participants engage in learning and practicing this skill conveys both the nature of the skills, and the way in which participants are invited to engage in trying on a new way of thinking.

Identifying and exploring themes

At the first gathering of the Facilitators Forum, participants were invited to imagine receiving this invitation to facilitate:

> *The four women who live in this home had been getting along just fine. They have lived together for three years now and we always thought they liked each other. Now things seem to be tense all the time. Every day one of the women is crying about something. Two staff quit in the past six months, saying that they just can't deal with these women any more. Can you come help us deal with this?*

Forum participants were invited to form small groups to consider what a facilitator might do next to explore both the invitation and the situation. Small groups played out the scenario, developing possible next steps, such as spending time with the women. These small groups were invited to invent stories about what a facilitator might learn as a result of the action. One group, for example invented this story:

> *I (the facilitator) visited the home on Wednesday and had dinner with the women. After dinner, I spent time sitting on the porch with two of the women. We talked about their lives as young girls. As we talked I learned that each had spent at least twenty years living in a large institution. Both had lost a parent in the past year. One of the women remembered the Jewish traditions her mother had taught her as a young child. I met two staff. One was new to her job and said she was just getting to know the women. Both staff were in their early twenties.*

Next, groups were invited to consider the themes that were emerging as they explored the situation. As groups reflected on possible themes, they were asked to think about the central ideas underlying the issues at hand. Groups were encouraged to consider whether this situation reminded them of any experiences in their own lives, and if so, what they might "name" that experience. Groups used their unique scenarios to generate possible themes. Some possible themes included: loss, grief, faith and traditions, growing up, home, family, roommates, and relationships.

Following this, discussions and exercises focused on ways to check out one's guesses about possible themes. Small groups then learned and practiced ways to facilitate conversations around these themes in a way that builds both a shared appreciation of the life experiences and identities of the women and lays the foundations for moving forward.*

Attending to who we are:
Bringing ourselves to our work

Participants notice that attending to these skills requires us to notice our own thinking, and consider whether our habits of thinking are useful to others and ourselves. Learning these skills causes us to notice our assumptions about people and events. We notice the habits of our minds and our hearts.

When we learned to think about the themes in a situation, it offered a way for us to bring our own lives and experience into understanding the life experience of a person receiving services. That brings more humanity into the conversation. It becomes a conversation about "us" and what any of us need in order to move on.

> We spent some time at one of our sessions focusing on the
> skill of "listening". We did some exercises designed to help
> us listen to our inner "chatter". For the next few days I
> just listened to it. I noticed my "chatter" was very critical.
> It was like having an entire Greek Chorus in my head. I
> started asking, "Do I really want to go around with these
> voices talking like this for the rest of my life?" I've been
> practicing being curious when I want to be critical. I make
> myself think of a question to ask, instead of letting that

---

*We are indebted to the author of Individual Service Design, Jack Yates, for teaching about the importance and helpfulness of naming and developing themes. For an overview of Individual Service Design, see O'Brien & Lovett (1998).

This is the January photo page from the *2002 Facilitator's Forum Calendar*.
Created by forum participants, the calendar is a collage of memorable
events and key people in the life of the Forum.

> *critical voice go on. It's hard sometimes, but I think it gets*
> *easier with practice.*

In the collective memory of those regularly attending the Facilitators Forum, one session is often remembered as pivotal in shaping
the Forum as a place to think and talk about "who we are". This session occurred at a January meeting, almost a year and a half after the
start of the Forum. Participants had been responding to the question: "What is your New Year's Facilitation Resolution?" Members
recall the palpable shift in the room as one member said:

> *I am re-focusing on who I am and the way I am in the*
> *world. I want to find more opportunities to be the person*
> *I am. I want to remember that if it was more about doing*
> *than being, we would be called Human Doings, rather*
> *than Human Beings.*

The gift of this comment opened the possibility for the Facilitators
Forum to become a container for holding our hopes and questions
about the connection between who we are and our work as facilitators. After these words were spoken, it became possible for participants to explore this new territory together.

The meaning of the connections between who we are and the work of facilitation expresses itself in rich variety at Facilitator gatherings. Participants talk together about developing a deeper appreciation of what they stand for as individuals, and how this connects with the work of facilitation.

> *This work, it seems to me, keeps coming back to who we are, and how we are together.*

> *This Forum has become a centering place for me. It helps me stay focused on who I want to be in my work and in this world. I'm thinking big. I'm talking huge. It's about social justice.*

For others, this connection between the self and the work expresses itself as emerging confidence in their unique style and way of being in the world. Participants share humorous and heartfelt stories about time spent trying to imitate another facilitator. Time and again, the group offers thoughtful feedback about the unique self and style that each person brings.

> *I spent years thinking I could never do this work because I couldn't be like this one facilitator that I admired so much. At one Forum gathering I shared this with another member. When I said, "I haven't yet found my own style", she just laughed in my face and said, "Girl, you are nothing BUT style". I hadn't thought of it that way. It made me start to think about myself in a new way. Now I have lots more confidence about who I am. In a strange way, this has opened me up to notice aspects of my style that I need to work on. I hadn't been open to that before.*

The poet, David Whyte, who writes so eloquently about work and identity, states the experience of many participants in the Forum when he writes (2001, p. 13):

> *Our competence may be at stake in ordinary unthinking work, but in good work that is an expression of ourselves, we necessarily put our very identities to hazard. Perhaps it is because we know, in the end, we are our gift to others and the world*

The Future of the Facilitators Forum

The Facilitators Forum was created out of the desire to expand the numbers and capacities of individuals willing to turn to one another to facilitate planning conversations around increasingly complex challenges. The individuals who have become a part of this effort have fashioned a community of learners that supports its members to learn together over time about what we do as facilitators and who we are as people.

The future of this community relies upon the continued diligence of its founders and members to set aside time from the busy demands of daily life to sustain this effort. It requires continued attention to attracting new and diverse participants. Members must support each other to continue to find new and richer meaning in the experience of the Forum. Most critical for future success will be the continued willingness to bring into the open the most central convictions about this work, and to find new ways to connect people around these convictions.

References

O'Brien, J. & Lovett, H. (1998). Finding a Way Toward Everyday Lives. In J. O'Brien and C. Lyle O'Brien, Eds. *A little book about person-centered planning.* Toronto: Inclusion Press. 1999. Pp. 113-132

Senge, P., et al. (1999) *The Dance of Change: The Challenges of Sustaining Momentum in Learning Organizations.* New York: Doubleday. Pp. 193-237.

Weick, K. Leadership as the Legitimation of Doubt. In W. Bennis, G. Spreitzer and T. Cummings, Eds. *The Future of Leadership.* San Francisco: Jossey-Bass, 2001.Pp. 91-102.

Whyte, D. (2001) *The Unknown Sea: Work as a Pilgrimage of Identity.* New York: Riverhead Books.

In Memoriam
Chaplain Allen R. Gunn

The Rhode Island Facilitators' Forum honors the life and work of our friend, Allen R. Gunn, who left this life as this book was completed. A tenacious networker and connector, Allen's dedication to facilitating true membership in faith communities throughout Rhode Island has enriched the lives of countless people. Members of the Forum have been inspired by Allen's unwavering faith in his Lord and his love for humanity. We are grateful for his presence with us.

14

Some Words Along the Way

MaryJo Alimena Caruso and Kathy Lee
with contributions by Guy Caruso, Karen Cross,
Terry Morris and Ruth Siegfried

In 1994 the Pennsylvania Developmental Disabilities Council funded the Circle of Support Mentoring Project. The intent was to utilize a small group of experienced and philosophically grounded facilitators as mentors to strengthen the foundation of person-centered values for people across the state while increasing the number of skilled facilitators. The mentors were given the charge of promoting the integrity of circle work and preventing perversions of the process for individuals wanting to know more about person-centered planning through gatherings, resources and hands-on technical support. People with disabilities, family members, school personnel and human service professionals sought out the mentors for guidance.

Joining together, the facilitators and mentors embarked on individual efforts initially focused on improving the quality of life through developing a circle of support. Each facilitator, focus person and circle had unique characteristics generating from their purpose or process in the attempt to make their person-centered plan move from a shared vision into a reality.

In the end, only two mentors, MaryJo Alimena Caruso and Kathy Lee, were able to complete the final three years of the project. To safeguard the process of person-centered planning, the mentors set out to create a piece that provided insight into the role of facilitator. MaryJo and Kathy gathered a diverse group of Pennsylvanians who have been facilitating plans for quite a few years. The result of their query is an unhurried conversation with unique individuals.

Think of this document as an opportunity to be privy to this conversation about person-centered planning and circles of support.

How we learned

One of the first things you may want to know about the facilitators is how we came to learn about person-centered planning and circles of support. Although it appears to be a rather straightforward question, and indeed was the first question we asked each facilitator, it seems difficult for some of us to clearly articulate a response. In fact, while many of the people we interviewed are active in person-centered planning as a facilitator, circle member, mentor or trainer, it was a struggle for them to think back to how they actually learned about it. A common response among interviewees was, "that was a long time ago, and hard to remember…"

Many of us have been drawn to person-centered planning through a personal calling. It may have been someone in our life that invited us to participate in his or her circle of support; initially, we may have come on board as a circle participant; or perhaps we got our feet wet by facilitating "even if we weren't exactly sure what we were doing."

> *My first exposure to it was when I was invited to participate in Peg's circle as it was forming. She was still a resident of the County Home. It was some time after that when I did some reading about it. My learning came from actually participating and seeing how it went. I remember those first sessions…going through her life…We were doing the flip charts about who was doing what and we were following up. We came together a lot in those early times. We came together to discover what Peg needed and started helping her change her life.*

For those of us who first learned about person-centered planning as a circle participant, it was a new experience to plan *with* someone we care about, rather than plan *for* them. The experience was powerful and has stuck with us through the years. Sometimes just being a part of it was enough to inspire a potential facilitator. One interviewee noted "I loved being a part of that circle and watching it happen…It became a real personal interest for me…I learned that if you know where you are going you have some shot of getting there." Many facilitators describe that time in their life as amazing and life changing. It helped a lot of us realize what was really important, such as how to listen to the dreams of someone you care for instead of making decisions for them based on your own frame of reference.

While it seems common to hear people in the human service field sharing stories of unsupportive co-workers or bosses, some of us found ourselves in very nurturing environments, and learned about person-centered planning from an agency director or supervisor. Some interviewees cited examples of bosses learning about person-centered planning, then encouraging others to use it as a learning tool or to offer as a resource for the people served through the agency. As a result, facilitators were supported to attend trainings presented by some of the "gurus" of person-centered planning or were provided with resources such as books or videos to help them learn more about the different planning tools. There were even those of us who learned how to facilitate by default.

> *One day we received a flier to go to a person-centered plan-*
> *ning training and nobody else where I worked was very in-*
> *terested. When the flier got to my desk, I decided to go. So I*
> *went to the training and learned. For me, person-centered*
> *planning fit like a new coat. It was just what I wanted*
> *and needed, but never heard anyone talk about before.*

Some interviewees learned about person-centered planning through mentors of the Circles of Support Mentoring Project who are often called upon to teach an agency how to facilitate a plan, mentor individual staff members or assist them in learning other person-centered strategies. There were even agencies that experienced a ripple effect, which sparked more learning about person-centered planning. As one person learned how to facilitate a circle, they in turn taught someone else, often through modeling and co-facilitating. Sometimes, even seemingly unrelated information, led us back to the philosophies and practices of person-centered planning.

> *Sometimes people would come to talk about different*
> *things such as behavior problems, but there was always a*
> *component of person-centered planning in whatever they*
> *taught us. My agency then revised our annual planning*
> *form to make it more person-centered and to make it more*
> *of a living document so it wasn't so cold. We included*
> *people's dreams. Now we can revisit the dream when we*
> *need to and not just create paperwork for the County.*

For those who were introduced to person-centered planning at the work place, having a boss who really embraced person-centered planning undoubtedly enhanced our learning. In addition, it was important to have a work culture that supported the planning and the dreams of the focus people. State initiatives, institutes and related events also provided the foundation to learn about person-centered planning. One facilitator originally learned about person-centered planning through a series of wonderful changes in the nursing home where she worked. These changes were the result of waiver funding for people moving into the community. At that time, it was decided that tools could be used to do planning with people who lived in the nursing home. The idea was to facilitate a smoother move to the community, although no one quite knew what tools were available and where to start to find them. Word of mouth led to connections with people who were doing person-centered planning and who were willing to come and teach those who wanted to learn. In this instance, learning about the process enabled the facilitator to use it to move people from the nursing home to the community.

In Pennsylvania, one interviewee recalled learning about person-centered philosophy through the related workshops on social role valorization (SRV) and PASS.

> We were doing PASS evaluations in Pennsylvania. During the foundation discussions, we looked at who the people were, we looked at their lives demographically and existentially, and at what their experiences had been. While we were doing people's "history" in the foundation discussions, it all started to come to me. We were hearing people's stories and listening to what they ideally needed. What I found is that when you look at the ideal way of meeting someone's needs, it leads away from the human service solutions and focuses on the individual. This process really helped me see people better and become more person-centered in my planning.

The Positive Approaches Institute also played an important role by introducing some of us to the people respected for doing the work –they hate to be called experts– and actually teaching us how to plan.

> My learning started at the Positive Approaches Institute. I would go to the trainings and then come back all worked up. I became known as a "Positive Approaches Junkie." People would see me coming and say "Here comes Miss Positive Approaches." I guess I overdid it a bit. I had to take about three steps back and calm down. I decided to stop learning and instead start applying what I had learned.

Some of us even got into the work by default. One facilitator recalled, "I sent Margie to the meeting and she didn't feel like she could do it, so she asked me to try." One of the interviewees did not even have a job role consistent with doing any type of planning –showing us that facilitators come from all walks of life. Even if we didn't set out to do person-centered planning as a part of our job, some accidentally stumbled into it!

> *My background is in housing support and fiscal informa-*
> *tion. I really hadn't had any participation in the planning*
> *processes. Once I learned about person-centered planning,*
> *it seemed to me that this was the way that planning should*
> *be done. It seemed natural to me that the person was the*
> *center and their thoughts and actions should be what*
> *everyone goes from—not the other way around. It made a*
> *lot of sense to me. Since then, I have facilitated or co-fa-*
> *cilitated about five or six plans. I have been a part of other*
> *people's planning when they ask me.*

Although each of us may have come to learn about person-centered planning for a different reason, many of us have been drawn to the work by some common themes, experiences and individuals. A majority of us had little (or no) formal training on how to facilitate a person-centered plan before doing one, except for reading some articles or monographs.

Regardless of how we came to know/do person-centered planning, somewhere along the way each of us has had the opportunity to meet up with and learn from those who are respected for their knowledge. Beth Mount, John O'Brien, Herb Lovett, Susannah Joyce and Michael Smull's names were echoed when facilitators reflected on their formal learning experiences. Pennsylvanians like Rosa McAllister, Beth Barol and the Circles of Support Mentoring Project folks (Thom Cramer, Jean Robertson, Kathy Lee and MaryJo Alimena Caruso), also continued to be mentioned as trainers and nurturers of facilitators across the state. All of them have deepened our skills.

> *I went to the Positive Approaches Institute and met some*
> *really wonderful people—people like Herb Lovett, Thom*
> *Cramer and Beth Mount. At that time, the main style of*
> *planning was Personal Futures Planning. I was encouraged*
> *to learn about it and then actually participate in a plan*
> *before I facilitated one myself. I served a young woman*
> *who was placed in a residential setting away from Blair*
> *County. Thom Cramer came down and facilitated her plan*

using Personal Futures Planning. It was an interesting process. I thought that it was a wonderful experience for the young lady.

By having the guidance of so many teachers, mentors and experts, we have had the opportunity to be exposed to a variety of different person-centered planning styles and techniques that all uphold similar values and philosophies. For each of us, that has meant having more tools in our toolbox from which to draw.

Having you guys (Kathy and MaryJo) come and do the training on person-centered planning and the one day follow-up still reverberates here in the County ... I've learned from Susannah Joyce and Michael Smull. I have connected with Inclusion Press. I have been amazed at the amount of information that is out there. I have had my mind opened by so many things. I have realized that person-centered planning is so many things. I have started to see it now as a lot of possibilities. No one style is better—it's trying to figure out what style fits that person's needs. Sometimes I have made mistakes. I started doing a PATH for a lady and it was too much—the details overwhelmed her. We stopped and went back to looking at pieces of the PATH. We made it simpler. Michael Smull talked to us about Essential Lifestyle Planning being a good base to start with. Since the training ... I use what is most flexible. You can pick and choose what maps make sense for you.

Each of us feels as though we continue to learn through intensive workshops, demonstration projects, retreats and hands-on experience. In addition, we feel as though our knowledge serves to weave us into a network, through which we as facilitators can offer support, mentoring and a forum to share common experiences with each other.

I knew this young woman whose person-centered planning story was just extraordinary. I also knew a number of people who were on her team. I got her permission to use her story and her plan in some of the training that I was doing.

I would present her situation to the group and then ask them to develop a plan around her story. Then I would take her story from two years later, after things had been

*moving for her, and share that with the group. It was
really dramatic because people would come up with these
huge plans for medical consults and psychiatric hospitaliza-
tion for medical changes. They would talk about dramatic
behavior plans and massive interventions in regard to her
family. Occasionally, people would even come up with the
idea that she shouldn't have family contact anymore because it was so destabilizing to her. What I showed them in
the end, was that she had a person-centered plan. That was
it. The things that she said were important were responded
to through the plan. All her Circle did was give her more
control over her life, give her attention that was not related
to being a paid staff person and get her involved in activities in the community where she had interests.*

*Without all of those other system-type interventions, she
became a really well integrated success.*

-Ruth Siegfried

The positives

Person-centered planning is the only thing we've given a name to
that actually puts the person in the center and respects their voice
over and above everyone else. Person-centered planning is a way for
systems and community people to join together, to bridge the gap
between what's available and what's possible.

Each of us appreciates the individualization that person-centered
planning promotes. We find it reinforcing to remember that person-
centered planning is about the focus person and not the organization that serves them. As a tool, the application of person-centered
planning is different for everyone. In fact, no two plans or circles
of support ever look alike. Using person-centered planning we are
reminded that this is a person who is unique. As facilitators, we
have experienced true joy watching a focus person have the opportunity to plan their own life as an individual, rather than as a person
caught up in a system. It is during those times that we experience a
transformation. People's goals begin to look more like the goals that
everyday people would have, not just something that the system
invented to make sure that regulations are met. It helps everyone to
understand that we are dealing with a person. With the old format,
we thought about the person as a number. It is easy to forget the
human side when you are dealing with system questions and paper

work. Person-centered planning causes us to return to a sense of humanness and reminds us of what's *really* important.

The values that helped us build a foundation and permeate the soul of our work, also play an important role in what we enjoy and respect about person-centered planning tools.

> *Behind person-centered plans and behind the thinking of the person who developed the tools, there were a lot of experiences and challenges that urged them to look at the question of values. Specifically normalization, PASS, PASSING and SRV training. Without these foundations, people may learn person-centered planning as a tool, but never fully get a foundation in the core values and vulnerabilities of people with disabilities.*

Person-centered planning also recognizes the uniqueness of the facilitator. For those of us who work with children, it helped to know that it was not just an "adult thing." For others who work with people that have been given many labels, we could stretch the tool beyond only assisting individuals with developmental disabilities. The individuality allows us to adapt it to our skill and comfort level. As experienced facilitators, we no longer feel the compulsion to pull out a flip chart and markers at every meeting. Sometimes, we enjoy just sitting back and listening to see what's needed.

As facilitators, we appreciate opportunities to "return to our roots" and remember what we've been taught. For example, one way to facilitate a circle of support effectively is to remember the importance of going back to the basics and putting the focus person in control. Simple things such as the location of the meeting and having invitations on non-agency letterhead are vital points. The group guidelines also help keep all members grounded. We have found power in participating in a process where "there are no boundaries, no hearing *that's not allowed* or *you can't have your dreams*." It's about finding the neat dreams and getting around the seemingly insurmountable barriers in creative ways. Some facilitators have deepened their understanding of person-centered planning by putting themselves in the shoes of the focus person, then doing a person-centered plan for themselves. For some, it is a difficult and humbling situation; many of the facilitators recommended it as a way to truly appreciate the process.

*I know that doing my own relationship map was pain-
ful for me. We don't think about it until we put it down
on paper and then we see that we don't have an extended
network. When we look at all of the paid relationships
in our own lives, we sometimes can have more paid than
non-paid.*

There are certain aspects of person-centered planning that appeal
to us, continue to engage us, and as a result make us stronger facilitators. The graphic process used in person-centered planning is one
aspect that draws us in. We like to take the time to map the pictures
and the concrete graphic view of a person's life. By doing this, we
have learned to really focus on the individual, who that person is
and their true essence. The graphic process allows us to create a
visual image that helps us connect with the circle members as well.
Then together, we can join in and find ways to help meet a person's
true needs and dreams. Many of us even have a favorite "map" or
question we like to pose to a circle of support to inspire the dream
and the vision for the future.

*I like the part where, towards the end, you talk about
preferences and non-negotiables. Being the bureaucrat for
so many years, we didn't listen. It was what we had and
it was how we made the person fit what was available. To
actually find out what is important to somebody is really
special. For one woman that I just met, it was being able
to have her two parakeets. She had been moved into a
nursing home and she wasn't able to have her parakeets
with her. She wanted to have her birds back and she
wanted to live somewhere where she could have a dog.
Those things meant the most to her. It seems fairly simple,
and yet for years we denied people the opportunity to have
any kind of pet. Changing that is the part that I enjoy.*

The permeability of the circle of support is also an aspect of
person-centered planning that facilitators identified as unique and
appealing. It is refreshing to work together, dream together and
celebrate together. There should always be room for new and old
people in the focus person's life. Often times, the person-centered
plan can be a way of hooking up with people from the past who
may have real significance to the focus person.

*People with disabilities lose so many people along their
paths. Circles act as conduits to reconnect them.*

It helps when circle members use their personal connections to make something happen. We live by the adage that it's not always what you know, but who you know. Circles of support work best when the circle is made up of loyal participants with wise advisors who remember the "question" and the person that brought everyone together in the first place.

One of the greatest rewards of facilitating is the knowledge we have gained over time. Many of us have been involved in some aspect of person-centered planning for 10 years. The things that really work are truly, truly, *truly* listening to a person and realizing what that person sincerely desires; learning what their true strengths and needs are, building in flexibility, looking at what connections that person needs to make to get the kind of life that they want. For us, person-centered planning is a way to support people. And we are most successful when we become really creative and think of things that work for the person not just what the system has to offer. We have come to realize that we are engaged in real person-centered planning and a true circle of support when we sit back and listen. Only then can a person be acknowledged and their preferences heard.

> *I think that anytime we sit and try to piece together a person's life, then take the next step to empathize with that person, I always gain so much clarity about why they are doing what they are doing. I am also able to see what needs to be done. I think that is missing for a lot of people... a basic understanding of who they are. You get that when you sit down and put it all together.*

> *I think that Peg's circle was the most successful. It went on for so long and changed so much of her life. It seems that in other planning, people come together frequently at first, then quickly lose interest, and things taper off. This is really frustrating. In Peg's circle that didn't happen. Even when we disagreed about the direction we should take, people continued to come together. I remember when Peg wanted to get a covered trailer to haul her electric chair to have greater mobility. All of the issues were talked about; Who was going to drive? What kind of insurance did she*

*need? Who would carry the liability? How would we raise
the money? We even talked about getting her a van as the
cart idea was getting close to $10,000 per year. It was a
frustrating time. The dream was there and it would have
been a wonderful thing. It just wasn't practical. But this
disagreement didn't destroy Peg's circle.*

- Terry Morris.

The threats

You must know by now, that as conscientious facilitators, we worry.
We worry about the focus people, we worry about our ability to
facilitate, and we worry about the external threats. Our enemies
span from the things we cannot control, like time, to the things we
wish we could control, like the human service system. The concern
we carry is sometimes not even something we are cognizant of on a
day-to-day basis, but it is always there. Being aware of the tensions
of person-centered planning is just a part of our nature and serves to
keep us faithful to the people and the process.

Most of us are still actively involved in person-centered planning
through facilitating plans, or through the continuation of relationships with focus persons and their circles of support. But the reality
is that folks are busier and busier. As the past few years have gone
by, facilitators are not as free to do the work of facilitating plans and
participating in circles. For some facilitators, the different initiatives
and the "politically correct" language that changes every few years
has caused them to become disgruntled. Others of us are concerned
that current options are just window dressing with little substance
underneath. Although our frustrations may be from varied sources,
some of us feel the very personal insecurity of being too few, for too
many. The tension of trying to do the "right thing" vs. what is asked
or required has eaten away at some of us.

*Not being able to deliver what people are asking for and
coming up short when people are trusting in us...trying to
work with what a person wants and what a family wants
when they don't match...Helping the family understand
that sometimes the goals are what the person chooses, not
what the family wants. These can be the most difficult.*

The feelings of inadequacy feed the recurrent worry of burning
out. It is a concern we have for ourselves, as well as our facilitator

friends. Many of us who have done a lot of person-centered plans have walked the fine line of falling into a rut.

> *If you do a lot of facilitating yourself, you may become uncreative and unlistening—almost institutionalized in your thinking.*

As a result, we look for ways to renew ourselves, build our skills and identify support. For most, if we don't have an understanding co-worker, we look for support through retreats and learning opportunities. These activities, like those sponsored by the Circles of Support Mentoring Project and facilitated by respected leaders allow us to regain perspective, revive our "values pulse," and reconnect to our support network.

Another threat to person-centered planning is the misrepresentation of the process and the participants. Words may be thrown around without recognition of what they mean. For example, a 'circle of support' is often interchanged with 'person-centered team' by people who may not know, nor care to learn, the difference.

> *I knew that there would come a day when we would have other buzz words that would become the new thing—and that made me sad. Terminology that we take for granted as being a part of circles and person-centered planning causes other people to look at me blankly. I have mixed emotions about moving away from our foundation and using new terms to describe person-centered planning. Sometimes though, we are overzealous about protecting pure person-centered planning language and we miss some of the good things that people are doing, have to offer or need. Sometimes by protecting the past, you lose your chance to embrace the future. We may lose some buzzwords and labels, but we all need to be on the same page. Most of the people coming out with degrees in Special Ed have never been with a person with a disability, and some even have problems or issues of their own. That is why I liked person-centered planning. It's not about what I want to make the person do, it's more about what they want in their life and hearing that.*

Some common questions/thoughts that have been pondered by those interviewed for this chapter include

- What happens when the system takes ownership of person-centered planning?
- If the system takes over by adopting/regulating/insisting on person-centered planning, isn't it actually systems centered planning? At times it just seems like a new name, but the same game.
- When we systematize something, it gets standardized. If we mandate that people do person-centered planning, there are so many abuses that can happen and it won't work. When the focus person doesn't have any one in their life except staff, there will be a price to pay somewhere down the line. Some paid staff tend to be fixated on what they know, which is human services, versus thinking "outside of the box"–something typical family and friends may do a bit better.

Many of us wear multiple hats such as case manager, program specialist, agency director or administrator, in addition to facilitator. As a result, we have experienced the lip service of person-centeredness that is contained within the regulatory steps of individual planning, goal planning, habilitation planning and life management planning. Our system-sponsored efforts always say that the person is a part of the team and the person is the loudest voice on the team, but this rarely happens. In the experience of most facilitators, system work means having meeting after meeting where goals are set, but no one knows what they are doing. We don't search for capacities, dream or engage community people in the process. A lot of the confusion with the system goals is that they are goals to which the group is not committed and they may not have any true relevance to the person. If ever there was relevance, it got lost along the way. For many of us, there is sadness and frustration in the systemic approach to planning for someone. Person-centered planning addresses the frustration and works because of the unifying dream.

> *This person hasn't had a vacation in thirty years and this year they got to go on vacation. That feels good. Compare this to his goal of learning to take bread out of the bag, which didn't mean anything to him.*

A systemic approach may not see commonalties or view people holistically. One of the greatest "injustices" that the facilitators have witnessed is that a paid provider may not see the worth of persons who have been coming together over time as a circle of support. As a result, service providers may be missing out on the opportunity to make room for other people in the focus person's life. These may include the people who hold the history, people of courage and people who can question why each person is involved in the circle.

Many of us also share a concern about who is facilitating person-centered plans. Of the facilitators interviewed for this chapter, none of us is a "certified person-centered planner" and agree that we never want a "certificate of expertise" to hang in a cubicle. However, while we shy away from the credentialing of facilitators, we worry that some people will be assigned to do person-centered plans as a part of their paid staff position without the training, support and best interests of the focus person in mind.

> *One of my gravest worries is the perversion of the person-centered planning process. There are so many pseudo-person-centered plans—it is running rampant and they are everywhere. We are not doing person-centered planning when we are…planning to move people out of state centers and other institutions. These plans are somewhere between the old process, which would take people and put them into slots and true person-centered plans.*

> *The biggest concern I have comes from the pressure from administrative people. To take something so creative and try to fit it into a system will make it lose so much. I fear the pressure from the system to do more, do more, do more will make things go really wrong. I know the struggle to make it be good can be a losing one when there is so much pressure from the system to do more.*

We are not so naive as to believe that our facilitator role involves imposing our values on the focus person and circle of support. However, the interviewees all recognize the need for a strong values base that keeps the process pure. We also recognize the risks to those values when the planning process is hosted by the system. These values are what support us to listen and strategize when a focus person dreams of a home of their own rather than just the offer of a space in an agency group home.

> *Where will person-centered planning fit in that? We are dealing with people with different gifts and dreams. Are we to stop thinking of them as having unique needs or that we can create a life that they would like? Or do we say, "You don't have any choice—you will get this many hours, or will be with these people or in this center.*

What happened to recognizing the individual needs of people? That is the greatest challenge. What happens when the system starts telling people that they have too much and then wants to take things away? People with disabilities and the people who love them need to be prepared to speak out.

Six to eight years ago, there were two projects that started in my county. In both of the projects, someone decided to use Essential Lifestyles Planning to determine what supports people needed in order to move into community settings. All of the case managers were supposed to facilitate the plans. Case managers sometimes went to the training sessions to learn how to develop a person-centered plan, but more often somebody from their office went to the training and then went back and trained the supervisors. Those folks then went back to their staff and taught them how to be facilitators of person-centered plans. None of them had any experience whatsoever, and yet they were training people in how to use these tools. What really got started was an entirely perverted version of person-centered Lifestyle Planning. This is similar to the game of telephone relay where something is whispered in someone's ear and it travels around the circle until it gets to the beginning and everyone laughs because it is not what was started at all. Even if Michael Smull had come and taught all of those case managers himself, it still would have been perverted because that work was not based on the right set of values. The facilitator understanding the values is essential.

Added tension arises around issues with paid staff. Many of us have struggled with staff turnover when paid staff, who have been active in a circle of support, are no longer employed by the agency initiating the person-centered plan. As facilitators, it causes us to look for ways that people can be welcomed to stay as circle members even when off the agency's payroll. We have also tried to balance the risk of adding the new paid staff hired to replace the turnover. One consequence of keeping the planning process permeable to new staff is that the focus person and circle members must continually tell the story again. It works well only when the paid staff is invited by the focus person. Benefits occur when paid persons have genuinely good intentions. The old circle members may feel that the constant welcoming of new staff is old hat, and as a result are guilty of thinking that new people are fitting in when they really feel left out.

Control. Money. Training. Values. Time. Our worries spiral around and around, but as conscientious facilitators, our greatest threats always return to what lies within ourselves. While we struggle with the issues, we also search for possible solutions.

> *I worry about the energy and time needed to do it right. I worry about the other people who are not getting planning done for them. The reality is that it is not possible to do this kind of work with a large amount of people. Finding and teaching other people is really difficult. I don't know the answer here.*

> *A big one is that we become complacent. We try to systematize something and we think that one training is going to change everybody—and that everybody will know how to support someone using person-centered planning. What is needed is ongoing training, mentoring and technical assistance—it can't be a one shot deal. Person-centered planning is so dynamic. What we learn about a person, and what we learn from listening and from watching them get the kind of life they want is so changing that we need to be very flexible.*

> *I worry I don't know enough. Learn as much about the person before you begin. You can't get the information from the file or even from other people. You need to spend concentrated time with them.*

The overall opinion maintained by the facilitators is that person-centered planning, however it is veiled and despite the threats, continues to be positive.

> *People who have received nothing in the past, they may at least get something through some type of person-centered planning.*

> *Mary had a terrific family that really loved her. Mary ended up having to go into a group home called an ICF/MR. There was another woman there with similar disabilities. The two were paired together because of the similarities of their disabilities not because they got along. Mary hated*

*it with every bone in her body. We had to try and make
something happen.*

*Mary was living in this home that she didn't like and was
going to a day program that she didn't like. The exciting
thing for me as a facilitator was that Mary considered
anything an improvement over her current circumstances.
The home she was living in was built to service people.
The doors were wide and the bathrooms were built so that
people could be helped in assembly line fashion. There were
no phones at the level where people who used wheelchairs
could reach. One of the first things that the circle did was
help Mary get a portable phone so that she could make
calls privately in her room.*

*One of the good parts was that her family was really
involved. We also got the mayor of the town involved. The
mayor was also the fire chief and the undertaker. He was
wonderful because he knew everyone in the community.
After we had a couple of meetings, he got to know Mary
better. When toast got burnt in the group home and the
fire alarm went off, this man came to Mary's home and he
knew her, and that was really neat.*

*It was fun for me to be the facilitator and be someone
from the outside. It was like a detective story. I had to contact people that I didn't know and invite them in. I really
struggled with the amount of time it took to keep things going. There was a woman there whom I helped to learn how
to take over when the time came for me to leave.*

*The good news is that the circle worked towards getting
Mary out of there. The Director heard Mary's story and
now he is working to get her out. Mary is going to be able
to have her own apartment near her parents. This will be
great because her parents are getting older. The support was
all there. It just needed to be organized.*

- Karen Cross

Sustaining the work

This is hard work. It can be joyful, fun and liberating but it is hard.
For many, this is the hardest work that we have ever done. It is
important to recognize that there are things that can help the work,

and the worker, be sustained. The first area is the recognition of the importance of relationships to the work. It is interesting that most of us were taught at our first jobs to remain aloof and maintain professional distance. In the work of the person-centered planner, it is important to feel. It is important to recognize that part of your job is to be a nurturer of relationships. Personal relationships will sustain the circle and the work. Safeguards are born out of the chance to mutually problem-solve with a group of people who genuinely care about the person.

> *Because members of a circle of support have come together freely, there is a drive that motivates people to say, we're coming no matter what. This battle cry protects the circle and gives it a taste of serendipity."*
>
> *The greatest safeguard to both the person and the process is when the relationships born out of and sustained by the circle of support are recognized. These individuals offer the greatest opportunity to return to the focus person's dreams and demonstrate an understood balance between "pie in the sky," and personal health and safety. True dignity of risk happens when the focus person is encouraged and supported through good times and bad by persons who genuinely care for them.*

Although this work is about gathering people together, it can be lonely. Often times there are only a few of us in an area who truly get it. It is crucial that we somehow find each other. And then more importantly, it is crucial that we bring others into the network. When we start thinking that we can do this work alone, we miss the guiding principle—it's about people. We cannot build an island, or even sometimes a pedestal, for ourselves and then go about trying to convince others to enter into relationships. We must practice what we preach.

We are starting to meet others who recognize the bastardizations of the process (i.e. when Individual Service Plan is whited out and Person-centered Plan is pencilled in). Even more importantly, we are meeting others who are inspired by circles of support.

> *Knowing people like the two of you (Kathy and MaryJo) and people across the state who are extremely committed to making sure that people are involved with others in ways that are truly person-centered, not just falling back on*

the system way of doing something or a prescribed format,
is so important. I do think that it is relationships with
people—whether that be people who have been the focus
person or facilitators, or people who have been involved
in any way with the planning. When I can continue those
relationships with people from across the state, that really
does sustain me.

There is sustenance in the process. When things are happening for a person; when the person is becoming accepted; being listened to, neat things start to happen. When the process of person-centered planning is embraced and wrongs are righted, the group gains an energy that is hard to stop. The rightness and respectability of the process also sustains us. It is this energy that will sustain us through the difficult times. We are kept afloat by the knowledge that when riding out the latest curve in the road, we will be led to a better path.

Person-centered planning gives us the answers to situations that we couldn't answer before. Sometimes this occurs when a member of a circle of support is able to reframe a situation by providing insight and information about the focus person.

There was a man who was considered an elopement risk
because he would often take off and be found breaking into
cars and putting them into gear. It wasn't until a circle
member recalled that the focus person enjoyed sitting on a
tractor during his childhood that they could put perspec-
tive into the focus person's behavior. The answers that circle
members are able to generate are often the "aha experience"
and may even result in righting a wrong. These moments
serve to lead circle members to be more involved in the
circle of support out of a drive to be a part of the answer.

Knowing that good things can happen in people's lives
makes things better for them, even if just for a short period
of time. It is not that person-centered planning is an end-
all and be-all, but it's a process that can open doors for
many people with and without disabilities.

Get rid of all of the paperwork crap that we do. Instead
of annuals and quarters, and goals and objectives, people
would have dreams and lives and revisit them on a peri-

odic basis. For many, it would be far more frequent than the current quarterly review. For other people it would be a coming together to ask, "How is your dream doing? Is there something more that we can help you with?" "I have always thought that people's live are a wonderful way to document that something is happening. These people that want to measure quality with standardized questionnaires because it is hard data are wrong. I want it to be a sharing of stories. If you need to count things, go through a story and find the important and meaningful moment in life.

Finally, it is watching people do the right thing that motivates us to continue on. Many of us have struggled in a system where we knew that what was happening for people was wrong. We also knew that there must be a better way to help people get the lives they wanted. Person-centered planning has provided one way for that to happen. For us "freedom fighters," this has been a more-than-welcome tool. The impossible dream does not seem so impossible now. We know, given a chance, that listening to people and doing what they want for their lives will work. We are also challenged through this process to do a check up on our own morality. Having to look deep at our intentions has caused some of us to view our own lives differently. This sustains not only our work but also our souls.

I've known that to see the rainbows, you have to know there's rain. I have seen a lot a lot of rain that most people have never seen. It is my job to show others what rain feels like, how you can grow from it and see the rainbows. I know that what glistens can be glitter or can be gold. I can tell the difference. I can see people who are true to the person vs. people who are fake or in it for the wrong motivations. I actually get comfort from knowing that some people just do person-centered planning because they are forced to, and there are others who genuinely know and love the person. It's like treasuring that fact that I have been able to walk with people and can now advocate for changes and then celebrate with them.

No matter how long each of us has participated in/ facilitated circles of support, it is important that there are people who check in with us along the way to keep us morally in line. That way we can ensure accountability to the person, not just the system or fiscal concerns. We all are responsible for remembering this and for reminding others.

An older woman, Ida, was living in a group home, and from the provider's perspective, she was not doing very well. We formed a circle of support around her and began a person-centered plan.

We discovered that Ida had a history that was tied to her ethnic Ukrainian heritage and people did not know about it. Because of the institutionalization, and just people not knowing who she was or what her history was, she became a "problem." She did not fit in and was not complying with what the group home wanted her to do.

We discovered that her language and comments were tied to her Ukrainian background. One of the circle members became Ida's champion and went to find out what some of these things meant. It led us to a tie with the local Ukrainian club. Ida was accepted there. She got reconnected to her roots and found enjoyment and peace through relationships of people—the people who shared her heritage. These people were able to accept her for who she was in a way that the human service system couldn't.

This champion also helped Ida get connected to relatives that she hadn't seen in many decades. She really seemed to have meaning in her life and the behavioral issues lessened to some degree. The champion became her ally and friend. The human service system never quite understood the importance of the roots in Ida's life, but did not stand in the way either.

Six months later, Ida died peacefully with a sense of culture and belonging that did not exist prior to the Circle. She was reconnected to her childhood and her identity, and was given back her heritage.

- Guy Caruso

The dream

It is always an interesting exercise to ask people who are "helpers" to the dream, to dream some for themselves. We concluded many of our interviews with the question, "What is your dream for person-centered planning in the next five years?" The dream, when it is about a process, can be elusive.

There were two distinct and different themes to our dreaming. Most people wanted the momentum to continue. More plans for more people. More people being taught about a person-centered philosophy. More families understanding, participating and leading. Within these responses was also a call to the values that guide the work. It was noted as important that people stay with the right values and principles.

> *My hope is that we will develop the values that are related to having a person-centered approach—honesty, respect, dignity, not saying things behind people's backs that you wouldn't say to their face, engaging the family members and honoring the role of relationships in the lives of people. The training in person-centered planning should be based on these values. This should be the soil in which we grow good facilitators.*

Along with wanting more opportunities, some people were clear about having a good result. They did not mean that every plan would lead to a perfect life, but rather that planning would lead to an everyday life filled with its ups and downs. There was mention of more natural supports and less system authority. There was hopefulness around more job opportunities and chances for love and affection for the focus person.

The dreaming also embraced a component of training or education. Many people recognized an on-going need to learn about person-centered planning and to teach others. There was mention of how some new direct care people are not even sure of what person-centered planning is.

We need to do some very intense type of training for people who truly get it. We need to find people who like people a lot, who understand about relationships and flexibility, and who understand that we need to look at a person's community for support, not necessarily what is available through a funding system. People need to have this intensive training so that they can then turn around and be mentors for other people. I think that is the way we are going to make change around the state.

And then there were a few who took it to the next step by saying that the dream should really be about a time when we don't need person-centered planning because we are person-centered to begin with.

> We are so person-centered in our approaches that we do not have to use any prescribed procedures. We all are so person-centered in what we do that we don't have to have structured planning with everyone, but that everyone does benefit from a person-centered philosophy.

The second view point of the dream came from a few interviewees who were concerned about the "systematizing" of the person-centered planning process.

> I hope it fails in the system and goes back to its original roots. It was meant for individuals to start thinking creatively about change. I don't see it as a human service tool. If it continues to stay in the system, it will get lost. When it is mandated across services it will lose its effectiveness.

Finally, the dreaming question brought forth a call to action. We will close with a quote that we believe says it all...

> We can make change happen. We can do it and do it well. We can honor people and their lives. We can make the people the most important thing—not the regulations, the administrators, the county office or other pressures. If we pull together and support one another, we can make people the driving force for change. There is a feeling of mutual respect and trust here now. People are willing to take some risks in order to make people's lives better.

15

Helping Staff Support Choice

Michael W. Smull

As more and more people with significant disabilities are moving from group homes to supported living, the challenges in supporting them in their choices increase. The staff involved with these individuals are often told to simultaneously support choice, build community relationships (and acceptance) and assure health and safety. Staff blessed with uncommon sense understand how to achieve this balance instinctively. However, many other staff members solve the perceived dilemma by only hearing the first or the last part of the message. They either support choice regardless of consequences or overly restrict people, in the name of health or safety. The middle part of the message, building community, gets lost in the struggle between choice and concerns over health and safety. What staff (and managers) often miss is that this is a balance, a balance that needs to be defined with each person supported.

In searching for ways to help people understand how to achieve a balance in supporting people I came across Charles Handy's "doughnut" principle.

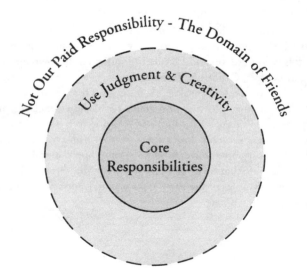

As adapted for use in supporting people with developmental disabilities, the doughnut principle suggests that there are three areas of responsibility that we can define with each person we support. At the center of the doughnut are the core responsibilities, those things that we expect staff to do without fail. These "core responsibilities" are typically a mix of issues of health or safety and those things that are most important to the person supported. The ring just outside of the core represents those areas where we expect staff to use judgment and creativity. They may continue to include issues of health and safety but they are in areas where staff are expected to try new ideas and not be punished if the ideas do not work. Outside of the doughnut are those areas that are not our responsibility, that are none of our business.

The boundary between core responsibilities and areas where people are to use judgment should be a sharp and clear. If this conceptual framework is to be helpful, sufficient time must be taken with staff to be certain that each person understands what responsibilities are within the core and which are in the area of requiring judgment. On the other side, the boundary between what is and is not our business, is deliberately kept "fuzzy". For example, what someone wears might be "none of our business" on a day to day basis but should fall into the area of "use judgment and creativity" when a person wears something inappropriate for a job interview.

The content of each area within and outside of the doughnut varies widely from person to person. Two people who illustrate how this works are Jon and Elizabeth. Jon lives in his own apartment in Benicia, California. Jon is a man with a great imagination who is also an eloquent speaker. He has found that traditional disability system employment programs (workshops, enclaves, and work crews) do not work for him and is trying to build a career as a speaker and consultant. Jon also has Prader-Willi syndrome and much of his support revolves around helping him maintain the independent life that he loves while staying within his very limited diet. Some examples of the three areas of staff responsibility inside Jon's life are shown here.

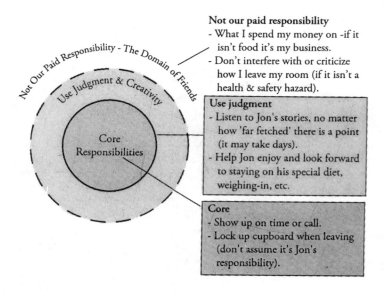

Not our paid responsibility
- What I spend my money on -if it isn't food it's my business.
- Don't interfere with or criticize how I leave my room (if it isn't a health & safety hazard).

Use judgment
- Listen to Jon's stories, no matter how 'far fetched' there is a point (it may take days).
- Help Jon enjoy and look forward to staying on his special diet, weighing-in, etc.

Core
- Show up on time or call.
- Lock up cupboard when leaving (don't assume it's Jon's responsibility).

Not Our Paid Responsibility - The Domain of Friends

Use Judgment & Creativity

Core Responsibilities

Elizabeth is a woman who one friend described as a busy lady who wants to be busier. People who met her during her recent presentations to the President's Committee on Mental Retardation and at TASH in New Orleans have commented on her charm and wit. Those who have taken the time to talk with her have realized how much we have to learn from what Elizabeth has to say. As this is being written, she is living with her family but this will change as soon as she can recruit a qualified paid roommate. Because Elizabeth communicates by pointing slowly to words, it is easy to not listen to how she wants to be assisted and Elizabeth needs a great deal of personal assistance. She relies on others for most of her personal care and eats using a G-tube. On the other hand she gets around quite well in her power chair and doesn't need anyone with her when she is off visiting during a conference. It will be critical for Elizabeth's life that staff understand their three areas of responsibility, some examples of which are shown on the next page.

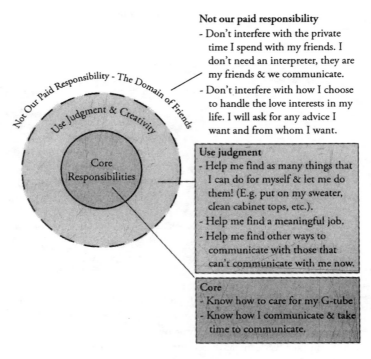

Not our paid responsibility
- Don't interfere with the private time I spend with my friends. I don't need an interpreter, they are my friends & we communicate.
- Don't interfere with how I choose to handle the love interests in my life. I will ask for any advice I want and from whom I want.

Use judgment
- Help me find as many things that I can do for myself & let me do them! (E.g. put on my sweater, clean cabinet tops, etc.).
- Help me find a meaningful job.
- Help me find other ways to communicate with those that can't communicate with me now.

Core
- Know how to care for my G-tube
- Know how I communicate & take time to communicate.

In the not too distant past we were quite comfortable in deciding where people with disabilities should live, who they should live with and how they should spend their time. Now we are trying to help people direct their own lives. We plan with people rather than for them and struggle to support the choices of each person. When we are careful and successful we help each person find the balance in their lives. A balance that reflects what people want, the resources available to them, and any issues of health or safety. Not surprisingly one of the lessons that we are learning is that we need to help staff find the same balance in the support they provide. This adaptation of Handy's "doughnut principle" provides a structure to help staff find that balance with each person they support.

16

Communication Ally
The "Missing Link" in Person-Centered Planning

Mayer Shevin.

Introduction

Imagine this:

> *You arrive, unaccompanied, at a party you've been told is being held in your honor. When you get there, you find that all the others are wearing formal gowns and tuxedos – everyone but you. There is an elaborate array of food and drink, but you are allergic to everything on the buffet. Periodically, the other guests start to engage in an elaborate, intricate dance, which you have never seen before, to music that you cannot hear. Hardly anyone speaks to you; eventually, someone does, but turns away before you reply. As the partygoers frolic on, you feel increasingly helpless and ghostlike...*

This nightmare scenario is a fair approximation of the experience that many people have at "their" annual team meetings and case conferences. Unfortunately, for many people, the meetings of "their" circles of support and the groups coming together for "their" person-centered planning are not much different.

Those of us with a deep commitment to community involvement and full participation for people with disabilities are often in the forefront of setting up circles of support and person-centered processes. Ironically, the same passion that may make us tireless advocates and supporters may lead us to "use up all the oxygen" at a meeting, leaving less opportunity for others to be heard who do not speak with our certainty or our fluency. I have attended many meetings over the years in which family members, friends and allies, each wishing nothing but the best for the person on whose behalf the meeting is being held, inadvertently but very effectively prevent that

---

*This chapter is taken from my article "On Being a Communication Ally," which was first published in the *Facilitated Communication Digest*. It is based, in part, on a series of workshops which Nancy Kalina and I have developed and presented collaboratively over the past several years. I gratefully acknowledge her contributions to both the analysis and the specific recommendations made here

person from having any but a token voice in the proceedings. It is often the most powerful and persuasive allies, who, "on a roll," move the process forward far too fast for the "guest of honor." Rather than having the opportunity to take ownership of the process, that guest of honor may end up "being processed."

This chapter is an exercise in undoing such inadvertent bulldozing, in order to make our practices consistent with our ideals. The specific "how-to" suggestions are located at the end of the chapter. The theoretical orientation at the beginning of the chapter and the general principles in the chapter's center form a necessary framework for the specific recommendations that follow.

Confronting fluency privilege

As we enter the 21st Century, the issue of *privilege* is slowly, and with much resistance, percolating into the consciousness of the population at large. In my hometown, there has been a major effort directed toward community-wide race dialogues; one of the most prominent features of those dialogues has been the acknowledgment by white participants (often for the first time in their lives) that they are the beneficiaries of white privilege. They come to recognize and talk openly of some things that they expect and feel entitled to in their neighborhoods, workplaces and daily interactions which cannot be taken for granted in those same situations by people of color.

Privilege is a loaded term in many ways. For most sorts of privilege (white privilege, male privilege, and heterosexual privilege, for example), the people who are least aware of its existence are usually those who are its biggest beneficiaries. The term smacks of unfair advantage (which it is) and of a vague moral "not-niceness" which tends to make most privileged people feel unfairly put-upon. Many well-meaning people feel accused of possessing a privileged status in one or more domains, which they have never actively sought for themselves. While such feelings are understandable, they must not be a barrier to action. One cannot truly be a social and political ally to marginalized members of the community without recognizing and owning one's privileged status in various domains.

To understand the role of a *communication ally,* which will be presented in this chapter, it is useful to focus attention on a form of privilege that, as yet, has no commonly recognized name. I will refer to it here as *fluency privilege,* which I define as **the advantages auto-**

matically accruing to people who are competent, fluent speakers of the standard dialect or dominant language of a given society.

For most Americans raised speaking English, the concept of fluency privilege may be a difficult one to grasp. Most of us acquired our privileged status at a relatively young age, and most of us have had few personal adult experiences in which our fluency privilege was not fully operating. Consequently, when we see others experiencing the social effects of a lack of fluency, we may be more likely to focus on other aspects of their circumstances which might lead to negative social consequences -- their immigrant status, perhaps, or their disability -- and we may not attend to fluency as a social issue.

It is often through dramatic personal experiences that we become conscious of some previously invisible privilege. Here are two ways in which the issue of fluency privilege was brought home to me.

***

Several years ago, my wife Mara and I, vacationing in the French town of Besançon, decided to take a canoe trip advertised in a local tourist brochure. She and I are both moderately experienced whitewater canoeists; we both speak, reasonably well, the French we learned in high school. We set off in the company of our guide, the driver, and several German tourists.

As we all rode in the shuttle van up the river to the place where our trip would start, Mara and I were increasingly apprehensive about what we saw. The river flowed quietly for the most part, but every mile or so it tumbled over two-foot or three-foot dams through narrow spillways. We asked our guide, an athletic-looking young man, whether we would be portaging around the dams. No, he assured us, we would be running them, and everything would be fine. The driver and the guide spoke for a time, quietly and rapidly; Mara and I tried to follow their conversation without total success; the gist of it was that the driver proposed the possibility of canoeing a different stretch of the river, which the guide rejected.

Mara and I tried to ask the guide again if he was sure that the stretch of the river we would be running was safe, and he brushed off our question with a breezy assurance. We all set out, with the guide and his partner leading the way to show us how to run the dams. The guide ran the first dam successfully; three of the other canoes, including ours, capsized. We were swept down the river, and I came closer to drowning than I ever want to be again; Mara and I have not been whitewater canoeing since.

In our angry conversation afterwards with the owner of the tour company, we learned that the young man guiding us had, in fact, never run that stretch of the river before. Although he was an experienced canoeist, our trip took place on his first day of working for the company. The owner agreed that running that stretch of the river with the water as high as it was had been a case of poor judgement.

The next day, as Mara and I revisited our experience, we recognized how we had felt powerless to negotiate the day before; we also saw the ways in which our lack of fluency had contributed to that powerlessness. Although we both spoke enough French to understand the guide, and to make ourselves fairly well understood, our lack of fluency limited the number of questions we could ask that the guide was willing to answer. He would have had patience for many more detailed questions if we were all fluent in the same language. We were limited in the specificity with which we could obtain information, and in the opportunity to engage in casual conversation (which might have told us, for example, that he had just arrived in Besançon the day before.) Mara and I were both clear that, had the interaction taken place in West Virginia or Colorado rather than in France, we would have been active participants in the decision not to run the river, rather than bedraggled victims of the guide's mistaken self-assurance.

***

Several years ago, I was operated on for oral cancer. For a week after the surgery, I breathed through a tracheotomy, was unable to speak, and communicated by slowly and shakily writing notes on a stenographer's pad. My mouth and throat were filled with a seeming ocean of mucus following the surgery; I relied for my survival on the wall-mounted suction machine, with its long hose and hard plastic mouthpiece. The hose and mouthpiece often clogged; I would clear them by dipping the mouthpiece in a glass of water. When that didn't work, and the hose or mouthpiece needed to be replaced, I had only a few minutes "breathing space" before I would begin choking.

One afternoon, the hose and mouthpiece both clogged, and I waited an endless-seeming 15 minutes until the nurse responded to my buzzer. When she asked me why I had buzzed, I started to write, "My suction is clogged -- the tube and mouthpiece need to be replaced." I wrote MY SUCTION IS. and the nurse started out the door, saying, "Oh, I see, you need a new mouthpiece. I'll get it for you." I knew that merely replacing the mouthpiece wouldn't work, and I was already gasping for air. I flung my notebook at her, and hit her in the back of the head. Startled and angry, she came back to yell at me; I kept pounding my pencil on the table-top and gestured, until grudgingly she returned my notebook to me. I scrawled my panic-stricken message in its entirety, making sure she did not leave until I was done. "Oh," she snorted, and with ill grace returned a few minutes later with my precious suction hose. I'm sure she went home that night to tell someone about the rude patient who had attacked her.

**

I am embarrassed to admit that, despite a focus on supporting the communication of people with disabilities throughout my adult life, and despite years of having considered these issues from a political as well as from a clinical point of view, it took dramatic events such as the ones I just described to alert me to the real power of fluency privilege. I am humbled by the knowledge that the occurrences I described above, which feel like major events in my life, are often the ordinary stuff of life-long daily struggle for many of my friends with disabilities and for the people with whom I work.

Since my cancer surgery, which left me with limited movement of my tongue and a hole in my soft palate, my speech has often been difficult for many people to understand. I pause in my speech in ways that are often misinterpreted as my being finished with what I had to say, and I may need to repeat a word or phrase several times, or spell a word out letter by letter, to make sure I am being understood. I speak slowly compared to most other people, and have a great deal of difficulty jumping into a conversation when many people are speaking at once.

However, these limitations to my fluency have not prevented me from continuing to be an assertive communicator in my family and in my professional and social communities. Despite my limitations, I possess a sense of entitlement, captured by the phrase, "I have a right to be heard." Is this because I began to experience limitations in fluency only after a lifetime of fluency privilege, acquired on my journey to my status as a native-English-speaking middle-aged professional European-American male? I often wonder what my situation would be today if I sounded the way I do, but did not have this deeply ingrained feeling that I have something important to say, and that the world owes me an audience.

Equity grows from the social uses of communication

Over the years, I have worked with many people with varying levels of communicative impairments. Like most other professionals I know, I began my work in this area assuming that the difficulties which people were experiencing primarily affected their ability to obtain information from, and convey information to, other people. Many professionals, teachers and speech pathologists in particular, focus their remedial efforts in these areas. But such an approach often ignores the reasons for communicating that have little to do with the conveyance of information, the reasons that most fluently speaking people, most of the time, are such eager communicators. People who have never communicated from a position of privilege often experience their greatest barriers with regard to these *social*, rather than *informational*, dimensions of communication. They include, among others:

- **Social connection:** When I get on an elevator with a co-worker, and I say, "Beautiful day, isn't it?" and he says, "Oh, it's great! This is my favorite time of year!" he is unlikely to have learned any new information about the weather, and I am unlikely to have learned anything significant about his personal preferences. What we may mean, at some level, could more directly be expressed by my saying to him, "You're a pleasant-looking person, and I'd like to experiment in a non-committal way with having a conversation with you," to which he could respond, "I'm agreeable -- let's see how it goes for the length of this elevator ride, and that will give us a basis for connecting the next time we see each other."

  Of course, nobody ever talks like that —we've been socialized not to— and that's why the weather is such a popular topic of conversation. We use the rituals of communication as ways of establishing social connections with each other. These rituals often rely on split-second timing, intonational nuance, and other features that are particularly challenging for non-fluent people.

- **Claiming a persona:** Many people my age have experienced the eye-rolling exasperation of our teen-aged children when we use words that were in vogue with young people the last time we checked. What we are trying to do at such a moment (unsuccessfully) is to tell our listeners about the kinds of people we are. It's as if we are saying, "Please notice that I am intelligent/ sophisticated/ witty/ sensitive/ folksy/self-confident/modest/ trustworthy/ loveable. etc." Increasingly, focus groups are used to help political candidates perfect the nuances of the ways in which they deliver their messages to the public. As one of their main tasks, these groups reflect back to the candidate the persona that he or she is projecting. Often, this persona is considered far more important than the actual content of the candidates' positions.

- **Making something happen:** When I answer a state trooper's questions after he has pulled me over for speeding, I am only minimally concerned with the informational content of what I say. My efforts are much more intensely directed at trying to work a kind of magic with my words that will somehow remind the trooper of the wonderful feeling he will experience when he sends me off with a warning instead of a ticket.

  Influencing outcomes is a challenge for non-fluent people even in two-person interactions; in meetings or other larger group processes, the barriers to a non-fluent person's full participation may sometimes feel insurmountable.

If we were to assume communication is only about the exchange of information, then we could conclude that what people with limited fluency need most are the services of expert clinicians. However, a shift of focus toward social uses of communication will lead the professional and lay-advocate alike away from the role of therapist, and toward the equally important but rarely recognized role of *communication ally*.

What is a communication ally?

Communication allies are people who use their fluency privilege on behalf of people who experience limited or impaired ability to communicate fluently. Their tools include their long-term experience and emotional comfort in settings where communication takes place. They also take advantage of the respect and deference that they are shown by others as a benefit of their fluency privilege. What they do with those tools is create a safe and empowered place for the communication of the non-fluent people with whom they ally themselves.

In a presentation called "On Being a Communication Ally," Nancy Kalina and I made a rough attempt to define the role of communication ally, specifically in the context of planning meetings or other activities in the organizational domain:

In a social situation or meeting, the communication ally is someone who has agreed to have, as his/her most important role, making sure that the situation is structured so that the person is fully **informed, heard** and **respected** throughout the proceedings. (Shevin & Kalina, 1997).

The communication ally, through his or her actions, serves to counteract both the *systemic oppression* (i.e., the disempowering and dismissive ways that institutions and their representatives treat non-fluent people) and the *internalized oppression* (i.e., the negative self-images and feelings of powerlessness) experienced by people who are not fluent speakers in a particular community.

The art of being a communication ally: General principles

Communication allies vary their specific actions depending upon the social circumstances in which they and the people they are allied with find themselves. However, there are some fundamental principles that undergird those actions:

Respectful assumptions concerning the speaker. In this role, it's useful to ground ourselves by being aware of the assumptions we tend to bring to our interactions with new students, clients or coalition partners. The key to this activity is remembering that these are *assumptions*; in other words, they are the starting points, the "default values" on which we act until we receive specific information to the contrary.

My personal assumptions are fluid. The last time I stepped back and considered what they were, this is the list I developed:

My Assumptions About My Communication Partners
- *They are highly intelligent.*
- *They have a deep interest in fostering relations with others (and possibly with me.)*
- *They have stories they would like to tell, if the circumstances are right.*

- *They have positive images of themselves that they wish to present as part of their communication.*
- *Regardless of appearances, they are paying attention to me when I interact with them.*

These are assumptions, not guarantees; but since we tend to find what we go looking for, my interactions with people tend to take on the respectful flavor of this list of assumptions.

Exercise

Reflection on Assumptions

Label a piece of paper "My Assumptions About New [Clients, Students, Patients, etc.]" and write a spontaneous list of assumptions for yourself. Then set it aside and go do something else. When you return to the list after a break, ask yourself:

- *Do I really assume these things, or does the list consist more of things I feel I'm supposed to believe, but don't?*
- *Do I tend to find what I go looking for in these people?*
- *Is that what I want, or would other assumptions serve us all better?*
- *What stands in the way of those other assumptions?*

Respectful listening practices. A communication ally is, most fundamentally, a respectful listener. I wish to place emphasis here on the concept of *respectful* listening, rather than the more general ideas of "good listening skills" or "reflective listening." By respectful listening, I mean the honor we give people by conveying to them, "your words are important to me, just because **you** are saying them."

Many of us have had the experience of meeting a famous celebrity, or a personal hero of ours. In such highly charged moments, we tend to pay attention to exactly what that person has to say -- even if it is only to rent a car from us, or order lunch. That's one snapshot of respectful listening. My friend Eugene Marcus summarized his advice on respectful listening in a single sentence:

> *Treat everybody like a visiting dignitary who may not speak your language very well."*

The practices of respectful listening are well known; for some people, however, they are second nature, while for others they are only mastered through thoughtful practice. They include:

- Dedicating enough time for the communication to unfold. Patience is increasingly important for all of us in our speeded-up world; for the person with communication impairments, time may be the single most important factor in gaining real access to the conversational community.

I learned an important lesson on this topic from my friend "Jonathan." I used to see Jonathan about once a week; I'd bring him over to my house where we could relax, and carry on a conversation using facilitated communication. At the time, I was the only person in Jonathan's life who facilitated with him regularly, so those two hours a week were his only real opportunity for extensive conversation.

Jonathan insisted on following an exact routine each time he came over. He would use the manual sign for "soda," and I would get him a can of Coke* from the refrigerator. He would drink it while lying on the couch with his feet up and his head resting on my lap. Only after finishing his Coke* would he be interested in conversing with me, and the can of Coke* could last him as long as 45 minutes.

After several weeks of this routine, I spoke to Jonathan of my frustration. "I hate wasting our limited time like this," I told him. "Isn't there any way we could hurry through the Coke* time?"

"No," Jonathan typed. "This time is important. When we are talking, I am in your world. When we are quiet, you are in mine."

"Oh," I said, and stayed quiet.

Dedicating enough time to respect the speaker's communication often requires postponing a conversation until a time when you can give it the attention it deserves, and making sure that such time is made available without significant delay.

It's useful to be aware of our cultural propensity of "filling in awkward silences" – and to resist that tendency. (This is not only a disability related issue, but one that also appears in contacts between members of different cultural and ethnic communities. For example, many Native American groups consider it terribly disrespectful to answer a question immediately – it means you haven't thought seriously before answering!) In practice, filling in the awkward silences may prevent the slow answerer from ever being able to find a break in the conversation that's long enough for him or her to respond.

- Making sure you have really understood what the person is telling you.

  Clarence was a 70-year-old man with whom I had a passing acquaintance at the state institution where I worked in North Dakota. He spent most of his leisure time hanging out at the facility's cafeteria, engaging staff in conversation when they were there on their breaks.

  Clarence's speech was almost impossible to understand, but that didn't stop him from trying. When I first got to know him, I would engage with him in the same way I saw most other people doing: I would say hello, smile and nod and say "Uh-huh" several times while he talked, and find the most convenient and inoffensive way to leave as soon as seemed polite. After several such conversations, though, I began to question what I was doing, and engaged in the more frustrating activity of telling him I hadn't understood him, and asking him to repeat what he had said. Often, he and I would struggle for five minutes so I could make sense of a single sentence. Sometimes I would have to leave before I understood, and I would apologize; I'd remind him the next time we met that we might have unfinished business.

  Was this frustrating? I know it was to me, and perhaps it was to him as well. But the effort seemed worth it -- because I had realized that my previous polite nods and smiles had symbolically meant, "I'm sure that what you're saying isn't worth hearing."

- Making sure you have the *full* message. Not only must you understand what you've heard; you must also make sure you've heard all there is to hear."Getting the gist" of what someone is saying may be enough in some situations, but it conveys little respect. Also, you may have missed the most important part, as I described earlier when I spoke of hitting the nurse with the notebook to get her to listen to my full request.

- Avoiding the sidetracking or appropriation of the conversation. Many of the habits of our everyday informal conversations can stand as barriers to respectful listening. These include interrupting, correcting real or perceived mistakes, "topping" someone's story with one of our own, and offering advice which has not been sought.

Most fluent speakers in a community have learned to continue their speaking assertively in the face of such obstacles. However, for the person with communication impairment or limited fluency, these interruptions and distractions, and the message of disrespect conveyed, may be enough to make further communication feel unsafe, or block it altogether.

Speaking respectfully. Although the roots of respectful speaking are contained in the practices of respectful listening, there are some additional issues which communication allies attend to, so that what they say and how they say it advances the safety and empowerment of the individuals they are supporting.

- Attending to the physical aspects of the communication. Much of respect in speaking is conveyed by the means of communication rather than its content. Such issues as physical proximity, positioning of the participants, eye contact, tone of voice, facial expression, loudness and pitch of speech, and time allowed between utterances all convey messages of differential power and respect.

Exercise
Physical Aspects of Communication

This exercise can be done by yourself; it is more effective done while taking turns and debriefing with a partner.

Think of how you might ask the question "What are you doing?" to a skilled glass-blower giving a demonstration at a craft fair. Now think of how you might ask the same question to a five-year-old you found drawing on the bedroom wall with crayons. How would your actions differ? (Consider such aspects as tone of voice, loudness, facial expression, physical proximity, how long you wait before beginning to speak, how long you wait before repeating or reframing your question, etc.)

Now think of how you would ask the same question to a disabled friend sitting and fiddling with a piece of string. Listen to what you sound like.

- Talking **to** people rather than **about** them. Nearly all non-fluent communicators (and many fluent ones with obvious physical disabilities) have experienced being talked about in their presence as if they were not there. This conveys a clear message of disrespect.
- Using questions in a respectful way. Generally, the person who asks the most questions is the one with the most power. Some of that power differential can be relinquished, and questions can be asked respectfully, by several means. The ally can invite ques-

tions as well as asking them (e.g., "Is there anything you'd like to know about me?"); he or she can ask questions for clarification, rather than in an inquisitorial, "let's-see-if-you-understand-what-I'm-talking-about" way; and the ally can ask permission before raising significant topics. (The social conventions of "If you don't mind my asking." or "Could you tell me." are markers that signify I am asking someone for something that is his or her right to bestow, rather than my right to demand.)

- Accommodative turn taking. Respectful communication is reciprocal, but true reciprocity is a complex issue when dealing with individuals who are non-fluent. On one hand, such people may require much longer than usual to get their messages across, and thus may need more than an equal share of the conversational time. On the other hand, non-fluent communication can be exhausting, and the person communicating may feel put on the spot if required to "hold the floor" for long periods of time. Accommodative turn taking should be attended to, but the details must be worked out anew with each individual.

Translating general principles into specific actions: the communication ally at the planning meeting

The communication ally who has established a respectful, reciprocal relationship with another person is well-positioned to support that person as a powerful communicator on his or her own behalf. Such support is particularly valuable in settings such as formal "team meetings" and circle meetings. Regardless of their structure, or the philosophical vision behind them, meetings *in general* have served to affirm the social distance between people with disabilities or other communication challenges on one hand, and the fluent communicators in their lives on the other. In those settings, people with communication impairments have typically been ignored; they have not been supported in preparing for the meetings to the extent that professionals and team leaders have; they lack official status; and they may be oblivious to the relative status in the hierarchy possessed by other meeting participants.

When I speak to groups about the role of communication ally, I am often asked, "Shouldn't *everybody* in the meeting be the person's communication ally?" In one sense, of course, the answer is *yes* —everyone in the group should be conscious of his or her ability to affirm the person's communication and support that person's empowerment. However, when I speak of the role of the communication ally in a formal setting such as a meeting, I am referring to the specific definition found above, where the communication ally sees that role as his or her sole function. In the formal setting of a team meeting, the communication ally is deliberately stepping out of any other roles he or she plays in the person's life as a way of focusing completely on supporting that person's communication.

To be effective as someone's communication ally in formal situations such as meetings, the communication ally must be active in that role not only during the meeting, but before and after it as well.

Before. In preparation for the meeting, some of the communication ally's tasks might include:

- Learn the person's **formal** and **informal** agendas for the meeting. It may be important to Lily that we talk about the logistics of getting adequate job training; it may also be important to her that nobody gets mad at her during the meeting. The communication ally should be aware of both of these.

- Tell the person what other issues are going to be brought to the meeting. If the person is to be an effective strategizer within the group, he or she needs as much information as possible in advance of the meeting.

- Brainstorm logistics. (Depending on the situation, the meeting's facilitator may or may not be involved in this discussion.) The discussion could include such questions as "Who else would you like to make sure will be at the meeting? Who would you like to be sitting next to you? How will you let me know you are getting scared or upset, or need a break?"

- Help the person prepare written materials in advance. Often the lowest-status person at a meeting is the only one who arrives without a written report, plan, list of issues, etc. By coming with a written agenda, list of questions, or an open letter to the planning team, the person is able to assert his or her official status as a primary player.

- Clear your own agenda prior to the meeting. You cannot attend the meeting both as the person's communication ally and as a passionate advocate for a specific issue in that person's life. If such advocacy is needed, find someone else to attend the meeting as the champion of that particular issue. If you are the only such champion available, then you should help the person find a different communication ally for that meeting.

During. The communication ally empowers the non-fluent person by creating the space for that person to process what's happening effectively, and to be heard throughout the proceedings. As the meeting progresses, most communication allies must work very hard to remain "in character." There is often a strong temptation to become an active participant in the meeting, forcefully representing one's own point of view. This is a dangerous tradeoff; short-term gains are obtained by sacrificing the opportunity for the person to actually become someone with a speaking role in his or her own life.

Some specific actions of the communication ally during a meeting might include:

- Monitor logistics. The ally checks in with the person being supported to make sure that seating, acoustics, and other aspects of the meeting support that person's comfortable and empowered participation.

- Make sure that agendas are reviewed at the beginning of the meeting. Often there are last-minute changes or previously unspoken agenda items brought to a meeting. The person who is not a fluent communicator should be apprized of this at the outset.

- SLOW IT DOWN! The greatest barrier to a communicatively impaired person's full participation in his or her own meeting is often someone else's impatience to get it over with so they can get on to something "more important." The communication ally is often well positioned to make sure that the brakes are applied on occasions when false closure is being imposed on a situation in which one or more people have unanswered questions, vague semi-commitments, or serious misgivings.

- Check in with the person. It's important to know that the person has been following the conversation despite obstacles such as rapidity, multiple simultaneous speakers, or use of professional jargon. The communication ally also keeps track of the person's comfort level with the discussion, and his or her agreement with what's being decided. In the heat of discussion during a lively meeting, it's the communication ally whose role it is to remind the group of the difference between someone's actual agreement and his or her silence being read as acquiescence.

- Take the person's "irrelevancies" seriously. I have been at many meetings when the conversation has gone more or less as follows:
  Team leader: "What progress has Joe made on his second and third vocational goals since last September?"
  Joe: "Pet store. Little dog."
  Team leader: "No, Joe, we're not talking about that now. we're discussing your vocational goals."
  Joe: "Pet store. Doggie."
  Team leader: "Joe, we can talk about that after the meeting. That's not what we're talking about now."
  Joe becomes silent, and walks out of the room while the rest of the team talks. Several days later, in a chance conversation with Joe's day habilitation worker, the team leader finds out that the day habilitation worker and Joe had visited a pet store during the previous week, Joe had played with the puppies, and the day habilitation worker had talked with the pet-store owner about the possibility of Joe getting a part-time job there.

  Had there been a communication ally present, he or she could have attended to Joe's persistent talking about the pet store, and explored more deeply with Joe why the topic was coming up in this particular discussion. Had that been the case, the entire team might have had the opportunity to help Joe think about an exciting work possibility.

- Negotiate modifications to support the person's full participation. Many of us live our lives following our Day Runners as we rush from meeting to meeting. Although we may complain of this, it's a pretty fair guess that for most of us in this situation, meetings feel like home. For other people, meetings may feel like ventures into alien territory. On their behalf, a communication ally may propose modifications to the meeting which allow the person's continued active participation. These might include taking frequent breaks, breaking out from large group discussions into one-to-one conversations where the person might feel more free to speak, or reprioritizing the agenda to focus on issues of greatest importance to the person.

- Press for details when needed. As meetings plod forward and participants get tired, there may be a tendency to become vague about time-lines, individual responsibilities, or follow-up meetings. The communication ally can be helpful in obtaining as much specific information as possible while the group is all assembled, and can help establish reporting dates and check-in points when specific information is not available. (This is another example of a place where the meeting-experienced person can be a strong ally to someone who is not.)

The role of communication ally calls for significant assertiveness; it calls for speaking out of turn, and for interrupting the smooth flow of routine. In my experience, most teams have eagerly welcomed allies taking on that role, *when the allies made the role they were taking explicit from the outset.*

After: Any of the professionals attending a meeting on someone's behalf could easily call other participants if they have misgivings, are unsure of exactly what got decided, or wish to check on the progress of various team members toward getting plans rolling. But what if the person on whose behalf the meeting was held was to have similar misgivings or confusion? Many of the people we support do not have the luxury of being able to initiate conversations or phone calls independently, and may need an ally's help in doing so. Also, "buyer's remorse," the opportunity to change your mind because you're having second thoughts, should not only be the prerogative of the privileged few. Some of the ways in which a communication ally can be helpful after a meeting include:

- Review the meeting minutes with the person after the meeting. A few days after the meeting, it's useful to check with the person to make sure he or she understands what's included in the minutes, and still agrees with what has been decided.

- Help the person monitor whether decisions reached are being followed up appropriately. Unfortunately, commitments made at meetings are sometimes not acted upon. I have sometimes attended meetings where wonderful-sounding goals are developed; someone then speaks up and reminds the group that nearly identical-sounding goals had been adopted, and then forgotten about, in the previous year. The communication ally can assist the person for whom planning was done in making sure things happen. A professional receiving a letter with a formal request for update information from a client that he or she serves is unlikely to disregard it.

Conclusion

The preceding section has emphasized the specific *actions* that a communication ally can take to support the empowerment of a person with limited fluency in structured settings. In focusing on the details of these actions, however, it's important not to lose the big picture. The spirit in which those actions are taken is more important than the specific acts themselves. If the communication ally "does all the right things," but does them in a way that keeps him or herself at the center of attention of the group, then the purpose of playing that role will have been defeated. Fundamentally, communication allies are people who refuse to continuously occupy the center, thus clearing the way for other people who have systematically been pushed to the margins. In doing so, the communication allies honor not only those previously marginalized people; but also the group process. Creating a space for all to participate in the process makes the importance of that process unmistakable; it can turn an ordinary meeting into a sacred place. Deliberately choosing to act as communication allies can be a challenging experience, leading us to behave in novel ways that may seem awkward at first. But in doing our work on behalf of the people with whom we ally ourselves, we create spaces in which being awkward is not a barrier to being powerful. As we do that work, we find that new freedom and power has been opened up for ourselves as well; we become both more skilled and graceful, and more fearless even in moments when skill or grace seems lacking.

Little of the work of the communication ally is overtly revolutionary or dramatically transformative. More often, in tiny, uneventful-seeming increments, non-fluent people become, over time, the engines driving their lives forward, and the deepest sources of information about their own destinations.

Reference

Shevin, M., & N. Kalina. (1997). *On Being a Communication Ally.* Presentation at the annual conference of TASH, Boston, December 1997.

17

Getting Beyond Sick
Overcoming Medical Obstacles To Development

Karen Green McGowan

Some 37 years ago, I stumbled into the field of developmental disabilities. I never intended to be here, I wanted to be a nurse-midwife delivering babies in the Kentucky hills. It was 1965, and I was hired to staff the newly organized "Diagnostic and Evaluation Team" at the middle-western mental retardation facility 10 miles from my home. The *real* hospitals were 20 miles away and working at one of them required me to regularly traverse the most dangerous road in the state. I had just been discharged from the United States Air Force. I was not enthused about this new job. The director of my nursing school told me I would ruin my career if I went to work in this facility.

There were 1200 persons living in the "state school" and the cost per person was $6 a day. The average zoo spent more money on their inhabitants than the state did in this institution. I was one of only six nurses on staff. I got the diagnostic team job because no one else wanted it. I had scarcely clapped eyes on a person with any type of disability before.

The facility admitted 130 persons a year and the D&E team also controlled the back door, supervising the small group of persons being readied for community transition. Meanwhile, residents were dying at the rate of 2-3 per month, most from choking on food or status epilepticus. Both residents and staff contracted Hepatitis C on a regular basis.

In the building that housed almost 240 people who couldn't walk, there were only 20 wheelchairs. Most of these were unsuitable for anyone, let alone a person with complex musculo-skeletal deformity. People simply moved from their beds to mats on the floor, always on their backs. Staffing ratios were dismal, often only one person to attend to 24 to 30 persons who could do nothing for themselves. Keeping the wards clean and smelling good was an almost impossible task. Meals were served from a large rolling cart of smashed potatoes, vegetable and mystery meat. The dietary department allowed only an hour before they claimed their cart back.

Person-centered planning was a generation away. Multi-disciplinary was the buzzword of the moment. The physician was the leader of the team. Most of the MD's on our staff could not qualify for a license to practice medicine outside the institution, and few could speak understandable English.

The term "multi-handicapped" was used to describe persons who didn't move well, and who often had complex seizure disorders and sensory deficits as well. At that time, we had no idea that the bizarre deformity patterns, such as twisted spines and limbs that would not bend or straighten, came as a direct result of lying on the back over time. Trunk and limbs fall in whatever direction gravity chooses to take them. No one knew that managing a person's position 24 hours a day and helping him or her to move actively is the antidote for the damage caused by movement deprivation. Neither did we know that food and other secretions are forced to struggle through a tortuous route in bodies squashed and twisted by the passing of years without proper support. The internal organs can never function well in corkscrew, horizontal alignment when our bodies were designed to drain internally in the upright position with the nose, naval and knees pointing in the same direction.

Meanwhile, not only were persons with any type of developmental disability perceived as a burden to society, the staff that worked with them were devalued as well. The first class-action court case was years away. Those who were court committed to state mental retardation facilities were treated as if "legally dead" and human rights were not recognized.

There were over 200,000 people in state operated DD facilities in the United States. Community placement at my facility really meant moving anyone over age 21 to a nursing home or to a county home in their community of legal settlement. You were more likely to be discharged in a hearse than to move to another setting.

In the early 1970's, parents began demanding "treatment", because mental retardation was perceived as a medical problem. The medical model was alive and well. "Active treatment" was the term of choice, and no one really understood what it meant. Please be clear that if I need my appendix removed, I wouldn't want a teacher to do it, but I don't get my whole life stuck in the medical model because my limbs or eyes don't move as good as they should. But if you were carrying the label "multi-handicapped", nurses and therapists were likely to dominate your future with doses of treatment that seldom made a difference. Most of them had no training or experience with people with strange looking bodies.

The most constructive change in our field came from families unwilling to choose between abusive systems or no service at all. While I cringe to characterize a facility that I was a part of for 7 years in that way, the fact is that no one's life seemed improved after living at our place for a few years. We were good at blaming the person with the disability for the problem ("that's the way they are, you know"), but in our guts we knew that no child or adult thrives in an environment without stimulus. With few staff around, the only role models were persons with bizarre survival behaviors, such as body rocking, squealing or acting out.

Parents were sent away and advised not to return for at least three months to give their child a chance to "adjust". Within months, a significant percentage of these newly admitted children died, more from the lack of human interaction than any other factor. My team was the gatekeeper for this facility. We did everything we could to prevent admissions, but few other services were available. Families were often at the end of their rope when they came to us.

But so what? In the 1960's, death was seen as a treatment option for persons with increasingly twisted bodies, persons who were seen as having no productive future. No one understood the impact of gravity and immobility on every part of the body and the consequences for every other organ, included the developing brain.

Person centered planning

In the mid-1970's, we created a process called 24-hour Planning, which focused on looking at what a person with complex disabilities would be doing if he or she were leading a life closer to the life of a person of the same age without disabilities. We distinguished "how" a person got assistance from "what" the person was assisted to do. The mission was to change the "how's" in ways that helped to reduce medical obstacles to participation without taking away the "what's" that made life worth living. So what if I have to roll places instead of walk? What will it take to get me there? So what if I have a tube to eat with, what will it take to taste some of that birthday cake? So what if I have a seizure or two in places where regular people might see me. What a good learning opportunity for them; they won't get so shook the next time.

Turns out, as people who didn't look like the rest of us began showing up in restaurants, rock concerts, shopping malls, regular classrooms and the like, they didn't get sicker, they didn't have more seizures, and they didn't break all their bones. They often became more responsive, slept less, communicated more predictably, and learned more from spending well supported time in the same places the rest of us do.

These changes came from the passionate and creative pursuit of two ideas.

• All people have similar needs. Services that ignore these needs create profound barriers to health and development.

• Function –what a behavior does for a person- is more important than the form of an intervention. Assisting a person with complex disabilities to move actively and experience positions in the same planes that the rest of us do is a full time health requirement that can't be met with periodic doses of therapy. Assuring that this assistance gives people access to real life experiences is fundamental.

At first, the ideas behind 24-hour planning and the practices that support people with complex disabilities to participate in real life were on the fringes of services. Not till the mid-1980's did it dawn on the field as a whole that each person with obstacles to development might have unique characteristics and needs. While we gave lip service to this as early as the 1960's ("The mentally retarded are more like other people than different), I don't think anyone really believed it then.

What every person needs

Basic human needs are the same regardless of the type or extent of a person's disability. We all need someone in our life who is passionate about our welfare and (probably) not paid to care about us. We need access to persons and places that stimulate learning. We need a place to live and help with things we can't do on our own. We need to be seen as valuable human beings with access to family and friends. We need chances to make mistakes and learn from them. We need to communicate with persons who understand what we are saying. We need to move our muscles and joints and bear weight on our long bones.

We also need touch and interaction that most of us may not recognize or talk about, but the need is there just the same:

*It is not words so much as acts communicating affection
and involvement that children, and, indeed adults require.
Tactile sensations become tactile perceptions according to the
meanings with which they have been invested by experience. When affection and involvement are conveyed through
touch, it is those meanings, as well as the security-giving
satisfactions with which touch will become associated. Hence
the human significance of touching (Montague, 1978, p.139).*

Unfortunately, if a person looks funny and has no formal way to communicate pleasure or distaste, tactile stimulation can be delivered in ways that are silly, useless and further dehumanizing. There are countless sensory stimulation rooms in use today that bombard their occupants with meaningless sound, light, smell and touch. Most of the time, these approaches help caretakers feel good when they don't know what else to do. Meanwhile, these approaches may cause the person to seize or pull into withdrawal.

Worse yet, many people are scared to touch an individual whose body is shaped differently at all. If that person carries a diagnosis of brittle bones (osteoporosis), she or he is really up a creek without a paddle. Many is the therapist I have talked to who says, "I am scared if I touch her she will break-I have had no experience or training with this type of person!" The therapist then resorts to the only thing that looks safe or logical which is usually passive range of motion.

This activity is much like going to your favorite exercise guru and asking: "Look, I'd like to change the shape of my body and my favorite activity is horseback riding. How many calories per hour credit do I get for riding a horse?" Responds the guru, "Zip –the credit goes to the horse".

The secret is in getting the person to move. Turns out, all we have to do is support the person in total opposition to gravity, and automatic movement mechanisms in the body tell her to weight shift, move her head and so on. Active movement is much more powerful than movement imposed by one body acting on another, such as that seen in passive range of motion, which, when done by persons without training and supervision, can actually cause harm.

This is a largely unrecognized but universal human need: to move and use the body and its parts in ways as close as possible to those used by the rest of us from the time we're very young. Lack of active movement tends to turn us all to stone as we age, which is one reason why getting older becomes associated with creaky joints and increasing health problems. Couch potatoes get junk in their arteries, joints that ache and refuse to work and stomachs and intestines that back up and refuse to function, much like a clogged plumbing system.

Infants born with obstacles to movement need help to move in the ways that nature intended. Getting the help you need to move and experience a variety of positions in your day is a need not only for persons with problems, but for the rest of us as well. When we do it too much, sitting on our rear ends tends to broaden that part of our bodies. Lying on one's back for too much time tends to let gravity reshape and flatten the surface most often exposed. Known as the "Secretary's Law", the rule is that the weight bearing surface will always elongate. If you don't believe me, watch how the shape of the rear end changes when a person sits down on it.

Form versus function

People with movement problems don't need doses of physical therapy a few times a week. They need physical management 24 hours a day seven days a week. We can't do this if we define people's needs through the eyes of the medical model; we have to express their needs in another way. Everyone in the person's life has to assume responsibility for managing these interventions. Physical therapists are one group who might be helpful in figuring out how to do this —or they may not be helpful if they lack proper training and experience.

The issue is physical management, a term that has come to mean assisting a person to move actively and experience positions in the same planes that the rest of us do. Coming to total opposition to gravity is what needs to happen by the end of the first year of life. Whether the baby does this on his own or needs a piece of equipment to make the position possible, the benefits include reshaping the hips and chest, putting calcium in the long bones, preparing the joints close to the body to support walking, reaching and grasping and other forms of trouble. Your baby is walking at 10 months! (You poor thing.)

Form versus function is a big issue in planning for anyone. We are likely to focus on the form of a behavior, rather than honing in on its function in the person's life. Everyone needs to move and experience a variety of positions across 24 hours that alter weight-bearing surfaces and change the force of gravity on the body. When someone has movement problems, it requires everyone's participation to meet that need.

If you and I are overweight, we usually have to change our life style 24 hours a day, seven days a week in order to change the shape of the body. The same thing holds true with persons who don't move well on their own. They need a range of positions across 24 hours that help with active movement, that change the way gravity works on the body, and that allow food and fluid to move from the top to the bottom of the trunk with the least interference. Physical therapy is a form of intervention. Moving in ways that are healthier for the person is the function. Turns out, the greater the degree of movement and the closer the person is to eating normally, the less likely the person is to die early.

If we get better at adapting the same set of rules about movement to everyone, regardless of the type or degree of developmental issues, we will come a lot closer to delivering what all of us really need. We are less likely to say that people need nursing care or physical or occupational therapy, and more likely to position the clinician as a helper in focusing everybody's attention on the universal need for movement and assisting everyone involved to figuring out how that need can be met for a person with a unique body.

Getting a real life

I will never forget visiting a group home a few years ago. There were six persons in the home, all of whom had complex developmental and medical challenges. None of these young adults could walk independently, several had complex seizure disorders, and all needed extensive assistance to eat safely. All had some degree of musculo-skeletal deformity.

I was there as part of a team to judge the appropriateness of service to this group, who were part of a class action court case. The staff seemed nervous and reluctant to share information about their routines. Finally, one staff member confessed that every Wednesday night there was a group activity with singing and swinging on the floor. John liked to swing his arms, Jerry was helped to twist from side to side because it reduced the tone in his trunk and limbs. There was some unique feature identified for each person during the activity, but none of this was in people's individual habilitation plans. The staff were reluctant to tell us because they thought it might not be seen as "active treatment." This activity was probably the most therapeutic thing that happened in these persons' lives, as evidenced by the exuberant participation of six guys who were often not responsive to other, more formal "programs".

Turns out, this kind of engagement in personally interesting activity is often the most effective way to deal with health challenges. I often ask if interventions with persons with complex issues can pass the Dead Person's Test. If a dead person can do it, it's not worth doing. "Tolerating side lying" does not pass the Dead Person's Test. I can take a person 30 minutes post-mortem, put them in a side lying position and they'll tolerate it just fine.

Most of the time, the reason persons with complex disabilities fail to achieve is that we don't recognize the conditions under which the behavior occurs in the rest of us, or we are demanding behavior that doesn't matter anyway. Tying shoes is an irrelevant behavior for me because I don't own any shoes with laces. As we age, middle age spread can make tying your shoes an uncomfortable activity and hence, one that you soon come to avoid. One of my professional friends says it this way: "If the person can't do it, will someone have to be hired to do it for her?"

Often it isn't what you do but how you do it that matters. Eating can be a therapeutic and stimulating activity with one caretaker, and dangerous and counter-therapeutic with another. The most health enhancing and growth stimulating activities can be tied to the things we all do when we are leading a real life. Making everyday living more therapeutic takes a little practice, but it is surely more interesting and a lot less work.

Why were such simple truths so hard to understand?

When we talk about the rules for person-centered planning, no group of individuals is as likely to be perceived as exceptions as those characterized as chronically ill or "medically fragile". It's worth thinking about what kept our field from seeing and acting on the simple truths that all people have similar needs and that interventions should be formed to assure meaningful function. The barrier to understanding is in how others see people with complex disabilities.

Persons whose records described them as having not only intellectual deficits, but many physical disabilities as well were seen as always needing the protection of the medical model. Doses of treatment, such as nursing care and physical therapy were the primary modality, with "failure to respond to a trial of therapy" becoming an indictment of the person rather than another example of the fact that three 30 minute episode of therapy per week can't work.

Doses of therapy are not effective for most individuals with disabilities affecting movement. The acute care approach is more effective for those recovering from surgery that affects limb function or ambulation, than it is for those whose 24 hour exposure to gravity defies a dribble of intervention now and then, no matter how good the therapist.

A good comparative test is to ask yourself how effective a reduction diet might be if done in the same way: you restrict your eating for one hour a day three times a week. Meanwhile, you can eat yourself silly in the other 165 hours and probably be stunned and disillusioned when you failed to lose weight. Remember, it is changing one's lifestyle that changes the shape of the body, whether the goal is weight reduction or avoiding deformity. Any person who does not move against gravity, bear weight on their long bones and expose all body planes to the relentless influence of gravity will suffer profound health consequences as a direct result. This holds true whether you have a significant neuro-motor disability or are just a couch potato with time and inactivity driving your hanging soft tissue in an avalanche toward your knees.

Because we fail to realize the parallels between regular folks and people whose movement mechanisms are damaged at birth, we see treatment as futile. When the medical model fails, then death is seen as the best outcome so at least families can be at peace. Few people realize that the failure is the model and not the persons subjected to it.

Children born with obvious disabilities and those whose developmental issues emerge early in life are the most vulnerable. They are likely to be seen as objects of pity or worse, as destroyers of their family's integrity. Being seen as a burden can be a pretty heavy load for any youngster. Families are not helped by the fact that most medical practitioners have little access to enlightened training about disabilities and, as a result, transmit attitudes that encourage the parents to seek out-of-home care.

Many of the secondary conditions associated with "medical fragility" are preventable. The essential component to planning for preventable health issues is the belief that the juice is worth the squeeze. If we believe that nothing will make a difference, then any effort is seen as scarcely worth it.

On the other hand, if we presume that every human has unlimited potential then our approach will be significantly different. When we talk to newborn infants, as good parents always do, we all know that the baby hasn't a clue as to what we are saying. Most moms and dads do so because it feels good, and some of them know that this is how language and self-esteem develop in young babies. Studies of infants nearly a century ago demonstrated the positive impact of "mothering" interaction, even when the mothering was provided by surrogates who were inmates of the same institution for the mentally retarded.

Overcoming the real obstacles to development

Negative beliefs about people are the most important impediment to giving people what they need to have a real life. I find it helpful to take an attitude about persons with complex disabilities and multiple health challenges that makes some powerful assumptions about their abilities.

Regardless of how "bad" a person looks, there is a competent person hiding inside and our job is to figure out how to find her or him.

I remember a 35 year old woman who weighed 30 pounds and was folded up in an accordion-shaped deformity pattern. Her face was tightly contracted and there appeared to be no expression and little cognition there. She lived in a 50 bed ICF, and was transferring to a group home. To ease the transition, I interviewed the Physical Therapist who usually helped her with lunch. The woman had an awesome reputation as a person who was very hard to assist with eating.

The food cart came clacking down the hall. The therapist became very anxious and I asked him what the problem was. He said that if he didn't get Evelyn her tray within 5 minutes, that she would make him sorry for the sin (actually, "There'll be hell to pay!" was how he characterized it).

Evelyn would sulk, scream and make helping her with eating take twice the time than if he did it her way (that is, promptly). She was characterized as profoundly retarded with no communication skills. I thought she communicated quite effectively. At least, if asked the question "Is this working for you?" I think Evelyn's answer would be a resounding yes!

Everyone communicates in some unique way.

Patrick was only five years old and he had no formal communication skills. He lived in a unit with a number of other youngsters with severe motor disabilities. One day he was noticed to be squirming and grunting and nodding toward another little boy who was about to fall out of his chair.

Stop doing things for individuals that they can perfectly well do for themselves. Why should the person perform if he or she can get us to do it for them?

I remember a 50 year old man that I was asked to see because he was aspirating liquids on a regular basis. He sat in his wheelchair with his trunk tilted forward and his head tilted back as staff poured fluid into his mouth without any help from him. He would cough intermittently and his breathing pattern would become labored. We fiddled around with a squeeze bottle to direct the fluid to the side cheek pocket where he could swallow it more safely. It suddenly became obvious that this gentleman was perfectly capable of pulling fluid from a straw without any help, particularly when his sitting position was as upright as possible. This was safer than having fluid dumped in his mouth or squirted to the side, but the staff had no idea that he already possessed the skill.

In 1967, I became an area administrator for the living unit housing the most handicapped and medically fragile persons in the facility. The Nursery was a living unit for 24 very young children and older youngsters who were particularly vulnerable to infection and other illnesses. At the same time, another unit, Two-East was coming into its own as part of a federal demonstration grant to look at new ways to provide services to those with the most physical challenges.

Tony was a 7 year old whose disability resulted from a brain hemorrhage at birth. He became a yo-yo, bouncing between the Nursery and the training unit. In the nursery he was fed on his back and he didn't have to do a thing but cough to keep food out of his airway. He had been transferred to Two-East to participate in the project. This meant that he had to sit upright at mealtime and, on his own, move his head to midline and neutral to get a bite of food. He did not like it because it was a lot of work. He would invariably spike a nice little temperature, and the nursery folks would demand that he be transferred back to them, where life was not so demanding. We soon had a war on our hands with the team physician being the rescuer or persecutor, depending on which side you were on. One day we got an agreement that, temperature or no, he would stay on Two-East and eat safely. When he finally discovered that the temperature spikes were not going to get him sent back to the Nursery, the elevations stopped. No point in playing to an empty house.

My job is not to protect the person from experience ("you poor thing") but to make experience a reasonable learning opportunity.

Children learn to stand up to avoid falling down. They perfect skills by practicing, practicing, practicing until they get it right. Persons with complex disabilities, particularly if they live in regulated places, seldom get any opportunities to take risks.

I remember one youngster with neuro-developmental disabilities who lived with a foster family with three teen-age boys. The boys taught her to climb stairs before she could walk. They placed her at the steps and facilitated her upward movement from behind. One foster brother held her at the ankles and lifted one knee at a time to the next step, while another brother coaxed her up from the front. Could this be a dangerous behavior? Perhaps. Did they do it anyway? Sure they did. They knew she could learn higher motor skills and wanted to be part of the action. Teachers, it turns out, come in all shapes, sizes and ages. Sisters and brothers, it seems, do not know when things are not possible.

Holidays were a lonely affair for most people in the institution where I worked, because few of our residents went home with their families. We encouraged our staff to take the children home if they were so inclined. One youngster with severe cerebral palsy went home with a staff member with five boisterous kids. I didn't mind that they gave Carl a horseback ride. It was the motorcycle trip that made me nervous. He, by the way, loved the experience. It is easier to get forgiveness than permission.

Persons with complex disabilities deserve to learn from the same types of discomfort that the rest of us experience.

Regardless of the degree of their disability, no child or adult has the right to become a tyrant.

I remember waiting outside the room of a 3 year old in the midst of a screaming fit 'cause things hadn't quite gone her way. She had severe cerebral palsy and a difficult to control seizure disorder. For 20 minutes she screamed and I waited. The minute she stopped, I went rushing in to give her the most lavish attention I could muster. Her other trick was to bite staff on the fleshy part of the shoulder as they carried her from one place to another. In this case, we simply taught the staff to carry her in a way that interfered with her opportunity to engage in the behavior. All children need to know what the rules of human behavior are.

In Toronto in the middle 1980's there was a residential program for young children. Twenty-four children lived in 6 person groups each with two sets of house parents who relieved each other in a live-in model. The children were integrated into a kindergarten setting, and others in regular pre-school settings. One little 5 year old named Danny was part of a Junior-Senior Kindergarten, which was a huge open classroom for 5 and 6 year olds divided into many activity areas. It was story time one day, and Danny was asked to join the story circle.

His label was "autism" and his favored activity was body rocking, screeching and squealing. As the story started, Danny launched into his repertoire. The 6 year old sitting next to him hauled off and smacked him across the chops, stating: "Not now, Danny, it's story time!" He never did it again. Because he was among a bunch of kids without disabilities he was subject to the same natural consequences that all children experience.

Most persons have a lot more skills than they want us to know about. People with complex disabilities are no different.

I remember teaching my 14 year old to do his own laundry. In the ninth grade, students change clothes for gym in a locker room and care a lot about how their underwear looks. I simply washed one set of underwear in something that bled pink. I was never asked to do laundry again. The skill is there, one simply has to provide the motivation to use it.

One of the things that happens to persons with complex movement problems is that their bodies change shape as they get older. Usually this is because they are using abnormal movement patterns or not moving enough. This becomes a problem when skills developed at an earlier age are now not possible as the body changes shape and loses function. Good clinicians, such as well trained PT's and OT's, know how to test for terminal skills and not be fooled by persons who like to play stupid. All kids (including those without disabilities) know this trick 'cause it gets them out of a lot of work.

I often refer to this as an understandable desire to keep calling "retarded room service.".

One section of the body that gets difficult to use well as the skeleton and muscles change shape is the mouth and tongue. Sometimes people hold their heads in one position and lose range of motion in the neck. This can cause the jaw to retract, making the lips and jaw almost impossible to close. Just try swallowing with your mouth open and realize how skilled a person has to be to accomplish it without lip and jaw closure. I truly marvel at some of the adaptive skills of persons with complex disabilities and don't feel they get the credit they deserve!

People labeled "medically complex" are not as delicate as they seem.

When I see persons in their 30's and 40's with complex physical disabilities and deformity patterns who scare service planners to death because they look so fragile, I am highly amused. No one seems to be willing to ask, "If these folks are so fragile, how come they haven't died already?" By virtue of their age, most have come through some pretty awesome life experiences, such as being tossed about by an arm and leg on one side from bed to cart to bath slab and back. Most have experienced 5 minute mealtimes being fed flat on the back with both the mouth and the airway open.

I remember meeting a 7 year old at a facility who weighed only 14 pounds and had been placed from an adjacent state. We were there as part of the discovery process, which is the mechanism by which facts are gathered for litigation. The rest of my party had wandered away. Ricky played half-heartedly with a toy supported by his distended belly. A direct care staff whispered to me so no one else could hear "I hold him when no one is looking". It was 1975 and staff in that private care facility were forbidden to hold or interact with the babies and young children who never got out of bed. We were able to yank this youngster out of this place and admit him to a hospital. He gained 10 pounds and grew 2 inches in a very short period of time.

Acknowledging humanity

Often when I have stood in a death watch over someone who looked really fragile, someone else slipped away instead. One of my mentors reminded me that we are all going to die someday, so get over it and do something productive in the meantime.

If we really want to hasten the inevitability of their death, we can steal a person's spirit by treating the person as though nonhuman, by assuming the person cannot feel or love or hate. Let me tell you the story that still gives me chills every time I think about it.

My little friend Tony (whom you met in an earlier story) was accepted as a student in a program in another state that was famous for its work with persons with cerebral palsy. We all knew, that Tony's brain was all there, in spite of his label of profound retardation.

Tony had a particularly tight bond with Kevin, a youngster on his unit who was, if anything, more physically involved than Tony was. Both boys were 7 years old and had been eye-ball buddies for several years. When Tony went to the nursery, Kevin did not thrive. We all knew that wherever one boy went, the other would have to go as well.

The two youngsters moved to the new program together and shared an apartment with a housemother who did her best to assist with their needs. They were both learning and doing well. We checked on them often since neither had any natural family involvement and we had moved them 350 miles from us.

One morning, I got a call from the program's physician. He told me that Tony had suffered another stroke, similar to the one that caused the developmental insult right after birth. They did not expect him to live. Another staff member and I rushed to be with him, arriving seconds after Tony died.

How were we going to tell Kevin? I finally took this anxious little boy on my lap and said: "Kevin, Tony has gone away and you won't be seeing him anymore. He's gone to heaven where he won't hurt anymore." The look on his face told me he understood exactly what I was saying.

My associate and I drove back. Within 24 hours, the physician called yet again to tell me that Kevin had just died "of a broken heart".

I just got goose bumps again.

What that taught me was that you can really screw up a lot with persons who seem very delicate, but as long as you treat them as real persons with feeling and attitudes and the same range of emotions as you and me, things will probably turn out OK. When you deny the person's humanity however, you are asking for trouble.

Reference

Montagu, A. (1978) *Touching, The human significance of the skin.* New York: Columbia University Press

Mutual Learning
Fine-Tuning the Process Of Person-Centered Planning With People Who Have Mental Health Issues

Susannah Joyce, Betty Boomer, and John Jones

An ongoing challenge in working with person-centered planning is to stay true to the inherent spirit and design of the process while still being able to adapt the approach, as needed, to suit each person individually. One of the reasons personal planning is so powerful and effective is because of its simple logic: learning about the person's preferences, passions, capacities and experiences, getting to know some of their dreams for the future, and determining what will help them to attain what they want —what my friend and colleague, Rosa Landes McAllister calls, "Describing, Dreaming, and Doing."

Person-centered planning has an everyday quality about it in the best possible sense; it can work for anyone. We have learned, however, that we have had to consider other factors in transferring a process created for people who have developmental disabilities to use with people who have mental health issues.

In the early 1990's John brought his experience as a funder and Executive Director of services for people who have developmental disabilities to his new position as Executive Director of the Canadian Mental Health Association (CMHA) in Waterloo, Ontario. When he started with the organization, the model used for planning with people was one that shares some of the values of more person-centered approaches, but only includes the person supported and a case manager, and involves filling out a number of forms to determine overall rehabilitation goals. At that time, CMHA focused on crisis intervention first, and life planning took second place.

John thought that the person-centered planning with which he was familiar would be a more effective way of helping people supported by CMHA. He believed that a person-centered focus would help people to explore a meaningful future and to reclaim more power and control in their lives. He also wanted to promote the inclusion of friends and family in the planning and use more general community resources to help people achieve their dreams. John was convinced that as staff were able to see people as more than their labels, it would change the ways in which they worked with them.

John invited Susannah to consult with CMHA to adapt *Gathering Together*, a handbook she had written about facilitating personal planning, to use with people who have mental health issues (for information visit www.realizationstraining.com), An editorial group was formed, consisting of staff and people supported by the organization, working in equal partnership with each other for the first time. They met with Susannah for over a year to determine which aspects of the process would remain the same and which ones needed some fine-tuning. Throughout this creative process an evolution occurred regarding how providers and users of the service viewed one another and themselves. People worked in mutual respect and collaboration and came to understand personal planning as a process rather than a model or tool.

One thing that we learned early on from people supported was that they had come to hate the word "goal", which was sometimes used interchangeably with "dream" in *Gathering Together*. They told us that goals were what other people had in mind for them, and when these were not reached, the person supported would often be blamed, or at least held responsible.

This conversation allowed us to think more carefully about the connotations of words like dream, goal, and vision. We realized that despite some professionals' discomfort with the newer terms (for example, several people were worried that "vision" might be associated with symptoms related to mental health issues) we needed to help people embrace the richness of language implied by dreams instead of the limitations of goals set by service systems.

Another important lesson involved how planning meetings were designed. Not always, but often, in planning with people who have developmental disabilities, the setting and length of meeting is determined primarily by family and the facilitator, with perhaps, some consideration for the person's preferences around the food served and the comfort of the surroundings.

We were now holding meetings with people who are used to sharing more opinions about their surroundings, and who frequently have a low tolerance for noise or for being the center of attention. We knew that we had to make a more concerted effort to include them in decisions about details like the location and especially the length of meetings. Now get-togethers are frequently only an hour in length or we have a break every thirty minutes or so, to help people feel less tense about having the focus on them, even when the focus is positive.

It has also proven more difficult, overall, to encourage people to include family and friends to help them plan. Often, people we support who have developmental disabilities don't seem to have a problem (that we know of) with having a group of people come together to share ideas about their future. Some people do not have language or communication to let us know what they think about the involvement of others.

People with mental health issues are more likely to express their concerns around inviting family or friends to make suggestions about their lives. While their fears may seem surprising at first to those who have been involved with person-centered planning, we need only reflect on who we would want, or not want, to attend our own planning meeting. We realize that being at the center of this process can place us in a very vulnerable position, where others may criticize or wish to assume control.

People supported through CMHA sometimes resist the inclusion of others in their planning because they believe that they have survived by compartmentalizing their life. They may have several friends or acquaintances, but can feel safer by keeping these relationships separate and often even unknown to one another. The mental health issues people experience can result in fear, lack of self-esteem, social isolation and feelings of rejection, which can reinforce an unwillingness to involve others in the planning. The reluctance of parents and brothers and sisters to reconnect with an estranged family member whose problems have caused serious rifts in their relationship, is another problem at times.

Staff also have some fears about initiating invitations to include non-paid people in the planning. Often coordinators have a background in providing direct support to people and are not used to the role of facilitator. They also worry that they could wind up doing family counseling within a planning group that includes non-paid people. We have found that training and support for staff are necessary to help them gain confidence in this area. We also try to assist people who are planning to see how a parent or friend can be useful to the process through their ideas, connections, or experience. We make an effort to assure the person that others are being invited specifically to be supports and that the values and ground rules of the process will be shared both at the time invitations are issued and at the beginning of the planning meeting.

Betty, who is the Associate Executive Director of CMHA, notes that because of the cyclical aspect of some mental health issues, as well as the less visible nature of particular problems, families and staff can sometimes forget to take the possibility of recurring symptoms into account when they plan with the person. This can result in greater disappointment when dreams aren't accomplished as quickly as they had hoped. The fact that medications can sometimes have a remarkable effect on someone's mental health issues (at least temporarily) also leads some families to keep seeing the dream as the disappearance of symptoms. This can make it more difficult for them to focus on a way of planning with the person that believes in dreams being realized now rather than waiting for the person to be "cured".

The cyclical aspect of people's lives can also keep them and their families in a state of constant tension, waiting for things to become difficult again. This can make it more challenging to feel relaxed or hopeful about planning. Betty suggests an analogy to someone who has cancer, with periods of remission and even some expectation that the disease may not return, but with no guarantee. There is always a worried watchfulness.

For families of people who have mental health issues there can be a fear of "rocking the boat." Things may be even for the person now, but there is a concern that aspiring to a fuller and more exciting life could trigger another difficult episode.

Of course, we often experience fears from parents of people who have developmental disabilities, but we have found that those concerns are usually more about the person's safety and acceptance in the community rather than fears of making the disability worse. Within CMHA in Waterloo it has been important for planning facilitators to make the time and effort to understand families' fears. We want them to see that someone leading a more fulfilling life, pursuing dreams and not just managing symptoms, actually contributes to the person's mental health.

There can be an extra poignancy for people and their families in looking at the past in planning. Often someone's mental health issues began in their teens or young adulthood and so a comparison of the Community Maps for their Past and Present can show major differences in their activities and relationships. Facilitators need to encourage people to believe they can reclaim a life that matters to them. It is also important for everyone to see how the past can work in favor of dreaming for the future, by remembering that the person is a multi-faceted and fascinating individual who is so much more than their mental health issues. Since it is the person and their family who hold the key to who the person was in the past, this information is often inspiring for staff, who only know the person as they are today, with their problems.

Sometimes people have had to take the dreaming in short spurts, just like the length of the meetings. Looking at their whole life can be overwhelming, so we try to be very conscious of the desired pace of the person in the planning. One person supported by CMHA did lots of dreaming, and then put the written plan in their drawer for a year before they were ready to proceed. These reminders to slow down at times, and to be sensitive about where the person is in their own planning process is another valuable lesson to bring back to planning with people who have other kinds of challenges.

We have learned to begin the discussion about dreaming in a general way, that includes everyone in the group, asking each person to speak a bit about how dreaming works in their life and what a few of their dreams are or have been. We have to be mindful, of course, that others don't become the main focus of this conversation, but we have found that by involving everyone in the topic, the person supported doesn't feel so much pressure as the only one talking about their hopes and dreams.

There are also significant differences in the service and funding systems that support people who have developmental disabilities and those that are in place for people who have mental health issues. In Ontario, services for people with developmental disabilities have been funded through a community/social service mandate, while the mental health services receive financial support through the health system, which still embraces a medical model.

Person-centered planning in mental health is seen as a "soft" service in a system that is still primarily treatment oriented, and so a more holistic way of planning does not always receive the credibility it deserves. Crisis planning, which CMHA in Waterloo still does (linking it to person-centered planning) continues to be seen as more important by most mental health services.

CMHA in Waterloo has called its approach to personal planning *Discovery*, and we have created an *Introductory Guide* and a *Facilitators Handbook*, both bearing this title. Betty has remarked, facetiously, that if the approach were called *A Comprehensive Functional Goal Plan*, many mental health professionals might be more comfortable with the process.

Funding priorities are still given to treatment more than community supports within mental health, so it is important for organizations like CMHA in Waterloo to share the success stories of people they support, who have used *Discovery* to make changes in their lives.

Many of these successes could be judged as insignificant by those who don't understand what life can be like for people who have mental health issues. However, achievements such as taking a bus alone again, calling someone to have coffee, or just getting out of the apartment without such intense fear can mark the beginning of a new phase in someone's life.

There have also been larger changes for people –going to university, writing and publishing an autobiography, developing careers such as welding or as a mental health professional, or reuniting with children after years of separation.

The change to a person-centered approach in planning has helped people with mental health issues to have better lives and to take back the power in their lives. It has also provided a new lens for seeing themselves as vital, talented people, deserving of love and respect. They realize that although they happen to have some extra problems, they are so much more than the labels assigned to them.

CMHA in Waterloo continues to share information on person-centered planning with other mental health services, and some have begun to use this approach, or at least offer it as another alternative to more traditional ways of planning within their organizations.

It is also important that we bring back the knowledge we have gained from planning with people who have mental health issues, to continue our work with people who have developmental disabilities. Issues of power and voice in shaping the process of the planning may need to be looked at more carefully, as well as the sensitivity we show when discussing such intimate topics as the person's past and their dreams. There is always more to learn about person-centered planning and one way to stay open to fresh ideas is to keep sharing this process with new people who can let us know what effect this attempt to help is having on their lives.

19

Sequoia
An Invitation To Senior Parents and Their Families
To Do Person-centered Planning

Sally Sehmsdorf

> *Viewing a grove of Sequoia, the trees appear to stand
> alone. A closer look reveals a parent tree surrounded by a
> family of maturing trees. Below the surface a network of
> interconnected roots share nutrients from the earth. That
> is their strength. Eventually the parent tree dies, and the
> grove continues. Like a Sequoia tree, senior parents and
> their families can develop an interconnected network that
> will sustain life in the future for their sons and daughters
> with disabilities.*
>
> *—The Sequoia flyer*

How and why we got started.

In 1999, our organization, the Center for Community Support,
partnered with the ARC of King County to offer senior families an
opportunity to do person-centered planning using PATH and Futures
Planning. Nancy Meltzer, at the King County ARC in Washington
State, had developed a Senior Family Network. She learned that
most senior parents whose sons and daughters were living with them
in the family home did not have plans for the future. Some still
needed to write wills and or develop trusts. In response, we offered
workshops to senior parents explaining person-centered planning
and offered to do a person-centered plan with each family.

To our surprise we had few takers. The reasons, we learned, were
complex. Senior parents were often facing chronic or long-term
illness, as well as the death of other family members and friends.
The thought of separation from their son or daughter with a disability who had by now become a life companion was painful. Some
families had strongly held values of independence; to ask other
people for support violated their sense of privacy and pride in self-
sufficiency. Some felt that their son or daughter with a disability was
their concern and their concern only. They were reluctant to talk
to any of their children: their children without disabilities for fear
of interfering in their busy lives and their children with disabilities

for fear of needlessly upsetting them by bringing up the unpleasant topic of death. Some, in order to deal with the challenges they faced, narrowed their focus of attention to the present, taking one step at a time yet carrying an unspoken and frightening concern for the future. Some admitted rather sheepishly to an underlying fear. If they were to get everything in place for the future, would they hasten their own death because they had nothing left to do?

When we asked what would be helpful to them in planning for the future, surprisingly they told us more information on wills, guardianship, services, and group placement. They wanted to know what would happen not what could happen. Person-centered planning calls up a kaleidoscope of colorful images: heart-felt dreams built on gifts and capacities in the person; laughter and sharing; food and companionship in the community. It's a far cry from the stark black and white numbered paragraphs of wills, trusts, and guardianship papers, and the formality of a law office.

Reflecting on our experience of parental disinterest in our offer, we noticed that we were privy to just one perspective: that of the senior parent or parents. They came to the workshops alone. We saw in some cases that the plans they did have for their son or daughter with a disability had been talked around but not about with other family members. More troubling was the certainty that surrounded their strongly held and unquestioned assumption that their picture of the future was obvious and shared by other family members. We wondered what people with disabilities and their brothers and sisters might have to say if they were part of the conversation. Other questions arose.

> How do we ourselves face loss, death, and vulnerability?
> What is the source of the courage to face the uncertainties of the future?
> What is friendship and why do we let people into our lives?
> What is hope and how can we encourage it?
> Under what conditions are people able to dream about a better future?
> How can we make future plans that respond to changes within the person as well as in the world around them?

We wondered what it would take to bring other members of the family together to have this conversation, and what such a conversation might look like.

> How could we support people with disabilities to dream and support their family members to listen differently, while at the same time honoring the wisdom, love and commitment of the elders?

> How would we deal with often favored, traditional service solutions that congregate and isolate people with disabilities?

> How could we encourage possibilities for people that are firmly rooted in the values of inclusion, contribution, giftedness, and friendship?

Who we are together matters.

Person-centered planning speaks to a bigger way of looking and living. Life springs from a diverse ecosystem of relationships. Too often planning becomes an isolated focus on a person alone and the relationships around them are not acknowledged as important. People think this solitariness is what "person-centered" really is. This kind of egocentric stardom leads to the mistaken assumption that a person's success or failure is only about their choices and not about our choices. One mother of a child with a disability powerfully reframed this assumption of individuality when she asked her friends,

> *Who will need to know John, and what kind of experiences will they need to have with each other so that someone in our circle will offer John employment when he leaves school? What do we need to be doing together over the next ten years for this to happen? (O'Brien, 2002)*

If part of our goal in person-centered planning is to further relationships, then we need to start by acknowledging our own. Who we are together really does matter, and to me this is another way of saying that person-centered planning is not done in a vacuum. If we can't acknowledge the gifts of those who have contributed to our work and our well being how can we see the gifts of people on whose behalf we work.

Bringing together the right balance of people is like setting up the colors on a palette. How we compliment as well as contrast with each other matters. Nancy brought significant gifts. As the mom of Adam, an adult son with a disability, and herself almost a senior,

she brought wisdom, empathy and heart. She was credible. Over
the years, she had built strong relationships with many families,
and senior families, were and remain, her passion. Nancy fiercely
advocated for them. These families looked to her when confused
and overwhelmed by government language and legislative issues.
They knew she was on their side, and they trusted her. In addition,
she brought an extensive knowledge of the service system and the resources of government and community. She had or could get all the
information they wanted or needed. Nancy says of herself that she
has a linear style and with that comes an ability to clearly articulate
just how it is that you get from point A to point B.

I asked Chris Bily to join us. I felt we needed someone who was
empathetic, creative, committed to community, experienced in
person-centered planning, a visionary, and a good listener. Chris, a
gifted visual artist, is all that. She makes people feel safe, welcome,
and special to her. She understands the art of cultivating goodness;
people's better sides flourish in her company. As the mother of
Errin, a beautiful young woman with a developmental disability, she
too brought the mother's heart.

I have a background in performance art, conflict resolution,
person-centered planning, circles of support, and a passion for
dialogue. I have benefited from many conversations with my colleagues at the Center for Community Support, Mary Romer and
Leah Preston Ing whose work is a constant reminder that we stand
with and for people with disabilities. Lastly I have had the good
fortune to have an occasional conversations with John and Connie
Lyle O'Brien.

A new beginning

*The seed is a kind of aperture through which the tree
gradually emerges... It organizes the process of growth
which eventually create the tree. Just so, our conversations
organize the processes and structures which shape our collective futures.*

—William Isaacs (1999)

The seed idea for Sequoia grew from a conversation about how
a circle of support could evaluate itself. In that conversation, I
thought about the possibility of replacing the mechanical metaphor
of evaluation, with its focus on external proof of objectives met,
with an organic metaphor, that of a thriving tree that maintains

its integrity while drawing from and benefiting its environment through the whole cycle of its life.

I began to wonder with Nancy and Chris what it would be like to think of person-centered planning as organic and growing? How might we design a conversation about planning by looking at the process organically? This was appealing because it undermined the idea that a plan, albeit a person-centered one, is finished once it is recorded. In reality it is a shifting conversation between people for the purpose of organizing action for change.

Nancy, Chris and I grew Sequoia in response to the special set of circumstances in which senior families in our community find themselves. Sequoia evolved into a series of workshops that provided a time and a place for open and respectful conversations that crossed generational and disability boundaries. We relied heavily on the values of person-centered planning. Belonging to family, and community, giftedness, contribution, and listening especially for the dreams of people with disabilities guided our process. We broadened the scope of the planning included the whole family before focusing more directly on the person with a disability. Finally we added to the person-centered planning methods that we knew by drawing our combined experience in the creative arts, group facilitation, and community building. We used graphic art, drama, games, and dialogue to slow the conversation down, generate different ways to ask and answer the most important questions, and create conditions for everyone's voice to be heard and understood.

In general the workshops were designed in three phases. First, an introduction to see if families were willing to try person-centered-planning, second, identifying dreams for the future, and third to honor dreams, as well as individual differences.

All the workshops were in comfortable settings in churches and community centers and lasted from about 10 AM to 4 PM. It was important to us for people to sense immediately that they mattered to us, that they would be nurtured in soul and body, and that this was a safe place to share what could be a difficult conversation. We greeted them as if they were special guests invited into our own homes. Good food was important, too. In the morning, we served hot coffee and home baked muffins set in our favorite dishes on a multicolored tablecloth with candles and flowers. In the afternoon specially selected or homemade lunches were offered to reflect quality and caring. Soft music played in the background. On the walls we taped quotes and poems on yellow, orange, and purple paper to evoke our purpose. Activities were planned for each workshop, but we were prepared to change direction depending on who came and what happened. At the end of day, we reflected on the values and how well they were represented. Were people included, heard, and respected? Were people listening to each other? Were people's gifts expressed and acknowledged? Were relevant topics brought up and talked about? Were people engaged and enjoying each other? How we were together mattered, and based on our reflection we designed the next meeting.

Eight families participated. Some families were represented by only a parent and one son or daughter with a disability while most brought sisters, brothers, uncles, aunts, cousins and their spouses. The following is a description of each workshop and what we learned.

> *A long-range goal to me is a direction that grows out of loving people, and caring for people, and believing in people's capacity to govern themselves. The way to know they have these capabilities is to see something work well on a small scale. When I speak about a social goal, the goal for society, and for myself, I don't say- 'this is exactly what it's going to be like.' I don't have a blueprint in mind, I'm thinking more of a vision, I'm thinking of direction and I'm thinking of steps, I'm thinking more in terms of signs pointing in the right direction...*
>
> *–Myles Horton*

Introducing Sequoia –first workshop

> *We don't set out to save the world; we set out to wonder how other people are doing and to reflect on how our actions affect other people's heart.*
>
> *–Pema Chodron*

At the introductory workshop we did not ask that all members of the family come, even though we strongly recommended it. Most of the time one senior parent, usually the mom, came accompanied by their son or daughter with a disability and often one other family member usually a brother or sister. Our purpose was to bring families together and provide them with an opportunity to tell their stories and break through the isolation, loneliness, fear and confusion we had learned that they felt. We also wanted to introduce person-centered planning as organic, growing and changing, and finally we were curious to see who might want to participate.

To introduce the concept of futures planning as organic, a large outline of a tree filled one wall. Facets of the planning process were written on different branches: "dreams for myself and my loved one", "community", "work", "leisure", "spirituality and the life cycle", "guardianship", "trusts", "wills", "services, and entitlements". To extend the metaphor, underneath the tree sat a large basket, a bag of soil, bulbs, and gardening tools: a rake, a hoe, pruning shears, and gloves. We invited everyone in the group to sit in a semi-circle facing the tree graphic. After introductions and sharing what brought us, we introduced our purpose to begin a dialogue about the future. We acknowledged that the conversation can be a difficult one but well worth the effort, and shared a sense of urgency. When families don't have a vision for the future, their most vulnerable members are at great risk of isolation and loneliness.

Future plans are like plants. Good tools and practice in using them are needed to grow good plans. For tools we drew from William Isaacs' dialogue practices of respect, voicing, and suspension of assumptions and from John O'Brien and Connie Lyle O'Brien's three dimensions of listening (1998). Listening, respect, speaking from your experience, and opening to possibilities are foundational to good person-centered plans.

Dialogue practices orient people toward deeper, more comprehensive conversation. Respect requires taking a second look, voicing means speaking from the authority of your experience, and finally, suspending assumptions means holding your judgments and your certainty at bay long enough to let new information in

These three dimensions of listening point to what it takes to listen to people with disabilities in light of a history that has failed miserably. They are crucial reminders of basic human courtesy.

- The first dimension asks us to consider, where we are listening from? Are we standing close enough to people to touch them? Are we accommodating their preference for communication?
- The second dimension asks us to pay attention to what we are listening for. Are we encouraging people to find their voice and speak for themselves? Are we attending to the details and dreams that disclose a person's identity and desires to participate and contribute?

- The third dimension asks us to listen with care. Are we conveying to the person that she or he matters?

To symbolize these practices, we introduced a talking stick– a piece of driftwood found on the beach. Whoever picks up the talking stick signals that he or she wants to speak and others to listen. It helped assure that every voice was heard, asked the group to discipline itself, and slowed the conversation down long enough to permit all of us to take in what others said. The presence of the talking stick helped people take turns and not talk at the same time, especially when families were talking among themselves.

In order to practice using the tools, and to begin grappling with the task of future planning, families were asked to describe a time in the past when they had faced a difficult challenge and to reflect upon what got them through it.

These conversations were awesome. Mothers and fathers, sons and daughters, brothers and sisters, shared stories and strengths, often for the first time. We were pleased to see that the person with a disability sat as a valued member of the family circle, not separated and protected but listening to and sharing stories and insights. Stories emerged of facing illness, losing jobs, and being teased. Sources of strength and comfort were identified as family and friends, a favorite pet, God and faith. Some found strength in developing plans and taking small steps with optimism and others acknowledged the courage it evokes to act while feeling fear. Family members attended to what they heard from each other, were moved and even surprised.

After lunch, people shared what gives them strength with the larger group. We wrote what they said on the roots of the tree, and talked about how we had just dug into the soil, uncovered the fears and released the energy for growth. Later, families who had already done person centered plans joined us and told their stories, sharing their vision for the future, their relief and often their tears. We closed the day by passing out purple, pink, and green paper leaves and asked for words that expressed what the day had meant. The leaves were gathered and taped to the tree with words like, "hopeful", "encouraged to get started", "just do it", "action", and "love".

Chris, Nancy, and I were moved by what we witnessed. We learned that people benefited from getting together, were inspired, and wanted to begin the person-centered planning process. We felt successful in creating an opportunity to experience trust, sharing, safety, inclusion and a greater connection to each other.

More questions surfaced for us.

> How could we accentuate the voice of people with disabilities even more clearly?
>
> What will we do to safeguard the sanctity of the dreams?
>
> What do family members have to do with each other in order to release the dream?
>
> Can we get both generations to come-parents, son or daughter with a disability and their brothers and sisters?

To extend the invitation to those family members who did not attend, we sent each family a letter summarizing the work they had done, inviting them and their family members back to two more workshops on successive Saturdays, and giving them a taste of what they might expect. Below is a piece of what we wrote:

> *We would like to begin by helping you clarify what it is that you want for your son or daughter, as well as, for yourself in the future. What is your dream? We would also like to ask the other members of your family the same question in another separate place in the room. We think it is important to differentiate your dream from theirs. We then invite both you and your family members to share the dreams, begin a conversation about your similarities and differences, and to chart action. Our hope is that your paths will merge. Mary Romer and Leah Preston from the Center for Community Support will join with us to facilitate a planning process called PATH (Planning Alternative Tomorrows With Hope).*
>
> *As you can see, in order for the two workshops to be successful, we need a commitment from you and your family to attend both Saturdays. This is a three way conversation that can happen only if all voices are there. If you think this sounds productive for you, please let us know.*
>
> *— Nancy, Sally, Chris*

Identifying Dreams –second workshop

*I've dreamt in my life dreams that have stayed with me
ever after, and changed my ideas: they've gone through and
through me, like wine through water, and altered the color
of my mind.*

—*Emily Bronte*

A total of eight families responded and completed the remaining workshops. Two families did not bring family members other than their son or daughter with a disability, others brought at least one sibling, sometimes a niece, and one family brought eight people: brothers and sisters, cousins, nieces and their spouses.

The intention in this phase was to voice, identify, and clarify dreams in the context of family and community. To evoke a family and community context as opposed to a disability only focus, we created two opportunities for families to draw closer, celebrate each other, and reach back into their collective history.

The first touched on family identity. Nancy began the check-in by going around the circle asking each person, "How are you and one of your family members alike?" The answers were hilarious and the person with the disability fit right into the family constellation clearly sharing the attributes both good and bad that defined them all. Later individual families (if enough people came) or two families together played a game, we adapted from a board game called "Life Stories". Chris made a deck of cards with pictures and questions on them. – "Tell about one of your family traditions?" "What would a perfect day be like for you?" "Where would you live if you could live anywhere?" "What has been the role of religious belief in your life?" These questions encouraged rich conversations about family identity, dreams, preferences and spiritual beliefs. People relaxed and had fun- important conditions needed to promote the dreaming we would ask of them later. The family member with the disability was just "one of" and not "separate from"- a joy to see. We ended the morning with poetry about family commitment and love, what brothers and sisters mean to one another, and comparing family traditions to a tall tree.

Lunch was delicious, with lots of lively conversation.

After lunch, brothers and sisters from all the families gathered in a group in one part of the room while all the parents gathered in another place. The generations were separated to allow the dreams to be expressed without influence from the other, and perhaps more safely and therefore more honestly.

Facilitators in each group asked typical questions associated with the North Star and The Dream in the person-centered process called PATH: "What guides this path into the future?" " What is the dream?" Graphic facilitators captured the images in color on large pieces of paper. People participating learned from each other's differences as well as similarities in both groups. Siblings listened to dreams from both their family member with a disability as well as those in other families that challenged their assumptions of what could be for a person with a disability. Brothers and sisters with disabilities enjoyed the encouragement and attention of their siblings. We encouraged everyone in the group to dream. Dreams abounded, revealing key aspects of individual identity. We heard dreams of...

> *moving to Mexico*
> *traveling to the Amazon with a son*
> *getting married, living in Seattle with a new husband*
> *a trip to Disney Land*
> *living in the same house and visiting friends on Broadway*
> *building a kayak*
> *living in a condo in New York*
> *working in a retail shop*
> *owning a business*
> *watching sports on TV with friends and family in my own house*

We took note that no one mentioned wanting to live in a program, a group home, or in intensive tenant support, and that the dreams of people with disabilities were in kind not the slightest bit different from that of their brothers and sisters.

What did parents dream? They dreamed of safety, stability, friends and contentment for all their children. In general, it was harder for senior parents to imagine the future. "It's hard to dream," they told us, "We think more about the reality". We gently nudged them asking,

> *What do you love most about your son or daughter? What are they interested in and good at? Imagine sharing them with the world.*

A safety net emerged as a central image, only then were they able to dream about possibilities:

my daughter playing monopoly with friends
my son, happy with lots to do
my son's ability for hard work appreciated
my son as a chef

For themselves they dreamed of sleeping in, moving to a country home, and spending a fortieth anniversary in Hawaii. They drew comfort from each other, feeling understood in ways that people often do when they share a life circumstance that unites them.

After everyone had gone home, Nancy, Chris and I reflected on what we had heard and asked ourselves...

> How can the perspective of each be shared in a way that is respectful, positive, helpful, and bring people closer to envisioning a future that expands possibilities while moving away from the limited choices offered by the traditional service system?
>
> What of the nightmare needs to be voiced?
>
> How can we model listening for and honoring the gifts and dreams of people with disabilities.
>
> We observed that one person with a disability was not as engaged as others and at times refused to join in. Could we listen differently to her gifts and include her more next time? She was an ardent Star Trek fan and spoke very highly of Captain Kirk and the Starship Enterprise. While some may have labeled her interest an obsession, we wanted to model respect.
>
> Another person with a disability voiced a dream of acting in front of an audience and a third took pride in helping others. What could we do to accentuate and honor these gifts for next time?
>
> How might we ground the dreams in possible action steps?
>
> Finally how would we deal with differences of opinion?

In the week between the workshops, I contacted as many people in each family as possible to see how they were doing and if there was any reverberation from the last workshop. I learned for the most part people were excited, expectant and relieved, but that there were also tensions and feelings of confusion, frustration, and hurt. As I spoke with some people I heard feelings and thoughts that would address positively the confusion, frustration and hurt felt by others.

Part of the work of the next workshop would be to provide a safe place to share those thoughts and feelings.

Beginning the dialogue

There is no greater power than a community {family} discovering what it cares about.... Ask "'What's possible?" not "What's wrong?"'...Be intrigued by the differences you hear. Expect to be surprised.

—Margaret Wheatley (2002)

In the final gathering we hoped to bring together the emerging paths of the two generations, share the dreams grounding them in possibility, honor people's gifts, learn from the differences, provide a safe place to reveal important thoughts and feelings, and finally see if any of the families wanted to continue on with the path process within their families and communities.

We opened the day as usual with good food and music, reviewed the tools of dialogue, and emphasized the three dimensions of listening. We talked about thinking in new and creative ways, and the importance of listening to the often forgotten voice of people with disabilities. We acknowledged and were encouraged by the love, courage, and commitment we saw from each of them for their families.

Chris had transcribed the dreams generated from the paths recorded last time on to little cards with images. The dreams remained anonymous to encourage creativity and suspension of judgment. In order to ground the dreams in possibility, we broke into three groups but not according to family, gave each group the dream cards and asked them to write down three steps to take toward realizing each dream. The brainstorm for each of the dreams would later be given to the dreamer to which it belonged. The ideas flowed freely. One group responded to a dream of having a Star Trek party. They came up with costumes, favorite foods with strange names to match the theme, and included themselves in the list of whom to invite. Another person's dream of acting resulted in sharing a connection with a theatre company. Families became resources for each other. It was great!

To display and honor the dreams, Chris made a multi-colored luminescent dream catcher out of a hula-hoop. She wove a jewel-bedecked spider web in the center and hung several red tags throughout to represent the dreams. After brainstorming action steps, people brought the dream cards they were working on and sat together in the large circle. To honor the dreams further and make sure they were heard, we made up a small drama. To honor the gifts of people with disabilities, we asked, Susie, the person who wanted to act, to facilitate the drama, and Doug, who loved to help, to help her. The skit took the form of question and response reminiscent of a Greek Chores. In turn Susie asked each person in the circle, "What is your dream?" They described the dream on the card in their hand and then in unison the group chanted three times "And this is your heart's desire, and this is your heart's desire, and this is your heart's desire." Doug then gathered the cards and taped them to the red tags on the dream-catcher. Finally we asked a family member to support, Larissa, as she cut out tickets with Star Ship Enterprise on them to give as gifts. To our delight she chose to join the circle and happily cut out the starships to give as invitations to her party. We noticed an engagement and a subtle change as we stepped into the background and Susie, Doug and Larissa stepped into the foreground to lead the group. Drama accentuates the human side of our aspirations. In this instance, dreams were voiced and heard; gifts honored. People with disabilities took center stage to facilitate and convey the dreams for all of us.

Lunch was pizza, salad and soft drinks. Every one was in a good mood.

After lunch we turned to the more difficult part of this conversation. In order to build small temporary communities of safety, we asked people to separate into three groups – one group made up of only parents, another of siblings and a final group of people with disabilities. Chris, Nancy, and I each facilitated a group. To start off the dialogues we asked in the privacy of each group, what had changed in their thinking or in the thinking of others since we last met? What did they need to let go of? What did they want most understood. What were the questions they were living with?

Interestingly, the **parents** group objected to the idea of letting go, and were hurt by what they understood as blame and judgment implied in the question. They told us they would not and could not let go. We had inadvertently touched a sore spot. After an apology and some discussion they concluded, they could think about what it takes to "let grow".

We noticed the dilemmas they faced underneath these words.

This is my responsibility. I worry about what I am passing

*on to the next generation. I'm trying to make it easier for
the kids left behind.*

*I'm exhausted. Our other family members don't know
about this paperwork.*

I can't do it alone.

*We know our children so well. Others often think they
know better but many are off base. We have to stand up.*

I want to respect my kid's choices.

*I don't want to impose my vision. I don't know how to deal
with future change.*

People with disabilities reflected on what excited them about their dreams. What they worried about. Who they turned to when their parents were away. Did they ever think about their parents dying? And, who listens to them?

Some people carried the burden of their parent's worry. They understood the concern about safety but wanted more out of life than safety. Others demonstrated that they understood much more than other family members thought they did, and some in their comments hinted of feeling isolated and lonely. One man said he couldn't imagine his parents not being around. Another said how lonely and sad he felt when his mother was in the hospital. Another man worried about a crisis in the family that no one thought he knew about. One woman knew that she would turn to her sister if her mother were gone. People imagined various living arrangements in the future- with a family member, friends, or a spouse in an apartment or house shared or of one's own. Some felt being understood was difficult and that people were often "too much on the go and too stressed to listen ".

The **brothers and sisters** shared the worry they felt about how long their parents could remain independent and as caregivers. Some felt confused about what their parents expected of them. Others mentioned concern for the well being of their sister or brother. They thought that their brother or sister could do more and be more independent if given a chance, but didn't know how to approach their parents without offending them. Some wanted to play a larger role. One person wondered, how assertive should she be? How much should she do now?

*I want my mom to feel OK about my assuming some re-
sponsibility. Responsibility, yes, but also an honor.*

On the question of where their brother or sister might live in the future, some siblings affirmed strongly that the person would come to live with them even if their parents were against it.

One woman shared how her sister with a disability had come to live with her for an extended stay. Since our last meeting on identifying dreams, she had called upon her other brothers and sisters and extended family members for help. They had come to a dinner at her house to talk about the dreams they had heard and lend support. She did not invite her mother, however. Her intention was to take some of the load off her mother during a time of stress but instead her mother felt hurt and excluded. We wondered together what her mother might be feeling and needing from her, and what she might say to her later.

Each group had a piece of a more inclusive picture. We knew we could not address all the complexity that the workshops up to this point had aroused but we hoped that people would leave with a deeper understanding than what they had come with. We also wanted to give them a chance to resolve some of the feelings of hurt and confusion.

In the last event of the day, everyone joined one big circle. We posed the questions, "Where are you now, what do you want most to say to other members of your family, and what do you want most understood".

What was shared was transformative. We asked sons and daughters to go first. One man said, "I'm not sure what to do, but I think about it a lot. I know I am the executor of the will but if something happened tonight, I wouldn't know what to do tomorrow." The parents, hearing this, later agreed to talk about the will and give him the information he needed.

A woman with a disability expressed a sentiment that others shared. "Mom wants me to lock up all windows and close the curtains. I do this even when my mom isn't there. It bugs my mom if I might not be safe. I know 911 is not a game." She then went on to enthusiastically voice her dreams. Other people with disabilities voiced where they wanted to live in the future. Sometimes this was a surprise to family members who thought they knew them well.

Sons and daughters, their wives, husbands, nieces, and in laws of one family told one senior parent who had been feeling left out, how much they loved her, what a wonderful support she had been to them, and how grateful they were to her for the solid foundation in life she had given them. They told her it was their turn now to support her and their sister. Other adult children expressed similar sentiments saying they wanted to be more involved in their brothers' and sister' lives. Some said they wanted their sister or brother to live if not with them very near them. All wanted to be more involved and closer.

A man with a disability who had come only with his mother felt the positive feelings and unity of the families who had many members present, and said he wanted to call his family together right away. He wanted to live in his own apartment and he wanted their support.

Some parents having heard a plea for more independence expressed wanting to give their children with disabilities more freedom and choices but didn't know how. Some expressed regret of not having made more planning decisions and shared the pain and confusion of planning choices in the past that had not worked.

We could sense the relief in the room. People were listening to each other and deeply moved by what they heard. All said they wanted to continue the dialogue, and most wanted to finish the path process within their families. Nancy, Chris and I felt privileged to be part of these families' lives. We don't know what the long-term impact will be. We do know that a deeper conversation about the future has begun. Our hope is to meet with each of the families in their communities and do individual paths that more clearly define the dreams, and the action it will take to make them come true.

To really see and listen, I have found, is not easy because, as the dimensions of listening indicate, you have to know what values guide your listening and what you are listening for: not data but dreams, identity and meaning.

In his book on dialogue. William Isaacs (1999) says that awareness is curative. I like that because it relieves me in my work of the lonely responsibility to fix people or situations. The best I can do is to try and create opportunities for myself and other people to listen and see what is already there. The responsibility (response + ability) is then ours collectively to act. Person-centered planning for me is an emergent and creative process that like the world at dawn gradually reveals itself to those willing to sit still and listen. If we are lucky we will get an inkling of our highest aspirations as well as our most profound human dilemmas.

References

Chodron, P. *When Things Fall Apart*. Boston: Shambala.

Isaacs, W, *Dialogue and the Art of thinking together*. New York: Doubleday Currency.

O'Brien, J. (2002). Great questions and the art of portraiture. This book.

O'Brien, J. & Lyle O'Brien, C. (1998). Learning to listen. *A little book about person-centered planning*. Toronto,ON: Inclusion Press.

Wheatley, M. (2002). *Turning to each other*. San Francisco: Berrett-Koehler Publishers.

20

Pathfinders
It's Never Too Late

Connie Lyle O'Brien, Beth Mount,
John O'Brien & Fredda Rosen

Pathfinders has made a world of difference for my grand-daughter, Shunelle, and for me, too. After the meetings, I feel so much more informed and enlightened in terms of understanding that possibilities exist in our communities for people with disabilities.

I never thought that Shunelle would be able to do the things she's doing right now. I didn't know that I could trust myself to allow her to negotiate the world on her own. But in the last few months, Shunelle has begun traveling to work, to therapy, the beauty salon, a favorite Chinese restaurant and my office on her own. She seems happy about her accomplishments and newfound independence. (Jeffery, 1999)

***

Pathfinders helped us put the emphasis on who Josh is, what he can do, not what he can't do, and his own particular loves, interests, values, and strengths. We began seeing him differently and thus with more hope and less despair over what he can't do… Person-centered planning helped us to focus on creating a community for Josh. I can't emphasize that enough. As we think about Josh's future, there's nothing more important that we can do for him than to help build a community around him because one of our concerns and fears has been his isolation and lack of friends. (Wolf, 2000/2001)

Shunelle and Josh have been among a small group of young New Yorkers finding their own paths into community life from segre-

We are grateful to the students and family members who have inspired us with their vision, courage, and determination. Special thanks to Vaulda Kendall-Browne, Christina, Lucia, & Ramon Rodriguez, Josh, Michael, and Roberta Wolf, and Phyllis Jeffrey for sharing their stories in writing. Thanks to Pathfinders staff, Carolann Granata and Debbie Lamothe for the example of their work and for their help in writing this paper. Thanks also to Kathy Broderick, New York State Office of Mental Retardation and Developmental Disabilities for her support of the Pathfinders Project.

gated school experiences. Instead of spending their final two years of eligibility for special education looking forward to catching special busses to day activity centers or sheltered workshops, this group of Pathfinders have rolled and walked from their homes to experience new connections and opportunities in their own neighborhoods and in the vibrant cultural and economic life that is a bus or subway ride away. They have been accompanied on their way by small teams made up of family members and allies from their schools and adult services. The work of their teams has been supported by Pathfinders, a project initiated and implemented by Job Path, an adult service provider committed to innovation in services to people with developmental disabilities, with co-sponsorship from New York State's Office of Mental Retardation and Developmental Disabilities (OMRDD), New York State's Developmental Disabilities Council, and New York City's special education program.

It is reasonable to ask what Shunelle and Josh and their fellow Pathfinders have to say about inclusion in community life. New York City's public schools enroll about 1,100,000 students; about 85,000 of these students receive special education services, and 20,000 of these students are served by District 75, a separate administrative unit, that among other programs operates 60 special education schools at more than 300 program sites. Some sites and schools are co-located with another of the city's more than 1,000 regular schools, but most high school students spend most of their time in a combination of self-contained class work and community based instruction near their school. Because schools specialize in particular disabilities or program purposes (transition, for example), most students are transported out of their local areas. (NYC Board of Education, 2001). The IEP's for all 96 Pathfinders participants identify a District 75 school as the least restrictive environment for them.

Like most systems, New York City's special education and adult services aspire to seamless transitions for special education graduates. However, the design of the city's adult service system for people with developmental disabilities makes continuing segregation the most likely outcome for District 75 graduates. Very large agencies operate a range of large Medicaid funded day programs backed up by clinics and specialized transport arrangements. Those family members who had considered the future after special education came to Pathfinders with the unquestioned assumption that a slot in an existing program represented the best possible alternative. Their questions were about how to marshal the necessary resources to avoid long waits for adult services and how to select a suitable day program from those on offer.

So Pathfinders's participants cannot testify to the benefits of inclusive schooling or the good effects of major system's change efforts. But we think that Pathfinders's students and their families witness the deep wells of capacity that can be tapped even in an enormous system bound to large scale, life-long segregation; even in a city that prides itself on being the nation's biggest, densest, fastest paced, most competitive, and most aggressive; even among families who struggle with poverty, language and cultural barriers, and a history of poor relationships with schools and professionals; even with students who most people have defined as too disabled to face the demands and experience the rewards of ordinary life. Almost every Pathfinders's participant has gained at least five things: some new neighborhood connections; a clear vision of their interests and gifts shared with family members and some of the staff that assist them; a plan for developing opportunities; membership in a supportive network of other people with disabilities and family members; and better informed expectations that the adult service system should provide them with individualized support to work and participate in community life.

Pathfinders's participants also witness the stickiness of segregated services. Despite good person-centered plans and an adult service system publicly committed to fund and deliver individualized supports for inclusive lives, almost half of Pathfinders's participants are hostages to segregated adult services or remain at home without day services because more individualized supports have proven too hard for adult service providers to arrange or sustain. Many who attend segregated adult programs do maintain the local connections initiated during Pathfinders, but it is their own energy and the support of families and community members that make this happen.

Change has not happened here because billion dollar systems have thrown their full weight into new paradigms of special education and individualized supports. Change has happened because a small group of teachers, school administrators, and adult services managers decided to work together, with leadership from the City's smallest adult service provider, to see what might be possible for a few students with disabilities and families who have been willing to explore new paths. Some of the people who have invested in and learned from Pathfinders hold key positions in their organizations as managers, administrators, and transition coordinators, and so its effects slowly multiply as these people work to re-align the systems in which they work. But this painstaking work is slow to shift an enormous system's inertia, and so we can only report on the way to small, fragile and significant changes in a very big and complex place.

The challenge of capacity thinking in New York City

Capacity thinking is the art of discovering the qualities that a person with a developmental disability can contribute to community life and then discovering people and places that value that contribution.

The city's scale and variety challenges the imagination and organizing skills of any reformer. There is the challenge of demographics. If its 309 square miles were a state, its more than 8 million inhabitants would make it the nation's 12th largest. Almost a million immigrants established themselves in the city in the past ten years, adding to a mix of racial and ethnic identities that counts 35% of the population as white, 27% as Hispanic, 25% as African-American, and 10% as Asian. (Census 2000). In 1990, Manhattan had the highest level of income inequality of any county in the US: the top income quintile made 33 times more than the bottom quintile. Average 1990 family income in a census tract between 85th and 91st streets was $301,000; average family income in a census tract between 145th and 150th street was $6,000 (Beverage, 1996).

Students in the city's public school system speak 140 languages at home. Sixteen per-cent of public school students identify themselves as white. More than half are eligible for free lunches (NYC Board of Education, 2001) and 62% of students have addresses in areas of concentrated poverty. (Campaign for Fiscal Equity, 2001).

There is the challenge of political and administrative complexity. Since the city's consolidation in 1898, borough governments have been in chronic conflict with mayors. And for 200 years the city has been in contention with the New York State legislature. Most adult services to people with developmental disabilities are administered by New York State's Office of Mental Retardation and Developmental Disabilities. Education is the City's affair, managed by a complexly decentralized bureaucracy that continues to struggle to provide adequate buildings and a sufficient number of trained teachers to meet the demand for high quality schooling. The administrators negotiating agreements around transition count their budgets in the tens and hundreds of millions and function as part of multibillion dollar systems responsible to different levels of government whose political leaders have conflicting agendas which may or may not coincide with the agendas of the people who administer public systems. Everything around Pathfinders has a highly charged political dimension.

There is the challenge of overwhelming variety. Yale University publishes a 2.5 inch thick *Encyclopedia of New York City*; Oxford University publishes a series entitled *The History of New York City*; Princeton University publishes a history of the city's water supply that documents a two hundred year history of power struggles between profit and public service (Koeppel, 2000). *The New York Times*, in addition to its stable of culture, entertainment, and food critics, employs six columnists to chronicle city life, including Randy Kennedy, whose *Tunnel Vision* column covers life in, on and around the city's subways.

Huge scale, diversity, variety, complexity and the special education and human service system's attempts to respond to them all challenge capacity thinking. Many District 75 students travel long distances from their own neighborhoods to work with teachers who may also commute a long distance to pursue community based instruction in a neighborhood in which neither teacher nor student lives. This matters because neighborhood matters to most New Yorkers. Neighborhood resources and relationships contribute significantly to many people's sense of identity and security.

Practicing capacity thinking in New York requires looking closely at the blocks around where a person lives and being able to spot places and people that might welcome that person's contribution. Sometimes this calls for people with the gift of seeing past obvious poverty and apparent difference and even danger spots to find the local associations and places where a good life goes on. Cultivating the art of finding the niches that escape the system's notice and assisting people with developmental disabilities to inhabit them along with their neighbors takes a systematic approach to person-centered development. The figure on the next page describes the Pathfinders' framework for discovering capacity in the social spaces that are far too small for the big systems to notice.

Person
Learn about...

...identity
...qualities
...environments
...skills
...challenges

Community
Explore...

...neighborhood
...what is on the block
...recreation options
...economic opportunities
...transportation options

Contribution
A Valued Identity
Support

Family
Listen for...

...values & identity
...connections
...resources
...neighborhood
...extended family

Service System
Create options...

...individualized funding
...family support
...service coordination
...individualized services
...collaborative agreements
among agencies

A person-centered development project

A relentless search to discover and mobilize hidden capacity threads
through the whole fabric of Pathfinders. In relationship to the city's
special education and adult service systems, Pathfinders as a whole
is designed as a person-centered development project (Mount, 1994).
In relationship to each student and team, Pathfinders focuses on
generating actions that challenge a deficiency view of person, family,
neighborhood, and city (Mount, 2000a and Mount 2000b).

Person-centered work holds both the worth of clear values and the
reality of uncertainty. The worth of specialized supports is measured
by their contribution to people's experience of five valued experiences: the respect that comes from playing a valued social role,
sharing ordinary places and activities, participating in relationships
and associations, making choices, and contributing to community
life (O'Brien and Lyle O'Brien, 1987). The valued experiences summarized
in the image on the next page indicate an overall direction for each
individual's unique search for a good life.

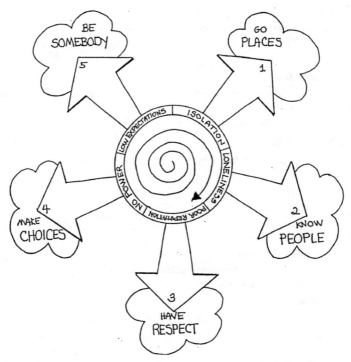

Uncertainty derives from two sources. First, people differ glorious-ly in their heritage and in their gifts and in their actual and potential relationships. Second, opportunities are unpredictable. Many people find their way to interesting and satisfying lives when preparation leads to an unexpected connection.

Person-centered work does not offer a programmatic answer. It defines a process that supports people to explore their interests and gifts and to search for opportunities to develop them. Understand-ing of each person's identity and gifts grows and changes as they design, try, and revise personally meaningful next steps in their particular circumstances. System managers can't mandate big quick-fixes full blown, but they can support the transfer of lessons from person to person and from place to place.

Person-centered development projects have four aspects:

- A focus question
- A working group that creates the space to explore new ways to act on that question

- Ways to learn and renew
- Forums that engage people with authority over important resources in the learning generated by the working groups

These projects develop recursively, like ripples in a pond. The energy and learning from an initial pattern of person-centered change generates interest and informs action among a wider circle of people. This wider circle revises and repeats the pattern in ways that energize and inform a still wider circle.

Framing a focus question

Person-centered development projects turn on a focus question that motivates a working group to learn together by changing the opportunities available to a growing number of people. For Pathfinders, the focus question is,

> **Could students whose current best option is placement in a segregated adult facility find paid and volunteer work in community settings, become involved in social and recreational activities in their neighborhoods, and develop new friendships and associations in their workplaces and neighborhoods?**

Notice that this question invites broad participation because it can be grasped from at least two starting points. Some people, including the originators of the project, see this as a question about the education system's and adult service system's capacity to provide effective assistance. For them, the ability of people with developmental disabilities and their families and their neighborhoods is not in question. Other people, including many of the people with developmental disabilities and families and school staff who have been active and successful in Pathfinders, take this as a question about what is possible for people with developmental disabilities who live in New York City. Either way of taking the focus question seriously will get people on the path with an attitude of experimentation. It is not necessary to convert to a belief in people's capacity before joining the work. It is only necessary to join with a genuine interest in discovering where the limits lie and a genuine interest in discovering creative ways to push those limits back.

Making space to work

Because continuing segregation is the typical result of the current system of special education and adult services, people who take the focus question seriously have to create a space to work outside the current system's habits and demands. The seed of Pathfinders was formed in 1993 when teachers and administrators from nine District 75 schools joined District 75 Transition Coordinators to learn person-centered planning by joining teams with 12 students and family members from their schools. Initially, a training course provided the necessary shelter from routine to allow new possibilities to emerge. School people and family members were able to give themselves sufficient time and space outside ordinary requirements to produce exciting results and important learning. The energy from this initial effort stimulated the development of a project to carry the work forward.

The diagram on the next page summarizes some of the new roles and connections some students have developed in their own neighborhoods through their participation in Pathfinders. The logo in the center of the figure expresses the project's values.

One parent vividly expresses the way this process developed in her son's life. Her account captures an important quality of the space necessary for Pathfinders to work. In this space, people collaborate outside their usual roles and boundaries. This involves school staff in moving from familiar territory to explore the opportunities available in Spencer's physical world. It involves Spencer and his family calling on their personal networks in new ways. It means suspending certainty that anyone, professional or parent, fully understands Spencer in favor of looking for new ways to decode his responses to changes in his expanding world. Notice that participation in the project accelerated a change that had already begun in Spencer's school.

> *Spencer and I were very fortunate to be in 373K (a District 75 school) with a Principal and Assistant Principal who were willing to listen to us and think differently. As the result of many failures to get Spencer to "adjust" to the inside of the school, we began to brainstorm together how to support him to be out in the community with good support. We finally found the right match between Spencer and a paraprofessional who respected Spencer and understood instead of just trying to control him.*
>
> *As we were involved in this brainstorming, we attended a person-centered planning workshop sponsored by District 75. Wow! This was it! We discovered that other people were thinking positively about the lives of people with disabili-*

Jason
Volunteering at
Kings County
Hospital
Taking an art
class

Jim
Working at
UPS
Playing basketball
on UPS league
on local league

Betsy
Volunteering at
Day Care Center
Taking yoga class
in the neighborhood

Andy
Working at
Medgar Evers
Day Care Center

Al
Volunteering at
Fulton/Cypress
Senior Center
Swimming at the
local YMCA

Dan
Volunteering at
Woolworth
Regular at neighborhood
Chinese restaurant

BE SOMEBODY
5

GO PLACES
1

LOW EXPECTATIONS · ISOLATION · LONELINESS · POOR REPUTATION · NO POWER

MAKE CHOICES
4

KNOW PEOPLE
2

HAVE RESPECT
3

Mike
Working at
Pathmark
Taking karate class
in the neighborhood

Mike
Working at
Project Sweep
Attending St John
Rec Center

Jessy
Working at
Day Care Center
across the street
from home
Walks to work with support
from family &neighbors
Bingo (without her mother)

Jackie
Volunteering at
Cobble Hill
Nursing Home
Swimming at the
neighborhood YMCA

Tom
Singing in his
church choir
Bowling on a
community league

ties, and we developed even better ideas for jobs and other community activities that Spencer might enjoy. Spencer's behavior did not just change over night just because we were thinking about creative options. However, we did find that we were more able to listen to and interpret his behavior and make better choices on his behalf.

Spencer got a job at the Barnes and Noble bookstore on the Pratt Institute campus. This was a good fit because we had connections there, Spencer loved the work, and he was able to dress beautifully which is part of his claim to fame. He worked alongside college students stocking the bookshelves. He loved it, and the students were very supportive of him.

We have learned that things do not just get better and stay better. Spencer's advocate, the store manager, left and was replaced by another manager who was not supportive of Spencer. Spencer picked up on the manager's negative attitude and engaged old tactics of acting out; so we began to look for another job. Spencer was still having outbursts, but they were far less frequent as he began to be more independent and form his own life.

When things fell apart at the bookstore, Spencer had already graduated from high school and we were already involved with an adult service agency that provides individualized support for community experience.

Spencer now works as a store associate in the shoe department at a K-Mart in Brooklyn where he has been employed for three years. (Kendall-Browne, 2000)

Investing in renewal

Person-centered development is a learning process for everyone involved. It is a matter of discovering and sharing new ways, not of transmitting pre-formed answers. Confusion and discouragement arise. New clarity and joyful surprises arise. And sometimes people get stuck on a plateau.

Pathfinders invests in renewal by creating habits and rituals among its participants. They share their dreams and visions. They devote regular time to celebrating good news. They routinely talk about what is working and what needs to be improved. They reflect on what they are learning from their efforts. They find occasions to tell others their stories and the lessons they have learned.

Over time, the ritual of sharing dreams and good news has had a powerful effect on many people with developmental disabilities. At large group workshops, a young woman who spent her first workshop in silence, head down, now demands her turn with the microphone. She says that hearing other student's with disabilities speak inspired her to use her voice. A very shy young man without speech, overlooked in last year's final workshop because of his usual reluctance to share with a large group, interrupted to bring forward the poster that expresses his dream and chose a team member to interpret it for the workshop. As the annual sequence of five workshops unfolds, each with its time and rituals for renewal, voices become more clear, signs more emphatic, shoulders straighter. These changes in communication reflect changes in what people have tried and changes in the support they experience from the people who love them and the people who teach them, changes that need to be given meaning by sharing them.

Creating forums

From the point of view of the managers of the systems whose routines define the life-chances of people with developmental disabilities, person-centered development projects can play the sort of role that Lewis and Clark played for Thomas Jefferson. They bring news of how to find previously uncharted destinations, appreciation of the good things to be found there, and estimates of the costs and risks of further development. The best medium for communicating a project's discovery is a forum. Forums allow face-to-face contact between those involved in a person-centered development project and those with authority over resources that matter to continuing and disseminating the project's work. Forums bring people together for creative problem solving; they are not structured as reports to decision-makers but as occasions to jointly design platforms for changes in the system's policies, practices, and programs that will multiply the benefits from the project's learning.

Forums make the most of the strength of person-centered development projects, which change what the whole system does for a small number of people who are actively involved in designing the change. Their efforts demonstrate new possibilities and identify the exact system rules, routines, and structures that block important next steps or make it difficult for others to follow the path. Forums set the problem of adapting the system squarely in front of its managers so that growing numbers of people will benefit from what project participants have demonstrated. Forums allow the kind of thinking that will influence decision-maker's agendas over time.

Some forums happen in large groups, but many involve a few interested people thinking together about how the Pathfinders's experience is relevant to their assigned tasks. Pathfinders forums have involved principals from District 75 schools, District 75 Transition Coordinators, regional OMRDD managers, and adult service agency managers in considering the implications of the Pathfinders's experience for their work. District 75 personnel say that their participation in Pathfinders has influenced curriculum for 14 to 18 year olds in at least one school, the ways in which several schools involve students and family members in IEP's, and some of the District's transition planning process. OMRDD and adult service managers say that participation in Pathfinders has influenced the ways they plan with people and families and strengthened their commitment to individualized supports and to "day programs without walls" (an individualized alternative to activity centers). The complexity of the systems makes Pathfinders one influence among many competing forces. The purpose of forums is to make that influence as clear and strong as possible.

The search for capacity

The Pathfinders's project offers students in their last two years of eligibility for special education two kinds of support: focused staff time and a person-centered planning process. When this support is successful, students have a team that includes members of their family, school staff, and adult service staff, a person-centered plan that guides their team in supporting their search for new possibilities, and the funding necessary to move smoothly to receiving individualized supports from an effective and well informed adult service provider.

Five themes define the core of the Pathfinders process. These themes guide the work of each student's team and structure each Pathfinder's workshop.

- **Build a capacity view** of the students and consequent expansive views of positive futures in community life.
- **Challenge deficiency thinking** –old ways of thinking about what the student can't do– and leave behind limiting views about the future.

- **Discover places, people, and associations** in the student's local community and consequently strengthen the student's involvement in these opportunities.
- **Increase expectations** of school programs and adult service agencies to provide individualized support for integrated community experiences.
- **Join with others to advocate** for resources and services that fit the student's vision.

Staff support

Two skilled staff (employed by Job Path at 1.5 FTE) support Pathfinders students and families by meeting them in their homes; helping them to arrange the assistance they need to participate in the project (interpreters, transportation plans, food preferences, etc.); supporting them to gather and maintain a working team; assisting them to do their part in following through on plans, filling out paper work that comes in unfamiliar languages; negotiating eligibility for adult services funding; locating and selecting an adult service provider; and tracking follow through by school and adult service staff. They are also available on request for school and adult service system staff to consult, to problem-solve, and to provide links to help. Their direct engagement with families on their own turf is one key to a much higher level of family and extended family participation in the Pathfinders's process than school personnel predicted.

Pathfinders's staff do not duplicate the efforts of system personnel. They do the many kinds of relationship work that often goes undone by overloaded teachers, service coordinators, and case managers. It is up to them to discover ways to shift the system's inertia, opening up small cracks in walls of routine that allow people to wiggle through and experience new possibilities. They help teams find ways to offer each member real opportunities to contribute to the student's success. They also bear the frustration that often goes with high expectations for people they care about in a system that often does not know how to keep its agreements with the people and families it serves.

Person-centered planning

Five times in each school year, from 12 to 20 Pathfinders's students and their teams gather from across the city for a daylong workshop. Project participation and team membership are voluntary. Teams include District 75 students, family members (usually one or two parents, sometimes grandparents, brothers or sisters, and occasionally aunts, uncles, and cousins), school staff, and, as graduation approaches, adult service staff sometimes join the team.

The meeting space reflects Pathfinders's staff efforts to create a welcoming and stimulating environment for creative work. The variety of meals and snacks mirror the participants's diverse cultural identities and provision has been made to accommodate different languages and modes of communication. There is a roving microphone to amplify each person's contribution to the large group's work. There is lots of poster paper, many multi-colored pens, and numerous graphic aids to encourage communication about personal capacities and positive visions for the future.

A team of experienced facilitators guides the process. They work to build a large group climate of trust and collaboration by making it safe and acceptable for every team member to share dreams, fears, achievements, reservations, discoveries and uncertainties. They support people to talk from their hearts and not just from their heads. They encourage clear, ordinary language and discourage the jargon, acronyms, and labeling that can trap people's thinking and create distance between those who label and those who bear labels. They invent ways to invite people to move beyond their roles as "Teacher" or "Mom" or "Assistant Principal" or "Transition Coordinator" or "Special Ed student" and into creative thinking and action for real change. They actively support students to risk speaking out about what really matters to them, in whatever form allows them expression. They structure the work of the students's teams and the work of the whole group to encourage an active search for capacity and opportunity.

The purpose of each workshop is the same as the purpose of each team meeting: to encourage, guide, and actively support each student, family member, and staff person to connect with local opportunities, discover capacities and make a positive contribution. From the first workshop, team members hear the stories of students, parents, and staff who have gone before them from the students and parents themselves.

Initial workshops support teams to construct personal profiles and a living account of what the student and those who know and care about the student see as a desirable future. (See Mount, 2000b for the details of this process and the graphic formats that support it). Later workshops bring people information about the ways the system works, about the everyday work of community building, and, perhaps most important, news from other teams about their discoveries, achievements, difficulties, and questions.

The level of mutual support that develops among students and parents outweighs the problems of many teams working in the same time and space. Teams have the opportunity to follow up on partially completed tasks as they meet between workshops.

The Pathfinders experience

Many Pathfinders want to reach out to other students and parents to encourage and inform their search for a capacity view. These two excerpts from a workbook for Pathfinders Participants (Mount and Lyle O'Brien, 2000) capture the experience from the point of view of a student and from the point of view of a student's father.

Hi, I'm Josh.

I graduated from high school a year ago...

I love geography. I love to look up places in the Atlas. I am a big fan of the weather channel, and I like to find the places discussed on the weather channel.

The mailroom job is perfect for me because I learn more about geography. I move around all day, and I sort and put things in order, which I love.

I am going on job interviews now as I would like to become permanently employed in a mailroom. I would like to work in a mailroom. My job coach goes with me.

One person in my Synagogue is writing a recommendation to help me get a job. He remembers my enthusiasm during my Bar Mitzvah.

Yes, you heard me. To the surprise of many people, I completed the requirements for and participated in my Bar Mitzvah at my synagogue. I memorized many of the songs, prayers, and Hebrew and I sailed through the service! I was so excited because I did so well. It was the first time I ever spoke in front of a lot of people, and everyone was so happy. People said such wonderful things to me. People never cheer during services, but everyone was cheering that day! It was one of the best days of my life!!!!!

I also have earned the 6th belt required of a Tae Kwan Do master. I am a member of a Tae Kwan Do School in my neighborhood. The whole place works together to help me earn my belts. I was amazed that I broke the board to earn my last belt. I was shocked, I couldn't believe it! Everyone cheered. It is a great feeling to belong to this group and be invited to all the great parties too. (Wolf, J., 2000)

***

Twenty-one years ago, my wife Lucia and I had a beautiful girl whom we named Cristina. When Cristina was only eighteen months old, our baby girl came down with meningitis. That bout with meningitis changed her life and our lives forever. After three days in the hospital, we brought her home but we had no idea what was ahead.

Needless to say, since early on, Cristina was overly protected not only by us, but also by everyone else in our extended families including her grandparents, uncles, cousins, and friends. Cristina was after all a very special child… For example, we never allowed Cristina to go outside and play with other kids her own age. We felt that she would be treated differently, maybe even with cruelty by the other children. In their innocence, they would not understand how she was different and special.

We always held Cristina by her hand whenever we took her out of the house. She soon grew accustomed to being treated this way. As she walked she kept her eyes very close to the ground, no more than two or three feet in front of her. She depended on us to be her own eyes and ears.

When I attended my first Pathfinders workshop about two years ago, I was outraged and couldn't believe the things I heard at that meeting. They talked about empowering young adults like Cristina to take charge of their lives. How could they? In my mind, this was all nonsense. Very discouraged, I came home and I told my wife that I was not going back to the second workshop.

Even though I was angry, I couldn't forget the things I heard. Could Cristina have an independent and productive life? Other parents and their children talked about their dreams and ambitions for their future, and these dreams were not that different from my own when I was their age. I went to the second workshop and I was in-

trigued but not yet convinced that Cristina could actually have all these things.

I wanted my wife to hear what I was hearing, so I brought her to the next workshop. I was almost to the point of letting Cristina dream about all these wonderful things for herself. My wife went through the same trauma and disbelief as I did.

In spite of our disbelief, we soon became believers... After hearing only words of encouragement and love from these unique professionals, we were more receptive to many ideas, including supporting Cristina to learn to travel using the bus and subway. She now travels from one side of the Bronx to the other on her own!!!!

Cristina just graduated this year, the year 2000, so we are moving into another chapter in her adult life. A year ago we feared reaching this milestone, but today we are far more hopeful. A year ago, we could have never imagined that Cristina would work at the Gap in Manhattan and travel there independently from our house in the Bronx!! Each step we took to build belonging and contribution to community life, both through volunteer and paid work, took Cristina one step closer to her dream of working at the Gap.

This journey toward community inclusion started the day we let ourselves brainstorm about community building. You won't believe what you will come up with if you ask yourself the same questions, and are open to new ideas! We have learned that Cristina is in the center of her future, and we have become the source of encouragement for her to continue to become more independent. Cristina dreams about living in her own apartment in New York City. She talks about her mother, sister, and I coming to visit only!!! Given all that has happened in the past year, anything seems possible when we have faith, determination, and take one step at a time! (Rodriguez, 2000)

Of course, there are some stories with fewer exclamation points. Segregation is sticky, and some families have traded uncertainty about whether adult service providers could learn to deliver individualized supports in a timely and reliable way for the certainty of a day activity program slot. Some students have not had a team member with the energy and ability to pull things back together and have lost their place in valued neighborhood activities. Some graduates remain in the training placements popular with the City's supported employment providers instead of moving on to the payroll as a full employee of the business they work for. These problems cannot be explained by individual disability or family troubles. They are clearly problems the service systems have to solve. And one consequence of Pathfinders is that the people with developmental disabilities and their families know that the problem is not their fault and they know that positive change is possible.

Pathfinders's participants –students, family members, school staff, and adult service staff– witness that searching for capacity works as a way to make it in New York. And, as one of the city's anthems has it, "If you can make it here, you can make it anywhere."

For information about Pathfinders, contact
    Fredda Rosen
    Job Path
    22 West 38th St
    New York, NY 10018
    (212) 944-0564

References

Beverage, A. (1996). Five important New York metro area trends. *American Sociological Association Footnotes, 24: 1*, 2-3.

Campaign for Fiscal Equity (2001). *The State of Learning in the New York City Public Schools.* (www.cfequity.org/ns-sta-1.htm).

Jeffrey. P. (1999, Spring) Letter from a grandmother. *Pathfinders, 1*, 4.

Kendall-Browne, V. (2000) Spencer's Story. In Mount, B. and Lyle O'Brien, C. (2000). *Lives in transition.* New York: Job Path, pp 8-9.

Koeppel, G. (2000). *Water for Gotham.* Princeton: Princeton University Press.

Mount, B. (1994). More than a meeting. Benefits and limitations of personal futures planning. In V. Bradley, J. Ashbaugh, and B. Blaney (Eds.) *Creating individual supports for people with developmental disabilities.* Baltimore: Paul Brookes Publishing. (Also in *A little book about person-centered planning.*)

274

Mount, B. (2000a) *Person-centered planning: Finding directions for change using personal futures planning*. Amenia, NY: Capacity Works (www.capacityworks.com).

Mount, B. (2000b) *Life building: Opening windows to change using person-centered planning*. Amenia, NY: Capacity Works.

Mount, B. and Lyle O'Brien, C. (2000). *Lives in transition*. New York: Job Path.

NYC Board of Education (2001). Facts about the New York City Public Schools. www.nycnet.edu/news/facts99/stats.htm#17.

O'Brien, J. and Lyle O'Brien, C. (1987). *Framework for accomplishment*. Lithonia, GA: Responsive Systems Associates.

Rodriguez, R. (2000). Challenge deficiency thinking. In Mount, B. and Lyle O'Brien, C. (2000). *Lives in transition*. New York: Job Path, pp. 16-17.

Wolf, J (2000). Hi, I'm Josh. In Mount, B. and Lyle O'Brien, C. *Lives in transition*. New York: Job Path, p. 23.

Wolf, M. (2000/2001, Winter). Who is Josh? Developing a capacity view *Pathfinders, 2,* 4.

21

Large Group Process for Person-Centered Planning

Connie Lyle O'Brien and John O'Brien

Sometimes the best road to inclusion runs through voluntary participation in a large group dedicated to supporting the creation and implementation of person-centered plans. Such a large group gathers up to twenty circles in one big room, each circle formed around one focus person, and meets at regularly scheduled times for up to a year or more. A facilitator team guides the whole large group by...

- Introducing the ideas and skills essential to person-centered planning.
- Defining a set of person-centered planning tasks for circles to work on in a self-managed way.
- Orchestrating the sharing of experiences and learning among the circles.
- Involving resource people who provide relevant ideas, information, and inspiration.

Between large group sessions, circles try out what they have planned and, if they choose, meet with skilled facilitators to work some more on person-centered planning tasks. The facilitator team checks-in with circles between meetings both as a form of support and as a way to design the next large group session.

Like any person-centered planning, the purpose of the large group process is to show forth and celebrate the differences among individuals and indicate fruitful connections between each person's capacities and the particular constellation of capacities available in their world. To read about the procedure and some of the results of two large group processes that support person-centered planning, see Chapter 20, which describes New York City's Pathfinders Project, and Chapter 21 which describes Sequoia, a process involving senior parents and their sons and daughters in Seattle.

Connie has learned directly from being part of the facilitation team for the Pathfinders project along with Beth Mount, Carolann Granata, Debbie Lamothe Sainte-Rose, Yvonne Oliver, and Fredda Rosen. The Pathfinders process convenes people for an introductory eight hour session at the beginning of the school year and for four hour meetings every two or three months. The examples in this chapter are drawn from the Pathfinders experience with a note from a team in Seattle who created their own version of the process with help from Connie.

Safeguards

Person-centered planning in a large group might seem like a violation of the axiom that the work must proceed "one person at a time". It is surely a more usual practice to gather around one person, in a place that is familiar, with the focused attention of skilled facilitators, and the assurance of privacy. But bringing familiar people to a public space shared by other circles of people with a similar concern for a better future offers focus people some real benefits. So far, the large group process –which we see as a means– has raised participants' expectations for "one person at a time" lives and supports –which we see as the desirable end of any person-centered planning process. So far, participants have gained strength from what they choose to tell one another about their dreams and fears, successes and disappointments.

There seem to be at least four conditions that safeguard the process from producing cookie-cutter futures and unreasonable intrusions on people's privacy:

- **Participation is voluntary.** No circle whose members place a paramount value on privacy could be required to attend, and people who find the process unhelpful can and do drop out. If they want them, more usual forms of person-centered planning are available to them, perhaps from other sources.

- **A team of skilled facilitators,** with knowledge of and commitment to personalized supports for community inclusion, take responsibility for designing, guiding, and re-designing the process. As with anyone who guides person-centered planning, the role of the facilitator team is to create a climate that supports people to listen to one another with respect and thus to highlight the uniqueness of each person's situation. The availability of skilled facilitation for circles with work to do between large group sessions supports circles to struggle with issues that are too complex or too sensitive for the time and space and level of facilitation available in the larger group.

- **Circles** include the focus person and at least one person who loves the focus person and usually others with a personal or work related investment in the focus person's future.
- **The group as a whole is diverse** at least in terms of past experiences and current expectations and, ideally, in terms of generations, community and family roles, income, race, ethnicity, and culture. And, the group as a whole is united by a common life transition and the circumstances of living with disability in a particular place and service system.

When is a large group process worth doing?

No planning process, whether supported by a large group or not, guarantees focus people personalized support from the service system. What planning can do is increase the chances for a positive future by supporting action that people can take with the resources available to them and clarifying what the service system can do to assist people in experiencing a good life. A large group process has an important contribution to make when focus people and their circles will benefit from...

... ideas, information, and inspiration that will raise their expectations about what is possible for people with disabilities and what works to generate new personal possibilities.

... improved skills in expressing their ideas about a desirable future.

... the opportunity to explore the difference between what is desirable and possible for them and what the existing service system is most likely to deliver if they simply put themselves in its hands.

... increased confidence in discovering and making positive community connections.

... encouragement to deal constructively with fear and work on a reasonable balance between risk and protection.

... the sense of belonging to a group with common cause and the opportunity to move out of feeling isolated.

The process isn't for everyone. Some people can't find the energy to participate, though others –like the grandmother who regularly made the long bus trip to large group meetings from the nursing home where she lives– overcome considerable obstacles because they find participation worthwhile. Some people are simply looking for a placement in a service that will manage things for them. They don't want to spend time making local connections and developing new opportunities; that is what service workers are paid to do. But it has been nearly impossible to predict who will come if invited, who will stick with the process, and who will take positive action. People have benefited despite initial skepticism about the process or serious doubts about the capacities of the focus people. People have moved from certainty that a focus person could not survive outside a specialized service building to delight at the person's success on a real job. Parents have found the process beneficial despite a history with schools or service providers that lead the professionals that know them to label them "overprotective" or "unworkable" or to predict that they will never come to meetings, much less participate actively. Sometimes our experience bears out these professional curses, but infrequently enough.

Local service capacities make a big difference to the results. Participants in New York City, where huge congregate services are the rule, have a much harder time realizing the vision of a real job than participants do in King County, Washington, where most of the system's funds are invested in individual supported employment. But in either setting, engaged focus people and family members find benefit in the large group process.

What the large group setting contributes

Many of the benefits that people experience come from the large group setting itself.

In the very first large group meeting, facilitators encourage Pathfinders participants to introduce themselves to the whole group and, after completing person-centered planning tasks, to share some of their work with the group. Those who can speak or whisper use a microphone; those who do not speak find other ways to make their unique presence felt. With encouragement and practice shoulders straighten, heads come up to allow eye contact with the rest of the large group, voices or non-vocal messages grow more vivid, and more and more hands reach confidently for the microphone. People display the posters their circles make with pride and excitement. Having these experiences together often gives parents, friends, and service providers –and often the focus people themselves– the chance to be surprised by changes in the competence focus people display.

As time goes on, participants learn from one another. Focus people may initially have only small ideas about their futures, or they may have big ideas that they fear to communicate. As they hear other people with developmental disabilities talk about their visions and what they have done to realize them, they have models that encourage them to be more bold and provide ideas about facing barriers and solving problems. At first, invited resource people with developmental disabilities who are a bit farther along in their journeys provide this modeling. As the year unfolds, the plans large group members make and the actions they take allow members to be models of positive action for one another. Whether it's riding public transportation alone, dating, joining a local association, or taking a job, when one focus person learns about another's accomplishments he begins to think, "If she can do that, maybe I can too."

A similar learning process happens among parents. When Vaulda, Spencer's mother, says that she carries a "mommy lump" of fear that her son with autism will be hurt as he makes his way around his community, most other parents can identify with her. When she goes on to say that she can't let her fear stand in the way of Spencer having a real community life, and then describes Spencer's days, other parents can look within themselves for the courage and problem solving ability to imitate her.

This learning involves more than discovering images of success. The stories people share provide useful information ("Oh, I didn't know Medicaid could pay for that.") and ideas for strategies ("I never thought of asking our pastor for job leads."). Models of acknowledging fear and moving on anyway, finding ways to pick-up after failures, and keeping on in the face of rejection or disappointment have particular relevance to circles who are trying to support better lives in a difficult world.

The large group also provides an appreciative audience for plans and positive steps forward and a supportive audience for stories of disappointment or failure. Group members spontaneously applaud or cheer one another's good news, express righteous anger when they hear of mistreatment, and cry when other's face sadness or grief. People thank one another for good ideas and honest expressions of feeling. Over time, many participants bloom in this atmosphere. After several sessions of seeing the positive reception other focus people receive when they share the graphics resulting from their circle's work on a session's person-centered planning tasks, a young man who does not speak and who had not come in front of the group before rolls to the front and proudly holds up his poster while another circle member reads it. The group cheers his accomplishment.

The large group offers people another source of contacts: job leads, referrals to a capable dentist who takes Medicaid, who to ask for help in unsnarling a problem with social security.

The facilitator's role

Large group facilitation is different from facilitating a plan with a single focus person. The role involves more effort in setting the stage by creating a respectful and positive working environment for the whole group; involving resource people who can supply inspiration, ideas, and information in a way that is relevant and credible to participants; and teaching participants about what they need to know about the process. It takes considerable forethought to define the person-centered planning tasks in ways that allow circles to self-manage their work. It takes self-discipline to coach circles during their work time without taking over the circle's responsibility.

Large group facilitators listen to participants as they work in their circles, during breaks, and as people are gathering. They listen for themes that need clarification or elaboration with the whole group. They listen for things that participants would benefit from telling and the large group would benefit from hearing. They create safe opportunities for participants to say whatever they want to the whole group: expressions of disagreement, anger, and fear are as important to hear as affirmation and positive feelings.

The facilitator team includes at least one person who makes it her business to check-in with participants between sessions. Facilitation team members may also offer help with further person-centered planning tasks or assist with problem solving. What happens after a session makes an important difference to the design of the next session.

Facilitators have less direct control in large group processes than they do when they work directly with a small group. Graphics may be less polished. A circle may take an excursion far from their assigned task. At least in early meetings, some people who don't appreciate the power of language may say things that make the facilitators wince. Initial ideas about the future may seem disappointingly thin. Some of these variations may be correctable within a large group meeting, but some will stand as they are. What is remarkable is the number of times that action and further discussion brings deeper understanding and positive results. Again and again, as the process earns the trust of its participants, we have been awed by the capacity of a large group that includes a nucleus of people committed to a better life for themselves and the people they love to nourish the whole group's growth. This has made us wonder if sometimes facilitators take on too big a role in person-centered planning.

These practices help the process along.

- Personal contact between a focus person or family representative and a facilitation team member before the first large group session provides participants with answers to initial questions, a chance to identify any special requirements, and a friendly voice or face to seek out on arrival.
- The physical environment should welcome people and support participants. Accessibility and accommodation to language or communication differences is essential. Food that reflects sensitivity to participant's religious practice or ethnic preferences adds to the welcome and celebrates the group's diversity.
- The group needs clear ground rules that encourage honest expression and respectful listening. The more facilitators are able to listen respectfully to expressions of skepticism or disagreement without discouraging the speaker, the sooner trust can grow.
- Encourage circles to pass around responsibilities for leading and recording the circle's work. Be sure that family members and focus people take their turns.
- As soon as one group has completed the large group person-centered planning process, invite "graduates" back to talk about their experiences and to identify what worked and did not work for them. Don't look for stories of perfection; people benefit from hearing how others have faced and dealt with difficulties and setbacks.

Why does it work?

Experience had shown us that a large group process can expand the benefits of person-centered planning. Then we came across the life's work of Albert Bandura, a social psychologist whose work on self-efficacy has stimulated much research and generated many applications (1997; 1995). It seems to us that self-efficacy theory explains much of what we have noticed and has the potential to suggest improvements in the practice of person-centered planning.

Bandura understands self-efficacy as people's belief in their capacity to organize and carry out the actions necessary to produce a desired effect. Research in Bandura's tradition demonstrates that people's beliefs in their efficacy influence (1997, p. 3)...

... what courses of action people choose to pursue

... how much effort they will invest in a course of action

... how long they will persevere when faced with obstacles and failures

... how resilient they are to adverse circumstances

... whether their patterns of thinking are self-aiding or self-hindering

... how much stress and depression they experience when they have to cope with difficulties

... how much they accomplish

Self-efficacy is not the same as self-esteem. It is a belief in one's ability to accomplish something despite difficulties rather than a sense of being valuable as a person. Belief in one's ability to achieve something does not assure success, but it does influence how hard and how long and in how many ways one works for an achievement and what learning one takes away from the effort, whether it is completely successful or not.

Many people with disabilities and their families and friends face a steep, rocky and slippery climb to a good life in community. Belief that they can figure out and then carry out a way to make that climb seems like an important resource for the journey. If we can modify the ways we do person-centered planning to increase self-efficacy, we should do so. (Shelley Dumas and her colleagues (2002) pursue this line of inquiry with participants in individual person-centered plans. We are grateful to them for connecting us to Bandura's work).

Research in Bandura's tradition identifies four kinds of experience that will positively influence people's belief in their efficacy if they have opportunities to think about the experiences in ways that connect the experience to their sense of efficacy (1995). These four experiences are:

- Acquiring the capacities to overcome obstacles through sustained efforts. Such tools include ways to think about and change goals and problems, skills, and the strength to keep going when things get difficult. Bandura calls these *mastery experiences.*
- Seeing people similar to themselves succeed through perseverance. Bandura calls this *vicarious experience* and notes that competent models transmit knowledge and teach skills and strategies

by the ways that they act and what they say about their thought processes.

- Experiencing acknowledged successes in environments where failure is unlikely and hearing other's express accurate confidence in their ability to manage changing situations. Bandura calls this *social persuasion*.

- Interpreting emotional and physical reactions to difficult situations as sources of energy for action or sources of important information about the task rather than interpreting emotional and physical reactions as reasons to give up or become despairing. Bandura discusses this influence of efficacy beliefs under the heading of *physiological and emotional states*.

Large group person-centered planning provides participants with opportunities to experience all four positive influences as well as the time and support to think through what they are doing in a way that can increase belief in their efficacy.

The process encourages people to focus on their capacities for positive action and allows a practice field for building new skills that affirms small positive changes from the first encounter with a microphone on *(social persuasion)*.

It provides people with models similar to themselves who embody important accomplishments as a result of dealing persistently with changing and sometimes difficult situations *(vicarious experience)*. As some participants take jobs or join in neighborhood activities, others learn of the rewards available and the possibilities for overcoming difficulties.

Sharing experiences across circles offers people different ways to frame the fear, tiredness, and feelings of being ground down by an implacable system that keep many people with developmental disabilities bogged down. They can think of these feelings and physical experiences as expressions of injustice, as reasons to keep working to make things better, as signals of a need for a new approach *(physiological and emotional states)*.

By design, the process encourages real world action that tests each circle member's abilities *(mastery experiences)*. As their first homework assignment, circles look for connections to local places, organizations and people. Resource people exemplify the struggle for good lives in community with personalized supports from the service system. Christina and her father share the learning from her experience of losing a carefully arranged volunteer job on her first day, finding another successful volunteer job, realizing her dream of traveling into Manhattan on her own to work at The GAP, losing that job and finding another job at a different downtown clothing store. As she and her father talk about the rewards of their difficult journey from overprotection and incompetence to achievement and a sense of possibility that now includes moving from her parent's home into her own place, they affirm their own sense of efficacy as they provide models for a new group of focus people and their families.

The process communicates by design that important changes will take at least a year of effort and more experienced people make it clear that things will sometimes be difficult, that successes may be partial or temporary, and that both persistence and thoughtful re-definition of strategy are likely to be necessary.

Throughout their time together, participants experience and talk together about the fact that drives the whole process: life with a developmental disability goes better when you have the support to define a clear vision and keep finding ways to work toward it.

References

Bandura, A. (1997). *Self-efficacy: The exercise of control.* New York: W.H. Freeman.

Bandura, A., Ed. (1995) *Self-efficacy in changing societies.* Cambridge, UK: Cambridge University Press.

Dumas, S., De La Garza, D., Seay, P. & Becker, H. (2002). "I don't know how they made it happen but they did": Efficacy perceptions in a person-centered planning process." In S. Holburn & P. Vietze, Eds. *Person-centered planning: Research, practice, and Future directions.* Baltimore, MD: Paul Brookes. Pp. 223-246.

From East to West: Large Group Process Comes to King County, Washington

Connie Lyle O'Brien and Marsha Threlkeld

Is this any way to get started? (Connie)

The rest of this chapter makes things sound so neat and orderly that I thought it would be good to describe the way the large group person-centered planning process developed by the Pathfinders project made its way from New York City to the Seattle area.

In October 2001, WISE, The Washington Initiative for Supported Employment, invited me to spend several days with them. They had heard me talk about the Pathfinders Project and asked me if I would spend one of my evenings with a group of students and family members who were in their final years of special education in a suburban high school. I like to tell people about Pathfinders and I enjoy meeting with people with disabilities and family members, so I agreed to what I thought would be a short talk followed by some discussion.

In the car on the way to the session, I discovered, to my horror, that I had misunderstood the evening's mission. WISE staff had gathered seven students and accompanying family members, friends, and professionals, not to hear about the process but to begin doing it. WISE staff, who are skilled facilitators of individual person-centered planning, were ready to support the continuation of the process. Each student came with between four and twelve people who assembled voluntarily at 7:00 on a week-day evening, with very little idea about what would happen.

After I picked myself off the floor, I decided we might as well give it a try and see what happened. So we did. The meeting was held in the school cafeteria where we shared a wonderful meal before starting the meeting (I didn't really get to enjoy the meal because I was too scared.) When we finished eating, students and their allies gathered together, each circle at their own table, with colored markers and a few sheets of chart paper stuck on a nearby wall or on tables stood on end.

Since I had prepared to give a talk, not facilitate seven groups of people at the beginning to try out person-centered planning, I was in kind of a daze. I started by briefly explaining the basics of person-centered planning and shared a couple of stories to illustrate what families and students in the Pathfinders project had to say about their involvement. The stories were success stories but each one included disasters or disappointments that people endured or overcame before reaching a dream.

Because we only had two hours to meet, I told the group that we would not be able to fully complete any one step of the plan, but that was OK because there would be other meetings to add or deepen ideas and to do the other steps in the person-centered planning process. We weren't planning to develop a perfect, full-blown plan this evening. Each circle created three posters: a relationship map, a places map, and a "what works"/"what doesn't work" map. Then each circle built on what they discovered by creating their maps and discussed, "Ideas about where in your community the student might share their gifts, capacities and preferences"

We took one step at a time and followed the same process each time. I explained the map or the question and told everyone to take 20 minutes to work on it. I said that someone in the group should volunteer to lead the discussion and another should volunteer to record. I also prepared people for reporting back to the whole group on what they had learned as they created the maps. As people worked I walked around listening and occasionally responding to a question for clarification.

We did the first two maps and then I asked circles to share something about what they were learning. People had been engaged in working on the initial maps, but the whole group's intensity increased notably as circles listened to each other. Spontaneous applause followed each circles' contribution. Every circle's presentation sparked ideas for others. Someone said "Oh, that's great! Susan's not interested in that exactly, but it makes me think of something that fits what she wants!" Students became bolder as they heard another student bravely state a dream or preference that they had been too nervous or shy to say out loud. "I never thought about doing that. That sounds like something I would like." When one focus person said that what he really wanted was a girlfriend, other students whispered or yelled, "Yeah!"

When our time was almost at an end, I asked everyone to take a few minutes and reflect on the meeting and identify "what worked" and "what could have been better".

It really helped to have the introductory ideas.
I wish there had been more time to hear what the other
groups were learning and coming up with. We learned a
lot from what other groups shared.
We really wish we'd had longer to work.
When do we get together again?

By the time I arrived at the WISE office the next morning, several parents had already telephoned to say how excited they were and how anxious they were to continue. One mother reported that her daughter had left the meeting elated and said,

That's the first time at a meeting that anybody wanted to
talk about what I was good at or wanted to do. It made
me feel good.

Almost one year later (Marsha)

These are our reflections on the year's work:

- Circles provided support to one another, offering ideas, resources and leg work on each other's behalf. Many heads, hearts and hands share the journey.

- The momentum generated by the process seemed to get everyone moving. If one team made progress, it gave the others confidence and energy to pursue their own dreams.

- There seemed to be less fear about trying new things. Having others progress forward at the same time gave confidence to all.

- The process has birthed circles which now have less involvement from the system. At this point, meetings consist of sitting in one big group, reporting back on progress, cheering each other on, and helping each other brainstorm for the next goal. Our presence is one of facilitator and less of teacher or leader. They have ownership over their group.

- Other individuals/families, upon hearing about the group and their successes, are now keen to start their own groups and begin the process.

- The positive things that have happened made it easy for individuals to get employment vendors to begin work on their behalf. In essence, the positive "hum" about the process has made employment service providers interested in serving individuals associated with the process. Being part of the project has added to their positive reputation.

Here is an update on the seven focus people:

Laura: Laura and her family have stepped away from considering placement in a sheltered industry. Laura worked this summer in a county funded summer youth employment position at a hospital. She has also connected with an individual employment vendor who will continue services with her. She has one year of school left.

Bethany: Bethany's family made the connection for a county funded summer youth employment position through the parks department. She also connected with an employment vendor who set up a summer volunteer position through the parks department's summer concert series. The agency will begin looking for a career position for Bethany in the fall, utilizing connections the family has with the city of Woodinville. Bethany has one year of school left.

Laura: Prior to this summer, Laura's school has sent Laura to a sheltered workshop as part of her school day. Laura and her family have decided not to proceed with sheltered industry. She worked this summer in a county funded summer youth employment position doing clerical work for a nursing agency. Laura made the connection to this job through her aunt and was supported by a work-study student. She has also connected with an individual employment vendor who will continue services on her behalf. Laura has two years left in school.

Daniel: Daniel's progress has been the quietest. His circle has been slow to build —on our initial evening it only consisted of his parents and a new residential provider who was off to a rocky start with Daniel. They have built a larger, more bonded circle and are now ready to talk about community employment. Daniel will not be returning to the workshop. Daniel has one or two years of school left.

Colin: Colin has employed the services of a master carpenter who designs and builds jigs to assist people with job tasks. Colin has had several pieces of equipment created to meet his needs. He worked very part time this summer in a clerical position, which will continue through the school year. He is interested in pursuing a clerical career and has two years of school left. His position was found through team connections.

Jasmine: Jasmine and her mother have had an uphill battle in moving Jasmine from the sheltered workshop. The school paid for Jasmine to go to the shop as part of her school day. Jasmine has worked this summer at a plant nursery. It looks as if this position will continue through the school year. The school has been involved in supporting her there, and she will not be going to the workshop this school year. Friends of the family and members of her church are involved in employment supports and will help to locate future jobs.

Tor : Tor and his team quickly found a position in the community. Initially the school provided supports and transportation, but Tor now rides his bike to work and needs little support. He has one year of school left.

Plans for the future include:

- Continuing work with the group of students and circles Connie helped us to begin. We'll also continue to work with the group of teachers from Kent who met with Connie (nothing could stop them now!).
- Increasing the number of groups. We have commitments to begin three new groups and are exploring the possibilities for two more.
- Some college work-study students worked with individuals this summer and things went really well. The work-study students offer a solid, but more natural style of support. The County DD system is interested in connecting college work-study students with these groups; providing extra manpower and support. We will look into that in the fall.

Here's a quote from Nancy, Laura's mother:

> *Thanks for the dinner and the transparent and open forum. I was encouraged. I am very thankful that there are a group of parents who are working through transition together. It makes the process seem less isolated and more supportive.*

Take care of your own lives, your own priorities as you help disabled adults work through their own lives. The vision for their future may or may not happen, but without a vision the people perish.
See you again in September.
Nancy

22

A Simple Half-Hitch

Debra McLean

> *It's naught but knots that tie me up,*
> *But for knots, naught binds me.*
> *The very same rope that gives me hope*
> *Could be the rope that winds me*
> *Belaying out, belies within,*
> *Be lies where truth be laying.*
> *The very words that seem so clear,*
> *Are knot, the words I'm saying.*

How work is so often the large knot that ties us to the community

I have always been inspired by the magic of seeing people not just bloom but burst into capability in the process of working. In my own patchwork history as a job developer and trainer, I have to say that the facilitative art of person centered planning has been as useful a skill as driving a car or reading. As a tool in figuring out job development and support strategies, it has rarely failed to show me what jobs might fit or how to proceed.

When people have had a very limited exposure to the diverse ways their fellow citizens earn money, it's hard for them to decide whether they want to go to work. But work is such an integral part of who we are and what we do that we can't give up on making good jobs a reality for people with developmental disabilities.

The benefits are obvious. I watch people, many of whom have never worked, go to work and see how soon they realize what being connected to a real job means. Their systemic exclusion from the world of work has affected and pained them, sometimes to the degree that they have ceased to ask for work, not because they didn't believe in or understand it, but because they felt it was a place they would never truly be allowed to be.

Most people with developmental disabilities have never worked or have held dismal underpaid jobs. They have lost hope in earning a living and so have the people around them, even those who knew them best and admired them. Their lack of work opportunity some-how got explained by their disability labels rather than the paucity of choices offered them.

Again and again, I have been struck by the secret of competence kept in the family. The secret is that the person is a learner, can do things, has interests, ideas, and methods of organizing their world –in spite of labels. Again and again, I have been moved by the way people's faces lit up as they told stories of competence:

He built a clubhouse with his brother in the yard.

She sorts all the cans by weight, even though she can't see the labels, when I bring the groceries home. One time she got mad at me and removed all the labels and wouldn't tell me which was which.

She puts all her clothes in the closet color by color.

The composite picture that families, friends, neighbors and sib-lings draw for me in the stories they tell gives form to the person's capability as a worker and shows very clear ways to pursue occupa-tions that fit them.

How work is that last stubborn knot to untie

People have sat through so many meetings, gatherings and encoun-ters, from the time they were very small and heard those dooming, damning words move from prophecy to painful reality…

will never work
low productivity
can't work
not interested in work
won't stay on task

In my experience, unwillingness to even approach the endeavor of developing a good job explains most unemployment among people with developmental disabilities. Just refusing to make a creative try explains more than those greater myths that people with disabilities can't or won't or shouldn't or don't want to work or that employers don't want them.

So many people have been excluded from the work force due to inaction justified by labels or perceived notions of incompetence that the possibilities for creating good jobs are wonderful. I believe all the people I work with are capable, and competent. I trust that their person-centered plan will identify both the right kind of job and the best strategies of support. Amazingly, each time it does.

Of course it's the people you know

There are many ways to get jobs. One is through the people we know. One person tells another person that a certain business is hiring, and to talk to a third person in a specific department. Friends or colleagues refer friends and colleagues to certain employers or call on their behalf.

Once people participating in a person-centered employment planning meeting identify definite skills or interests that can be tied to specific occupations, I ask people to name actual people they may know in that type of work. I have found that I, a stranger, in a particular town, could move swiftly through local social networks by following the names given to me at the meeting.

"I'm here because Mary Smith, told me to see you. Your name came up because her son, Eric, is looking for a job. He's very enthusiastic about Xerox® machines." Even if that business hasn't got an opening, I can continue on a personal intertwined trail by making my last question, "Who else should I talk to?" That way I always have a personal connection with the person in the next business.

Sometimes the connection is as immediate or quick as the family's pastor saying at the planning meeting that he never realized Joe's interest in construction and he would talk to the builders in his congregation on Sunday.

Sometimes it was a matter of following connections through the social networks of the town. A person tells me to talk to the next person in a similar business who refers me to the next and so on.

It's *also* who you don't know

Employers often hire people they don't know, based on common interests and skills. Employers hire people who are enthusiastic about their particular type of work.

> A woman who loved to arrange her vast collection of purses at home was pleased to be hired to arrange purses in a local store.

> An employer hired a woman to run a large noisy machine. She was someone who didn't talk but spent a great deal of her time yelling and pounding on tables. When a switch was placed on the table, near where

she sat in her wheelchair, she could run an automatically fed paper-shredding machine. She did this in a
large print shop that had many noisy machines, yelling
happily all the while. The employer commented, "You
know, when she is in a good mood she's a great worker,
when she's in a bad mood she's a really great worker".

A person's productivity is always a matter of job match plus the
support and structure that ensure success. The job must have elements of tasks that the person enjoys doing and can do independently or be re-structured so that the person can do independently.
In addition to kinds of occupations that might fit the person, I
collect clues for how to teach and structure the job through the
person-centered planning process.

Process

Assembling a group of people who know and like the person, I use
a variation of personal futures planning to get an accurate, quick
sketch of a person so that we can start job development immediately
after a short hour and a half of planning. I listen to the stories people share and record them. I am not a passive listener: I ask specific
questions regarding the person's habits, places, interests, and loves.

I use five basic maps to collect the wisdom of the whole group and
come up with five ways to begin work.

- Gifts, Strengths, Capacities → Rough Resume.
- Works/ Doesn't work for the person → Strategy for support, non-
  negotiables in the workplace and in the way the job is developed.
- Possible dream jobs, tasks → as many different categories of
  work environments the group can think of based on the first two
  maps.
- Personal Connections → as many actual local businesses and
  people connected to them as the group can think of.
- Resources → as many agencies, entities and people as the group can
  think of who might be interested in partnering to realize the plan.

I consider all stories about a person from the point of view of good
work for the person.

A woman who loves to meticulously paint her fin-
gernails a different color daily, exhibits her accurate
eye, steady hands, patience and careful dexterity She
was also the only one in the house who could find the

polish bottles amid the familial clutter. She became a
valued worker in the accessories section of a department
store, organizing and putting away stock. She can always tell customers and co-workers where everything is.

Perceived barriers to employment provide further information for
implementing a successful plan. If a person "can't be left alone at
all", I want to know how far away a person can be before it's too far:
next chair? next room? The activities people pursue on their own are
clues to occupational preferences and interests even when they are
the reason for others saying that a person needs constant supervision. A man I met "could not be left alone" because he persisted in
removing the light switch covers and molding from the walls, truly
a problem for his family, but a gift to the remodeling company who
eventually hired him.

Look beyond attributes: It's neither positive nor negative

It's not enough to describe a person as "kind" or "friendly" in
looking at attributes that will make a difference at work. Collect
specifics.

Tell me about "friendly".

She loves to stand at the church door and greet people.
She smiles at everyone and shakes their hands.

versus

He never forgets a person's name or face, he will be sure
to say hello and greet them personally"

or

She has a great memory for birthdays and special events
and loves to buy and mail cards for them.

All these different attributes and skills fall under the heading of
"friendly", but make a difference to what jobs might best suit a
person.

Inherent in all the stories concerned people tell are clues to genuine occupations. If a genuine occupation exists, then we can locate
the employers and share the good news. Clarity about a person's
interests makes it unthinkable to appeal to an employer on the basis
of charity or disability —as in "I'm representing an agency that has a
person in it with a bunch of labels, who has never worked in his life,
doesn't talk and would somehow be a worker in the most entry level
position you have because..." Clarity about a job that will really

suit a person writes a script about strengths, common interests, and community connections. "I'm representing a person who is very enthused and quick at molding removal. I'm wondering if we could talk. Mary Jones gave me your name."

Regarding dreams

I look closely at dreams and feel it is important to ask not only "What is your dream job?" but also "If this was your dream job, what would you be doing?" Inherent in people's descriptions of their dreams are the essential elements of jobs that might fit them. The details of these dreams are particularly useful in sketching out a direction of possible occupational categories to locate.

When Dan, a man with autism and blindness spoke about his dream job, he said he wanted to be a dentist. There was silence. Such a dream seemed impossible. In answer to the second question –"What would you be doing if you were a dentist?"– Dan described his vision, "I would feel and pull your face, and then I would go away and play the piano for you, then come back and fool around with your face some more". Dan was talking about dentistry and was also talking about music. From a job development standpoint, he was reminding us of his manual dexterity and skill at playing the piano. Matching fingers to specific keys and auditory acuity were prominent features of the stories his family told about him. Building from this realization, Dan ended up taking computer key boarding at a community college and became a transcriptionist. He loves the sound adaptation on his computer that says the letter of each key as he presses it. He was motivated and interested in acquiring this new skill, and he uses it as a way to earn a living.

Another person, Jeff, spoke eloquently about his love for elevators. Impressed by his passion, I neglected to ask him the second question, "If you were working with elevators what would you be doing?" He was hired by the state of Oregon to operate an antique elevator at the State Capitol building . He charmed the interview committee with his knowledge about the history and mechanics of elevators. For the first two weeks all was well. Then reports of wild and irresponsible elevator driving came back from Jeff's employers. Jeff was running the elevator too fast and sometimes without lights. He began to also leave the elevator unattended in order to explore the rest of the building. After discussion, observation and training, we all decided that this was not Jeff's dream job. Elevator operation is more about sitting calmly in a small confined space with occasional machine operation than it is about pursuing an interest in elevator lore. Jeff left the job and another person who was interested in needlepoint and word-find puzzles took the elevator job and proved highly successful in it. It was an important lesson to me to carefully consider the essential elements of the person's dream when considering job matches.

Both the person and the group of people concerned with the person have crucial information about job interests and conditions of job success. It is important to consider all the nonverbal information given by people regarding interests and preferences, as well as the stories told by people who know and care about them. Job tasks and routines are a collaborative effort among the person, the employer and the employment specialist. This collaboration is rooted in the person-centered plan.

Regarding resources

It is most effective to strategize from person to the resource rather than from the resource to the person.

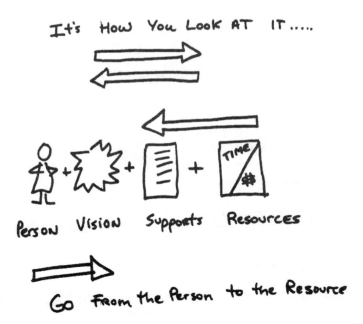

Too often planners begin with the resources available from a single source. The adequacy of this amount becomes the focus of discussion and often turns into a barrier to even commencing a search for the right job. Social service workers might begin a planning meeting with a conclusion, "We know Bob might like a job but there is not enough money available to support him."

This blocks the process and ignores the fact that the support, time and resources available depend on the vision and person, the type of job located, and the strategies devised for support. Resource development is most effective in partnerships, and resources can come from a multitude of sources, much the way college students utilize a range of funding to pay for their education.

Supports

I don't define support by units of human supervision. I let the person and the job define the support strategies needed and refine them accordingly. When I think about supports and strategize their implementation, I collect the information from people who know and like the person. What family, friends and neighbors have figured out about how to live with, teach, support, and communicate with the person provides keys to success in the workplace from non-negotiable requirements to subtle nuances.

> *I have to take my medication every morning.*
> *He sharply hits his own chin when he's not happy*
> *Raised eyebrows mean "I need a break"*
> *He's memorized every Golden Oldie since 1967*
> *If you sing it, he'll learn it.*
> *When she cooks, we put ingredients in small bowls, set up*
> *left to right and she just moves down the counter*

This information tells me how to structure and arrange supports so the job makes sense to the person, can be quickly learned and does not depend on simply having a job coach present. The role of the coach or employment consultant is to set up successful strategies in the work place and to communicate their use and importance to the employer.

Follow up and perseverance

Follow-up and follow-through are critical to success. After the plan is outlined at the meeting, it becomes a blueprint for job development and job design. A plan unrealized is often a plan unattempted.

The most common failure I encounter is beautifully crafted plans that never led to action.

Some basic math

$$\text{Person } (3e+3c/3p)B^2 = \text{Success}$$

Look at the person first: Consider who they are, what they do, where they live, what's important to them, what strategies and supports will succeed.

Multiply that by 3E: Empowerment, Encouragement, Employment. Consider: People need information and the encouragement, education and empowerment to act on it. Plus 3C Community, Communication, Collaboration

Divide by 3P: Persistence, Patience, Perseverance. The process of locating jobs takes continual process, work, and investment over time.

Multiply the whole thing by B^2 : Belief. Believe that the right job for the person exists somewhere in their community and, once it's located, the person will be able to do it.

SOME BASIC MATH

$$\left(\frac{3E+3C}{3P} \right)^{B^2} = \text{Success}$$

3E — Empowerment
Encouragement
Employment

3C — Community
Communication
Collaboration

3P — Persistent
Patience
Perseverence

Belief

23

Vocational Profiles

Anne O'Bryan

An important part of person-centered planning is assuming that most people will be interested in having a full adult life. In our society this includes the expectation of a job and career as a necessary option. Supported employment is a way of ensuring the probable success of that choice.

The Vocational Profile is the person-centered plan used in supported employment. Ideally, supported employment (and Vocational Profile planning) would follow on from broader person centred planning. Thus, an understanding of how someone wants their life to develop in general would naturally contribute to the creation of employment supports to achieve specific career goals. However, for some people with clear employment priorities or even just access to an employment service, supported employment may come before broader life planning. This should not keep someone from additional person-centered planning. People will grow and develop throughout their lives, and planners need to remain involved and flexible. Beginning the career of your dreams will likely lead to raised expectations in other parts of your life, and supports must be available to realize a growing quality of life in each person's home, social relationships, hobbies, leisure, education and lifestyle.

What is supported employment?

There are many definitions of supported employment; this is the one I prefer (O'Bryan et al. 2000):

> A person is hired and paid by a real employer.
>
> The job done meets the person's requirements and the employer's required standard.
>
> The person and the employer receive just enough help from a support organization to ensure success.

The supported employment service invests time to learn about each person; their interests, routines, skills and potential skills as well as potential support needs. This makes up each person's Vocational Profile and results in a description of the individual's ideal job. The Vocational Profile aims the supported employment service at the job and career opportunities that reflect the person's preferences and strengths. It also describes which work places are most likely to naturally provide the required support, such as clear tasks, a supportive atmosphere and helpful co-workers. Once the person has been hired, the service provides a variety of supports to the person and their employer which complement what is naturally offered in the workplace. This support can include teaching someone to walk to work, or to take public transport, or to arrange for a taxi, or to assist the person to find a co-worker willing to provide a regular lift. It will also include ensuring that the employer's induction suits the person and, wherever necessary, supporting the person and the employer to adapt teaching strategies, methods of assistance or the workplace layout. For people with more complex needs, it may also include specific individualized training, such as systematic instruction. Once a person has successfully begun employment and is working independently of their coach, the service's role is to stay in touch with the person and their employer just enough to ensure ongoing success and career advancement.

What should supported employment be like?

The Association for Persons in Supported Employment has developed *Ethical Guidelines for Professionals in Supported Employment* as basic human principles to follow (DiLeo et al):

- People receive assistance as unique individuals with varying interests, preferences and aptitudes.
- There are sufficient options related to each individual's interests and desires in life in order for them to exercise control and autonomy over their life's direction.
- Services are always dignified, age appropriate and enhancing.
- People have the opportunity to actively participate in all their chosen pursuits of life.
- Individuals are provided opportunities to develop skills of interest and use in their lives by discovering their capacities.
- People have access to diverse individuals in social contexts in order to build friendships, working relationships and networks of individuals to share places, interests or experiences.
- Services are designed to support persons in natural settings in ways that minimize artificiality or restriction.
- At all times, the individual receiving supports is the central driving force in the development of options and decisions.

- Employment should be an option for any person interested in working, regardless of label, support need or perceived functioning level.
- Jobs developed reflect personal interests, preferences, abilities and life goals as well as employer needs. The decision to take the job is made by the individual based on reliable information.
- Existing supports natural to the work environment are maximized for training and ongoing support. Best training practices and technology appropriate to the setting and culture are used.
- Efforts to provide a holistic and integrated life service support are made. The individual's family members and friends are involved.
- Persons have the opportunity and support for career advancement that may provide additional responsibilities, compensation and challenge.

How can person-centered planning using the Vocational Profile make a difference?

Many people have described the Vocational Profile process (Callahan and Garner, 1997, Mcloughlin et al 1987, DiLeo & McDonald 1993, Leach 2001). The Vocational Profile is a way of gathering information about each person's interests, skills and potential skills (as well as support needs) which aims job developers at the ideal job for each individual. It differs from many traditional employment assessments because it assumes anyone who wants to work is employable. It is at its most effective when seen as an investment to help someone learn about and achieve their career goals. It should not be imposed on people who know what they want and need minimal support to get a job.

This discovery strategy is useful for anyone with complex support needs or past difficulties in achieving successful employment. A relationship between the applicant and employment specialist is built up over time from conversations, observations and spending time together. This relationship results in a comprehensive picture of the job applicant which provides the basis for an individualized job development process. This profile captures what has been discovered and underpins all planning and job development.

Gathering the information

The profiler should use a variety of methods to learn about the person in a variety of environments. A good way to begin is to spend time with the person - talking with them, their family, friends and staff. Accompanying the person to a variety of work places and community establishments also helps. Observing the person's reactions to people, places, and activities can add information about potential career directions and indicate those most preferred by the person.

Talking to people who know the person well may produce additional information. Discussions can provide important ideas about the person's interests, experiences, habits and skills, especially if these are hidden or no longer practised. Of course, each person should suggest people to contact and give their consent for doing so.

Another way to gather information is through short job tryouts in a variety of real work places. Tryouts should take no longer that two weeks and may take no more than two hours - whatever time it takes to find out the person's interest in the particular job and level of comfort with the particular workplace atmosphere. Job-related preferences, stamina and speed can be observed, helping to narrow down types of settings, jobs and co-workers. On-the-job learning can also be explored, resulting in ideas for aids, adaptations and training strategies where needed.

Developing the Profile

Listening to and learning with the job applicant is an important part of developing the knowledge to support job and career success. However, a clear, attainable written vision is necessary to realize future success. The information is recorded in everyday language in sections that relate to the person's preferences, experiences, skills and support needs. These factors then influence the development of a job that is well suited to the person. Mcloughlin et al suggest the outline on the facing page.

These elements guide employment specialists to develop a job that reflects the interests, skills, potential skills, resources, hopes and supports available to a person. Recent focus on self-determination encourages vocational profilers to prioritise a person's preferences over the more static information gathered in other areas and to assist people to complete the profiles themselves (Wehmeyer 1992, Martin et al 1993, Kilsby and Beyer 2002). The profile does not follow a rigid formula but rather focuses attention on all areas which may help the person explore what is already there to assist them to become a successful employee. Where there are gaps in the profile, the employment specialist can work with the person to identify strategies to develop the

Vocational Profile Outline

Personal

  family and friends in the person's life

  support available through these relationships

  neighbourhood description including available services, transport and employment

  detailed description of how the person currently spends their time (e.g. 7:00 am -10:00 pm)

Educational

  school history and achievements

  work training achievements

  use of community resources

  recreation and leisure training and achievements

Experience of Work

  formal and informal work performed at home or for others

  sheltered employment

  paid work

Present skills

  domestic (personal care, home care)

  community (using shops and services, transportation)

  recreation and leisure

  academic (reading, maths, time, money)

  mobility (walking, sitting, lifting, carrying)

  sensory (hearing, sight)

  communication

  social interaction

  physical health

  vocational

Learning and performance characteristics and preferences

  ways the person learns best

  helpful adaptations

  preferred length of instruction

  preferences for working alone or as part of a team

Preferences

  types of work the person wants to do

  what the person enjoys doing at home

  observations of the kinds of work the person likes best

  observations of the types of social situations the person likes best

Connections

  potential employers amongst family, friends or neighbours

  family or friend contacts for employer leads

Flexibility or accommodations that may be required

  habits and routines,

  specific preferences for hours, location, work environment, compensation, transport, co-workers, adaptations and assistance

  physical/health requirements

  communication and behavioural support requirements

profile further. The completed profile helps aim the job developer at the ideal employment situation for the person.

Using the Vocational Profile

Carol is a woman labelled as having a severe disability who at age 30 lived in a long stay hospital in London. At that time she received an Industrial Therapy Assessment which summarized previous Health Care reports. The assessment reported that Carol had shown little or no interest in activities and that she became very agitated and generally disruptive in work situations. Because Carol uses a wheelchair, the assessors decided that most packaging tasks in the sheltered workshop were not suitable and assigned her to place completed bags of parts into big boxes. The way Carol responded to this assignment led the assessors to conclude that she was unsure about what to do, reluctant to complete the task, and required constant prompts. Eventually, she got so agitated that it was necessary to remove her from the situation. The assessors summarized Carol's work potential this way:

> *Carol is unsuitable for this type of work and probably any type of work which requires her to produce at a consistent level. She seemed to have little understanding of what was required and displayed little interest. She is unable to work in a busy environment where others need to concentrate. Her concentration level is very low as she was easily distracted away from the task and appeared at various times to be staring into space. The offer of a cup of tea on completion of the task proved not to be an incentive despite the fact that Carol is usually rewarded with a cup of tea for good behavior.*

Carol has now worked for four years in an office that manages school meals. She is involved in organizing the menus, developing promotional campaigns for the children and sending out all correspondence. Reflecting her sense of her self, she is pleased to be a member of a lively team of well-dressed individuals. Her success, which began with the creation of a careful vocational profile which is summarized on following pages, demonstrates the falsity of pessimistic expectations.

A look at the Carol who shines through the vocational profile shows that the conditions of her previous assessment couldn't help but justify pessimistic predictions about her ability to hold a real job. To produce new results, we need new ways of understanding who people are.

Key Points from Carol's Vocational Profile

<u>Domestic information</u>

Carol has strong connections to her parents and her aunt. While they are elderly and would not be able to provide support on a daily basis, their support of the employment process will be important to Carol.

Carol lives with 3 other people with learning difficulties. She wakes to an alarm clock, bathes and dresses with support and attends a day centre 5 days a week. She leaves for the day centre at 8:30 and returns at 3:45. Carol watches TV for relaxation and receives communication support from a Speech Therapist at home. At 7:00 she shares her evening meal with her housemates, then watches soaps until she goes to bed at 10:15.

Carol is close to her key worker, but has not developed friendships with the people she lives with. She occasionally attends the local Gateway club [a social club for people with learning difficulties].

Currently Carol uses the swimming pool and leisure facilities every week. She particularly enjoys shoe shops and is well known by all the sales people. Carol also enjoys going out at night to the local theatre or cinema and for a meal at a restaurant or drink at a particular pub.

Carol lives in a quiet residential area of similar properties that border on a large community park. Most amenities are a short bus ride away. There is a popular shopping centre within easy reach and a wide range of public services, including libraries, swimming pools and colleges. Bus and rail services are available and travel is easy. Carol has her own car and all staff are registered as drivers.

All types of employment are available near Carol's home, including retail, public service, private sector manufacturing, transport and all the service industries.

<u>Educational information</u>

Staff have focused on basic living skills since Carol was a child. Carol undertook light industrial work in industrial therapy and at a day centre. When she was clear about the purpose, she was keen and enthusiastic about the work When she did not understand what was required, she had difficulty in the work setting.

<u>Work experience</u>

The profiler developed his knowledge about Carol's work by spending time with her at home and by finding out about the specific tasks she had done at the day centre and at a local cafe once a week. Carol is extremely particular about her room and possessions. Her clothing is always clean and pressed. Carol does a lot of ironing for herself and others. The house vacuum cleaner has been adapted to clip on to her chair so that she can vacuum the downstairs. At the day centre Carol packaged drainpipe pieces for a local manufacturer. At the cafe she provided a washing and ironing service.

<u>Present skills</u>

Carol is able to use one hand, her head and chin to dress, clean and do some cooking.

She uses accessible facilities and prefers longer bus or car rides because it takes her quite a while to get in and out of the vehicle.

She has acute hearing and vision and takes a keen interest in everything happening around her. She communicates very effectively with a Rhebus book and some Makaton [a form of sign language].

Carol's strength of personality makes her well liked. She usually has a relaxed manner and lets people know if something is bothering her. She is rarely ill and is enthusiastic about working.

Being around lots of people in a busy warm environment enhances Carol's learning and performance. She learns fast, usually with just a demonstration. She prefers to then try the task herself with support provided only when she requests it. She does need support to get to and from work.

Carol feels pain if the temperature in her environment drops below legal standards for warmth.

Work preferences

Carol wants to work near or with computers.

Her appearance is important to her and she enjoys being with glamorous people of her own age.

Her parents think a busy office environment would suit her.

Carol is very social and primarily likes doing things with others.

She is interested in TV soaps and music on the radio.

At home she organises bills, insurance forms and other correspondence into piles in her room.

She also enjoys ironing.

Connections

Carol's connections are most likely to come from the potential employers near her home. There are many public and private sector administrative opportunities.

Flexibility and accommodations

Carol's place of employment must be warm and wheelchair accessible. There must be enough space for her to get around and all tasks must be in easy reach.

Carol will need support for all personal care.

Occasionally she may lose concentration and require a gentle touch on her right hand and a point back to her work. Carol needs clear instructions and may need support to return to work from her tea break as she has a passion for cups of tea.

She will work slowly while she is learning tasks and should not be put under pressure to speed up while learning.

Carol receives Benefits and she will require excellent benefit advice in order for her to earn an income as well as continue to be healthy and safe.

Ideal job

Working in a large office with a very social team of fashionable people of her own age.

How do we greatly increase the number of people at work?

Sadly, Carol is an exception. She is one of a growing but still far too small number of people with learning difficulties who have the support they need to hold real jobs (DoH, 1999).

A person's postal address is the strongest predictor of whether she will have the same opportunity as Carol. In some places, employment specialists are committed to seeing past labels and difficult personal histories to discover the capabilities, interests, and supports that make for success at work. Global assessments of severity of disability become insignificant as specific details of the exact assistance a person needs come into focus. Once the ideal job and the necessary supports can be clearly specified, people can work together to overcome the many barriers that still stand between people with learning difficulties and real jobs.

England's government has set a clear objective in *Valuing People*, it's policy statement on supports to people with learning disabilities [intellectual and developmental disabilities]:

> ***Moving into Employment*** *To enable more people with learning disabilities to participate in all forms of employment, whenever possible in paid work, and to make a valued contribution to the world of work.*

Making progress toward this objective calls for big changes in the ways agencies relate to each other and in the way the benefits system works for people. But these changes will only make a difference if people and families and service organizations can find what they need to get people to work (see O'Bryan, Simons, Beyer, & Grove, 2000) .

People and their families need

Good information about what job and support options are currently available in their area.

The expectation of all professionals that most people will wish to have a career and that it is possible for people to have satisfying jobs and careers in ordinary community workplaces.

Job coaches and other champions who will find out each person's ideal job and develop job and career opportunities from which people can choose.

Job coaches and other champions who will work with government people, such as New Deal Job Brokers and Benefit Advisors [staff in generic agencies responsible for helping people get work], to successfully support people into the work they want.

Good chances to influence local developments and decisions which will affect people's job and career opportunities.

Service organizations need

Adequate long term funding aimed at career success for people, including people with significant needs for assistance.

Clear policies that define the organization's purpose in terms of assisting people to work in real jobs and focus their energy on the kind of individualized job development and support that Carol's situation exemplifies.

Support from a network of other practitioners and researchers and people with disabilities at work to get around barriers such as the benefit trap.

Effective ways to continuously improve the effectiveness and efficiency of their practice. (The Quality Network, 1998).

Conclusion

Person-centered planning, in the form of a vocational profile, provides the necessary link between policy objectives and real life. Competently constructed vocational profiles provide the foundation for facing and dealing with the many problems that keep people from work, one person at a time. As service reforms take hold, fewer of these problems will be generated by government policy and agency practice. This will make the work of developing good jobs easier, but it will not diminish the importance of planning thoughtfully with each person.

References

Callahan, M. and Garner, J.B. (1997) *Keys to the Workplace: skills and supports for people with disabilities.* London, Paul H. Brookes.

Caven S. Mcloughlin, J., Garner, B. & Callahan, M. (1987) *Getting Employed, Staying Employed.* London: Paul H. Brookes

DiLeo, D. & McDonald, R. (1993) *Partnership and Collaboration: Supported Employment Service Co-ordination.* The University Affiliated Program of New Jersey

DiLeo, D., McDonald, R, & Killam, S. Ethical Guidelines for Professionals in Supported Employment. Richmond, Virginia: THE ASSOCIATION FOR PERSONS IN SUPPORTED EMPLOYMENT.

DoH (1999) *Facing the Facts - Services for People with Learning Disabilities: A Policy Impact Study of Social Care and Health Services*. London: DoH.

Kilsby, M. S. and Beyer, S. (2002). Enhancing self determination in job matching in supported employment for people with learning disabilities: An intervention study. *Journal of Vocational Rehabilitation, 17,* 125-135.

Leach, S. (2002). *A Supported Employment Workbook: Using Individual Profiling and Job Matching*. London:Jessica Kingsley.

Martin, J.E., Huber Marshall, L. and Maxon (1993). Transition policy: Infusing self-determination and self-advocacy into transition programmes. *Career Progression for ExceptionalChildren 16,* 53-61.

O'Bryan, Anne, Simons, Ken, Beyer, Steve and Grove, Bob (2000). *A framework for supported employment*. York: Joseph Rowntree Foundation.

The Quality Network (1998). *Our Lives: A framework of outcomes for services used by people with learning disabilities*. British Institute of Learning Disabilities and the National Development Team.

Wehmeyer, Michael, L. (1992). Self-Determination and the education of students with mental retardation. *Education and Mental Retardation, 27,*302-314.

24

Some Beginnings
Person-Centered Planning In The Midwest

Jack R. Pealer Jr. and Sandra Landis

Novelty doesn't come easy to the Midwest. A city in Indiana describes itself as "The Crossroads of America", and for several years auto tags in Ohio carried the sub-title: "The Heart of it All". One subtext of both of these slogans is that here is the place where things don't change too fast, where you can count on patterns being, tomorrow, pretty much like you found them today.

Since about 1983, the two of us living in Ohio have had a chance to try out the innovation that has now come to be called "person-centered planning" in this part of the United States where things new are often things suspect. Jack is still working with a formal organization that tries to support people with developmental disabilities. Sandy turned her efforts, several years ago, to the puzzles involved in the restoration to vigor of communities in southeast Ohio that have long been bypassed by industry and the economy.

The vignettes that follow in this chapter are about early work involved with personal planning with citizens of the Midwest who were said to have developmental disabilities. Most of this work took place between 1983 and 1990. So, while "person-centered planning" is *au courant* in 2002, with the idea finding its way into state laws, public policies at various levels, and agency advertising, this was all new just a short time ago. We were privileged to learn about the ideas and processes central to person-centered planning through our association with Wolf Wolfensberger and PASS, through our friendships with leaders like John and Connie Lyle O'Brien, Beth Mount, Jack Yates, and others, and through circumstances of our respective work that, in effect, forced us to consider new ways of thinking and acting with people whom we were supposed to help. So, here are some glimpses at the early days, somewhere in the heartland.

Getting to know people at New Castle

> *This task force is: to reduce the on-campus population of New Castle State Hospital to its certifiable capacity; to develop appropriate residential placement opportunities consistent with individual client (sic) needs; to plan for*

community services for those people who leave New Castle State Hospital.

— Commissioner, Department of Mental Health (1983), paraphrased

Connie Lyle O'Brien and John O'Brien have recalled that a part of the history of what has come to be known as person-centered planning lies in the work of members of a "normalization teaching community of practice" that gathered during the 1970's and 1980's around the teaching and use of PASS (Wolfensberger & Glenn, 1975). Lyle O'Brien and O'Brien remember:

> *Through the lenses provided by PASS, the originators of person-centered planning learned difficult lessons. They learned that opportunities for improvement which are evident to people with disabilities and those who care about them as people are very often obscured, ignored, or dismissed by powerful people in their lives as "impossible" or "unrealistic" based solely on the untested assumptions of the powerful person (p. 9).*

The story of our involvement with people who lived at New Castle State Hospital in 1983 is an example of an effort to test, at least for a couple of days, the "untested assumptions" of some people who had power over the lives of 150 people living at New Castle. Our purpose was to help state-level officials meet some of these people face-to-face. Our hope was that such meetings would make a difference in how those officials carried out their official-dom.

In 1983 the Indiana Governor's Commission on Mental Health decided that it was an important time to revise goals that had been set for the Indiana Department of Mental Health. One of the newly revised goals said that Indiana would see to it that all of its state-operated hospitals or other institutions would be certified to receive Medicaid payments for services to patients/ residents. Another goal dealt specifically with the New Castle State Hospital; it was intended that the "strain" on the population of New Castle would be relieved by means of a reduction of the hospital's population from 350 people to 200 people. This meant that 150 people who lived there would have to live elsewhere.

The job of planning how these 150 people would be chosen, how they would move, and where they would live after they left New Castle was concentrated within a Task Force organized by the Department of Mental Health's Division on Developmental Disabilities. The Residential Programs Director for that Division, Michael Morton, was an experienced teacher of PASS, a member of that community of practice about which Lyle O'Brien and O'Brien have written. Because of that experience Mike worried about how the New Castle Task Force would go about making the necessary plans for the 150 people who had to leave the hospital. He worked with other like-minded Indiana colleagues to set this goal for the Task Force: to develop an understanding of the needs of the residents by getting to know those people as well as Task Force members could before decisions about the people's future lives were to be considered. This meant that upper-level officials of the Indiana Division on Developmental Disabilities (including its Director) and Department of Mental Health would come to New Castle and spend a significant amount of time —more than just a few minutes— meeting and getting personally acquainted with a few people who were members of the group that had to leave. The plan was that each official would be introduced to one person at the hospital and would be with that person, to share the person's experience, for several hours over a period of three days.

Michael Morton thought that having someone from outside Indiana to help design, oversee, or facilitate this experience would be necessary. He called us, and we agreed to come to try to help.

New Castle State Hospital (New Castle) opened in 1907 as the Indiana Village for Epileptics. Over the years, the name and apparent mission of the hospital changed so that, while many people who came there because they had epilepsy remained, by the 1970's the major identity of the hospital was a long-term institution for people with developmental disabilities. In 1983, the hospital had many old buildings scattered across its grounds north of the city of New Castle. This meant that the people we were to get to know were also scattered. We decided to divide the Task Force (12 of them agreed to come) into four groups, with each group to spend time in a different "unit" of the hospital. There, each group member got to meet and share life for a few hours with someone who was, it was thought, likely to be leaving New Castle sometime soon. This meeting-and-sharing took place over parts of the first two days in the places where the residents from New Castle usually spent their time. At intervals during this time, each group would re-assemble for conversation about the experiences they were sharing and the people they had met.

We invited colleagues with PASS 3 experience to serve as either group leaders or additional group members, so that each group would have 5 or 6 members. We did this because we wanted the groups to have a thoughtful conversation about the lives of the people whom we met. We knew that such a conversation would be enabled through a process derived from PASS's conception of "model coherency", and we needed leadership of that kind of conversation. Lyle O'Brien and O'Brien (2000) describe this process:

> *Two simple questions guided these discussions, which often moved the group to surface and work through significant differences among themselves. These questions are, "Who are the people served?" and "What are their most important human needs?"... By adding only one question to these two, "What would have to happen to meet these needs?", Jack Yates developed a format for engaging staff in reviewing their own program, which he called Program Design Sessions... Exactly because these questions are so simple, facilitating a discussion that moves below superficial comments and cliched understanding requires great mastery on the part of the group leader (p. 12).*

Those are the questions we asked of Task Force officials from the Indiana Department of Mental Health as they shared hours with people at New Castle. Task Force members found themselves thinking about experiences and questions like:

- If I lived here, it looks as though someone would have to escort me everywhere I go. Am I that much of a bother?

- John sleeps a lot. John has a "severe behavior problem." Is there any connection between the two? How distressed are the others around John because he sleeps a lot? Are they grateful, sometimes? John doesn't seem to like others around. Is anybody doing anything about this, other than just staying away from him? What do his "program plans" say?

- A man described as the "ultimate bureaucrat" walking hand-in-hand across the hospital grounds with a man who is described as "severely retarded". Walking hand-in-hand is probably not good form in downtown Indianapolis. This kind of personal contact may be quite a new thing for the "ultimate bureaucrat".

- The "canteen" is open between 8:00 a.m. and 4:00 p.m., Monday through Friday. Can I not be thirsty on Sunday afternoon? What if I am?

- Are there ever fire drills when people who live on the second floor slide down the big tube on the side of the building? What would that be like? If it's enough fun, would people want to do it more often?

And, they did it! Despite all the fears by us, the out-of-state experts, that folks would rise in protest and transport us 40 miles east to the Ohio line, they did what we asked. Men and women in business suits sat on beds in wards, stood in day rooms, waited through long hours when nothing (at least on the surface) was going on, ate meals in the hospital's dining areas. And they talked to each other during the group intervals.

And, at least while they were there at New Castle and for a while after, they resolved that there were some essentials that had to be thought about when the planning occurred—when they were deciding about where and how 150 people were to move from New Castle. Those essentials included the following "needs", from the Task Force's Report (Morton, 1983):

- New separate services are not needed. We need: to extend an invitation to people with disabilities to participate, and to extend ourselves to give the support that will make it possible.

- People ought to have as much control, influence, and autonomy in their lives as possible. Whatever is possible, it will be much more control than they have now.

- New homes are needed —real homes, not just places where we could confuse placement with community participation. If changes must happen to people around their homes, then there must be changes in those places. People shouldn't have to move to get something better.

- There have to be ways to help people learn to work —ways to support the start of careers.

- People's families have to be involved in our planning, and we have to do whatever is necessary to make that happen.

- We'd like people to experience joy and closeness to others.

- We need help in learning to recognize the gifts —the potentialities— that other people have to offer.

It may be that these words from the New Castle Task Force report seem commonplace now. In some ways we hope that they do. They were not common words or phrases for state-level officials to use, in 1983, to describe the rules-of-procedure for planning what was then called "deinstitutionalization". At the end of the three days that the Task Force spent at New Castle, we declared a success! We re-stated our initial understanding that planning or decision-making roles carry with them an obligation for the planner-decider to know the people whose futures are on the line. If the quality of planning rises as personal acquaintanceship with the subjects of planning increases, we thought that we had improved the odds that the Task Force's decisions would really help the 150 people who were being planned for. We believed that the experience together offered planners the chance to see someone at New Castle as more than a line on a spreadsheet or a folder reviewed in the file room. We were at least a bit more confident that, as the Task Force went forward with its work, at an important juncture a member might say something like: "Well, you know, I know John a little bit. And, if other people are like him, then they'll want more friends, good food (especially pizza), pleasant and comfortable rooms, and plenty of privacy. Maybe we'd better think more about that."

We see the brief work of the New Castle Task Force in 1983 as a precursor of person-centered planning. We see this in three little ways. First, the days at New Castle introduced, just a little bit, a few of the people who would move directly into the fashioning of decisions about what their lives would be like. At least a little, these decisions would connect to people's experiences and maybe their aspirations. Second, planners were received and took part, although just for a little bit, in the circles of relationships to which a few residents of New Castle belonged. The hand-in-hand walk between someone who lived there and the "ultimate bureaucrat" didn't last long, but it did occur. Third, the vast system of agencies, contract, budgets, laws, and politics that surrounded New Castle was willing, for just a little bit, to be shaped by the diversion of its attention to just one person. Everything could stop, just for a little bit, so that the quietness of a walk or a meal could have its say while plans were being made.

Did these three days change things a lot, either at New Castle State Hospital or for the 150 people who were supposed to leave? It depends. New Castle State Hospital no longer exists. It does not show up on the State of Indiana's listing of hospitals or developmental centers. So, in 19 years all 350 of the people left for other places. It is doubtful whether the three days at New Castle had a lasting effect on the New Castle Task Force or its eventual decisions. Such is often the outcome of plans. The days had an effect, though, on some who were there. They led some of us from the middle of the country a bit further on toward an understanding of what eventually became known as person-centered planning. And, we cherish a small hope that a walk, hand-in-hand, across the grounds made a lingering memory for the "ultimate bureaucrat".

History isn't destiny, but it matters

> *Herman can learn and has learned many things. He can read and write and find his way about the community quite well. He has had more difficulty in adjusting his social outlook and making the necessary adaptation to the mores of the community to be able to flow smoothly along in mainstream society. Herman has, on occasion, over-stepped the boundaries of moderation and found himself rebuffed. He is, however, proving to be a most resilient person, ever optimistic, and he will continue to grow and add more chapters to the history of his life.*

> – *Personal Histories*, OHIO SAFEGUARDS, 1990

We wrote the paper, *Personal Histories,* in the first place because we were trying to help people who were responsible for "planning" in the lives of other people who had developmental disabilities. In the early 1980's one of us (Sandy) worked intensively with a small organization in southeast Ohio. That agency, Residential, Inc., began its self-examination by asking the nearly 30 people with de-velopmental disabilities whom the agency helped support what they thought about their lives and what they hoped for in the future. Residential Inc's story has been told by John O'Brien, who reports the reaction of agency workers and managers to the self-examina-tion:

> *It was bad news. The better we learned to listen to the people we serve the more clearly we heard them say, "It's not working for us. We don't like where we are living and we don't like the group of people we are living with." It smashed us. We had a clear mission and were working very hard, we liked the people we served and they liked us, but what we were doing didn't really fit their needs. (O'Brien, 1987, p. 5)*

The leadership of Residential, Inc. responded to their shock by, among other actions, re-orienting the way that they helped the people whom they supported to make plans for improvements in their own futures. It may be hard to recall now that the very idea contained in the previous sentence was nearly revolutionary in 1982 –not writing the plan but helping people make a plan, not planning for how to get by from day-to-day but planning for how to reach out towards something a lot better. Again, O'Brien (1987) recalls in full the changes that were attempted.

> One thing that Residential, Inc. leaders learned quickly, though, was that their own workers, who were now in the role of "planning-assistant" with people with disabilities, did not know very much about the people they were supposed to assist. Especially, the workers did not know the life experiences –the personal histories– of the people they were trying to help. So, Sandy developed the original version of the suggestions for studying and recording other people's personal histories to guide planning assistants as they worked with people with disabilities on this new thing: making workable plans for brighter futures.

Suggestions for exploring and recording the personal history of someone whom we're assisting to plan (latest revision)

Why assemble a personal history?

Most of us don't make plans because we are paid to do it; at least, most of us don't make plans, for our own lives for involving the lives of others who are close to us, on a commission basis. Usually the plans we make for ourselves or people we love are just results of thoughtfulness and conversation about what we want, for ourselves or people we care about. We might actually not think about that so much as planning as just good common sense. What makes it so is that we experience it first-hand. It is part of our day-to-day life. It is about our past or about our children's future. We don't have to study anything to learn our own history or, usually, the experience of someone we care about. We remember it, with the help of our family and friends.

This kind of remembered or intuitive knowledge is probably missing from a relationship that we have with someone else because we have a job-related responsibility to that person. Information about the past of someone with a disability is often unknown to anyone other than the person herself. Developing a written summary of someone's history is, then, a way of making up for helpers' absence of close personal or intuitive knowledge. We also think that such a summary is an essential part of a way of creating and carrying out useful action with and on behalf of the other person.

As we see it, there are five more-specific reasons for developing a written personal history of someone whom we are going to help with planning:

- If we develop a personal history with a person, we will be better able to make plans that will take advantage of the strengths and capacities that the person has demonstrated in the past. There are bright spots in everyone's life (more in some lives than in others, of course), and part of our aim in planning is to figure out how to increase the number of such bright spots. It helps if we know what the person's previous good experiences have been so that we can make a plan that builds on them.

- Working on a personal history will help us try to avoid the repetition of experiences that have been hurtful or damaging to the person. One way to begin thinking about this is to study the kinds of experience patterns that seem to be common among people who have been rejected or otherwise systematically hurt by others. Wolf Wolfensberger has, for many years, described this experience pattern as "the most common 'wounds' of devalued (and especially handicapped) people" (e.g., in Wolfensberger and Vanier, 1974). Investment of a few hours in listening to this description and reflecting about its implications is, we think, important preparation for those who want to write a summary of someone else's history. People with disabilities are likely to have been hurt—often quite seriously and frequently. Serious study and reflection about the pattern of those hurts helps us understand things that have happened to someone that, if possible, we don't want to have happen again.

- Developing, with the person who is the subject of the story, a written history makes room for that person's point-of-view (and those of the people who are close to that person) about the difficulties or weakness with which the person contends. There is always plenty of opportunity to read about others' (e.g., professionals') points-of-view about someone's problems. The perspective of the person himself could add depth to our understanding.

- Many people with disabilities go through life carrying with them, as it were, a story that they had little hand in shaping or recording. That history –the one told in agency case records– may be neither enhancing to the person nor accurate. If we write a personal history with the person whom we are assisting we can help assure that the person's own version of her story is written and heard. This can also mean that the person's own story can, then, be carried with him, instead of or in addition to case records, if he moves to a new place or enters a new service or when the faces (i.e., of assistants) change, as they inevitably do.

- Researching and writing a personal history of someone we're trying to assist is a valuable learning experience for the writer and for potential readers. It's likely that most of us would seldom be willing to trade past experiences with someone who has been socially devalued. As we learn more about the lives of people who have been devalued we may recognize even more clearly the anguish that many people endure throughout a lifetime. We may also find ourselves acknowledging our own parts in bringing about such anguish. It's important, we think, to learn the story about how things have been, so that our understanding about what really matters and our conviction about how things could be can be strengthened.

How to do it

Here are some of the many ways to research a person's past. The most helpful ones will probably be combinations of several approaches, such as:

- Encourage and help someone to think and talk about their own story. Try to think of ways to organize answers and to be more certain that you have not left important parts of the story untold. We found a guidebook to this process that has a useful pattern of questions for someone to consider. That guidebook is entitled *Your Story: A Guided Interview through Your Personal & Family History* (Gift to the Future2000, 1992, unfortunately out-of-print now) A check with genealogy or family-history sections of libraries or bookstores may yield similar guidance.

- Try at the beginning to think of ways to publish the history –in photos, in drawings, in words or stories, on tape, on a web site, on a CD or DVD, etc. If you think about the presentation of the history from the start, you'll be less likely to miss important information.

- Have conversations, interviews, or correspondence (e-mail may work well) with people who are close to the person now or who have been close to her in the past. Think like a journalist, remembering the rule about: what, when, where, why, how questions. Be ready to do some digging. Important questions to think about with regard to talking to others may include:
  - What ties these people together? How active or intimate a part of each other's lives have these people been? What experiences have these people shared?
  - What does the informant know (and how well) about the life of the person? Especially, what experiences can the informant relate that are unknown to others (e.g., human service workers)?
  - Are there stories that reveal this relationship –"tell" about it with special clarity.
  - What does the informant, as a person who has or had a close connection with the person, hope for in the person's life?
- Read (with permission from the person) written material compiled about the person. This might be in the form of letters or journals. Very likely there will be lots of written, official case records. Especially when you review case records you will want to pay special attention to issues like:
  - Where, and in what kinds of places, has the person lived?
  - Has the person been set apart from natural relationships and familiar places (e.g., sent away from home and family)?
  - For how long or during which periods of his life has the person been set apart?
  - What did the person miss out on? What did she get more than her share of?
  - What things about the person get the most attention? What kinds of interests or capabilities is he portrayed as having?
  - How current is the information? How continuous is it—are there unaccountable gaps or periods of time with no information?
  - How and with whom has the person spent her time? Has she been educated or undereducated?
  - How much experience does the person have at choosing, risking, succeeding, failing?
  - How and why did this person come to be where she is now? Can you trace a path backward over the past years?

- What, in particular, is happening to or for this person at this place now? Are there difficulties that need to be overcome?
- What is the meaning or implication of any diagnostic labels? What past responses have there been to the various labels attached to the person. (It is especially important to think and ask about this if the labels are ones that have led to the exclusion of people from their homes, neighborhoods, or communities.)
- What solutions have been proposed for the person in the past? How well have past solutions worked to reduce or eliminate difficulties?
- What general portrayal or image of the person emerges from these materials? How relevant (or irrelevant) is this information to the person whom you've come to know?

The answers to questions like these will shape any account of the person's personal history that you devise.

- Try some things that may help you in making inferences and arriving at judgments about someone's pattern of experience. For example, you might consider:
  - Learning about the things a person saves, treasures, or regards as very important. Perhaps these are photos, clippings, places, certain people, songs, or collections. Conversations about these, or help in building or securing them, promote understanding that you might not reach any other way.
  - Making a diagram of the important events in a person's life. Note the ups and downs, as the person thinks and talks about his life and as others share (or maybe debate) about what they know. Keep this diagram and add things that you discover and regard as influential.
  - Helping make a picture of a person's relationship life. Graphically display who's close now and who has been close to the person before. Where do people stand? How many other people are in the picture, and what is the connection of each of them with the person whose picture it is?
  - Reflecting about events or situations in the past and their possible connection to current experiences and aspirations the person has. Are there some situations that should not be repeated? Are there other experiences that should be? What has brought strength in the past? Might it do so again?

- Writing down stories and drawing images that simplify points in the personal history. Can you convey important ideas through simple portrayals of particular memories, moments, events? Are these represented, for example, by favorite holidays, pastimes, trips, foods, hopes, etc.?

A person's personal history can be recorded and made useful in many ways: in narrative summaries, on tape (or other) recordings, in electronic media like CD-ROM's or DVD's, through the use of charts or other graphics, in photographs, in scrapbooks, in journals or stories or poems, or in a combination of these and other means. We have seen personal histories summarized in murals, collages, banners, and quilts. The means for recording and preserving someone's history are limited only by the boundaries of imagination. The form the history takes, however, is, for us, less important than the learning that comes to the subject of the history and to the historian.

We learned, for example, from a man named Don that "I don't want to go back" (repeated, on every meeting). The place where he had been, nearly 20 years before, was so offensive and frightening that he reminded us with great discipline: "I don't want to go back." We knew that, whatever was planned, it couldn't include anything like "back". Don also let us know: "I belong on Gracely Drive." Gracely Drive is the street where Don lived, more than 30 years before he went to the place that became known as "back". That let planners know that Gracely Drive was the goal. That's where Don belonged. If we hadn't learned some history from Don and from others who knew him, we might not have figured that out.

Our test for a good personal history is simple. First, does the history we've uncovered and recorded portray a person's life honestly and with respect? Second, does the history offer insight into the person's current interests, relationships, aspirations, and burdens? Finally, does the history meet the standard that its writer would probably require for her own personal history?

Are dreams kept in drawers?

> *Killing me softly… should be about our children sitting in*
> *non-workshops, having their communication systems taken*
> *away while our person-centered plans and dream plans are*
> *in some drawer…. It could focus on how it feels to watch*
> *the hope that we had when our children were in school*
> *fade as they become adults.*
>
> -from an e-mail message

> *I talked to (Jacques Maritain) about the question which*
> *bothered me, that in his whole philosophy, I didn't find*
> *any access to the concept of* PLANNING. *And he asked me*
> *if this was a different, an English word for accounting. I*
> *told him no. And if it was for engineering, I said no. And*
> *then at a certain moment, he said to me… "Now, I finally*
> *understand…It's a new species of the sin of presumption,*
> *planning."*
>
> – Ivan Illich

At first, we thought that it would be easy. Or, if not easy, then at least rational, straightforward –linear. Many of us in the Midwest, like many others elsewhere, had learned that there was a certain way to get organizations like those supporting people with disabilities to change. That the way we had learned did not seem to work very well did not seem to matter.

Perhaps we should explain. We learned a story about how change occurs, especially in public-service arenas that are dependent on taxes and politics. We came to title this story: "Distressing the Monarch." The story begins with the idea that, in order to get something to change (let's say to get more flexible funding for long-term supports for people) you first have to cause pain, discomfort or distress to the person who's at the head of a particular organization. You have to make the monarch uneasy. The monarch might be the governor, the director of an agency, a cabinet minister/ secretary/ director. The starting place is to cause distress, by organizing, writing letters, making visits, doing all of the things that experts in politics recommend. The monarch, feeling distressed, will (as the story goes) pass the distress to someone else, if possible; that someone is likely to be lower in the hierarchy. The passing of the distress has to be seen as something akin to the transmission of electric current. Lightning hits the throne and is conducted away. The distress or unease gets conducted, then, through a series of lower-level stops, because each manager/ director/ supervisor/ courtier acts in imitation of the monarch. Finally, the distress reaches a level from which it cannot be conducted further. Functionaries at that low level are skilled in processes that somehow dissipate the energy that was captured in the initial charge of distress. Some of these processes involve drafting policies or convening meetings to write formal plans. Sometimes the ones at the lower levels of a hierarchy know tricks that will actually relieve the cause of the initial distress for one or a few people, and this is a reason for hope. (Cynics might say that providing occasional relief is a form of intermittent reinforcement to keep people believing in the usefulness of the "distressing the monarch" story.) The moral of this entire story is that, in order to get things to change, you first have to distress the monarch!

In the early and middle 1980's, some of us thought that we had found new tools for starting the chain-of-events the above story tells about. We learned about Personal Futures Planning. Conduct of personal planning with a critical mass of individuals or families in a given area (a town, a county, a state) would systematically introduce new visions from people with disabilities and their allies into public discourse. Systems could not help but be affected, in ways we wanted, by the vaccination with positive ideas that came from these plans, could they? Well....

For several years between 1984 and 1990 the Developmental Disabilities Planning Council in Ohio awarded funds to groups with the intent that those groups would try to do two things: a) to improve support for at least a few people with developmental disabilities, both for the sake of that improvement and as demonstration that improvements could be devised and put into effect; and b) to explore the connections between planning with and for an individual and planning by and for a service organization so that we could use those connections to achieve what was called "system change." We worked on some of those projects, and we used Personal Futures Planning as one of our major tools.

One of these projects used personal planning as a way to figure out how conditions in the lives of some people, who lived in a number of Ohio counties, could be changed so that "severe" or "challenging behavior" would be a less-frequently applied label for those people. Working under the direction of Wade Hitzing and the (then titled) Ohio Society for Autistic Citizens, one of us (Jack) both facilitated personal planning sessions for dozens of people and families across Ohio and tried to teach personnel who worked more directly with those people and families about how to conduct similar planning for others. Again, our aim was to make things better for these people, both through the planning that took place and through the training in positive behavioral supports that was made available to support workers. Our second aim, though, was to assemble data, arising from the personal-plan records and from the teams that produced them. We wanted to convert the data from many places into white-papers or policy documents that would help us distress the monarch (state officials) in order to bring about changes in the system of support for people with disabilities.

It's not our purpose here to evaluate that work; we're only trying to remember it and tell a bit of its story. We recall the young man who was the focus of the very first Personal Futures Plan gathering that was held as part of the project. The group, which became, at length, a circle that included this man, met in a conference room at a community college in western Ohio. The facilitator (Jack) was terrified, at least in part because we had asked local officials to select for planning purposes the people supported by their agencies about whom they worried the most. And, the description of this man was that he was the one who "tried to burn down the workshop." Over a period of four or five hours over a two-day time, though, this man, without using many words, persisted with us in drawing out a portrait of the future that at least partly satisfied him. It took a long time to get to that future. The picture changed a lot as years went along, as it does for most of us. Nearly fifteen years later, we were privileged to attend this same man's housewarming, at his own house, which included a garage for his pick-up truck. (At the original planning session, the vehicle pictured was a red Firebird. People change their minds.) Several of the helpers and guests at the housewarming were people who were in the room at the community college fifteen years before. This man's story continues, and we believe that it is different now because, in part, of the gathering years ago. And, his story inspires others toward similar ends. The bits of data that were collected about this man with the intent of fueling a systems-change effort have been lost along the way. Lots of things about systems look about the same as they did fifteen years ago. That doesn't mean that we failed to stimulate change; it just means that change occurred in ways that were not linear and that we, believing the story about

distressing the monarch, didn't anticipate. Planning, as Jacques
Maritain noted, is full of presumption.

As part of a second project in Ohio between 1987 and 1992 we
worked together to (as the title of the project stated) "train design-
ers of individualized services" in a number of Ohio communities.
Again, the idea was to affiliate with local agencies, conduct personal
futures planning with a number of people who were connected with
those agencies who wanted to develop such plans, teach the others
involved with the agencies about personal planning, and gather
information that would bring about changes in service systems. We
managed some of all but the last one.

A man, who was affected by an earlier head injury and who
was living in suburban Dayton, was unhappy in the suburbs and
residing with someone else whom he didn't choose. He made his
unhappiness known to the organization that supported him, in ways
that the organization could not tolerate. When we started talking
with the organization, this man, and his family, the man's life was
moving in the direction of increased restriction. Personal planning
and follow-up conversation led all of us to understand that this man
thought he would prefer a smaller, quieter community and that he
would really like to try living by himself. We were able to help point
the support agency in some new directions, and the agency located
a single apartment in a nearby small town. The man lived there with
evident contentment until his illness and death eight years later.

A man and woman in northern Ohio had histories of institutional
life and, after leaving the institution, met and were married. They
lived in an apartment in a small city; all of the other residents of
the apartment building carried disability labels as well. The couple
wanted to establish a home elsewhere and they wanted better jobs.
They were eager to call together people they trusted, most of whom
worked for the agency that provided supports to them. The record
of the planning session was remarkable, in hindsight, because the
house that supporters found for them to rent was a nearly-exact
copy of what they had described and what had been drawn on the
chart-paper during the planning sessions: one floor, two bedrooms,
fenced yard for the dog, washer and dryer, reasonably large kitchen,
near work, etc. Two years later they learned about dining rooms and
decided to move to another house down the street where they could
have more friends over for meals. People learn. Visions change.
The support organization was willing and able to keep up with the

changes because many of the organization's personnel were, by this time, part of the circle.

We could fairly say that neither of these stories led directly, though, to changes in the way that service systems operated. The stories are both examples of stretching policy and practice within acceptable bounds. Both the man in the Dayton area and the couple in northern Ohio represented change at the margin of systems. It turned out that service systems are resistant. We knew this, I think, but hadn't learned another change-story. That—another story about how change happens—is what we found, developed, and started to tell as a result of our work with people, families, and organizations using personal futures planning.

Near the end of his essay, "Standing by Words," Wendell Berry wrote:

> I come, in conclusion, to the difference between "project-
> ing" the future and making a promise. The "projecting" of
> "futurologists" uses the future as the safest possible context
> for whatever is desired; it binds one only to selfish interest.
> But making a promise binds one to someone else's future. If
> the promise is serious enough, one is brought to it by love,
> and in awe and fear. Fear, awe, and love bind us to no
> selfish aims, but to each other.

In place of the "distressing the monarch" story of change, consider the following diagram:

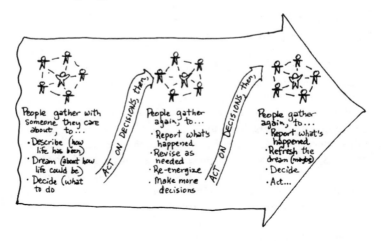

This is one way that person-centered planning works. People gather with someone else they care about, and they make some decisions about what to do to make life better. They check themselves from time to time by gathering again, reporting to each other, and making new decisions. There are, we think, two important messages we hoped to send by means of this diagram. One is that what goes on between the gatherings –what the diagram calls "Act on decisions"– is most important. Gathering and talking and writing things down are helpful, but what really matters is whether, in the spirit of Wendell Berry's observation, people keep their promises –whether they do what they say they will do. If they do, they will learn something, and that something becomes the basis for reporting, re-examining, and deciding to keep on or to do something else. The energy and essence of person-centered planning is in the doing.

The second thing to notice about the diagram –an arrow– is that its length is bounded only by the side of the page or by the space that it occupies. The actual length of the arrow is unknown, in every instance. When we start to make plans and act on them to bring about a brighter future with someone, we have no idea about what direction we'll be going and no idea about how long it will take. That can be discouraging to people who have been asked to fulfill annual or quarterly objectives, who have been asked by someone else to demonstrate progress lest there be censure or withdrawal of resources. When we start to use person-centered planning, of whatever style, with the consent of someone else, we're likely to be getting involved with that person for a long journey. If we will make that journey, who knows where we'll find ourselves or what we will see along the way? We may find people picking out dining room sets, looking for a house in the country, or buying a new pick-up truck, or maybe running for mayor.

There is nothing worse, though, than empty promises. Another thing we've thought about person-centered planning is that it's likely better not to start if we don't have the capacity to carry it through. Hopes and dreams are powerful. They are also fragile. We have to treat them with care. We have to be willing to go where they lead us. As the mother whose e-mail we quoted at the beginning of this section alerts us, dreams don't belong in drawers.

References

Berry, Wendell. (1983). Standing by Words. in *Standing by Words: Essays*. San Francisco: North Point Press.

Gift to the Future2000. (1992). *Your Story: A Guided Interview through Your Personal & Family History*. Rhinebeck, NY: Gift to the Future2000.

Illich, Ivan. (1989). *Part Moon Part Travelling Salesman: Conversations with Ivan Illich*. Toronto: Canadian Broadcasting System.

Morton, Michael. (1983). *Report of the New Castle State Hospital Community Placement Task Force on Getting to Know Some of the People Who Live at New Castle State Hospital*. Indianapolis: Indiana Division on Developmental Disabilities.

O'Brien, Connie Lyle., and O'Brien, John. (2000). *The Origins of Person-Centered Planning: A Community of Practice Perspective*. Lithonia, GA: Responsive Systems Associates. (Also in this book.)

O'Brien, John. (1987). *Embracing Error, Ignorance, and Fallibility: Competencies for Leadership of Effective Services*. Lithonia, GA: Responsive Systems Associates.

Wolfensberger, W., and Glenn, L. (1975). *Program Analysis of Service Systems, 3rd edition*. Downsview, ON: National Institute on Mental Retardation.

Wolfensberger, W., and Vanier, J. (1974). *Growing Together*. Richmond Hill, ON: Daybreak Publications.

25

Thinking About Support Broker Roles

Michael W. Smull

As service systems increasingly embrace the principles and practices of self-determination and individual funding, people are looking at the roles of those who have been traditionally known as case managers or service coordinators. The expectations that many had of service coordinators in the late '70s and early '80s have been buried under increasing numbers of people to support and endless paper to complete. As we change from service coordinators to support brokers (or whatever new label is adopted), we have the danger of just changing the labels without changing what happens. Unless the underlying structures are changed, including reducing the volume of paper and the numbers of people each support broker works with, the changes in roles and expectations needed to achieve self-determination are doomed. Real change needs to begin with an understanding of the desired outcomes and then move to developing the structures to support it. We need to begin by asking what do support brokers need to know and do?

I could say that the support broker's job is to help people have their own lives where they are supported by and contribute to their communities. While this is true, it is also too glib. "Sound-bite" advice is often a good way to help people remember complex ideas, but the ideas have to be explained first. If I had the opportunity to briefly explain what I meant, I would talk about roles and responsibilities mixed with values, gifts, and talents.

At its core, the work of a support broker is about partnership, partnership with those supported and those involved in their lives. Partnerships are built on a foundation of respect and trust. Unless people with disabilities and their families feel respected, the trust needed to share what is important and to take the risks inherent in growth will be absent. Without trust there will be no partnerships. Real success is easier with (and usually requires) a series of interlocking partnerships. Partnerships are needed between people with disabilities, their families, those who provide the support, and those

First published in *Impact, 12* 4, (Winter 1999/2000)

who do the planning and funding. These partnerships require effort to establish and maintain. Some of what follows begins to describe what is necessary to create and sustain them.

It begins with listening

Everybody involved in these partnerships must feel that they are listened to. Compromise is often required and disagreements will sometimes occur, but everyone must feel that the service broker/support plan facilitator has listened to them. While everyone has ideas and important contributions to make in developing and implementing service plans, those involved must keep in mind that the individual with disabilities is the expert. They need to listen to what the person says with words and behavior about how they want to live, and act on what they say. They have to be careful to distinguish between what the person wants and what others want for the person. And they need to understand that what someone asks for may be limited by what they have tried. What someone is saying that they want is based, in part, on their experiences. People need opportunities to try things to see if they will like them.

After the person with disabilities, the most important people to listen to are family members. In many instances they were the only advocates who were present before the support broker met the person and they are advocates who will be there after the support broker is gone. Part of the role of the support broker is to help to maintain and enhance their relationships with the person as part of their work in representing the person. They need to understand and take into account the family's perspective. Where what family members want for the person is different from what the person wants for himself or herself, they need to understand why. Where there are differences that are substantial, they need to negotiate a compromise that maintains the relationship while creating a balance that works to the person. While there are notable exceptions, among the things that most people want and need are continued good relationships with their family.

Plans as frameworks for learning

The support plan that is developed with the person is a focal point at which many efforts and ideas come together and are represented. A support plan should begin with recording the learning that resulted from listening and that describe what will be done to act on what was learned. The plan should:

- Reflect what is important to the person.
- Describe a balance between what is important to the person and any issues of health and safety.
- Make clear the responsibilities of those who support the person in moving toward his or her desired life.

The plan should describe the direction of the journey and the destinations along the way. The plan must, however, be viewed as a work-in-progress, base on recognition that learning is continuous and the partnership ongoing. Plans should provide a framework for recording the ongoing learning that takes place, and describe what will be done whom in response to the learning.

Helping find a balance

Few people, regardless of the presence or absence of disability labels, have a perfect life. What we all seek is a life has a balance that we see as positive. The support broker's job can be seen as continuously working toward a balance that works for the person, a balance between what is important to the person and what is important to those who know and care about the individual, and between what is important to the person and any issues of health and safety. It is important to remember that this is a journey, not an event. The best balance that can be achieved today is the starting point. As the person grows and changes, as others' perceptions of the person change, as our understanding deepens, opportunities for a better balance arise. Self-determination is not about a single effort; it is about pushing for the best immediate outcome, looking for new opportunities, and continuing to listen to the person. In seeking a balance that works for the person, the order in which you answer questions matters. For example, it is important to learn how somebody wants to live before you look at where. It is important to learn what would make the person happy, and then determine how they can be healthy and safe within the context of being happy.

It's about control and possibilities

Support brokers have to be able to facilitate the use of individual budgets. Skills in managing money are important, but money is only where it starts. It is really about control. If people can use and move their public dollars as makes sense to them, they are more likely to be listened to and achieve a balance that makes sense. Doing this requires that the public funding be seen as not just a way to buy services, but also as a way to leverage changes in the services available. With enough flexibility, money allocated to buy services can assist people in building community. Sometimes this occurs by paying people to "bridge" or "connect" with everyday community settings. Sometimes it occurs when coworkers are paid to provide the needed support. But, it all starts with seeing possibilities. The best support brokers are not trapped by what is; they lead a process where people go beyond the boundaries of the system and see the possibilities in the community.

It's not just one person's job

A service provider's response to this list of responsibilities and activities may well be, "'This is the ideal, but we'll never be able to afford it." If the support broker is the only one to do all of what is needed, it is unlikely that there will be the funding to have enough support brokers with all the needed skills and community connections. Central to achieving self-determination in service coordination is, again, partnerships. If the work is done in partnership, the broker does not have to be the only one doing it. With support, there are families, self-advocates, and service providers who are developing and implementing remarkable life plans. Ongoing, continuous learning is essential to success and can only happen in partnership.

Conclusion

Much of the creative thinking (and learning) about helping people live lives of their choosing, and be supported by and contribute to their communities, is happening within existing service systems. Whether part of more traditional service systems or part of new self-determination initiatives, successful service coordination depends on looking for opportunities to develop productive partnerships, listening to persons with disabilities and their families as they identify what they want and need for their lives, developing and implementing balanced plans, leveraging resources effectively, and seeing possibilities. It is about making sure that the truly important work in building a life is happening.

26

Person-Centered Teams

Helen Sanderson

Person-centered planning can be a life changing, enriching experience. It can also be a distressing disappointment if nothing changes. Lisa's plan described how she wanted to live by herself, ride a motorbike, have friends and go to Cyprus. She invited her sister and staff to plan with her to achieve her dreams. Then her key worker was moved to another staff team. Other 'priorities' engulfed the team and nothing changed for Lisa. She could not understand why she did not move immediately, and became angrier at having to continue to share a house. Lisa became violent. The psychologist was called in to help with her 'challenging behavior'.

Official interest in person-centred planning is creating a planning epidemic. We need to invest in these plans being implemented, or risk leaving people disillusioned and cynical. Or in Lisa's case, understandably bitter, violent and depressed.

Implementing plans means moving from planning to action, reflection and back to action. In our early efforts with person-centered planning we assumed that the hard work was developing a creative plan that truly represented the person. We assumed that once you had the plan, implementation would be straightforward. Our assumptions were wrong. As Beth Mount says,

> In many ways, finding capacities is fascinating and creating a positive future is exciting. The long-term benefits of implementation are rewarding but the process of solving problems over time is just plain hard work. There is no way round it.

We have learned that there are many conditions that make change more likely in people's lives. Where people are supported in services, these conditions include effective leadership, a team that is committed to the person and a service that is flexible. For many individuals, staff are the only people involved in putting the plan into practice. Our track record of services implementing plans is variable. There are many reasons why teams of staff have failed to implement plans.

Thank you to Jo Harvey and Charlotte Sweeney for their contributions to developing person-centered teams.

After the meeting had finished, Doreen's team simply lost momentum. They saw person-centered planning as additional to their work rather than central to it. Implementing person-centered planning is not the icing on the cake – it is the cake.

Successful implementation will require different strategies for different teams. For some teams, like Derek's, it required strategies to embed the planning within team meetings and staff supervision. Nadeen's team developed an implementation plan that described how the team kept the plan alive. Our challenge is to discover ways that the spirit of the dream and vision can inspire other actions, rather than just achieving goals. Teams need to change how they work to make the plan a living document that defines and guides their actions.

For many teams and organizations, putting person-centered plans into practice requires a change in thinking about support staff. This means managers being person-centered with staff. This chapter addresses how we can support team managers and teams to become powerful levers for change, which complement the other conditions for change. This work is based on research in developing **person-centered teams.** A 'person-centered team is one which sees its purpose as supporting an individual to achieve the lifestyle they want as part of their local community; who are characterized by a willingness to listen and learn continually; and who highly value personal commitment and relationships with the people they support.

This chapter presents and illustrates a ways of building person-centered teams, beginning with a change in thinking that results in a change in practice.

A change in thinking

Being person-centered with staff

Some of the fundamental principles of person-centered planning are that we involve people in all decisions about their life, build on their existing skills and interests, identify what support they need and provide it. Developing person-centered teams extends those principles to staff. This means that managers and team leaders need to:

- Involve support staff in decision-making that affects them.
- Discover the existing skills and interests of staff and see how these can be used to support people using the service.

- Find out what support staff need and discover the best way of providing it.

This is a change in thinking about power. John O'Brien and Connie Lyle O'Brien suggest that when organizations operate by having 'power over' their staff, support staff typically mirror that relationship with the people they support, acting as if they are in charge of them. All relationships within organizations need to be based on 'power-with' rather than 'power-over'.

> *Power over others is the most common and familiar form of power. People expect its use, feel uncomfortable in its absence, fear the uncertain consequences of denying it, and easily fall back upon it in times of stress... But power over others poisons the relationships necessary to support people with disabilities in taking their rightful places in community life.*

Most organizations operate by having power over their employees, who are instructed what to do and then are checked on to ensure that they have done it. On John's first day as a support worker he was given the policies file, told to read it, and then sign a sheet to say that he had read them. Then he was given a list of tasks that needed to be completed by the end of his first week, and told his first day off would be the following Tuesday.

It is easy for professionals and support staff to assume the same relationship with the people who use the service. 'Power over' people can poison relationships and extend to demeaning, dishonest practices. Suki loved to thread beads. She has a job working from home making necklaces that were given to the 'bead man' every Friday night. There was no 'bead man'. Whilst Suki slept the staff unthreaded the necklaces and gave the beads to Suki to start again the following week. This was cruel 'power over.' There was no respect or honesty for Suki. 'Power with' arises from mutual respect and a willingness to listen and learn from each other. It is about co-operation and sharing, questioning and negotiating. In management terms, this is described as using a participative approach and building semi-autonomous teams.

Moving towards 'power with' challenges the organization at all levels. As with person-centered planning, the process of developing person-centered teams begins with getting to know people, their skills, interests and support needs, matching these as closely as possible to what the person using services requires. The person using services always takes priority in this process. We all know of situations where a service user supports Manchester City and attends all their games, until there are staff changes and suddenly the service user is an avid Manchester United fan and follows all their games. In person-centered teams staff's interests do not dominate what the person using the service does. The person-centered plan identifies what is important to the person, and then staff's interests are used to support actions and activities, not the other way around. In traditional planning with 'strengths and needs' lists, the service user's strengths were supposed to be used to meet their needs. In person-centered teams, the support staff strengths and interests are used to meet the service users needs and desires.

The team and team leader have three important interfaces: with the individuals they support, with the community and with the rest of the organization. Their characteristics reflect the values, skills and understanding required to support people effectively, build bridges into the community, support each other and influence organizations

Characteristics of a person-centered team

- Sees the team's purpose as supporting people to achieve the lifestyle they want and to contribute to their community
- Highly values personal commitment and relationships with the people they support
- Sees itself as being 'with' people not 'over' them
- Reviews itself not the people it supports
- Invests in community connections
- Continually tries new ideas and evaluates whether it improves the support it is providing to achieve the team's purpose

Characteristics of an effective person-centered team leader

- See themselves as coaches who bring out the best in people
- Create an environment where team members can identify and solve problems on their own, delegating real power and responsibility
- Demonstrate and articulate the values of the organization
- Look for ways to use staff's interests and strengths in directly supporting people
- Share decision making
- Have a clear vision and direction
- Encourage personal involvement with the people being supported

To become effective person-centered team leaders, people need to identify their coaching and training needs. Team leaders must find their own strategies for building a person-centered team.

The following describes an approach based on research on person-centered planning.* Examples of how teams worked to implement plans are shown to illustrate this process and clarify why a change in practice as well as thinking is required.

A change in practice

The process for developing person-centered teams is described as a sequence. In reality, different teams will be at different stages. Each stage may need to be revisited several times over a team's 'life'. When existing team members leave and new people join, the first stages will need to be revisited. Stage 3 is where the issues of person-centered planning begin to be addressed.

Each stage begins with a question, followed by goals for the team to address the question. There are practical ways and examples of how teams have achieved the different stages.

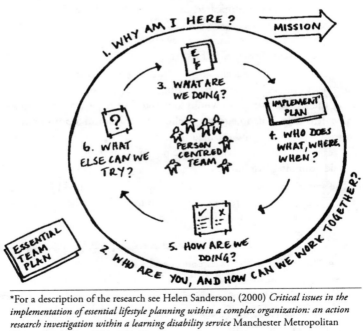

*For a description of the research see Helen Sanderson, (2000) *Critical issues in the implementation of essential lifestyle planning within a complex organization: an action research investigation within a learning disability service* Manchester Metropolitan University, UK unpublished Ph.D.

The person-centered Team Development Model

Stage 1 - Why are we here?

This stage is about clarifying values and direction. All teams need to be clear about the values and direction of the organization. This is more than just reading a mission statement. It involves providing an opportunity to think and talk about what being ' person-centered' means, and what the principles and philosophy of the organization mean in practice.

If the organization is going though a change process the team needs to discuss where the organization is now, why change is required and what it is changing to. Finally, support workers need to be clear about what their personal values are, where these may differ from those of the people they support and what the practical implications of this are.

The team who support Liz and Jen spent a half-day thinking about their purpose. They did this by asking themselves, 'What is the purpose of our team, what are we here to do?' Once they had agreed on a statement that communicated this simply, they chose pictures to illustrate it. This poster is displayed on their office wall. When they have difficult decisions to make, they consider whether the decision would take them closer to or further away from their purpose.

A team, which was developing volunteering opportunities, spent part of a development day 'envisioning success'. They imagined what their successful team would look like and recorded this graphically. This helped people to think about their team in a positive way from the beginning and enabled them to share their expectations of the team in a collaborative way. The poster is on their office wall to provide ongoing inspiration.

The success poster on the following page was developed by the VOX Team, Oxfordshire Learning Disability NHS Trust and facilitated by Jo Harvey & Charlotte Sweeney

Team Goals For Stage 1

- Share the organization's direction and values
- See its purpose as supporting people to achieve the lifestyle they want, within their community
- See themselves as being *with* people, not *over* them and valuing personal commitment

- Reflect on their values and how these may differ from the people they support

<u>How Teams Have Done This</u>

- Attending values-based training
- Devising their own team mission statement developed from the organization's mission statement
- Setting aside one team meeting every other month to do values exercises to reflect on their values and the impact this has on their day to day work
- Using individual supervision sessions to explore what one issue (e.g. power-with, choice, relationships) means to the person and consider the practical applications of this in their work
- Describing graphically the purpose of their work by doing a 'Purpose Poster' or an 'Envisioning Success Poster' (Like the one below. See a larger color image at www.inclusion.com.)

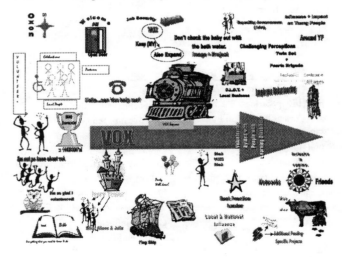

Stage 2 - Who are you? How can we support each other and work together?

This stage focuses on building trust within the team to answer the questions 'Who am I? ' 'Who are you? ' and 'How can we support each other and work together?'

During this stage individuals identify their strengths and look at how they can work together in the team. This stage involves clarifying the support that each member of the team and the team leader requires. There is no prescription for this. As well as addressing support issues, the team needs to be clear about what autonomy they have, how they make decisions and how far they can use their own initiative.

The example below is adapted from the team plan developed by the Supported Lifestyles Directorate Management Team, Oxfordshire Learning Disabilities NHS Trust. This team meets on a monthly basis to manage the operational and development work of the directorate. The plan was facilitated by Charlotte Sweeney and Kathy Brown. They began developing individual introductions using a 'Reputations Exercise'. The team then worked on a communication chart, as this was an area of development the team had identified. The plan ends with identifying what matters to the team as a whole and as individuals. We have only included issues that relate to two team members. The complete plan refers to each of the six team members.

Team Introduction

Charlotte	Jo
Thoughtful in supporting	Confidence and clarity
Can explain things logically so I can understand them	Forces us into action
	Very positive
Helps pull things together	Often calm but not afraid to challenge forcefully when faced with situations that she sees as unjust
Systematically thinking	
Knowledgeable and explains things well	
Keeps the momentum going	Makes sure we get things done
A good person to approach for information	Gets things moving
	Calming influence
Organized	Bubbly enthusiasm
My other buddy and thinking partner	Supportive and enthusiastic always
Helps me to clarify my thinking	Lively and innovative
Methodical and deep	Tenacious 'rotweiler' tendencies don't give up
Logical	

Communication Chart

When Charlotte is ...	She does this	She wants this
Bored	Day-dreams, switches off, doesn't talk.	Kick me, change subject, & let me say something.
Embarrassed	Go quiet, look down at feet – dwell on it for hours – get preoccupied.	Leave me, let me talk through when I am ready -help me put it to bed.
Inspired	Jiggle about, talk fast, nod lots, arms go like windmills.	Agree with me -possibly calmly; help me turn ideas into action.
Worried	Frown, go quiet & thoughtful.	Give me a chance to come back later when I've thought things through, don't pressure me but let me talk when I am ready
Angry	Go very quiet, sulk even, opt out, look annoyed	Leave me alone till I calm down.
Pleased	Smile lots, feel benevolent, talk more.	Talk to me, two way reinforce and join in.

When Jo is ...	She does this	She wants this
Bored	Look switched off, maybe yawn and don't contribute.	Bring me into the discussion.
Embarrassed	Go red and quiet.	Leave me until my acute embarrassment has gone then let me speak.
Inspired	Talk a lot or try to butt in with my idea, jiggle about in my seat and wave my arms.	Listen calmly to my idea and talk it through with me.
Worried	Hold my arms across, be defensive & go quiet.	Listen carefully; don't dismiss it as nothing.
Angry	Either go very quiet or look very unhappy or burst out with it, in a very aggressive manner.	Listen to what I have to say but in a calming way. Don't aggravate me by arguing aggressively with me.
Pleased	Grin a lot, look animated.	To ask me what I am so pleased about, because I always like to talk about things.

Things That Matter to Us All

What Matters to Us	How we support each other
That team meetings are useful & productive.	Everyone attends 8 out of 12 meetings.
That we are action focused & follow things through.	We set clear objectives with timescales and monitor these.
That we keep the team plan alive.	Review and update every three months.
That we all feel safe to ask for help when we need it. We can admit that at times we do not know the answers.	Recognize each others strengths & accept our weaknesses without judgement.
That we have fun together.	Make time for celebration both in & out of meetings & getting to know each other.
That we apply the principles of 'Thinking Environment' e.g. Respect, honesty, equality	Don't indulge in destructive gossip or have hidden agendas.
That we celebrate our successes & learn from things that did not go so well.	Build regular time into our meetings for this.
That we are all committed to the same vision	Revisit this every year.
That there is a mix of personalities, strengths & preferences within the team.	Find out what these are &make sure that we build in opportunities to use them.

Things that matter to individuals in the team

Things that matter to Charlotte	How we support her
That some team members share my values .	These individuals spend time working & chatting with me outside meetings.
That I find my own way of doing things.	That others are clear with me about what they want me to achieve & then let me find my way to get there.
That I have good professional working relationships with colleagues.	That I deal with my working & personal relationships separately.
Sometimes I like to think aloud and may not express myself very clearly.	That others give me enough time to finish what I am saying even if I am not making total sense. Be patient.

Things that matter to Jo	How we support her
Relying on other team members to deliver what they promise.	That we do what we promise Jo.
Having people around to inspire, support, listen and think with.	Let me stay connected after I leave.
That we do not spend all our time talking, but actually get things done.	Ensure we stay action focused. Know who are best people to help with this.
	Smaller working groups that have clear objectives.

Team Goals For Stage 2

- Identify their strengths and interests and find ways of using these to support each other.
- Look at ways that their strengths could be used within the organization, e.g. people with interest or skills in training being utilized or people contributing to relevant working parties.
- Know what support they need and how they can be best supported.
- Know what they have autonomy over in decision making.
- Agree how decisions are made in the team.
- Decide what the boundaries of innovation are .

How Teams Have Done This

- Using a formal assessment, e.g. Belbin's team profiles, Team Strength Audit, Myers-Briggs type indicator etc.
- Doing a plan on their own life and sharing that with the team, e.g. ELP relationship map or any other map from Personal Futures Planning, sharing their dreams and nightmares from MAPS or PATH.
- Developing an 'Essential Team Plan' which describes what support they want from each other, what support they want from their team leader and what support their team leader wants from them.
- Setting team ground rules about how they communicate with each other, how decisions are made and what the boundaries are
- Developing a team 'doughnut', which identifies the teams core responsibilities to the people they support and to each other and where they can use their judgment and creativity in their work.
- Identifying different team roles in team meetings according to each person's strengths.

Stage 3 – What are our goals?

This stage looks at three questions: Who are the individuals we are supporting? What is our role in your life?, How can we support you? These questions are answered with the people the team is employed to support.

The answers are described in person-centered plans. An effective person-centered team can get good results out of almost any method of person-centered planning. It is the attitudes and values that are important, not the technology of planning.

All styles of person-centered plans generate actions. Essential Lifestyle Planning and Personal Futures Planning also specify what people need to have in their lives everyday. The goals for teams in this stage are to ensure that the specific actions from the meeting take place and to ensure that people get what they need and want on a daily basis. This is more complicated to achieve.

Team Goals for Stage 3

- Get to know the individuals they support and discover together what lifestyle they want and what contribution to their community they may like to make.
- Have clear goals to help the individuals to achieve this.
- Be clear about their role in supporting the person and what support is required.
- Know who is important in the person's life and how they can be supported and encourage to maintain and develop their relationship.

How Teams Have Done This

- Assisting the people they support to make a personal portfolio if they want to.
- Using any of the person-centered planning styles.

Stage 4 – Who does what, when and where?

This stage takes the plan and the goals and asks 'Who needs to do what, when and where to make this plan happen? It also returns to what was learned in Stage 2 to ask 'How can we use our interests/talents to support the individuals?'

Some teams have achieved this by developing an implementation plan.

Mark lives with five other people, supported by a staff team of twelve led by Gail. Gail used some aspects of 'active support', a planning process which structures how staff use their time, in implementing the plan.

The team members use simple planning sheets for each week. The sheet incorporates what is important to the person from their essential lifestyle plan, including the times of the day when this matters.

Activities that can happen at different times of the day are written at the side of the sheet.

At the beginning of each week a team member plans that staff will provide individual support to each person at specific times throughout the week. Gail tries to take into account the skills and interests of staff and Mark's own preferences for particular members of staff. The sheets are displayed on a pin board, and activities are ticked off as they happen. If Mark chooses not to do the activity a particular day, staff put a cross, along with a brief explanatory note.

Each day one member of staff acts as shift co-ordinator. The person reminds other staff members of their responsibilities and checks that the routine tasks get done.

Team Goals for Stage 4

- Each member of the team to know what their role is in ensuring that the plan happens and that the person gets the lifestyle or moves closer towards the dream as expressed in that plan.
- Each member to have explored how any of their strengths or interests could be used in this.
- The team to agree what structure and support they require to implement the plan.
- The team to decide what it will take for them to ensure that the plan stays a living plan and how it can be monitored with the person themselves and their advocate.

How Teams Have Done This

- Doing a GANTT chart to project plan their actions.
- Developing an implementation plan for each person.*
- Deciding when to evaluate each goal and planning these into forthcoming team meeting agendas.
- Having it as a standing agenda item for each team meeting and supervision session.
- Completing a Team Path to ensure that the goals that they are responsible for from the person's plan happen at the right time.

---

*For further information on Implementation Plans see Michael Smull and Helen Sanderson. *Essential Lifestyle Planning :A facilitators guide.* Available at www.nwtdt.com

Stage 5 – How are we doing?

The final stages involve looking at how individual plans are being implemented and how the team is working generally by asking, What is working? What is not working? How well are we listening to the person? How are we using our power? This reflection is powerful when it happens on a daily basis by individual team members and in a less frequent but more formal and structured way for the team as a whole.

Some services require a planning review meeting to reflect on actions. Circles of support review how they are doing at their regular gatherings. Regular reflection is vital. The person themselves and their family must be central. Tom meets with the team leader each month to give his views on how things are going in relation to the plan. The team leader feeds back on Tom's views at team meetings.

It can be helpful for external people (for example independent facilitators, care managers) to keep teams on track. Karen's mum and the care manager meet every six weeks with someone from the day service and short-term support service to review the plan and problem solve any issues.

Traditionally it has been the team leaders role to monitor the team's performance. Using a person-centered approach means that we find out what works best for each team and team leader rather than using a standardized approach.

Reviewing progress requires that we look both at what is being done, how things are done and whether this reflects what is in the plan.

It is much easier to count activities than to see whether the person's preferences for the pace of their life are being honoured.

- In Kath and Derek's team, the key workers took responsibility for checking that the plan was being implemented and then reporting back to the team at a team meeting each month.
- In Simina's team, the team leader collated information from the team's paperwork, and worked alongside the team for a few shifts each month and reported back to the team in team meetings.
- In Tom's team, each member was responsible for feeding back on a particular 'theme' or part of the plan at their individual supervision each month. This was then discussed with the team at a team meeting.

It is vital that teams share their successes and barriers with implementation groups and senior managers.

This stage needs to be a continual process and cycle of learning.

Team Goals for Stage 5

- Continually examine the fit between the team's activity and what is important to the person.
- Recognize that people's jobs are complex, and that there are tensions between choice, safety and risk.
- Have a forum for reviewing how the team is responding to those tensions.
- Have regular opportunities to review larger, ongoing problems together and bringing in outside help where necessary.
- Celebrate achievements.
- Give feedback to senior managers about policies and procedures that limit people receiving the service they want.
- Give feedback to senior managers about the effects of organizational changes on the team and in the lives of the people they support.

How Teams Have Done This

- At each team meeting each person says one thing that has worked well and one thing that could be improved about the support that the person has received over the last two weeks.
- Bringing in an outside facilitator or member of the community team to help with large or complex problems.
- Have one team meeting a month for administration and one for review and planning.
- Use the doughnut exercise to review how the team is supporting an individual with a particular issue in their life (See Chapter 15).
- Review what is working and not working in the person's life and share this information with managers and implementation groups.

Stage 6 – What else can we try?

A plan is never completed. The process of implementing a person-centered plan begins with learning through a structured process of asking and listening. People continue to grow and change. As what is important to them changes, and as our understanding continues to deepen, the plan should change. On-going learning needs to take place on two levels: what we are learning about the person, and what we are learning about ourselves and the support we provide. Each style of planning provides a particular 'lens' to look with someone at his or her life. If you started with Essential Lifestyle Planning then using other styles of person-centered planning are vital to add to our understanding of the person and creating a picture of the future.

As well as learning about the person we also need to continue to learn about ourselves, how we work together, and find ways of improving the support we provide.

In the North West Training and Development Team every team meeting starts with sharing something that is working well in your work life and something that is working well in your personal life. We have half an hour to do a 'development exercise' that deepens our understanding of ourselves, each other, or the heart of our work. In this way we continually learn about each other, and develop the relationships between team members.

Team Goals for Stage 6

- Identify what they are learning about the person.
- Find new ways of listening to the person and their dreams for the future.
- Review new ideas and evaluate whether they improve the support people receive.
- Generate new ideas and plan how they can be tried and evaluated
- Develop the team's understanding of each other and the way the team works together.

How Teams Have Done This

- Every couple of months using a 'map' from Personal Futures Planning to help look at the person's life from a different perspective if the original planning tool was ELP or PATH.
- Put the ELP into landscape. Reformatting the plan so that the text of the plan covers half of the page and encouraging people to write on this as they learn about the person.
- Use the learning log to record day-to-day information that focuses on what we learned rather than simply what has happened.

- Support the person to use the accessible learning log if they want to record their thoughts about their day or week.
- Use a style of planning that has a different focus on the person's life.
- Incorporate development sessions as part of team meetings
- Have retreats to re-energize the team.
- Team building.

Conclusion

Person-centered planning is a process to enable people to get the life they want and to make their contribution to the community. Investing in staff and team leaders is essential for lives to change.

The plan needs to be seen as a living plan, which grows and changes and does not wait, inert until a short time before the next prescribed review. It needs to be constantly re-visited, so that teams can consider the progress they are making together as a group, as individual team members and most importantly, with the person themselves. If person-centered plans are to be living plans, they need to be part of every way that team works together. We need to ask how implementing person-centered plans has changed team meetings, supervisions sessions, the ways that staff schedules are drawn up, and most importantly, the way the team sees and works with the individual.

Keeping plans alive is rooted in continual learning. This continual learning happens in three directions: what the team learns about the people they support in the context of their community, learning about how the team implements the plans and learning about how the team can effectively work together. The six stages to develop person-centered teams provide a framework for this learning, action and reflection.

> *The effectiveness of a plan depends on a support group of concerned people who implement the dream by learning to solve problems, build community, and change organizations together over time.*
>
> *—Beth Mount*

27

The Challenges of Person-Centered Work
How Two Agencies Embraced Change

Patricia L. Fratangelo and Jeffrey L. Strully

> *So many large community services are really just institu-*
> *tions broken up and scattered around. No amount of good*
> *will, regulation, or monitoring can ever make either a*
> *large institution or its smaller community analogs a home.*
> *I often despair that these so-called community services will*
> *never change as they work under the misperception they are*
> *just fine as they are.* (Lovett, 1996, p.29)

For more than 60 years, well-intentioned family members and professionals have established community organizations to serve people
with developmental disabilities. The desire to provide good services
and the requirements of state agencies, who have played an increasing role in paying for services, have led most agencies to implement
local services based on models developed elsewhere. While these
models vary with time and place, they embody a common pattern,
which we will define in order to describe the baseline conditions
from which our two agencies have transformed.

Until very recently, program models for residential and day services have been disability-specific and group-based. First, an agency
implements a program model by acquiring property, then it hires
supervisors and staff people, then it chooses people, who may be
strangers with little in common except a label, to fill the number
of available slots. While program developers thought about how
many people would live in a home, its floor-plan and furnishings,
and its staffing patterns, they usually paid less attention to the ways
routines and rhythms would be shaped to match each particular
resident's life (Smull, 1999).

The decision to support people as a group, dictates much of a
household's organization. Dinner will be at five o'clock for the
household, even though for the first 33 years of one person's life dinner was always at six-thirty. Because everyone can't bathe at the same
time, one person is assigned to bathe at eight in the evening instead
of showering in the morning after breakfast. A person shares a room
with a stranger, although before moving she had her own room.

The worker responsible for scheduling may not experience these events as significant, but the person placed in the group –away from family and familiar routines, living with people they may not like– experience these efficiency measures differently. Shortly after the residents move in, problems develop. One person starts to throw food when required to eat dinner at five o'clock. Another person angrily yells at staff who prompt her to take an evening bath. A third person hits his roommate for touching his prized possessions. As problems multiply and increase in intensity, staff tighten rules, get help to implement behavior plans, and call for medication to control "mental health problems". Eventually, a person who lives under this group regime either loses their individual spirit and succumbs to the setting's demands or fights even harder for what is important to them. Those who keep their spirit and decide to resist are often defined as disruptive or disordered and, if available control strategies fail, referred to a more restrictive setting.

Staff and managers are more likely to see the individual people as being or creating problems than they are to question the design of their program. This all too familiar scenario blocks the changes necessary to deliver person-centered supports: Programs created for groups become the machinery which keeps an organization thriving. Effort goes into keeping that machine properly lubricated so that it will run efficiently (Schwartz, 1997). The people using the service are the nuts and bolts necessary to keep the machine running smoothly. When a person becomes unmanageable, the machine's efficiency is reduced. That person can be discarded in favor of a new person, with the hope that the new person will function properly and get the program machine back into proper working order.

Too much effort in the developmental disabilities' field goes into trying to fix the wrong problems. Until an organization questions the way its programs are designed, staff and managers and boards will waste energy looking for the perfection that will make their group-based program work like a Swiss Watch. They will spend countless hours and dollars hunting for the perfect group match and mix, the perfect person-centered planning technique, the perfect behavior plan, the perfect job description, the perfect staff training and motivation package. This futile search for the perfect program machine will continue until leaders find the insight and the courage to get people throughout the organization to ask two questions and take the answers seriously as a demand for real change in the way we offer services:

- Why do we usually see it as the person's problem if they cannot conform to the program that we set up?
- Why don't we understand these situations as our program's inability to do what people need and then re-create our supports from the ground up, starting from individual people we know or get to know?

Our two agencies –Onondaga Community Services (OCL) in Syracuse, New York (Pat) and Jay Nolan Community Services (JNCS) in the San Fernando Valley of Los Angeles, California (Jeff)– have worked for twelve and ten years to learn the lessons that come from understanding and changing the limits imposed on people with developmental disabilities by group-based programs. We strive to center our organization's work more on the people we support, rather than the systems that we operate. We focus on learning to listen to behavioral problems with a different ear (Lovett, 1996). We struggle to align our efforts with people with disabilities and family members, not with today's most popular version of state of the art group-based service models.

These commitments enable us to walk down a different path with each person we support, seeing the many problems we experience along the way through a set of lenses that show us how we can better adapt and adjust to better match each person's changing situation. These commitments demand that we design services one person at a time, a practice that has taken us into new territory for our agencies and for the systems that pay for and regulate us. Group-based residences and day programs are a thing of the past for our agencies, but the search for effective ways to sustain person-centered work goes on.

Our agencies support people with varying needs, but most of our work serves people who challenge the system in multiple ways. Earlier in their lives, many were abused, neglected and exploited. We see these people as spirited individuals who worked hard to fight against services that did not work for them. They were not always successful. Many have suffered the brunt of behavioral plans, behavior controlling medications, and, often, multiple moves from placement to placement –all to serve the system's interest in gaining control of them without changing its ways. We are determined to change this pattern in the lives of the people with developmental disabilities who trust us to support them.

Our approach is simple to state: we focus on individual people and figure out what each person wants and needs to have a good life, and then we arrange organizational resources to support each person in a way that works for them. Creating the organizational capacity to do this simple thing calls for much more than small changes. It has taken organizational and personal transformation.

After briefly describing the changes in our organizations, we will each tell the story of how change happened for one of the people we support. Each of these people has taught us a lot, but neither one is "typical" of the people we serve. Our purpose has been to work one person at a time, so fully describing what has happened would take many stories, one for each person.

The agencies then and now

Onondaga Community Services (OCL)

In 1990, OCL supported people through traditional group living arrangements that were designed around disability. The homes were structured and staffed according to state of the art ideas about what constituted a good group home. The people we served and their staff lived through many variations of the group-based services pattern that we described above.

Though there were problems, group home staff worked hard to deal with them and, for a time, most people thought that the group homes offered people the best possible support, given the extent of their disabilities.

As new people were referred, OCL began to spend more time getting to know people as individuals and personalizing services for new people. Each new person supported by OCL moved into their own home with a support structure that enables the person to live effectively. Some new people lacked skills in cooking, personal care, and budgeting, and some had behavioral or medical problems. Many required 24-hour support. Staff and families of people in the group homes began to notice that some of the new people had more needs for support than some of the group home residents. This realization raised a new question.

> If OCL can develop personalized arrangements for new people coming in, why can't we do the same for people we already know who live in a group home?

Taking this question seriously began to spread a change in mindset throughout the organization. People began to question the assumption that a person had to have a particular set of skills to live in their own home. It became clear that all a person needs is a desire to live the life that can be theirs if personalized supports are available. Once people at OCL learned to recognize this desire and work with the person to develop proper supports, the transformation was on. People in the existing group homes got the option of more personalized living arrangements and the numbers who chose to move into their own homes steadily grew.*

Today, OCL serves about 75 people with a combination of supports that may include residential, supported employment, day support and service coordination. Which services a person gets from OCL depends on what each individual requires.

OCL supports 38 people to live in homes that are personalized for their unique situations. Many of these people need 24-hour support and several also require personal care. No one must live with another person with a disability, though some people choose to do so. A large percentage of people now share their lives and homes with ordinary community members instead of people with similar labels. These life-sharing living arrangements are based on the personal interests of those involved. Sometimes a person or a family member recruits a housemate; sometimes the person and family look to OCL to assist in recruiting a suitable housemate and ensuring a good match.

About 35 people a year receive personalized vocational supports from OCL. Depending on a person's interests and needs, he or she can work competitively or volunteer in the community. OCL does not have a congregate vocational site, but rather supports people in many ordinary community places.

Jay Nolan Community Services (JNCS)

Founded and governed by the families of people with autism, most of whom had no community alternative to institutionalizing their sons and daughters, JNCS has been committed since its founding to never terminating service to a person because of that person's behavioral challenges. The family members who govern JNCS have a long standing desire to assure that their agency's services reflect the state of the art.

---

* For more about the changes at OCL, see Fratangelo, 1994; Fratangelo, Olney, & Lehr, 2002; Olney, M., Fratangelo, P. & Lehr, S. (2000); O'Brien, 1996; Warren et al, 1999.

In 1992, JNCS served 65 people with autism in 13 group homes, 140 people in three "day behavior management programs," and offered an array of segregated and congregate recreation, respite, and family support programs.

The agency was in fiscal crisis. Morale was low and tension was high among staff, management, and the Board. People lived out most of the pattern of problems generated by group-based programs (except exclusion from the agency). These problems were particularly intense because so many people experienced major communication impairments and behavior that was injurious to themselves or others or damaging to property.

A comprehensive review of JNCS by a team of nationally recognized experts brought these chronic difficulties into focus and catalyzed a process of organizational transformation led by an alliance between Board members and Jeff, a review team member whom the Board recruited to lead the agency.

Within three years, JNCS closed all 13 group homes and moved people to their own homes, one person at a time. Responsibility for designing, overseeing and modifying personalized supports rests with each person's circle of support.*

All three "day behavior management programs" closed and the people involved now receive personalized day supports, including supported employment.

Most segregated family support activities have also been redesigned to support people to participate in community settings.

These changes were based on trying to understand who people were, listening to each person, helping people find their own dreams and then walking with people to achieve their dreams.

Today JNCS offers three types of support —supported living, personalized day support and supported employment, and family support— to a total of 650 people throughout Los Angeles County and surrounding counties including Santa Clara County. **Susan's story (OCL)**

Susan started life without a disability, but as an infant she developed a serious infection that left her with a seizure condition and profound cognitive disability. She lived with her parents until she

---

*For more about the change process, see Hulgin, 1996; O'Brien, Leary, Hitzing, Savarino, & Sousa 1995. Learn more about jncs at www.jaynolan.org

was five. At age five she went to an institution where she lived for twenty-eight years in living units with many other people with challenging behavior. Susan developed a reputation as demanding and self-abusive.

Susan and one other person from the same institution came to live with four other people from our community when OCL opened it's second group home. The Selection Committee had worked hard to match the six people so that they would be compatible, but on day one the problems began as people in the house, including Susan, damaged property or lashed out at one another.

Susan was very jealous and demanding of group home staff attention. She became agitated and angry when staff went out with another resident and she was not included. She often stood at the front door and pounded on the window or wall unit until it was damaged or broken. After replacing many windows, we installed Plexiglas. Staff tried to keep Susan away from the door and tried to sneak out of the house to avoid scenes. Susan also took her frustration out on other residents. She would hit, bite and throw things as people left and again when they returned.

We discovered that the person who moved with Susan from the institution did not like Susan. When the two of them were left at home, they engaged in hitting, hair pulling, biting, and screaming. Sometimes this behavior would spill over and involve residents.

Susan has limited verbal skills and is not easily understood by many people. She could not say, "I want to go out more" or "I do not want to live with so many people" or "I do not want to live with this person." As staff became more reflective and better able to listen to the messages in Susan's behavior, they associated much of Susan's difficult behavior with her not being as busy as she wanted to be. When someone left the house to do something, Susan wanted to be part of whatever was going to happen. But she could not always go out because of the needs of the other members of the household.

We tried medication to control her behavior. The meds may have slowed her down a bit, but it became clear to staff that Susan's behaviors were not going to change until her situation changed. This deeper understanding helped us comprehend our part in the problem. Instead of thinking of Susan as a person, we were trying to fit her into a group that she didn't want to join. The design of the group home was working against us and Susan was not willing to compromise her desire for supports that suited her.

Susan's support needs were complicated: she required 24-hour support, had difficulty communicating and dealing with frustrations, lacked most self-help skills, was unable to do housekeeping or take her own medications, could not cook or budget, and required help with personal care. Our staff vision for Susan had changed, but it still was not clear how to set up a living arrangement where she could be successful.

OCL staff, along with Susan and her family, struggled for months to think out a different method of support. Even though other people were succeeding with personalized support from OCL, Susan's parents doubted OCL's ability to provide the amount and kind of support she would need outside a group home, and so did some of the staff who worked with her day-to-day. Despite their doubts and our uncertainties, we kept trying for an understanding that would support Susan in a better way. Carefully considering family and staff doubts gave us a deeper understanding of the assistance and safeguards Susan needed in her new life.

Persistently pursuing these key questions together helped us arrive at some of the answers and to enlist Susan's family in allowing the change.

- What does Susan's life and history show us?
- What are her preferred personal daily rhythms and routines?
- What people bring out the best in Susan and what people bring out the worst?
- What places bring out the best in Susan and what places bring out the worst?
- What situations bring out the best in Susan and what situations bring out the worst?
- How is Susan vulnerable?
- What safeguards can be put into place to reduce the risk from her many vulnerabilities?

We wanted to discover what made Susan's life most pleasant and minimized her agitation. We wanted to eliminate things that caused her distress. As we re-visited the key questions, we kept coming back to the mismatch between our group-based program and Susan's life: Susan had not chosen the people she lived with and she continued to dislike them as much as they had come to dislike her. The paid people who spent most time with her did not believe in her ability and only saw her inadequacies. We knew it was critical to find people who truly enjoyed Susan.

Susan moved from the group home into her own place in 1996. She lives there with a non-disabled housemate and has back-up support from paid staff. She attends a day service provided by another agency. A personal care aide assists her daily with her morning routine. Susan no longer has to compete for attention because she is the focus of her support. All of the non-disabled people who have been housemates to Susan got to know her either in a paid role or socially before deciding to live with her. They share a normal household and a typical lifestyle of working separately and living together.

Susan is happier and more content than she has ever been. Her problem behaviors have decreased dramatically. Comparison of records for a random month in the group home with those of a month in her new home, show that she is enjoying life with less personal stress. For example, in the group home in June, 1994, Susan hit, bit, banged on and broke windows, or banged on and damaged property 12 times in 30 days. In June, 1998, two years after moving there were only two indications of arguing (no hitting, biting or damaging property). In June, 2000, there were no notable incidents.

Susan teaches us that to effectively support a person whose behaviors threaten us, we have to take time to discern what the person is trying to communicate and to understand the person more deeply. People with this deeper knowledge of the person have both a full awareness of the person's vulnerabilities and a powerful desire to work with the person to create a situation that is truly better. This knowledge underpins the kind of personalized supports that give a person their best chance at true security.

Jim's Story (JNCS)

Jim has taught us a lot these past seven years about person-centered planning and support. Most of all, Jim has taught us to "walk with people" especially during dark and difficult times. Jim has also taught us to listen. Listen not only to the words, but to emotions and feelings. Listen to and honor Jim's concerns. Finally, Jim reminds us of the absolute, critical importance of personal relationships. Sometimes walking with Jim means running very fast to keep up with him and sometimes it means paying attention to the little things that only show up when we slow way down.

Jim lived in a JNCS group home for many years. Then things got out of control and his medication level became more and more dangerous to him. He was admitted to a state institution on a temporary basis so that physicians there could safely stabilize his medication. Once Jim was in the institution, state and local authorities decided the level of violence Jim exhibited barred him from living in a community setting.

Jim's dad and mom fought state and local authorities in court to win the right for Jim to return to the community, and finally achieved their goal in the fall of 1992. At that time Bob (Jim's dad) came to JNCS and asked that Jim be returned to our agency and be placed in one of our group homes. The JNCS Director said that Jim should indeed come home, but that he should move into his own place with appropriate support rather than into a group home. Though he had doubts, Bob agreed as long as we hired Mike, a long time support person for Jim.

The first year after Jim moved into his own home was a major challenge to everyone. Jim destroyed, broke, or ripped out lots of things. Tens of thousands of dollars went to replace or repair walls, windows, windshields, sinks, appliances, and bathroom plumbing. Jim went through more than 30 different staff people. A number of staff members ended up in the hospital with injuries Jim caused. Other staff were fired for myriad reasons. Mike, the key staff person, hung in with Jim, but he had some significant personal problems of his own, including addiction. Mike made several errors in judgment which placed Jim at risk and had to go. Jim had trouble connecting with staff, and the few times he did connect with a staff person, the staff member left him for one reason or another. People were afraid of Jim or Jim was afraid of them. It was a very, very difficult year for everyone.

At the beginning of the second year, a crisis occurred with Jim's support people. All three staff had to be terminated at once. Because, through all the chaos of the first year, we had managed to learn some more about who Jim was and what he wanted, we were able to use the staffing crisis to find three new support staff whose attitudes seemed more in sync with pur deeper understanding of Jim.

These three people turned out to be the right match. Their personalities and their respectful way of listening to and being with Jim were exactly what he needed. Over time, they formed a good working relationship with Jim. It is not credentials or training that made this relationship work, it is who these people are when they are with Jim. The way they relate to one another allowed Jim to get to know and care for them and for them to get to know and care for Jim.

Six years later, these same three people continue to work as Jim's support staff. Property destruction has decreased almost to zero. Injury to staff is almost non-existent. Jim is happy. Jim lives with less violence in his life and in the lives of the people who support him. His parents are happier and under less stress.

Jim uses facilitated communication (Bicklen, Morton, Berrigan, & Swaminathan, 1992) and is almost independent in his typing: support at the shoulder or shirtsleeve is enough for Jim to express his views on life. He communicates with a lots of different people including his mom and dad, his support staff, and several other people.

Jim's circle meetings have become opportunities for good conversation and a chance to think with Jim about the future. Jim has had several jobs and is most interested in returning to school. He has had several dates with a young lady he has known for years and cares about greatly. He and his dad go to happy hour every week. Life is not perfect for Jim, but his life is headed in the right direction. Today we don't spend time with special incident reports, property destruction, and staffing challenges. Now we discuss where Jim wants to go on vacation, or what classes he wants to take in school, or when he is going to see Jenny. These questions are closer to the questions that Jim has always wanted to discuss.

What have we learned?

In both agencies, the transition from group-based services to person-centered supports happened as more and more people adopted new ways of seeing people with disabilities, new ways of thinking about supports, and new ways of acting. We can describe some of the tools that moved our transformation forward:

Tools for transformation

Dreaming of Desirable Futures People with disabilities as well as their families, friends, allies and supporters deserve to have vibrant, beautiful dreams for their future. Dreams that are bright and multi-colored. Dreams about doing things you always wanted to do. Dreams of ordinary and common experiences that allow a person the opportunity to live every day to it's fullest. Dreams that are not only recognized and heard, but shared by people who are willing to work to bring dreams into reality.

Person-centered planning Person-centered planning is not a one time phenomena but a way to stand with people over time, listening carefully to them, validating their hopes and dreams by taking action with them, and learning to know them more deeply. Our ability to listen this way depends on the relationships we form with one another. Person-centered planning is about walking with a person day in and day out over time as the journey of life unfolds.

Circles of support A committed group of people have a much better chance of achieving dreams and avoiding nightmares than a lone individual does (Mount, Beeman & Ducharme, 1988). The circle comes together as the person with a disability joins willing family members, friends, co-workers, neighbors, supporters, and allies to support and protect a good life. The circle brings imagination, strength, help, and wisdom to the personal direction a person works to take.

Zero rejection An agency commits to stand with the person no matter what challenges they have. We work to improve our understanding of who the person is and what the person wants. We adapt support structures to enable the person to live life more fully. (Smull & Burke-Harrison, 1992)

Outcomes

Some of the notable results of our agencies' transformation from group-based programs to personalized supports include these:

- Many people and their families say that people's lives have significantly improved
- People are living with less violence
- Behavioral incidents have decreased significantly
- Medications have often been dramatically reduced
- Staff turn-over has decreased significantly
- Staff injuries have decreased
- Premiums for Worker's Compensation are lower
- Families are happier and more satisfied
- Staff are happier
- People are moving forward with their dreams
- JNCS has increased its net assets from about $200,000 to more than $800,000. OCL went from running a $200,000 deficit to running in the black

Lessons

After more than a decade of doing this work –in a smaller agency and a larger one, in a medium sized community and in one of the most populous areas on the planet– we would list the lessons we have learned like this:

- *All* people can live in their own homes. It is not dependent on skill level. It is dependent on support level. Willing people can develop supports to enable anyone to live effectively in their own home. Sometimes it takes time and trouble (remember Jim's first year).

- Listening to people is essential. Staff must learn how to listen both to words and behavior to discover something about the desires and interests that make a person uniquely themselves. So many professionals think they have heard what the person wants after a brief talk. Such superficial listening leads to placing people in slots. We need to avoid preconceived notions of what people need and take the time to listen with open ears and an open heart while being willing to change our typical service structure to enable new things to happen.

- Behavior is truly a form of communication, though it can be terribly misunderstood. Like Herb Lovett (1996) we must find the will to listen differently to behaviors that confuse or threaten us. A person does not usually bite someone, damage property, or hit themselves or others for no reason. Unless we take the time to understand the deeper, more personal reason behind a particular person's behavior, we may never get to the root of the problem.

- Power and control must rest in the hands of the person and when appropriate his or her circle of support. Decisions must be made at the individual level not at the agency level. Professionals have been tagged as the experts for people with disabilities and for what they need. Our experience shows that professionals need to let down our façade and learn to trust the real experts, the people who come to us for support and those who love them. Together, this partnership will undoubtedly know more about what the individual needs than any one professional can. We need to respect the person and their support circle as we work to develop the services around them.

- Being in the community is not the same as being part of the community. A person can live in a wonderful house on a nice street and have a nice job, but if no one knows them, says hi to them, or wants to be with them, life can be very lonely. We need to ensure that each person is supported in growing numbers of relationships in the communities and activities that are of interest to him or her (Walker, 1999).

- Relationships and friendships are at the heart of the matter. Relationships are the glue that holds communities together. Relationships are the lifeline to happier lives and more satisfying existences (Amado, 1993; Amado, Conklin & Wells 1990). People with disabilities are sometimes less able than others to initiate, develop and maintain relationships on their own. Each person needs thoughtful staff and others in their lives to recognize the importance of personal relationships with other community members. Our role is the on-going work of helping people stay or become connected to people, places and associations where they are citizens, members and friends (McKnight, 1987).

- The people we support can be some of the most wonderful teachers we have ever experienced. Susan and Jim are just two people who taught us how to listen differently, how to stand with a person over time and how to change service systems to meet individual needs.

- Families can start to see their sons and daughters in new and exciting ways or be challenged by this new experience. Both Susan's and Jim's families were hesitant about a more personalized service. Both families knew the challenges their son and daughter presented and neither family had experienced anything but group-based programs. It took many discussions and experiences, over time, for their parents to realize that different support would give Susan and Jim what they needed to thrive.

- Existing systems of accountability, regulation, and funding –which were built for group-based programs– do not prohibit the development of personalized supports. Our agencies use the same funding streams and are accountable to the same regulations as other providers, we just use them differently. Regulations can and do adapt to person-centered work. Under existing regulations, effective power and control can rest with the person with a disability; a home can belong to a person, not an agency; support systems can be tailored around individuals, not the regulation staff quota for a group residence. We have made this happen through negotiations.

- Managers face new demands that call for significant personal learning. It was simpler when the pattern was simpler: place the person into the open slot. Now managers worry:

  - *Is the right person supporting the right person, in the right way, in the right situation?*

  - *Are we doing what we said we would do?*

- Changes in organizational rules, procedures and policies can encourage the new ways of thinking necessary for personalized support. For example, changing staff roles from skills trainers to community connectors made an important shift in staff attitudes and behavior.

- Changing internal policies away from agency control and toward giving the person effective control of agency resources sets the framework for generating personalized supports.

- Regular retreats, discussions, and opportunities to learn from leaders in the field and discussions with the board, parents and staff provide opportunities to touch more of the realities of people's lives. This opens minds to new possibilities.

- There are no pat answers and it isn't easy to figure out solutions to complex human problems. Sometimes all we can do is to continue to walk with people through dark or dangerous or confusing times. Plans will not always work out; we must expect to have to rethink and refocus. From time to time we will need help to find new ways of approaching problems. The trust that provides the foundation for our work sometimes grows slowly because of past bad experiences with people like us.

- The excitement of moving from a group-based program to a person's own place is the first and almost the easiest step. It is more challenging to maintain excitement about quality on a day to day basis. Person-centered work is only as good as you are today. Some days will bring joy; tomorrow or the day after will bring new issues. That is what life is all about.

- The human service empire changes slowly. People with disabilities continue to be socially devalued, mistreated, and abandoned. But Sue and Jim show that good work can be accomplished if people join together to enable it to happen. We plug ahead and negotiate our way through all the red tape and bureaucratic tension that threaten to drag us backward into group-based programs.

Working in a person-centered way requires continual flexibility that arises from deep respect for the person. Respect creates the willingness to slow down and listen more deeply so that it becomes possible to discover new ways to understand a person, stepping into their shoes and trying to see life from their perspective. Respect creates the willingness to hold on to a vision for a person. Respect motivates acknowledging and picking up after mistakes. Respect keeps us from blaming a person's disability or difficulties in life and encourages us to acknowledge our responsibility to join in changing structures and practices that keep people from the life they deserve. The respect that founds good support informs our heads, but it has its source in our hearts.

> *There is no such thing as a value-free way of working with others. The challenge is to keep ourselves honest and to consider what values we actually use in our work, not just what values we say we have. (Lovett, 1996, p. 30)*

References

Amado, A. (1993) *Friendships and Community Connections between People with and without Developmental Disabilities.* Baltimore, MD: Paul Brookes Publishing.

Amado, A., Conklin, F. & Wells, J. (1990) *Friends: A Manual for Connecting Persons with Disabilities and Community Members.* St. Paul: MN: Human Research and Development Center

Bicklen, D., Morton. M.W., Gold, D., Berrigan, C. & Swaminathan, S. (1992) Facilitated communication: Implications for individuals with autism. *Topics in Language Disorders, 12* (4), 1-28.

Fratangelo, P. (1994) Creating supports based on a person versus the system: A story of organizational change. *TASH Newsletter, 20* (3) 16-21.

Fratangelo, P. Olney, M. & Lehr, S. (2001) *One Person at a Time: How One Agency Changed from Group to Individualized Services for People with Disabilities.* St. Augustine, FL: Training Resource Network, Inc

Hulgin, K. (1996) *Jay Nolan Community Services: The challenges and dilemmas of quick conversion from group homes to supported living services.* Syracuse, NY: Center on Human Policy

Lovett, H. (1996) *Learning to Listen: Positive approaches and people with difficult behavior.* Baltimore, MD: Paul Brookes Publishing.

McKnight, J. (1987) *Regenerating community.* District 1, Massachusetts Department of Mental Health

Mount, B., Beeman, P. & Ducharme, G. (1988) *What are we learning about circles of support?* Manchester, CT: Communitas

O'Brien, J. (1996). Deliberate-fire: An account of organizational transformation of Onondaga Community Living, *TASH Newsletter, 22,* 1, 27-29. (Download from http://soeweb.syr.edu/thechp/rsapub.htm)

O'Brien, J., Leary, M., Savarino, C., Hitzing, W. & Sousa, M.E. (1995). *The transition to supported living: Realizing the moment and moving on.* Syracuse NY: Center on Human Policy, Syracuse University. (Download from http://soeweb.syr.edu/thechp/rsapub.htm)

Olney, M., Fratangelo, P. & Lehr, S. (2000) Anatomy of commitment: An in vivo study. *Mental Retardation. 38,* 3, 234-243.

Schwartz, D. B. (1997) *Who Cares? Rediscovering Community.* Boulder, CO: Westview

Smull, M. (1999) Positive rituals and quality of life, In J. O'Brien., & C. Lyle O'Brien, C, (Eds.) *A Little Book About Person Centered Planning.* Toronto: Inclusion Press. Pp. 51-54.

Smull, M., Burke-Harrison, S. (1992) *Supporting people with severe reputations in the community.* Alexandria, VA: NASMRPD.

Walker, P. (1999) From community presence to sense of place: Community experiences of adults with developmental disabilities. *Journal of Association for Persons with Severe Handicaps, 24* (1), 23-32.

Warren, B., Doherty, M. Fratangelo, P., Goodfellow, R., Kendall-Brown, V., Messier, H., Johnson. M., Mount, B., Rosen, F., Tomaszewska, T., Tilbe, S., & Woods, N. (1999). *Searching for excellence and promoting systems change. Committee on person centered planning for systems change recommendations.* Abany, NY: New York State Office of Mental Retardation and Developmental Disabilities.

28

Planning with People
The Development of Guidance on Person-Centered Planning from the English Department of Health

Martin Routledge, Helen Sanderson and Rob Greig

Following the publication of the White Paper, *Valuing People*, in March 2001, the Department of Health commissioned Martin Routledge and Helen Sanderson from the North West Training and Development Team to prepare good practice guidance on person-centered planning. This guidance was issued in January 2002. This chapter describes the thinking behind the guidance, outlines some of its content, and describes national and regional supports for its implementation. The guidance reflects thinking about how to diffuse complex innovations within organizations given the experience of implementing person-centered planning in a number of other localities.

Valuing People and person-centered planning

Valuing People (DoH, 2001) is the first English White Paper specifically relating to people with learning disabilities since 1971. It has been widely welcomed as a comprehensive statement of policy with detailed and challenging objectives which, if achieved, would strongly progress inclusion for people with learning disabilities. *Valuing People* is explicitly cross government in its approach and it pushes to ensure that people with learning disabilities gain access to a range of opportunities linked to other policies, for example in housing, employment and education. The implementation structure includes

---

A Glossary for North American Readers

People with learning disabilities: the label adopted by government agencies to replace "mental handicap". In the US, people with learning disabilities would be officially labeled "developmentally disabled" or "mentally retarded."

Commissioning: public authority function responsible for planning and contracting for services; separate from service provision.

Care management: the publicly accountable process of establishing eligibility, assessing need for services, and specifying the package of services that will meet assessed need. Similar to "case management" or "service coordination".

White Paper: An English White Paper is a statement of Government policy, but is not legally enforceable as that would require an Act of Parliament. Statutory guidance accompanies the White Paper and defines expectations of what public bodies *must* do.

a national Task Force advising ministers, a section of the Department of Health focussing on delivery of the policy (Disability Policy Branch), a Director of Implementation (Rob Greig) with a national support team and modest development funding. Local responsibility for implementation is largely placed upon 150 Partnership Boards that bring together local specialist and non-specialist commissioning and service providing agencies with people and their families.

Valuing People does not closely define person-centered planning. Instead, it defines the function that person-centered planning serves as an important tool for changing the culture of services so that services can achieve the White Paper's objectives. Partnership Boards are required to develop person-centered approaches and to make person-centered planning available. Some priority objectives are set, with time-scales, including the use of person-centered planning to support the modernization of day services and to support people in the transition from childhood to adulthood.

Among a range of specific requirements placed on Partnership Boards, and reflected in a formal policy circular [LAC(2001)23], is the expectation that they produce a framework for person-centered planning by April 2002. The White Paper promised guidance for Partnership Boards on the development and implementation of the framework. Accordingly, this guidance was prepared under the supervision of a steering group made up of national person-centered planning experts, the policy leads from the Department of Health, representatives of key statutory organizations, and people linked to other important policies. External advisors included John O'Brien, Michael Smull, Pete Ritchie and Jack Pearpoint.

Developing the guidance

The first fundamental question we faced was should there be official guidance on person-centered planning at all?

Warnings echoed around when we considered how to approach the development of the guidance. A very early question was "should it be done at all?" Some of the people we consulted answered in the negative. Some family members, self advocates and other people already involved in facilitating planning felt strongly that as soon as person-centered planning entered "serviceland" its power as a means of helping people achieve self determination would diminish. At worst they argued, it would be corrupted and perverted, becoming "..another thing done to people by professionals".

Those who advised against making person-centered planning the subject of government guidance were concerned that tools that should rightfully belong to people with disabilities, their families and chosen allies would become professional property. They predicted that organizations would perpetuate existing forms of services and supports by simply re-labelling current professional activity as "person-centered". These concerns seemed reasonable to us because we too have seen Orwellian situations where services undertake bizarre activity in the name of inclusion and person-centeredness.

On the other hand, we knew many staff and professionals making honest attempts to form true partnerships with people. We also had direct experience of the power of person-centered planning in the hands of those serious about helping people to pursue their aspirations. We also weighed the fact that, to date, person-centered planning has only reached a very small minority of people. Thus, without a more broad based and systemic dissemination effort, person-centered planning would continue to benefit only a few people.

Our conclusions from these various debates were:

- The genie is out of the bottle –person-centered planning has entered the language, things that people called person-centered were going to happen no matter what and we would do better to try to influence things in the right direction.
- We and others know something about how to introduce complex changes into organizations, including some learning from implementing person-centered planning in organizations (Routledge & Sanderson, 2000; Sanderson, 2002) . Many people of learning and integrity were willing to help us to develop useful guidance.
- It is not enough to advise people on how to complete a person-centered plan, we would have to pay serious attention to advice on implementation, key issues of context and complementary activities so that person-centered planning will support the development of person-centered approaches and thus make a positive difference in people's lives.
- It was crucial to consult with stakeholder groups as much as we could within the time available in order to hear issues and concerns and seek to incorporate these in the guidance.

To define specifications for the guidance, we reflected with our steering group and our advisors on probable barriers to useful and effective implementation of person-centered planning. We defined our goal as outlining strategies that will minimize barriers and take maximum advantage of the opportunities for change presented by the White Paper. The steering group agreed on these guides for our thinking.

- Success is *not* defined as lots of people with plans but as more and more people getting the lives they want. Hence we would consider how person-centered approaches can support achievement of the major and sustained cultural changes necessary to reach the White Paper's objectives. To do this it would be necessary to link person-centered planning to complementary elements in the overall White Paper implementation strategy at local, regional and national levels.

- The guidance needs to include strategies for local implementation and define the supports that will increase the chances of local success.

- The guidance needs to gain a balance between sufficient prescription to ensure some action in the right direction while allowing for different local contexts and the creation of multiple strategies for implementation. Early drafts, which offered a great deal of detailed advice, made way for a final version which provides principles and a well defined approach to local analysis and action planning.

How easy is person-centered planning to adopt?

Valuing People requires changes in organizational culture and practice. There are very real dangers, however, that the introduction of person-centered planning will avoid the challenges of deep change. If decision-makers treat person-centered approaches as simple changes, they are almost guaranteed to fail because they will neglect a careful and well thought-through implementation effort. It is easy to visualize a situation where quite significant efforts still fail to contribute to major shifts in how people are supported and, in fact, generate damaging cynicism.

So a key implementaion question is: **What kind of change is the introduction of person-centered planning and how can we maximize the chances of a successful implementation?**

There is a great deal of research on the kinds of changes that are easy to bring about in organizations and those that are not. The work of the late Gerry Smale (1996), from the National Institute of Social Work, guided our strategic thinking. He talks about the "adoptability" of innovations: there are some characteristics of particular changes and sets of circumstances that make it more or less likely that the change will take root and flourish. We adapted these questions from Smale to analyze the change person-centered planning calls for...

- To what extent do people see the change as better than what went before?
- How far is the change seen to fit with existing values, past experiences and current needs, for example of professional groups, local families etc.?
- Is the change seen as complex or difficult?
- Can it just be added on to existing activity?
- Can the change be tested in a limited way?
- Can people see the impact of the change?
- Are there "enthusiasts" in influential roles who will put significant energy into bringing the change about?
- Does the idea appeal to people who have the power to promote change?
- Does the idea require significant changes in relationships?
- Can the change be adapted to local circumstances?
- Can the change be brought about with few additional resources or are there resources which can be used for the purpose?

Because local contexts are different, local planners need to answer these questions about person-centered planning for themselves. However, there are intrinsic features of real person-centered planning which make its adoption quite challenging. For example, it requires changes in relationships, not just procedures, it usually comes into conflict with some existing practices, it can't just be added on, etc.

On the other hand, a superficial understanding of person-centered planning is *very* adoptable. Who would not want to describe what they do as "person-centered"? Hence, we can expect to see the words "person-centered" being attached everywhere –this is the easiest thing in the world to do.

However, those people seriously interested in the possibilities of person-centered approaches and person-centered planning will think carefully about the adoptability questions and let their answers guide their actions. The questions encourage a serious analysis of what it will take, in a particular place and set of circumstances, to properly implement this innovation. Answering the questions can give important clues as to what activities will be needed locally, who will have to be enrolled or supported, what will be an appropriate timescale for implementation, and what types and sequence of training and development activities will work in this place and time.

In considering the context into which the guidance would "drop", we identified factors we believe to be present to a greater or lesser extent across the country:

- Despite some serious attempts and recent improvements in many areas, we lack a history of effective partnership between service staff and people with learning disabilities and families. The lack of a tradition of power sharing will lead to difficulties for professionals and their agencies in shifting towards planning approaches which aim to promote a partnership in which people and their families are powerful. Also this history may lead families and self-advocates to take a defensive and sceptical position towards the introduction of person-centered planning. Linked to this history, many people view planning with people as the province of the professional and see individual planning as necessarily associated with assessment for the allocation of state resources. This raises issues about the proper relationship between person-centered planning and care management.

- To realize the benefits of person-centered approaches, many organizations will have to change existing practices in respect of resource allocation, operating procedures, priorities for staff activity and strategic planning approaches. Organizations must shift in order to promote the creative problem solving needed to undertake and deliver on person-centered planning. It is important to ensure that people not see person-centered planning as a panacea which can substitute for other necessary change activities.

- Public services in the UK are currently driven by a political desire for measurable targets. Deliberate efforts to build capacity for person-centered planning that makes a positive change in people's lives could run counter to a way of defining public accountability that favors reports of increasing numbers of plans completed and lacks ways to assess the quality or impact or ownership of the plans.

- Smale (1996) warns against using a "simple linear approach" when the innovation is complex and involves significant changes to existing relationships, but the pressure to deliver on White Paper targets might tempt policy makers to look for simple solutions.
- The shift towards person-centered approaches and planning will come up against a combination of real and perceived scarcity of the time and money necessary for training and supporting facilitators, engaging in person-centered planning, and taking action to implement people's person-centered plans. One source of perceived scarcity is the belief that any significant changes for people will require a major increase in specialist service resources.
- Knowledge and experience of the aims of and approaches to person-centered planning is limited. Though person-centered planning has a twenty-year history, its level of penetration into localities and organizations is very limited and there have been very few efforts to systematically implement person-centered planning at the scale of whole organizations or localities. So there is not a great deal of local tradition or knowledge to build upon. We fear that the lack of a clear agreed definition of person-centered planning could lead to the re-labelling of existing activity or to poor local interpretations.
- Several theorists of change management (e.g. Kotter, 1996) suggest that major change in organizations requires a build-up of strong forces which make the status quo untenable –a "positive pressure for change". Since most localities lack powerful, well-organized family and self advocate groups who are pushing for the adoption of person-centered approaches and many service commissioners and providers believe that they are doing as well as they possibly can within the limits of existing budgets for specialized services, it is not clear how widespread this pressure for change is.

Setting Smale's adoptability criteria against our context analysis might seem to make gloomy reading. Our intention, however, is to realistically identify possible difficulties in order to shape a strategy with a chance of working to produce cultural change over time. The groundswell response to the White Paper provides energy for change.

The guidance*

The guidance explains the role of person-centered approaches and planning in the implementation of *Valuing People*.

> People with learning disabilities and their families should expect everyone involved in providing or commissioning services to accept *Valuing People's* key principles of rights, independence, choice, and inclusion. They should also expect all professionals to work from a person-centered approach.
>
> This means
>
> - Direct service workers should enable each person to be involved in activities that express their choice and independence as valued community members
> - Service managers should base the running and improvement of services on careful listening to people with learning disabilities and those who know them best
> - Care managers and other specialist professionals should respond creatively to informed choices about how a person wants to live and how they prefer to be supported
> - Commissioners should invest strategically in developing systems and services that offer assistance which uphold people's rights and support independence, choice and inclusion
>
> A person-centered approach may seem an obvious way to operate but evidence gathered in *Valuing People* shows there are important limitations in the design and delivery of most existing services when they are measured against the White Paper's principles (pp. 6-7).

The guidance identifies the responsibility local Partnership Boards have for developing and implementing long-term strategies to change the culture and practice of services.

> Partnership Boards and their members are responsible for long-term strategic change in the design, management, and delivery of services and for commissioners, managers, professional specialists and direct service workers daily practice. Person-centered planning will play a significant role in assisting the Boards to bring about the new approach and the necessary shift in culture and practice to help people lead the lives they want within their communities (p 7).

The guidance defines both person-centered approaches and person-centered planning and sets out the differences between the two terms. Our notion is that while good person-centered planning

---

This section includes direct quotations taken from the guidance, inset in smaller type. Excerpts from the text have been organized for this chapter. To see the context for the quotations here, download the guidance document from www.doh.gov.uk/learningdisabilities There is an accessible version of the guidance available at the same address.

becomes gradually available to people, service organizations should work to become increasingly person-centered in all of their activity –i.e. adopt person-centered approaches. The shift to person-centered approaches should be aided by person-centered planning but not dependent upon it.

> When we use the term "person-centered" we mean activities which are based upon what is important to a person *from their own perspective* and which contribute to their full inclusion in society. Person-centered planning discovers and acts on what is important to a person. Person-centered approaches design and deliver services and supports based on what is important to a person. Hence person-centered planning can promote person-centered approaches

> **Person-centered planning** is a process for continual listening and learning, focussing on what is important to someone now and in the future, and acting upon this in conjunction with their family and friends.

> This listening is used to understand a person's capacities and choices. Person-centered planning is the basis for problem solving and negotiation to mobilize the necessary resources to pursue a person's aspirations. These resources may be obtained from someone's own network, service providers or from non-specialist and non-service sources.

> **Person-centered approaches** are ways of commissioning, providing and organizing services rooted in listening to what people want, to help them live in their communities as they choose.

> These approaches work to use resources flexibly, designed around what is important to a person *from their own perspective* and work to remove any cultural and organizational barriers to this. People are not simply placed in pre-existing services and expected to adjust, rather the service strives to adjust to the person. Person-centered approaches look to mainstream services and community resources for assistance and do not limit themselves to what is available within specialist learning disability services. They strive to build a person-centered organizational culture (pp. 11-16)

The guidance identifies the different styles of person-centered planning and emphasizes what they have in common by identifying key features and clarifying what person-centered planning is not.

> The most common planning styles in use in the UK include Essential Lifestyle Planning, PATH, MAPS, and Personal Futures Planning. These different styles of person-centered planning, and others developed from them, are all based on the same principles and share the same key features. All start with the person's capacities and what is important to them and end with the necessary actions. They differ in the way in which information is gathered and whether emphasis is on the detail of day-to-day life or on longer-term plans for the future. It is important not to spend energy debating what is the *best* planning style but consider which style might be

best used in particular circumstances. Styles can be used to complement one another. Similarly, ideas about person-centered planning continue to evolve. There must be space for innovation and development in policy and practice (p. 15).

There are five key features of person-centered planning that help to distinguish it from other forms of planning and assessment.

- The person is at the center
- Family members and friends are full partners
- Planning reflects the person's capacities, what is important to the person now and for the future and specifies the support they require to make a valued contribution to their community
- Planning builds a shared commitment to action that will uphold the person's rights
- Planning leads to continual listening, learning and action and helps the person to get what they want out of life (pp. 13-14)

Person-centered planning is **not** the same as

- Assessment and care planning under section 47 of the 1990 NHS and Community Care Act. It does not focus upon questions which determine eligibility for resources from statutory services to meet legally defined needs, though when services are required such mechanisms may well be triggered. Though service responses are likely to play a part in supporting a person to achieve their personal aspirations, person-centered planning is not constrained by them. Assessment and Care Management is greatly assisted by person-centered planning undertaken independently of it.
- A review of service provision, although it can form a helpful basis for reviews and ensure they are based on what matters from an individual's point of view (p. 18).

The purpose of differentiating person-centered planning from assessment and service reviews is to discourage people from simply re-labeling these service activities as person-centered planning. We intend person-centered planning to have some independence from these activities, while they can be complementary and connected. Though valid and necessary, these service routines are inevitably constrained by the availability of service resources and organizational priorities. We were also concerned to place person-centered planning in a wider context of strategic service development. The guidance recognizes that person-centered planning cannot carry the full weight of the changes that are the responsibility of local Partnership Boards and some of their members in their roles as service commissioners and service providers.

Person-centered planning ...cannot substitute for quality leadership, adequate resources efficiently and effectively used, skilled and energized staff or service development work and system changes (p. 19).

Real change happens when leadership manages the tension between a service's current capacities to develop person-centered approaches and people's informed choices about their lives and the services they receive. Valuing People's objectives provide a way to gauge Partnership Boards' effectiveness at delivering person-centered approaches.

When the delivery of services lags significantly behind people's informed choices about their lives, negotiating and problem-solving activities will take much longer. For example, a young person who wants to take a job on leaving children's services will find it far easier to negotiate for a suitable care package in a service that has built up a strong and effective supported employment service. In a system without such a service the young person might well encounter care managers and service providers who define their choice as "unrealistic" or "excessively costly".

It will therefore be necessary for service development and systems change to take place alongside the development of person-centered planning. Partnership Boards must not wait for many plans to be completed before they take action to increase employment opportunities, broaden choice and control in housing or promote direct payments. Rather, they should use the lessons from person-centered planning in conjunction with local service development projects and system changes (p. 20).

The guidance emphasizes the crucial role of people with learning disabilities and their families.

In most localities, support for people, families and circles to undertake their own planning is very limited. Partnership Boards should invest in such developments as part of their person-centered planning framework. Such a move is an important test of the Partnership Board's commitment to power sharing (p. 39).

[Partnership Boards should...]

- Give people the assistance they need to do their own planning. This may be of different kinds depending upon the individual and their circumstances. It could involve providing people with training in person-centered planning and materials for their use.

- Fund people who are independent of services to be available to help people facilitate their own plans and/or to broker responses to the aspirations emerging from plans.

- Local statutory agencies could provide their own staff to help people with aspects of planning, separating this from the function of assessment and eligibility. This assistance could take various forms, including trained plan facilitators or workers who have knowledge about local resources, opportunities and provisions (p. 40).

[Partnership boards should build leadership capacity by...]

• Providing training, support and materials for families to learn about person-centered planning and what it could mean for them, and how to get involved if they want to.

• Allocating resources to other means of building people's strength and power - in particular support for advocacy and self-advocate/ family leadership development by commissioning *Partners in Policy Making* type leadership courses (p. 41).

Our strategic thinking was shaped by the positive but frustrating experience we had with small or very small scale efforts to develop the knowledge and skills required to support positive changes. Like many others who have engaged in effective person-centered planning, we found that people's lives can change positively and sometimes dramatically. But we were frustrated by the slow pace and limited scope of change. As facilitators we often felt like lone evangelists. We were constantly explaining what person-centered planning is, and dealing with myths and scepticism. Our intensive efforts changed the lives of only a small percentage of people. There were some ripple effects, but not enough to create the sea tide of organizational change necessary to make *Valuing People* a reality in the lives of most people with learning disabilities.

Our reading of research on organizational change suggested the importance of introducing an innovation at all levels across an organization. This 'depth and breadth' approach promises more success than implementing a 'depth' strategy alone. Accordingly, the guidance provides advice on effective approaches to implementation in organizations and localities, recommending a "depth *and* breadth" approach to developing capacity to offer high quality person-centered planning and increasing demand for services that take a person-centered approach.

Experience suggests that it is better to introduce person-centered planning gradually. Trying to create person-centered plans for everyone quickly is likely to lead to lots of plans but little positive change in people's lives. At the same time it would be wrong to deny people with learning disabilities and their families the chance to take some steps towards more person-centered services and supports.

A depth and breadth strategy should be used. The depth strategy invests in high quality training and support for facilitators over time to learn about implementing person-centered planning. Therefore a small but increasing number of people in the service have in-depth person-centered plans that are implemented. What happens to everyone else is addressed by the breadth strategy. This makes introductory training available for everyone so that people can decide on actions to further develop person-centered approaches, and get started with some aspects of person-centered planning (p. 60).

Intensive initial training is a pre-requisite for developing competent facilitators, but experience suggests that it is unlikely to be sufficient on its own.

In the UK to date, person-centered planning facilitators have benefited from a range of supports including:

- "Buddy" systems.
- Mentors/ coaches.
- Action learning sets.
- Making time within teams for problem solving and staff supervision.
- Stakeholder days or "away days".
- Learning about organizational change.
- Learning from best practice.

[Communication, inspiration and reinforcement are essential to changing organizational culture. People throughout organizations should join the people and families who use their services to...]

- Review different roles and responsibilities, identifying where there are opportunities for staff to make their work more person-centered.
- Review policies, procedures and practices to ensure that these enhance rather than hinder person-centered approaches.
- Review communication throughout organizations and seek opportunities for these to reflect person-centered principles - for example in newsletters.
- Organize staff development and training activities to implement actions from reviews of person-centered planning that has taken place.
- Review all training courses to ensure that they reflect person-centered principles and practices.
- Develop new ways of sharing information about person-centered planning outside of organizations – with community groups, non-specialist services etc.
- Consider learning and sharing with other organizations, formally or informally – visits, exchanges, joint projects and study tours (p. 63).

The guidance describes a framework for Partnership Boards to use in developing their local strategies. This framework includes...

- A clear statement of purpose of how person-centered planning will be used to deliver *Valuing People* objectives.

- The establishment of a person-centered planning implementation group which includes key local stakeholders. This should be a sub-group of the Partnership Board and be chaired by a person with effective authority.
- An action plan for the local development of person-centered planning.

[The key aims of the framework are…]

- To offer increasing opportunities for people with learning disabilities and their families to plan and to have the supports and services they receive designed around what is important to them now and in the future.
- To provide a way that commissioners and providers (specialist and non-specialist) can learn how their services and systems need to change in order to respond positively to the aspirations of people and their families. Boards should give an explicit commitment in their frameworks to report back on this learning (p. 24).

The guidance calls on each Partnership Board to set up a local implementation group whose tasks are…

1. Undertake initial identification of what is working and not working well in respect of the ability of the local service system to deliver person-centered approaches, including person-centered planning, and plan phased action for improvement. Based upon this review the implementation group should:

2. Develop and deliver a local program for training, development and support including:

   - An introductory overview of person-centered approaches and planning, including people with learning disabilities and their families.
   - An ongoing training and learning process for people facilitating and implementing person-centered plans.

3. Support service development projects in *Valuing People* priority areas by integrating, implementing and learning from person-centered planning.

4. Work with strategic commissioning, care management, specialist professionals and provider services to build person-centered approaches, including the use of person-centered planning.

5. Support and respond to initiatives from self-advocates, families and provider agencies.

[As implementation efforts progress, Partnership Boards should seek evidence to answer four key questions about their efforts to implement person-centered planning]

- Are people doing it?
- Are people doing it right?

- Is it changing people's lives for the better?
- Are services learning from implementing person-centered planning?

Supporting local implementation

Implementing *Valuing People* is clearly the responsibility of local people, working in Partnership Boards that include representatives of all of the key stakeholders. This delegation to local decision-making and control reflects the current government's approach to policy. However, the evidence developed in preparing the White Paper revealed huge variations in practice and performance across the country. So *Valuing People* provides for national leadership of the implementation effort by a Director of Implementation who leads a small team of Regional Advisors, the Valuing People Support Team (VPST).

The VPST does three kinds of work.

- The team provides support and advice to the more than 150 Partnership Boards in England. Through developing close working relationships and mutual trust, the aim is to perform a developmental support function –being a 'critical friend' in relation to the work of the Boards and bringing in external help and advice to support them in defining and pursuing their local change agendas.

- The team influences national policy makers across government departments and regional delivery mechanisms. Using the evidence of people's real experiences from its work with Partnership Boards, the team works to ensure that mainstream policies in areas like housing, education and employment reflect *Valuing People* aspirations and their delivery directly benefits people with learning disabilities.

- The team acts as a focal point for the *Valuing People* agenda, often in a public relations context, maintaining its profile and building agreement of a clear understanding of its content.

The team believes that the central implementation challenge is to achieve change in the culture and behavior of organizations. Culture change is the source of sustainable changes in service procedure. Though many people think that procedure change is sufficient to improve people's lives, it is not. Based on this belief, the team's early work has focused on three short-term objectives, namely:

- The development of strong partnership arrangements at a local level, so that Partnership Boards have a broad base of membership and operate in an inclusive and action-oriented manner.
- The development and delivery of person-centered approaches to service and person-centered planning.
- Local organization and strengthening of a variety of forms of advocacy.

Though all team members are deeply rooted in the learning disability field, each comes from a different background and brings different kinds of expertise and knowledge. Regional Advisors each take a national lead on specific issues, co-ordinating national initiatives and being a resource for Team colleagues. Martin Routledge took the lead on person-centered planning and Helen Sanderson was contracted to support this task.

The objectives of the first twelve-month person-centered planning implementation support program are:

- To match support activity and its phasing to the requirements placed upon Partnership Boards by the White Paper and person-centered planning guidance.
- To invest resources in a combination of centrally and regionally based activity, aiming to provide direct assistance regionally while building capacity and learning in key areas centrally.
- To make effective use of the national and regional development agencies with experience and expertise in person-centered planning. The limited budget is therefore largely invested to stimulate rather than directly deliver activity.

The initial implementation effort involves training, providing materials and stimulating, supporting and sharing good practice. The first twelve months' work has three phases.

Phase one: Getting started (January – March 2002)

This phase helped Partnership Boards understand the task of developing a framework for person-centered planning and take their initial steps. There were eight regional conferences and each Partnership Board was invited to send a team of four people with lead responsibility for implementing person-centered planning, including a person with a learning disability and a family member.

Before the regional conferences we worked with members of one Partnership Board to pilot a framework for local implementation of person-centered planning. From this we learned what people were anxious about, which parts of the guidance were challenging, and what specific help people wanted. From the pilot effort, we developed a range of practical materials to help other partnership boards.

- Stories of good practice.
- Detailed sample training plans.
- Techniques for analyzing current practice with ideas for practical next steps.
- Contact details so that people can build their networks.

The conferences were designed in collaboration with a stakeholder design team who chose to structure them following the large group intervention methodology, Real Time Strategic Change (Jacobs, 1994). The conferences walked people through what was required of them and introduced them to practical approaches to going about their task. The team responded to questions, and the event offered an initial opportunity for networking across local areas. We worked hard to make the experience of the conference congruent with the creative problem solving required to develop and deliver person-centered approaches. Hence, the events were creative. Groups presented songs, poems and dramatized their vision of how lives could change through person-centered approaches. One memorable song replaced the twelve days of Christmas with the twelve days of person-centered planning! People left holding a graphic template on which they had recorded their first steps for delivering a local framework. Evaluations suggest that most participants found these sessions very useful.

The question time at the conferences demonstrated that people felt anxious about evaluating the quality of planning and outcomes. In response the VPST gathered information about different approaches to assessing quality and presented this information at a conference.

In this initial phase the VPST began preparing materials for a web site to complement the resource guide we prepared as part of the guidance. We commissioned short briefing papers on key topics, identified existing useful materials to reproduce and link to, and planned a discussion forum

Phase 2 - Building capacity and competence (March 2002-present)

Our challenge is implementing an innovation that is important but not easily adoptable - person-centered approaches and planning. Therefore the implementation strategy involves spreading information about person-centered planning and approaches across the breadth of the country, whilst developing the capacity for learning from in-depth person-centered planning. Phase 2 activities include these:

- The VPST has worked with some of the leading consultancy and training agencies, supporting the design and subsidizing a national program of training trainers to deliver local workshops that build awareness about person-centered approaches. This initiative aims to increase local capacity to inform people about person-centered approaches and make practical tools and techniques available. These courses are based on learning from previous course designs and delivery and the experiences and needs of some of the organizations we have worked with in recent years. In addition to the awareness raising itself is a menu of practical courses and tools to follow up people's interests, for example communication "passports and dictionaries" and methods for self advocates to take control of their meetings.

- Experience has shown us that some families and people with learning disabilities prefer to learn about person-centered approaches separately from professionals. The Joseph Rowntree Foundation has commissioned the preparation of information about person-centered planning for families and people with learning disabilities. The VPST have worked with some of the development agencies to design a one day awareness course that uses these materials with families. Graduates from the family/ self advocates leadership course *Partners in Policymaking* have been central to this design process. We now intend to develop a similar course with and for self-advocates.

- The roles played by care managers and other specialist professionals in relation to person-centered planning are important in assuring that people get the paid services and specialist support they require. Care managers, for example, need to think about person-centered approaches in respect of their assessment and care planning activities and work out practical ways to link with person-centered planning led by family members, self-advocates and others. The VPST has worked with development agencies on short courses for care managers on practical approaches to practice in more person-centered ways. Our next step is to design a local process to review and develop specialist professional practice in support of person-centered approaches.

- Training and consultancy groups continue to provide in-depth facilitator training courses. The VPST continues to discuss the implications of the variety of content and different lengths of these courses with the "community of practice" of trainers and consultants. We plan to build on initial experience and develop ways to train and support families and self advocates to facilitate person-centered planning.
- The Joseph Rowntree Foundation has commissioned a work book, *People, Plans and Practicalities,* which local implementation groups will use to review and further develop their activities. It will offer practical examples and tools based on experience in implementing person-centered planning.

History suggests that many people think that all that's necessary to effect change is to offer training courses. In reality, training is only one component of the journey to person-centered approaches. The influence of peers, managers, reading and other study materials, coaching, mentoring, and seeing other people put person-centered approaches into practice also play important parts. At an organizational level, work to change practice with individuals needs to be complemented by attention to service development and strategic change.

Our implementation strategy attempts to influence in each of these areas. At first, people seize upon what they are familiar with, what seems adoptable, and what they can do relatively easily. Through phase one and phase two implementation activities, a growing number of people have begun to move past these initial, low demand tactics for dealing with the guidance. This naturally generates a demand for training. As we respond to these training demands, our consistent message is this: for every day invested in training, at least the same amount of time needs to be invested in providing on-going support for people in new and better ways.

Opportunities to learn with experienced facilitators and get skilled coaching are emerging, informally through communities of practice and more formally through train the trainers programs in some of the major styles of planning (so far, Essential Lifestyle Planning and PATH and MAPS).

The VPST members for each of the regions are developing their own programs to support the development of person-centered approaches and planning and to incorporate these within service change strategies.

Building on a long history of training and development work, the North West Region is testing multiple ways to support the people responsible for delivering on the promise of person-centered planning. Other regions will adapt these initiatives for their own use.

- A tool for reviewing initial frameworks for implementing person-centered work is now available to local groups who decide to undertake self-evaluation.
- There is now a regional support network whose early activities include testing the review tool and the *People, Plans, and Practicalities* workbook in order to strengthen strategies and action plans; setting up training courses; convening person-centered planning facilitators and family mentors to strengthen the regions' community of practice.

Phase 3 - Capturing and sharing new learning (to begin in Winter 2002)

In the third phase of the implementation strategy, we will continue to build and support capacity to deliver high quality person-centered planning and promote person-centered approaches to service.

Family members and self advocates as person-centered planning facilitators. Some entrepreneurial and tenacious self-advocates, circles and families have reclaimed person-centered planning from services. This turns our traditional approaches to how budgets are used, and who benefits, on their head. Where self advocates and families want to lead their own planning, we need to learn how to respond, support and sometimes simply keep out of the way. This shifts power and creates tension.

Parallel national initiatives will gather family members and self advocates to collaborate with us in designing the next steps toward effective ways to train family members and self advocates who want to become person-centered planning facilitators.

The implications of person-centered approaches for specialist professionals. A design team of care managers, health and other specialist professionals, families, self advocates and staff is creating a large group event to explore the contribution of specialist professionals. Like detectives, participants will search for what good practice exists, what guidelines may be helpful for professional staff, and how this information can be shared. Having the whole system in the room to develop understanding and learning on this may lead us to a different place than working in isolation with different professionals. One of the author's experiences as an "associated health professional" demonstrated that it is easy for a professional group to be more concerned with maintaining status with colleagues from other professional groups, than with assessing the possibilities for joint contribution.

We will also create ways to capture and share what people are learning from their implementation efforts by **supporting the emergence of communities of practice.**

> *Communities of practice are groups of people who share a concern, a set of problems, or a passion about a topic, and who deepen their knowledge and expertise in this area by interacting on an ongoing basis* (Wenger & Snyder,, 2000).

Skilled practitioners are developing new insights into planning and implementation. Our knowledge of person-centered planning is not static. Books and articles document our journey so far, but what is being learned quickly surpasses what is formally recorded.

Sharing knowledge also requires interaction through story telling, networking, and informal coaching. Communities of practice exchange information, celebrate successes and problem solve about difficulties. Some already exist, using different names –for example, there is a learning community of trainers in Essential Lifestyle Planning that has a website and meets annually to share developments.

The VPST is investing in support to emerging regional communities of practice including:

- **Facilitators.** VPST will assist people practicing and training in person-centered planning to gather for a day every 6-8 weeks. The first part of the day is for structured problem solving using an action learning set approach. This will be followed by a long lunch for informal sharing and networking. The afternoon offers an opportunity for shared learning on a topic chosen by the community. People can attend for the whole day, or whatever part of the day appeals to them, perhaps just for lunch. The learning from the day will be shared via a website, which gives other interested people an opportunity to learn and for shared learning across regions.

- **People implementing person-centered approaches and person centered planning within organizations.** This network is linked to the first one and will focus on how to ensure and sustain the effective implementation of person-centered planning over time and how to maximize impact within and across organizations.

Sharing learning across regions is important. The VPST is exploring the idea of an annual conference designed by members of different communities of practice to celebrate and share learning. The website is another opportunity to link what people are learning.

Alongside communities of practice, other ways of supporting learning and problem solving are emerging. In the South West Region the VPST advisors are arranging 'surgeries' [sessions in which people can seek advice] where people can meet with an experienced consultant. In the North East a consortium of seven authorities has jointly requested bids for a support program.

Will it work?

How will we judge the success of the person-centered planning guidance and associated implementation support strategies? It is difficult to define success in a way that allows easy and credible measurement. We also know that the implementation of public policy is subject to many mediating forces independent of any specific policy and its associated support measures. We have already discussed the far from ideal context for the introduction of person-centered planning and aspects of the innovation itself which will make something other than superficial adoption difficult. We went into the task of designing the guidance aware of these issues but believing we could offer something that would have beneficial impact. Learning from the effectiveness of the implementation strategy and changing it as a result of this will be crucial.

We have thought a lot about the "unintended consequences" of our efforts to support the implementation of the guidance. Smale (1996) says:

> *To be partially successful in introducing an innovation it is necessary, but not sufficient, to have the new idea in place, being used by those who are supposed to use it, and for it to have the intended impact...*
>
> *A major argument for improving our capacity to manage these (change) processes is to reduce the harm that unplanned, uncontrolled or mindless innovation can cause by identifying unintended consequences...*
>
> *"To be successful the innovation still has to be relevant by the time that it is adopted and not causing or precipitating significant counter productive, harmful, unintended consequences.*

We actively seek feedback about the actual course of implementation at the local, regional, and national level in order to adjust our strategy for supporting implementation. We will expand out ability to do this as regional networks and our various communities of practice gather strength.

We recently invited a national leader in the development of learning disability services, Peter Kinsella, to offer his early "reflections from the field" about the impact of the guidance, 6 months after publication. He offered the following brief analysis:

Positive impact	Possible unintended consequences
Made people sit up and take notice about person-centered planning	*Promoted a planning process as more important than the outcome in many areas*
Putting it on local agendas	
Senior managers talk about it	
Agencies have committed resources to it	*Produced an inflated person-centered planning economy: too many people spending too much money and having too high expectations*
Given ideas to people as to what they can or should do	*Given the impression that if you either do as you are told or follow the instructions then certain things will inevitably happen*
Vastly increased the amount of training of staff in person-centered planning	*Got much too focused on the technicalities of training*
Legitimized the work of people who would previously have been described as ideologues	
Given a real chance of many of the other parts of the White Paper becoming a reality	
Focused some people's minds on including families in person-centered planning	

We will continue to seek this kind of feedback from others and do so continuously in order to ensure that we use the various means at our disposal to minimize the unintended consequences and maximize the positive benefits of this national initiative. We are determined to do this. Despite the many obstacles, there are increasing numbers of people and groups who are willing to think and act together to ensure that person-centered approaches are increasingly influential in services and supports. Ultimately the strength of these groups is likely to be of much more importance than government guidance, but we hope that the guidance and the activities to support its implementation will play a part in building this strength.

References

Department of Health (2002) – *Planning with people – Towards person-centered approaches*. London: DoH. (Download from www.doh.gov.uk/learningdisabilities).

Department of Health (2002) *Valuing People: A new strategy for learning disability for the 21st century – Implementation Guidance*. LAC (2001) 23 (Download from www.doh.gov.uk/learningdisabilities).

Jacobs, R. (1994). *Real time strategic change*. San Francisco, CA: Berrett-Koehler.

Kotter, J. (1996) *Leading change*. Cambridge, MA: Harvard Business School Press.

Routledge, M. & Sanderson, H. (2000). *Work in progress: Implementing person centerd planning in Oldham*. Manchester: Northwest Training and Development Team. (Download from www.nwtdt.com)

Sanderson, H. (2002). A plan is not enough: Exploring the development of person-centered teams. In S. Holburn & P. Vietze, Eds. *Person-centered Planning: Research, practice, and future directions*. Baltimore, MD: Paul Brookes Publishing Co. Pp. 97-126.

Smale, G.G, (1996) *Managing change through innovation*. London: HMSO.

Wenger, E. & Snyder, W. (January-February 2000) Communities of practice: The organizational frontier. *Harvard Business Review*. (Reprint 00110).

INCLUSION PRESS ORDER FORM
24 Thome Crescent, Toronto, ON Canada M6H 2S5
Tel: 416-658-5363 Fax: 416-658-5067
E-mail: inclusionpress@inclusion.com
WEBSITE: http://www.inclusion.com

Nov.2002 Listing

Inclusion SPECIAL PACKS...

◎ **PATH in ACTION PACK**
- 2 Path Training Videos [(Path in Action + Path Training) + Path Workbook]
$150 + $15 shipping/pack   _____ _____

◎ **All Means All PACK**
- Video: All Means All, plus & book: All My Life's a Circle
$110 + $10 shipping/pack   _____ _____

◎ **Friendship PACK** (1 book + Video)
- [Friendship Video + From Behind the Piano/What's Really Worth Doing]
$ 60 + $10 shipping/pack   _____ _____

◎ **Inclusion Classics Videos PACK**
- Videos [With a Little Help from My Friends + Kids Belong Together]
$ 90 + $12 shipping/pack   _____ _____

◎ **Inclusion Classics Book PACK**
- Books [Action for Inclusion + The Inclusion Papers]
$ 30 + $7 shipping/pack   _____ _____

◎ **Petroglyphs PACK**
- Petroglyphs Book and Video on Inclusion in High Schools - from UNH
$ 60 + $10 shipping/pack   _____ _____

◎ **When Spider Webs Unite PACK**
- When Spider Webs Unite - Shafik Asante - Book and Video
$ 80 + $10 shipping/pack   _____ _____

◎◎ **The Person-Centered Planning PACK (new)**
-2 books by O'Brien/Lyle O'Brien: Implementing Person-Centered Planning
+ A Little Book on Person-Centered Planning
$ 40 + $7 shipping/pack   _____ _____

◎ **The Education Book PACK**
- Inclusion: Recent Research & Inclusion: How To - 2 Books - Gary Bunch
$ 40 + $7 shipping/pack   _____ _____

◎ **The Community PACK**
- Members of Each Other & Celebrating the Ordinary
2 books - John O'Brien & Connie Lyle O'Brien
$ 40 + $7 shipping/pack   _____ _____

Books

◎◎ **Implementing Person-Centered Planning - Voices of Experience**
      Edited by John O'Brien & Connie Lyle O'Brien $25 + $5 shipping

◎◎ **Hints for Graphic Facilitators**   **Jack Pearpoint** $25 + $5 shipping

◎◎ **One Candle Power**   **Cathy Ludlum + Communitas** $25 + $5 shipping

A Little Book About Person Centered Planning $20 + $5 shipping
     Forest, Lovett, Mount, Pearpoint, Smull, Snow, and Strully

All My Life's a Circle Expanded - Circles, MAPS & PATH $20 + $5 shipping
Path Workbook
     - 2nd Edition Planning Positive Possible Futures $20 + $5 shipping

Celebrating the Ordinary   O'Brien, O'Brien & Jacob $25 + $5 shipping

Members of Each Other   John O'Brien & C Lyle O'Brien $25 + $5 shipping

Action for Inclusion - Classic on Inclusion $20 + $5 shipping

The Inclusion Papers - Strategies & Stories $20 + $5 shipping

Lessons for Inclusion Curr Ideas for Elementary Schools $20 + $5 shipping

Inclusion: How To   Classroom Strategies - Gary Bunch $25+ $5 shipping

Inclusion: Recent Research   G. Bunch & A. Valeo $25 + $5 shipping

Kids, Disabilities Regular Classrooms   Gary Bunch $20 + $5 shipping

Reflections on Inclusive Education $15 + $5 shipping

Each Belongs - Hamilton-W Catholic School Bd - J. Hansen $20 + $5 shipping

From Behind the Piano, by Jack Pearpoint **& What's Really Worth Doing**
     by Judith Snow **- Now in ONE Book *** $20 + $5 shipping

When Spider Webs Unite Diversity Inclusion- Shafik Asante $20 + $5 shipping

Yes! She Knows She's Here Nicola Schaefer's NEW Book $20 + $5 shipping

Dream Catchers & Dolphins Marsha Forest & J Pearpoint $20 + $5 shipping

It Matters - Lessons from my Son - Janice Fialka $15 + $5 shipping

Do You Hear What I Hear? - Janice Fialka & Karen Mikus $15 + $5 shipping

The Careless Society - John McKnight $25 + $5 shipping

Who Cares - David Schwartz $30 + $5 shipping

The All Star Company - Team Building by Nick Marsh $20 + $5 shipping

Changes in Latitudes/Attitudes The Inclusion Facilitator $20 + $5 shipping

Petroglyphs - Inclusion in High School from UNH $20 + $5 shipping

Treasures - from Univ. of New Hampshire $20 + $5 shipping

Circle of Friends   by Bob & Martha Perske $25 + $5 shipping

Unequal Justice   by Bob Perske $25 + $5 shipping

Perske - Pencil Portraits 1971-1990 $30 + $5 shipping

Inclusion – Exclusion Poster (18 X 24 **)** $10 + $5 shipping

Inclusion News   **(free with book order)**

Inclusion News in Bulk (box of 100) $50 – includes shipping in NA

◎◎   **New**

Videos & CD-ROM

◎◎ **TOOLS for CHANGE**
The CD-Rom for Person Centred Planning
        Pricing is dependent on a licensing agreement.
        To obtain licensing information check our website,
        http://wwwinclusion.com   E-mail or call us.

◎◎ **ReDiscovering MAPS**
        Charting Your Journey - NEW MAPS training video   **$100 + $8 shipping**

PATH in ACTION
        Working with Groups -Training Video for PATH   **$100 + $8 shipping**

PATH Training Video
        Intro Training Video - An Individual Path {Joe's Path} **$75 + $8 shipping**

PATH Demo Video
        U Dayton Ohio - Video of PATH Workshop   **$55 + $8 shipping**

Celebrating Marsha
        (32 minutes of edited clips from Oct.7,2001)   **$50 + $8 shipping**

Each Belongs
        (30 years of Inclusion-15 min. celebration in Hamilton)**$50 + $8 shipping**

All Means All - Inclusion Video
        Introduction to Circles, MAPS and PATH   **$100 + $8 shipping**

When Spider Webs Unite - Video
        Shafik Asante in Action   **$75 + $8 shipping**

Everyone Has a Gift
        John McKnight - Building Communities of Capacity   **$75 + $8 shipping**

New MAPS Training Video (Shafik's MAP)
        Shafik's MAP - MAPS Process - Step by Step   **$75 + $8 shipping**

Friendship Video
        Judith, Marsha & Jack on Friendship   **$55 + $8 shipping**

Petroglyphs Video - the High School video -   **$55 + $8 shipping**
    Companionto/images from the Petroglyphs Book - **Packaged with book - $60 + $8 shipping**

Dream Catchers
        Dreams & Circles   **$55 + $8 shipping**

Miller's MAP
        MAPS in Action   **$55 + $8 shipping**

With a Little Help from My Friends
        The Classic on Circles & MAPS   **$55 + $8 shipping**

Kids Belong Together
        MAPS & Circles   **$55 + $8 shipping**

Together We're Better (3 videos)
        Staff Development Kit   **$175 + $12 shipping**

**Tools for Change
the CD**

**Tools for Person
Centered Planning**

*Cheques, Money Orders, Purchase
Orders Please.*
• **Prices subject to change without notice.
Shipping prices for North America only.
Elsewhere by quote.**

*** Shipping: Books: $5 for 1st + $2/copy; Videos:
$8 for 1st+ $4/copy. OR 15% of total order cost
- which ever is less for customer.**

Order NOW: TOOLS for CHANGE CD-ROM

*An exciting multi-media Training Guide with resources galore for your
staff. Presentation ready. A practical, usable CD-ROM featuring
slide shows, graphic overheads, video clips, articles. Introduces 'tools
for change' that were developed by Jack Pearpoint, Marsha Forest
and John O'Brien. Essential for 'trainers' using Person Centered
approaches, MAPS, PATH, Circles or just dealing with day to day
change. Includes articles and overheads that can be printed.*

INCLUSION PRESS
24 Thome Crescent • Toronto • ON • Canada • M6H 2S5
Tel: 416-658-5363 Fax: 416-658-5067
E-mail: inclusionpress@inclusion.com
WEBSITE: http://www.inclusion.com